I0818827

ALEXANDRA FULLERTON

THE ULTIMATE GUIDE TO CHANEL BAGS

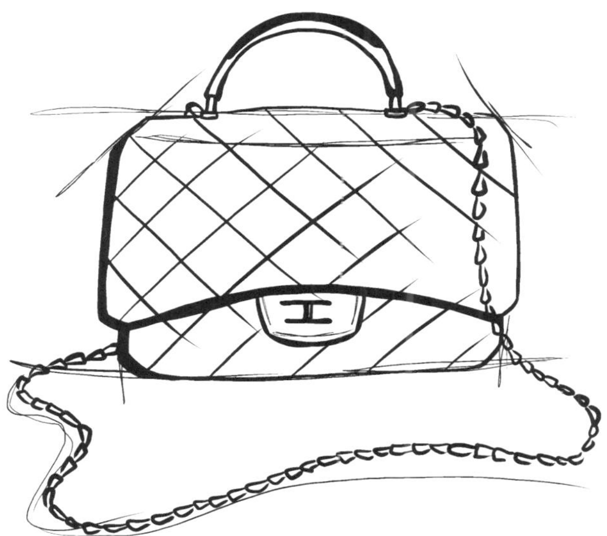

teNeues

Next page: Magazine advertisement featuring Chanel bags, UK, 2000s

Pages 4/5: Visitors to Paris Fashion Week carry a Paris-Hamburg Shipping Container *minaudière* and double flap bags, 2019

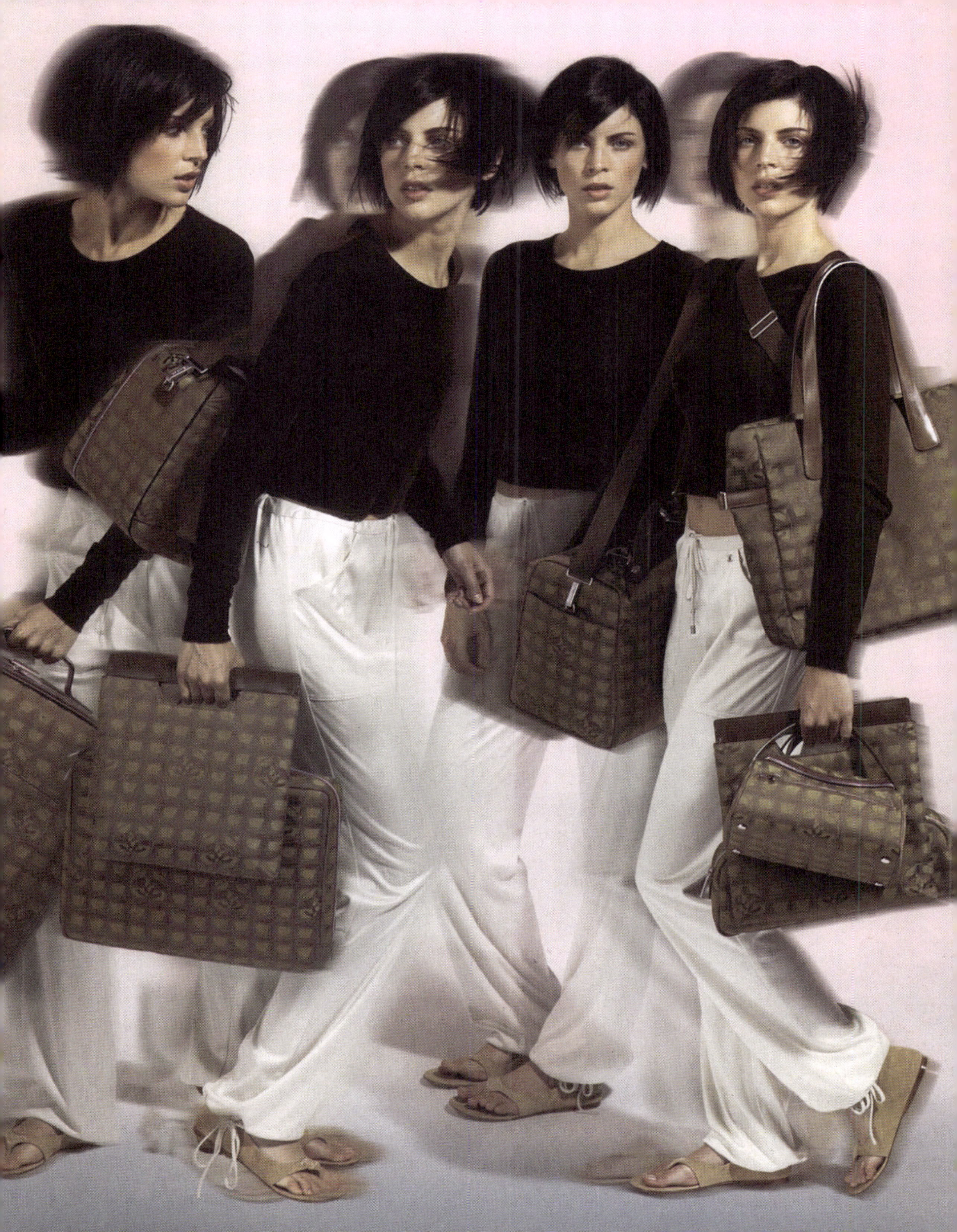

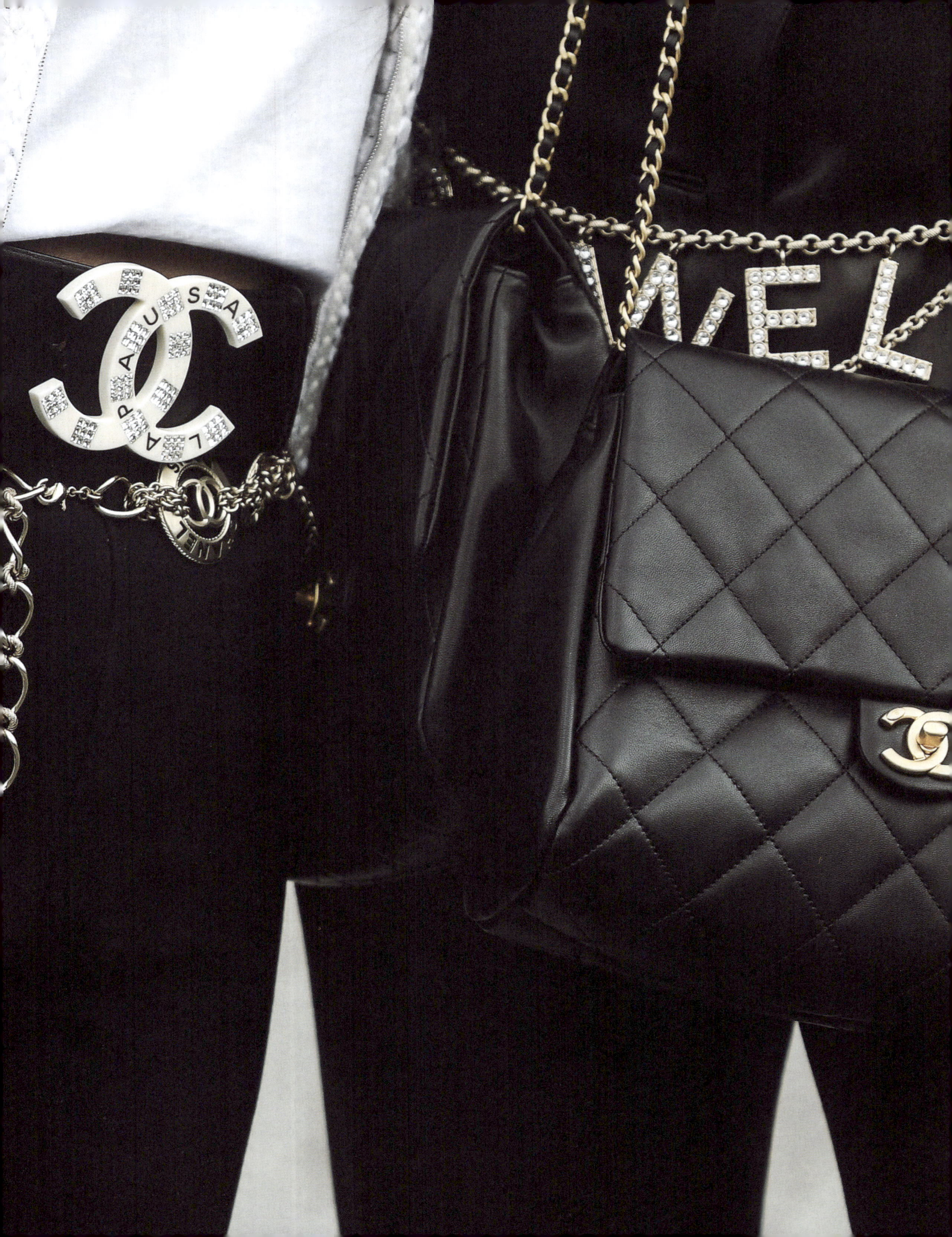
LA PAUSA

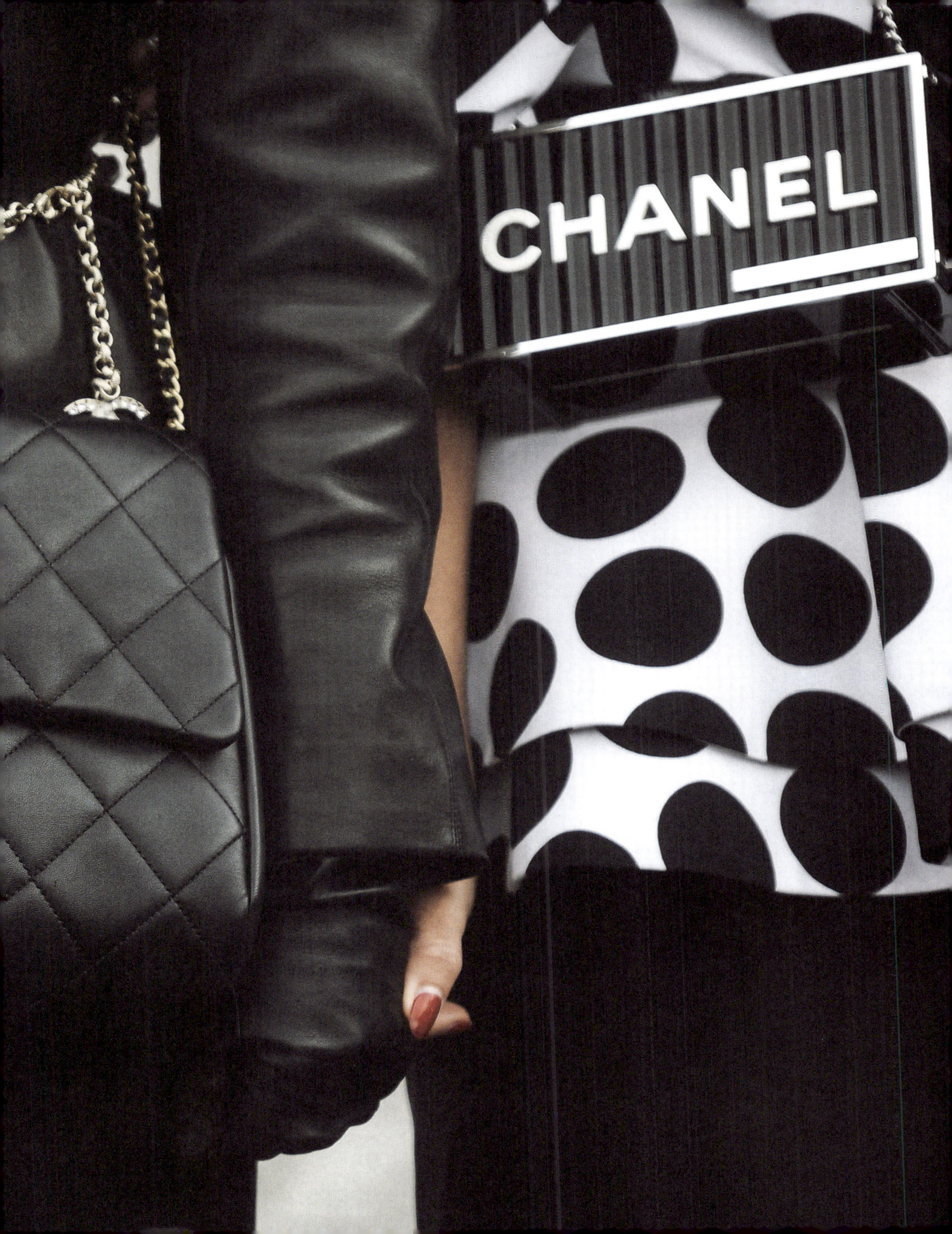
CHANEL

Whether you are manifesting your first Chanel bag or are a seasoned collector, this book pays tribute to the maison that changed the style of the 21st century. Gabrielle 'Coco' Chanel created some of the most game-changing designs in womenswear, and her legacy still resonates today.

From Mlle Chanel's original 2.55 bag to the Boy bag and limited edition *minaudières*, this volume showcases Chanel's legendary bags and the stories behind their creation.

The *savoir faire* behind each It Bag is revealed, along with tips to ensure you secure an authentic Chanel bag on the pre-loved market. Go beyond the catwalk: discover the bags that shaped pop culture and became fashion icons through appearances in film, TV and music.

Next page: A model strolls down the runway showcasing a vanity case adorned with a pearl strap during the Chanel Womenswear Spring/Summer 2024 show in Paris, 2023

Pages 8/9: Gabrielle "Coco" Chanel and her companion Arthur "Boy" Capel, accompanied by Constant Say, enjoy a day at the beach in Saint Jean de Luz, 1917

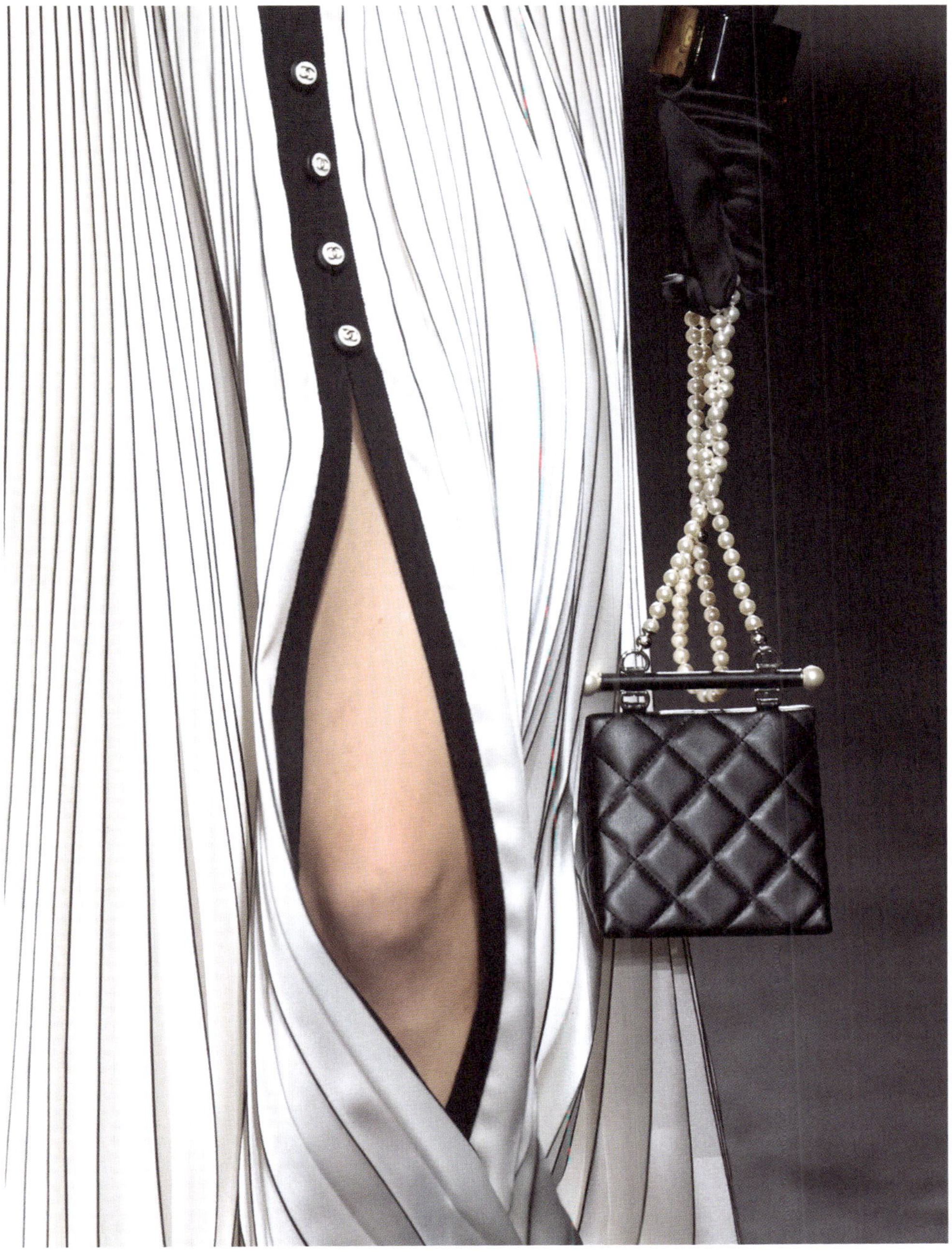

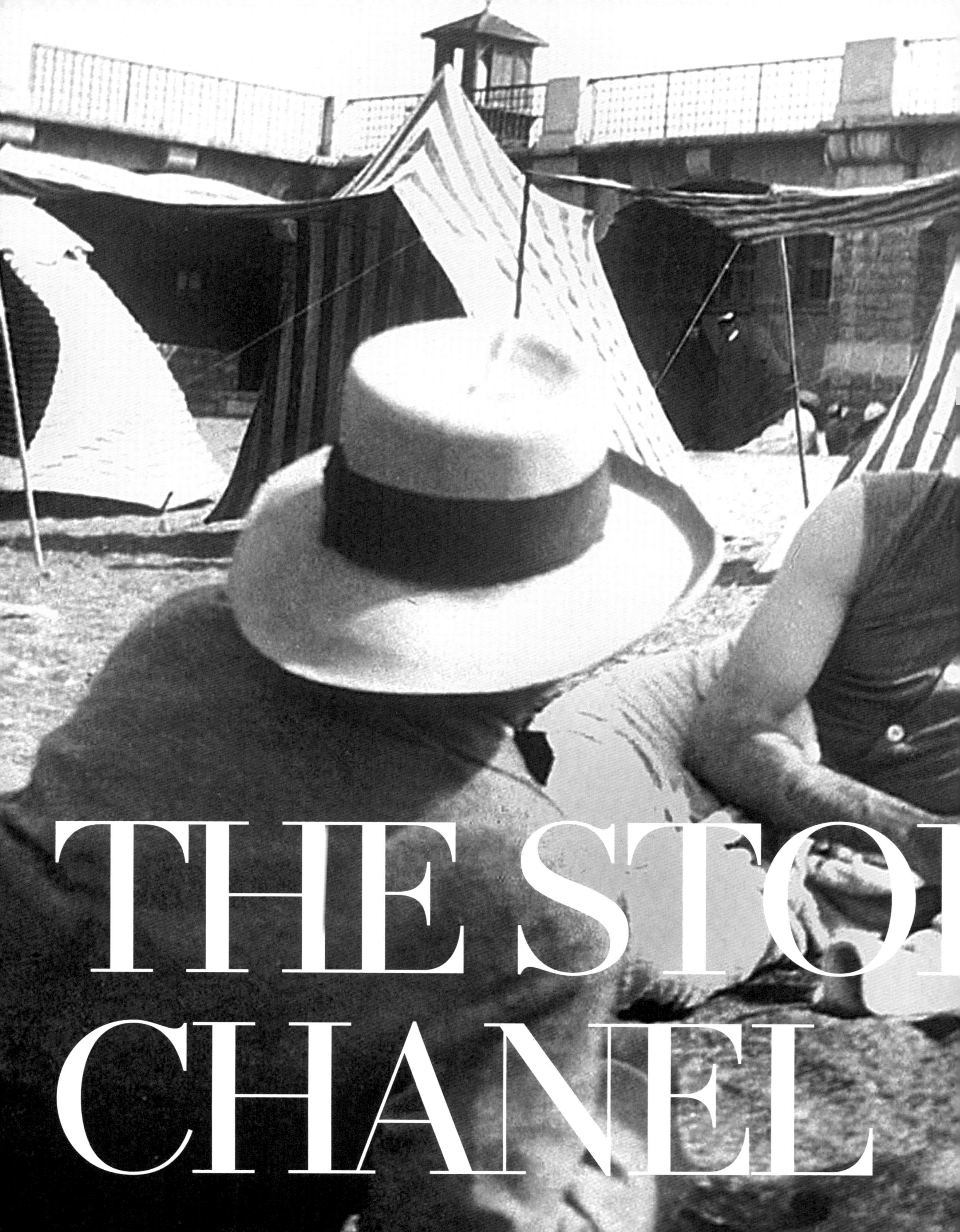
THE STO
CHANEL

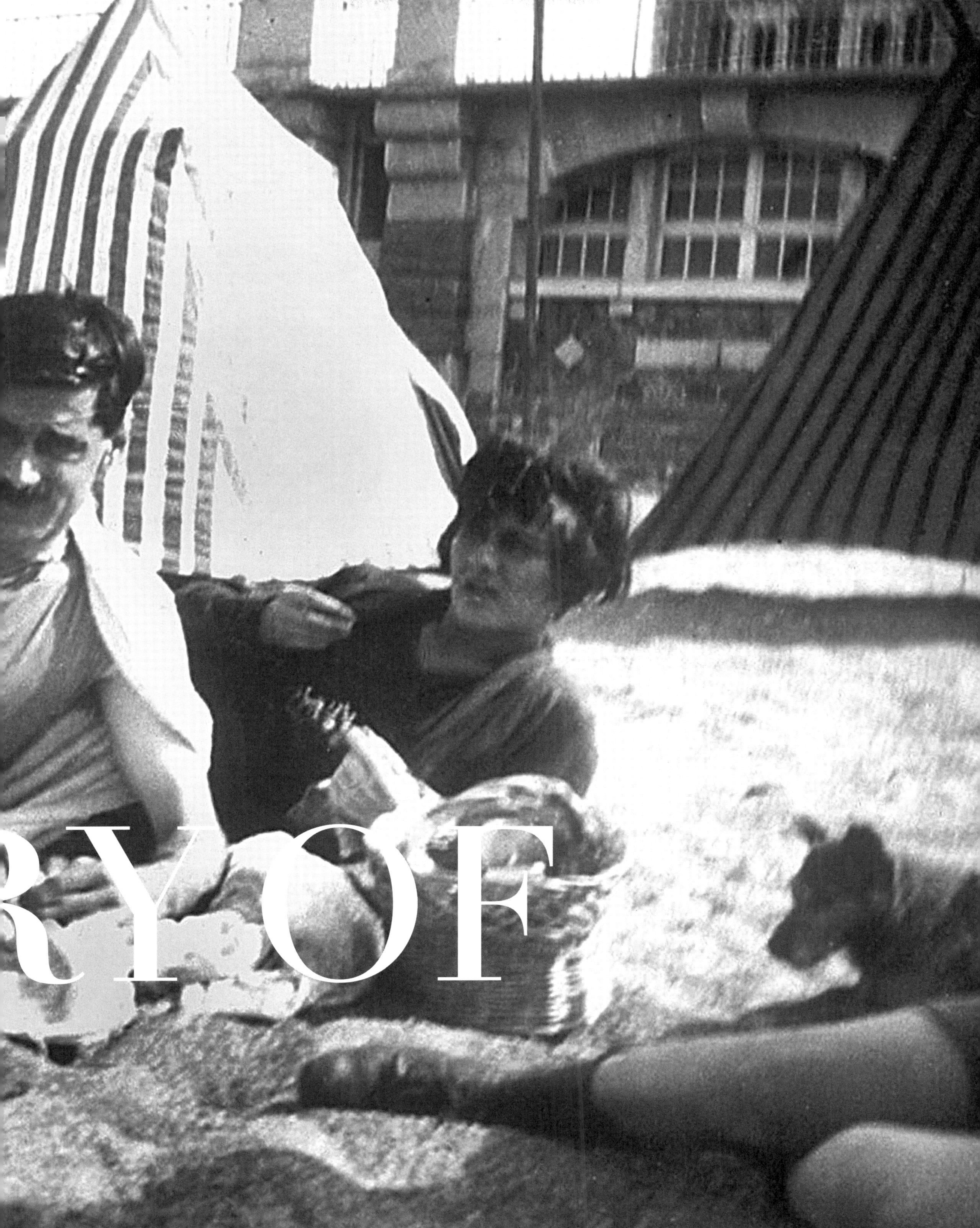
RY OF

COCO BEFORE CHANEL

Without Gabrielle 'Coco' Chanel's designs, women's fashion would look very different today. Perhaps we would have arrived at a similar aesthetic, but it might have taken far longer to develop the ease, practicality and stylishness that everyone has access to and wears today. The little black dress, freedom from corsets, logomania, jersey daywear, signature scents *and* an array of iconic handbags: they were all products of Chanel's inimitable mind. The *maison* she founded has a legacy that is still responsible for creating startling fashion moments. But how did Chanel rise above her humble beginnings to become the fashion world's original influencer and a name synonymous with high-value luxury goods?

Gabrielle Bonheur Chanel was born on August 19, 1883 in a charity hospital in Saumur, a small town in western France's Loire region. Her mother was a laundry worker and her father a traveling salesman. At the time of Chanel's birth they were unmarried, which was frowned upon in the late 19th century, although the couple did marry the year after Chanel was born. Chanel and her six siblings lived in a modest one-room apartment until her mother died when Chanel was just 11. Her father sent his three daughters to live in an orphanage at the convent of Aubazine while the boys became farm hands. Later in life, Chanel was known to give a different version of her upbringing, retelling her history with her father moving to America while she moved in with two aunts.

In reality, life in the orphanage would have been tough. As part of The Congregation of the Sacred Heart of Mary, Chanel would have lived under a strictly disciplined regime, with meager food rations and little love from the nuns. However, she did learn to sew and embroider during her six years in the convent. When she turned eighteen, she moved into a boarding school for Catholic girls in the town of Moulins, where she found work as a seamstress in return for her board. Her sewing skills would serve her well as her future career evolved. After clocking out from her day job, Chanel would sing in a cabaret after dark, where she earned the nickname Coco, perhaps after her repertoire, which was apparently limited to *Ko Ko Ri Ko* and *Qui qu'a vu Coco? (Have you Seen Coco?),* although Chanel always insisted that Coco was a childhood nickname bestowed by her father.

Next page: Gabrielle Chanel graces the pages of *Vogue* magazine, 1954

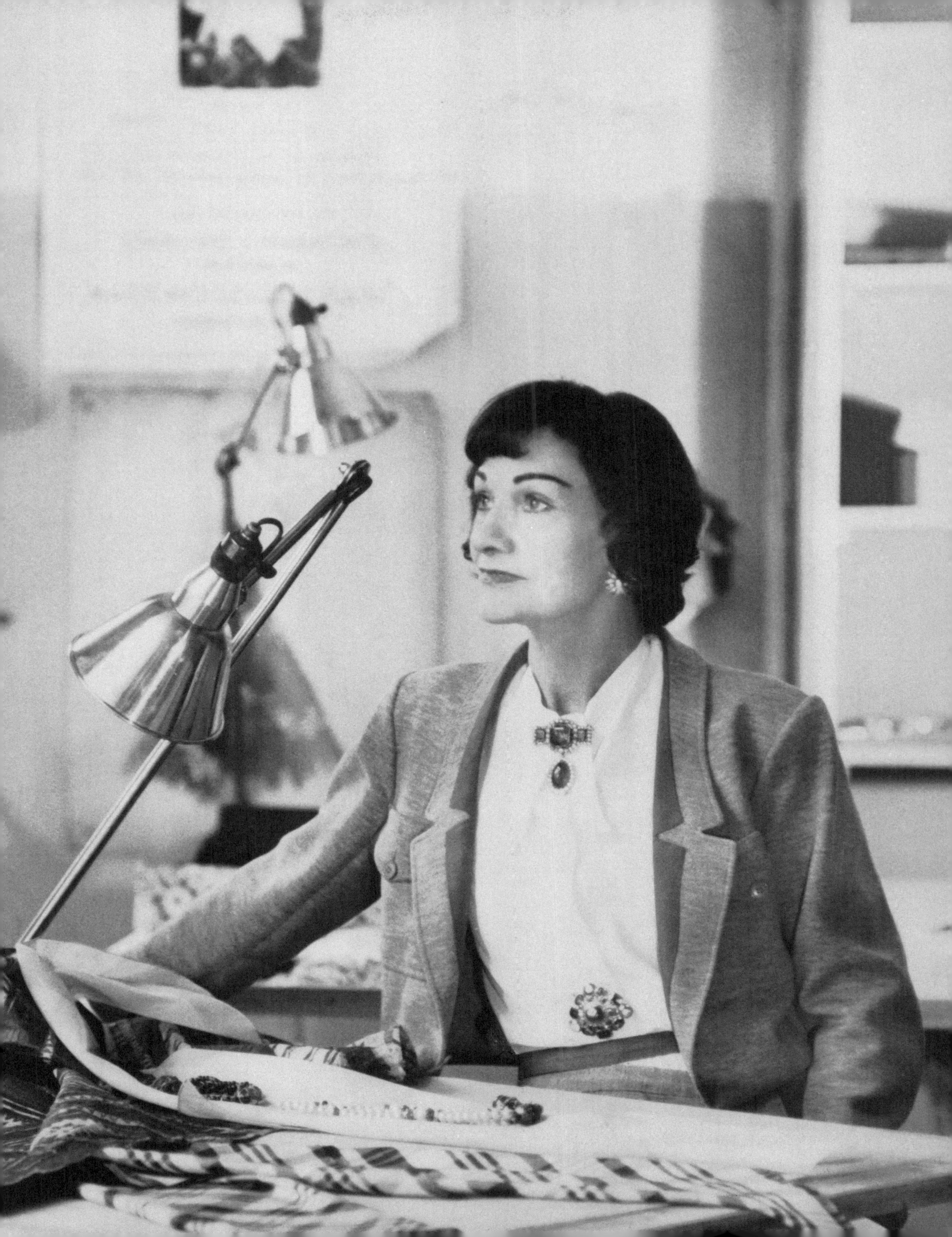

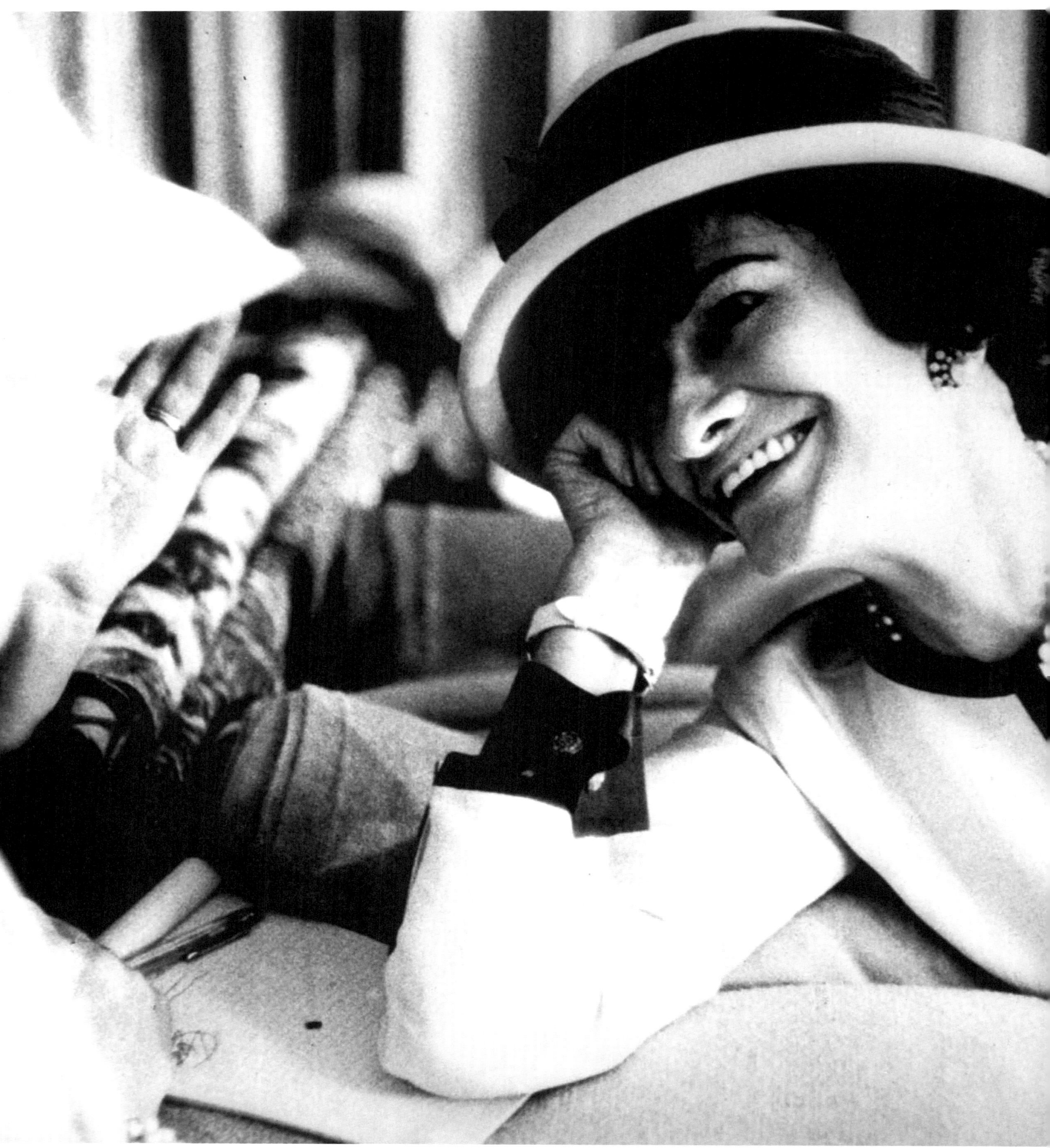

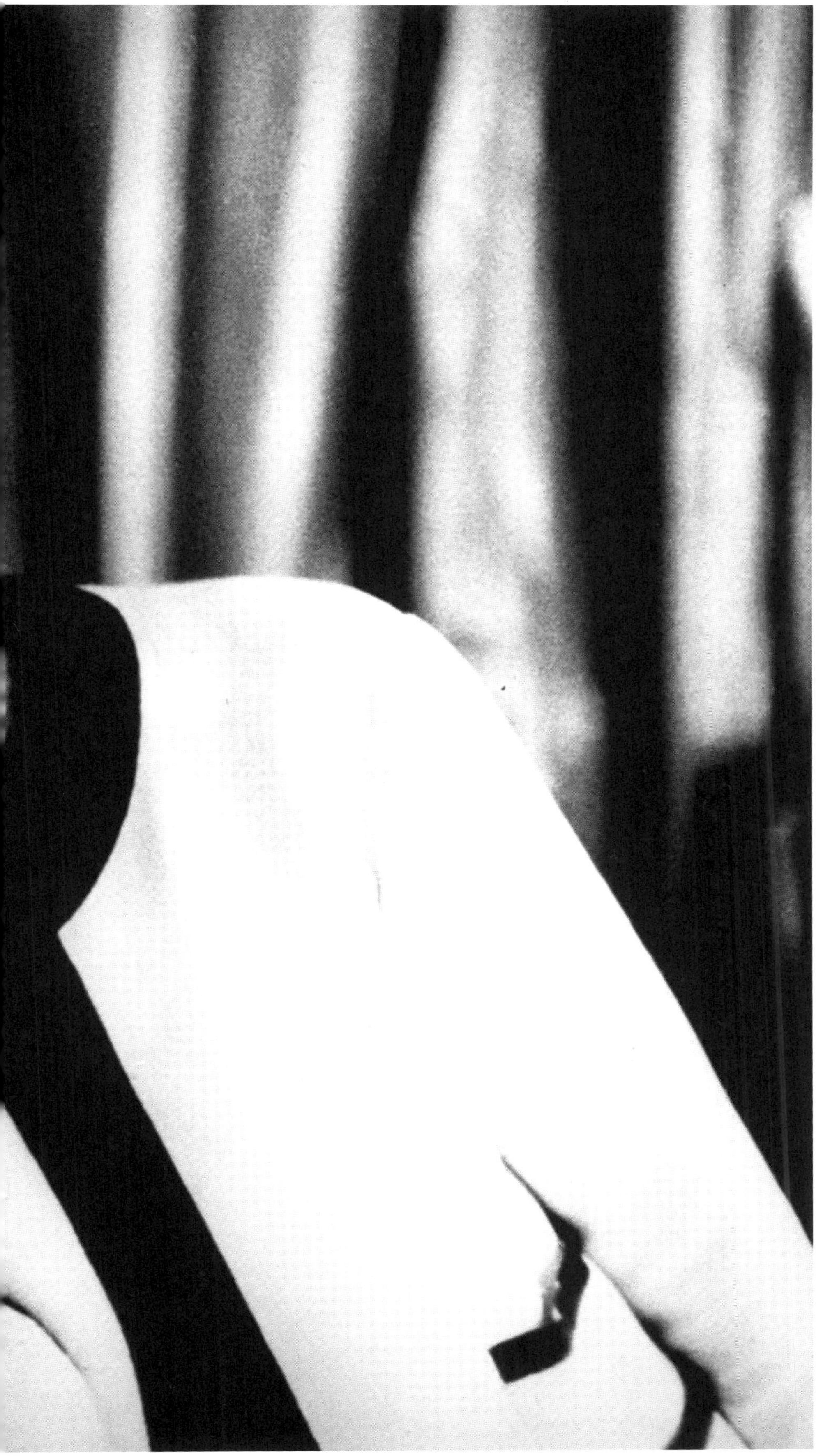

Fashion designer Gabrielle “Coco” Chanel, early 1950s

While singing, Chanel became a favorite with the nightclub's military clientele. The officers overlooked her lackluster voice and fell hard for her gamine looks. One suitor, Etienne Balsan, was a former cavalry officer and heir to a textile fortune. Balsan removed Chanel from the cabaret and installed her in his chateau in Royallieu as his mistress, where he gifted her with jewelry and dresses and provided her with a lavish lifestyle far removed from her convent days. While with Balsan, Chanel started to make hats. Perhaps her early forays into millinery were simply a way to fill her days, but her sleek feathered confections meshed with Chanel's own style *and* the incoming flapper look of the early 20th century. Balsan helped Chanel on her entrance into business by funding a millinery boutique in Paris, which opened in 1910. Chanel's hats were a wild success and were worn on stage and by French socialites in her circle, which helped to cement Chanel's name in high society and gain press coverage.

It was while living with Balsan that Chanel was introduced to his friend, Captain Arthur Edward 'Boy' Capel, an upper-class Englishman. Capel and Chanel became lovers, and she left Balsan to move to Paris. Capel funded the next stages of Chanel's fashion empire; having already opened *Chanel Modes* as a hat shop at 21 rue Cambon, Capel then funded the designer's first fashion boutique in the chic seaside resort of Deauville in 1913. Chanel was known as a milliner, and as another clothing business was already registered at rue Cambon, Chanel was limited to hat sales at that store. However, in Deauville she introduced sporty jackets and jerseys (including the *mariniere* Breton top), expanding her products beyond accessories to clothing perfect for walking, playing tennis and golf. Chanel already understood the importance of advertising and employed her sister and aunt as models—they paraded around town to promote her designs. In 1915, Chanel followed the Deauville boutique with a store in Biarritz, housed in a villa rather than a traditional shop, where she introduced her *couture* business. After just one year, sales were so brisk that she was able to pay back Capel's investment; however, their romantic relationship failed.

While her personal life faltered, her career was flourishing. Chanel bought the building at 31 rue Cambon, and, unrestricted by the other tenants, she registered her business as a *maison de couture* in 1918. Other Chanel boutiques were opened on the same street that sold accessories and jewelry as well as fashion and fragrances. Rue Cambon is still a place of pilgrimage for fashion fans today.

Instead of the ornate fabrics and stiff silhouettes that characterized early 1900s fashion, Chanel's designs made use of more relaxed materials like jersey (previously used only for men's underwear) and simple shapes that allowed women freedom of movement. Released from corsets and bustles, these were clothes that suited the burgeoning emancipation of women after World War I. For the remainder of her career, Chanel continued to introduce game-changing garments and accessories that are still wardrobe staples. The Little Black Dress was one such piece, which Chanel created as a solution for afternoon-through-to-cocktail-wear in 1926. Black was rarely used in fashion at the time because it was associated with mourning, service—and nuns. But the lack of adornment on Chanel's creation made it a versatile staple and "the frock that all the world would wear" according to US *Vogue*. Chanel's best-known fragrance, No. 5, was launched in 1921, and by 1935 Chanel employed around 4000 people, mostly women.

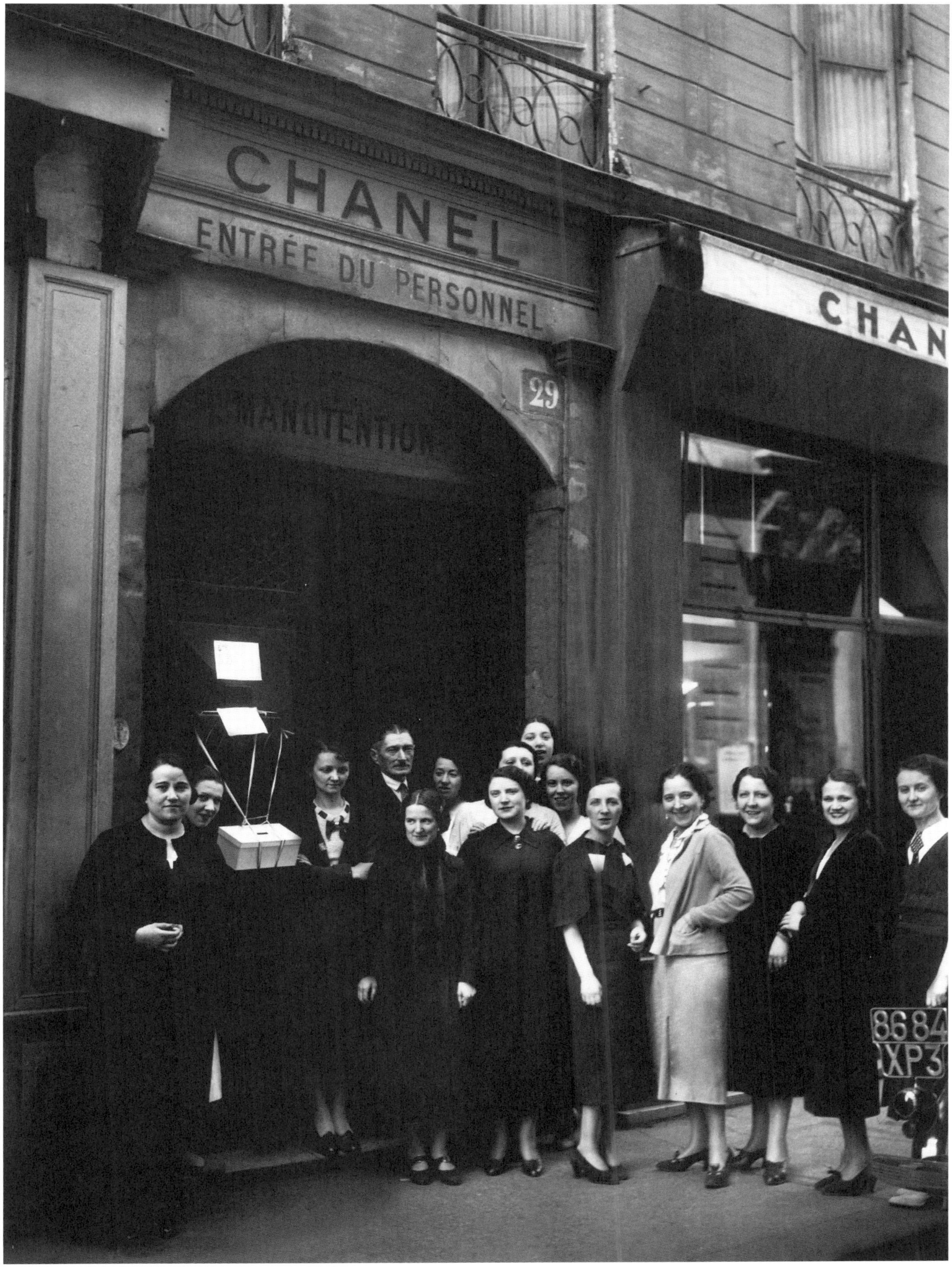

Previous page: Employees at the Chanel fashion house in Paris, 1938

This page: Gabrielle Chanel (1883–1971), circa 1932

Next page: Karl Lagerfeld's inaugural year at Chanel. In 1983, Lagerfeld commenced his role as chief artistic director at Chanel, where he and his team prepared for the Fall/Winter 1984 runway show at the Chanel studio on rue Cambon in Paris.

Pages 20/21: Virginie Viard and Karl Lagerfeld observe the finale of Chanel's Spring/Summer 2019 fashion show in Paris on October 2, 2018

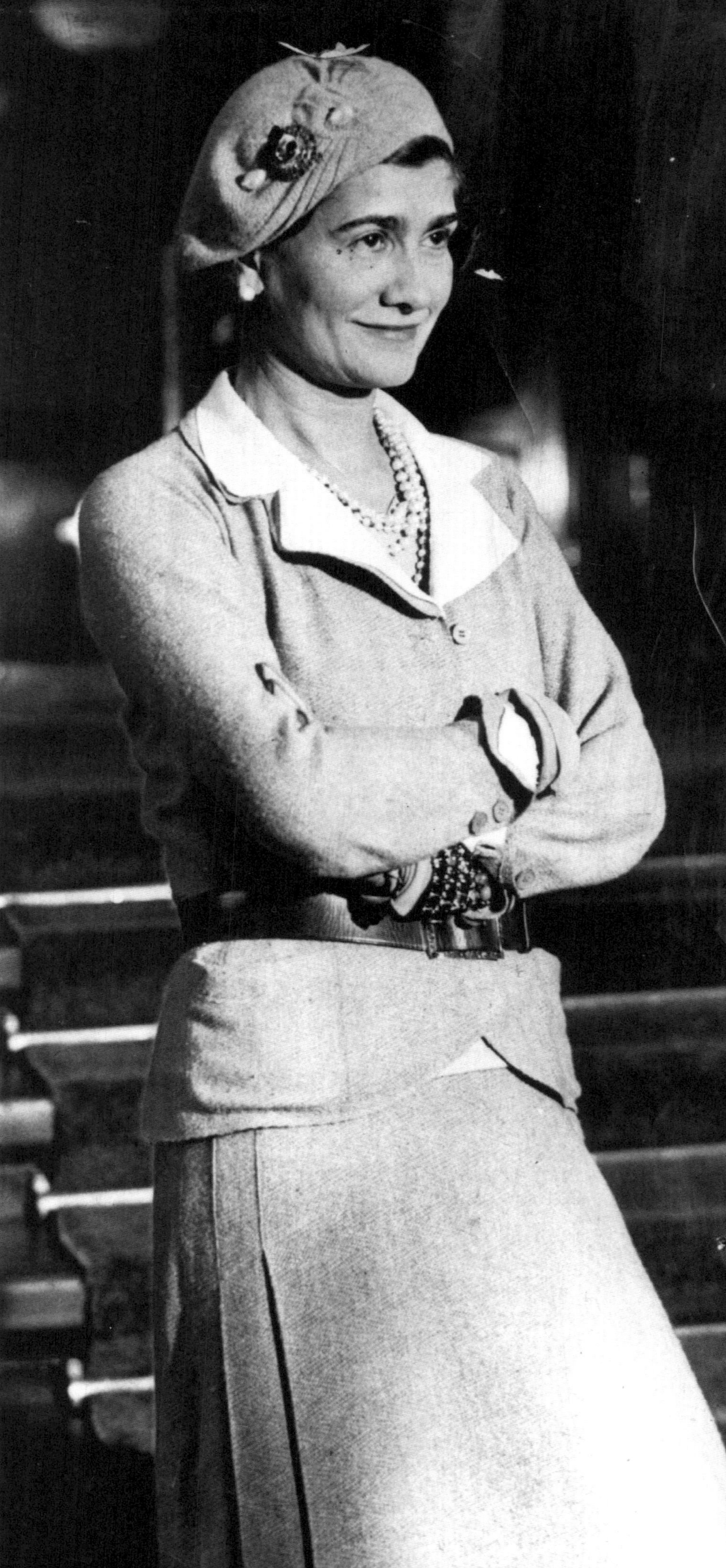

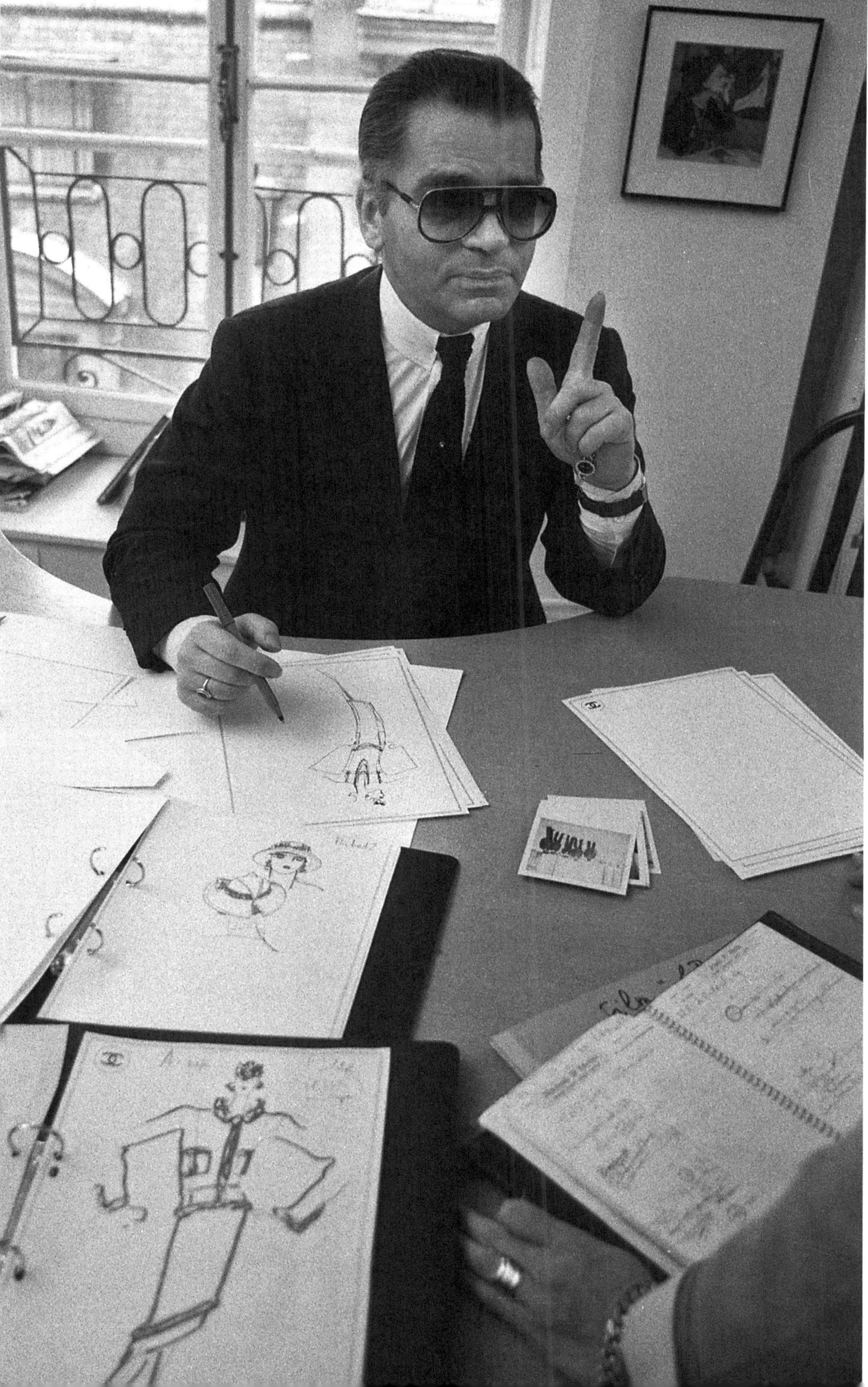

Her evenings were spent at the epicenter of high society which saw her rubbing shoulders with aristocrats (including the Duke of Westminster, a future lover), artists (such as Picasso), politicians (notably Winston Churchill) and composers (such as Stravinsky).

However, the world was changing, and when World War II broke out, Chanel closed her stores, leaving only one perfume boutique open and putting her female employees out of work. She moved into The Ritz hotel, which was the preferred residence of the German military during the occupation of Paris. She started an affair with Baron Hans Gunther von Dincklage, who was an active Nazi agent, and Chanel filed charges against the Wertheimer family, the Jewish directors of *Parfums Chanel*. Documents declassified in 2014 show that Chanel was engaged as a German spy, and in September 1944 she was arrested and interrogated about her involvement in German intelligence. It was said her connection to Churchill saw her speedily released, although the discovery of an alleged membership card for the French Resistance movement in 2023 may mean she was actually a double agent instead.

After the war, Chanel fled to neutral Switzerland, where she lived quietly until she moved back to Paris in 1954 and reopened her couture house to tepid praise—particularly from the French press. At the time, Parisian fashion was dominated by male designers—Christian Dior, Cristobal Balenciaga and Jacques Fath—and, ever true to her feminist manifesto, Chanel wanted to bring back easy, wearable designs that reflected the lifestyle of post-war women, not the "illogical" looks of her male competitors. In later years Chanel was interviewed by *Life* magazine and mused, "Why did I return? One night at dinner, Christian Dior said a woman could never be a great couturier." Chanel handily proved him wrong with her later work, and in 1955, she introduced the iconic 2.55 bag. In 1957, Chanel was awarded the Neiman Marcus Award for Distinguished Service in the Field of Fashion and was described as "the most influential female designer of the 20th century." She was perhaps the most influential *designer*, period. Chanel was also included in *Time* Magazine's 100 Most Influential People of the 20th Century, the only fashion designer to make the list.

Chanel lived through epic social and political change, and while the turbulence obviously affected her personal life, it also influenced her design legacy. Chanel's approach to dressing was undoubtedly feminist and in line with the minimalist movement of the prior century. Chanel was the first designer who truly understood that creating her own celebrity myth could help her sell handbags. Her way of defining how women dress—making clothes that *she* wanted to wear—still resonates today.

Chanel died on January 10, 1971 at age 87 in the suite at the Ritz where she had made her home. In the years following her death, her couture house soldiered on and continued to create collections. Herve Leger was at the helm in 1982, and Chanel's house DNA was firmly established. The interlocking double CC logo (said to represent her relationship with Capel)... her favorite flower—the camellia (which was synonymous with courtesans)... her lucky number 5... the lion's head motif that represented her Leo birth sign... the dedication to beige and black... quilted finishes (echoing jockey's jackets)... chain details (a nod to the *chatelaines* carried by the nuns)... humble jersey and hard-working tweed... all these motifs were sewn into Chanel's legacy and continue to be instantly recognizable as Chanel today.

After some time in the doldrums, the arrival of Karl Lagerfeld in 1983 gave the *maison* a new lease on life. After her death, Chanel's clients were mainly older women, and it was far from the behemoth brand it is today, but Lagerfeld's direction reinvigorated the house of Chanel.

Born in Germany on September 10, 1933, Karl Otto Lagerfeld also glossed over elements of his childhood and background, suggesting different birthdates for himself and differing nationalities for his parents. After a childhood largely unaffected by World War II (his father was a member of the Nazi party) and a penchant for continuously sketching, Lagerfeld entered two fashion competitions run by the International Wool Secretariat. They led to his first appointment in Paris as Pierre Balmain's assistant and apprentice, before his first artistic director role (at Jean Patou) in 1957. Lagerfeld worked as a freelance designer for Chloe, Valentino and Fendi—one of the first to do so—before arriving at Chanel. From the start, Lagerfeld initiated a bold change in the house's look. Chanel's signature skirt suits saw shortened hemlines, in line with the 1980s penchant for mini-lengths, while shoulders were padded and heel heights raised. Jewelry was supersized and bag shapes shrunk to create the decade's signature look, which was copied across other designer labels and budding high street brands. Initially controversial because they often clashed with Gabrielle Chanel's own views, the changes were a commercial and financial success.

Lagerfeld's direction helped Chanel become relevant again and achieve the status and respect the *maison* maintains today. Lagerfeld oversaw the minutiae of every element of the house, from design to shooting the campaigns as a photographer, from 1987 onwards. He was awarded the British Fashion Council's Outstanding Achievement Award in 2015, presented by US *Vogue* Editor-in-Chief Anna Wintour, and remained at the helm of Chanel until his death on February 19, 2019. With the house's top spot vacant, Virginie Viard was appointed creative director.

Viard had worked alongside Lagerfeld for over thirty years after joining Chanel as an intern in 1987 and being promoted to Director of the Haute Couture studio in 1997, after which she headed the Ready to Wear studio in 1999. The designer had an intrinsic understanding of all things Chanel, and Lagerfeld once said that Viard was "my right arm... and my left arm." With reported revenues of $19.7 billion in 2023, Chanel was booming when Viard left the house in June 2024. For the next six months, the fashion world was abuzz with rumors of her successor. After an agonizing wait to find out who would hold fashion's most coveted position, it was announced in December 2024 that Matthieu Blazy, formerly of Italian leather goods brand Bottega Veneta, would take the reins.

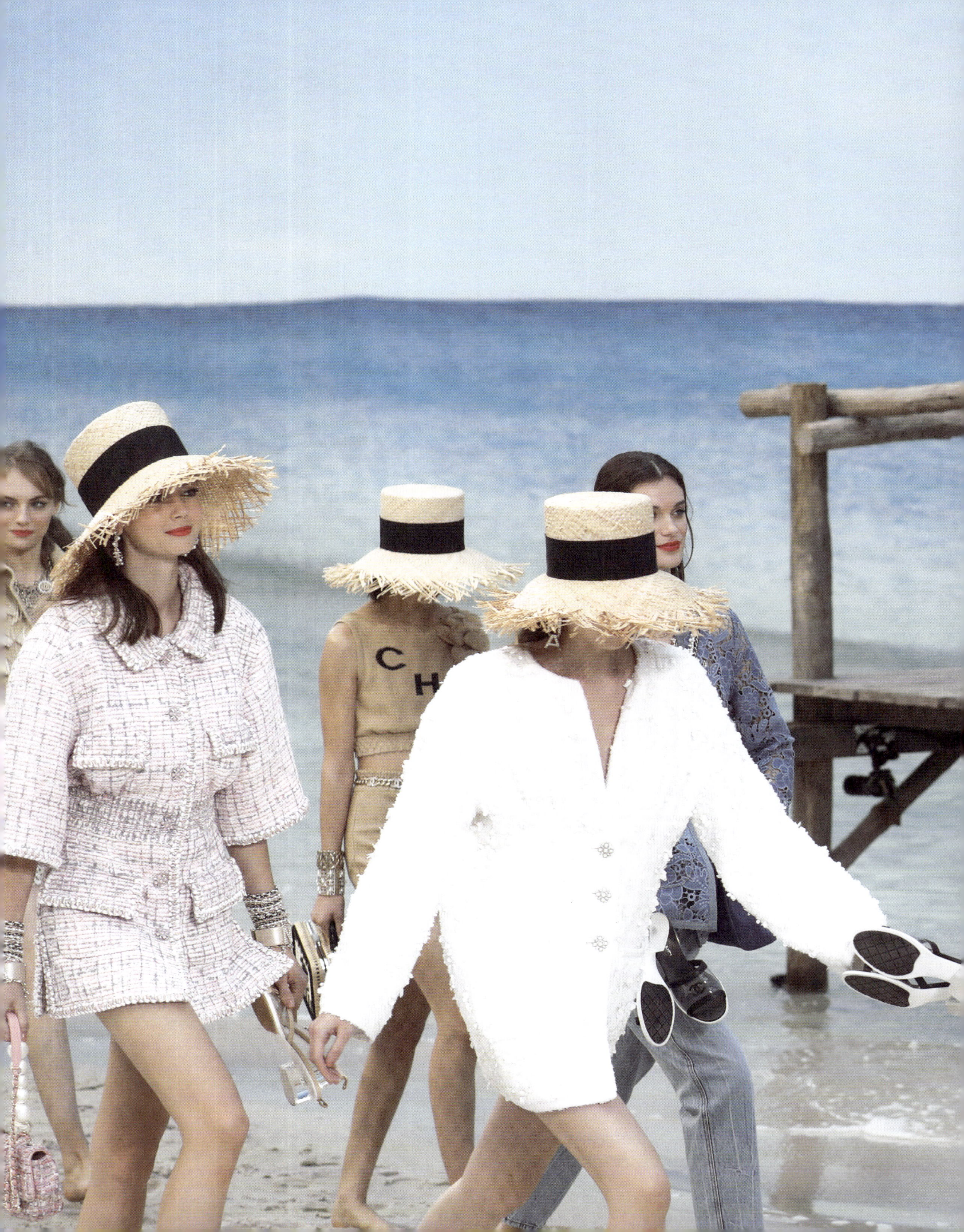

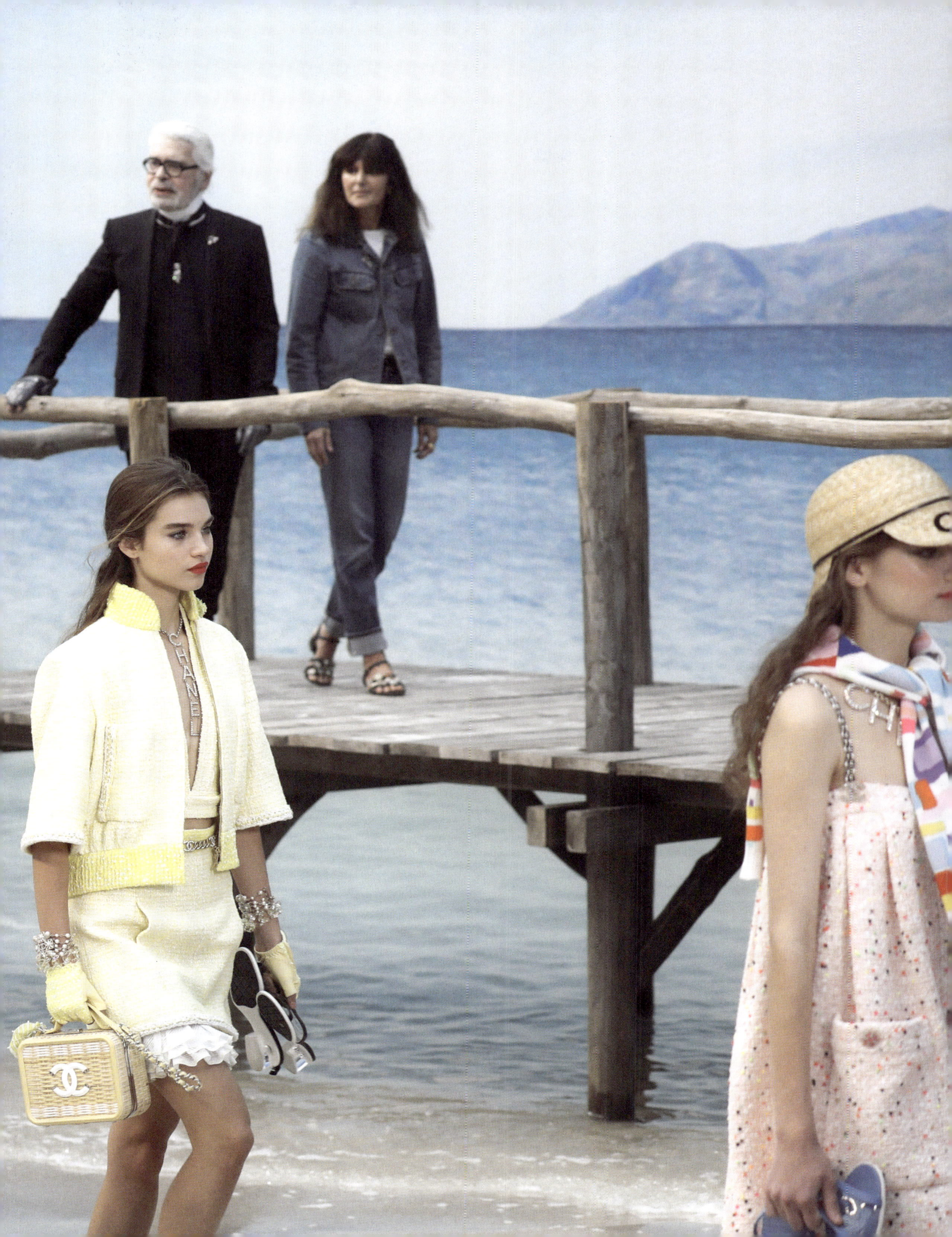
CHANEL

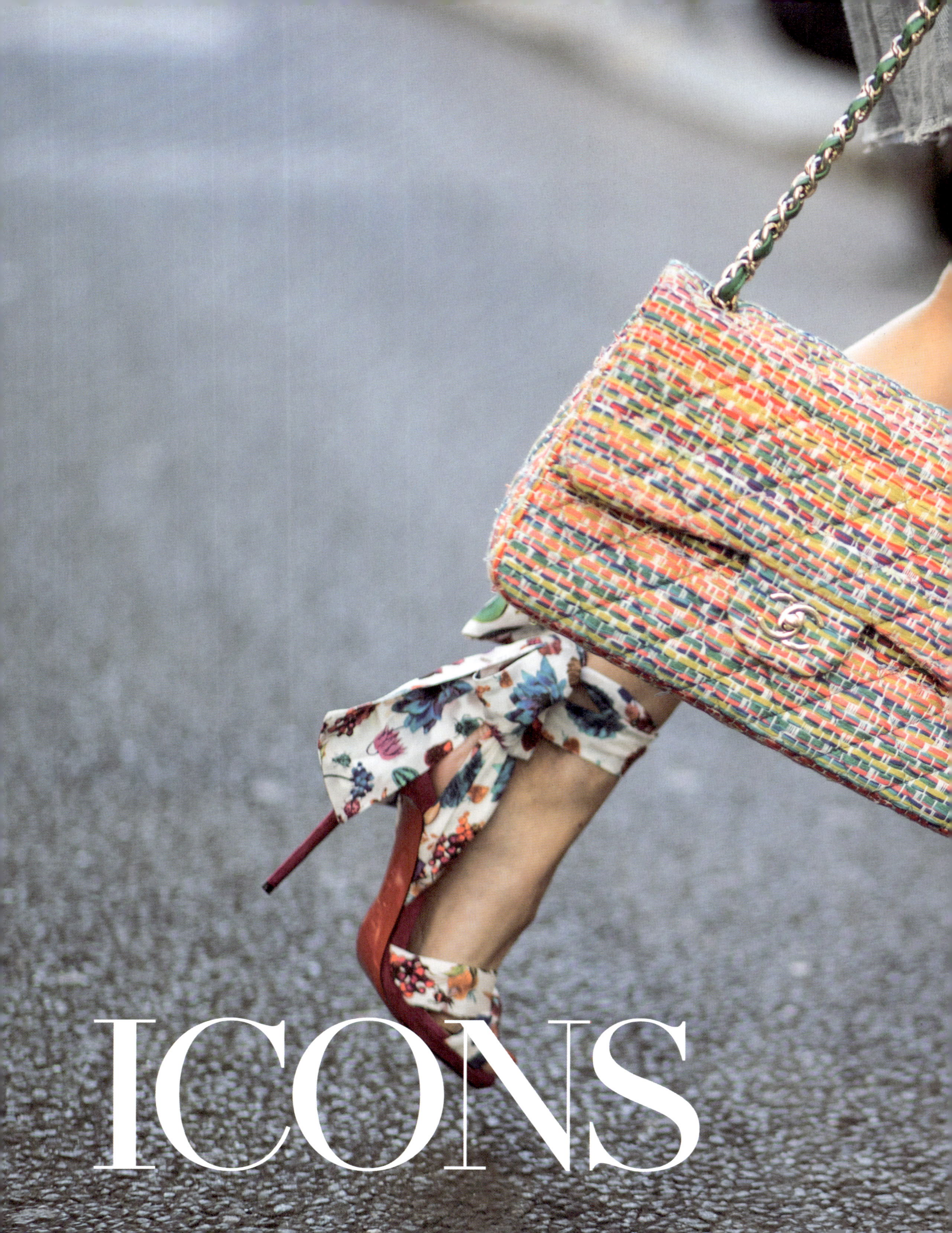

ICONS

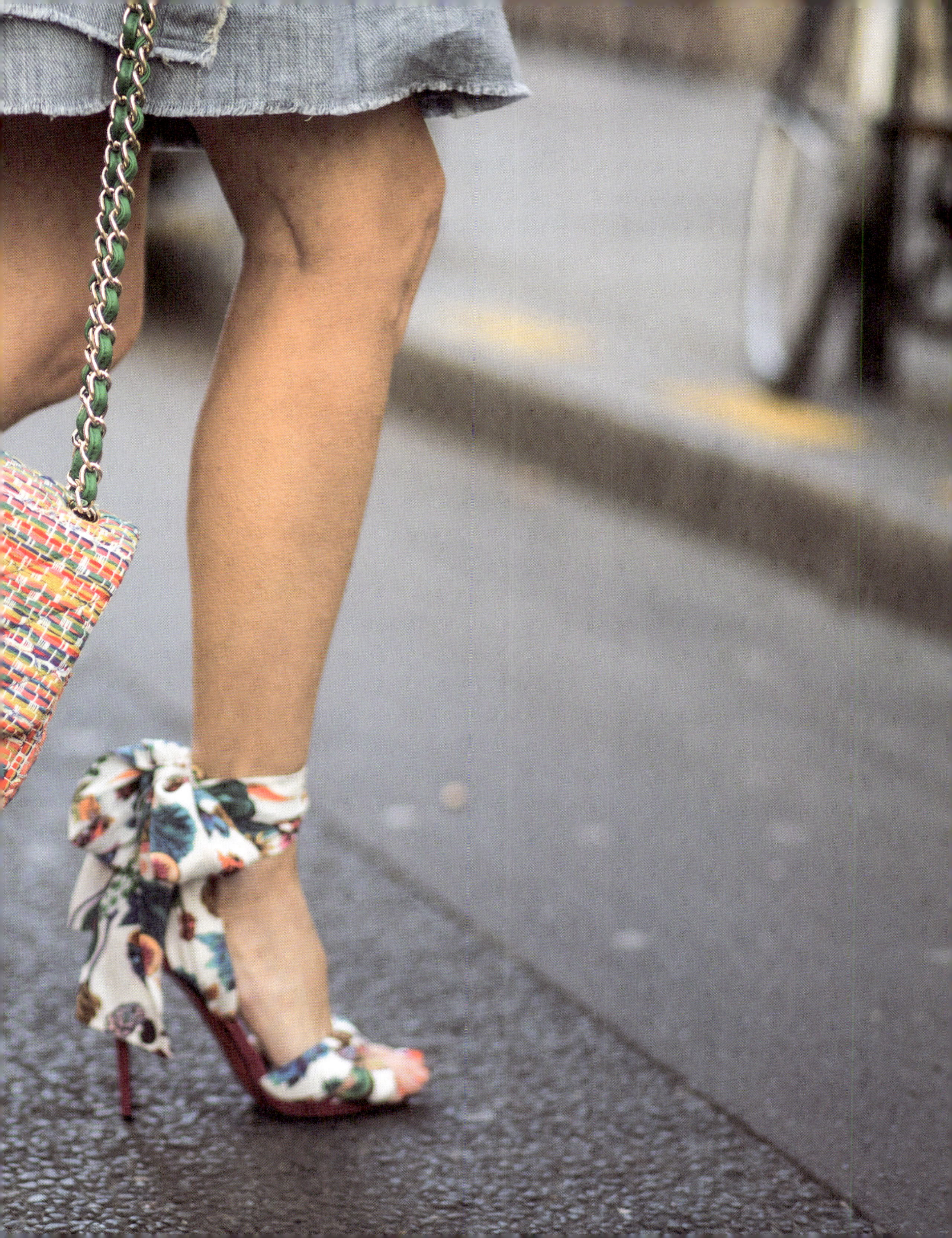

2.55 AND 2.55 REISSUE

Throughout her life, Chanel was fascinated by numerology. Five was her lucky number. It was emblazoned on the first outfit in her comeback couture collection (shown on February 5, 1954) and is the name of the *maison's* most famous perfume, No. 5. Chanel stood on the 5th step of the mirrored staircase at rue Cambon to oversee her presentations, and her most legendary handbag was named 2.55 after the date of its creation—February 1955.

Although arguably the most famous, the 2.55 wasn't Chanel's first bag. In 1929, a soldier's satchel inspired Chanel to create a bag with a shoulder strap, allowing the wearer to keep her hands free. This version influenced the 2.55 and, like so many of Chanel's signature styles, was a reaction to the dress code of that era. Beginning in the 1800s, handbags were mainly the preserve of aristocratic ladies. They were often hand-held, sometimes nestled in the crook of the wearer's arm. Other than military men, only lower-class women used shoulder bags, but the boxy, masculine shape carried by higher-class women restricted the wearer's movements and looked unattractive to Chanel. With the triple whammy of aesthetics, lack of practicality and breaking down expected class signifiers, Chanel saw that women needed a better way to carry their belongings *and* look chic while doing so. The 2.55 solved all three problems, providing an elegant shoulder-strap bag that left the wearer's hands free *and* was acceptable for society ladies to use.

The details of the first 2.55 bag combined several of Chanel's favorite tropes. Its story reflects the semiotics of Chanel's life, making it more than "just" a bag and providing some justification for the price tag. While the original 2.55 cost approximately £170 in the 1950s, their prices kept pace with inflation until around 1990. However, Chanel bags have appreciated at a rate far outstripping inflation since then. Today, a new bag costs around £8500 ($11,000/€10,200), with prices of pre-loved bags available through resale retailers hovering around £3000 ($3,900/€3,600) depending on size, material and condition.

Chanel's first bag employed quilted wool, and quilting has become synonymous with the Chanel look. It represents the quilted jackets worn by jockeys and the quilting on the horse's numnahs (the pad worn underneath the saddle). Balsan bred racehorses; Capel was a polo player, and Chanel often attended horse races. The quilting reflects Chanel's fondness for all things equestrian, although some believe it represents the stained glass windows in the orphanage or the quilted cushions in Chanel's apartment. The first iteration of the 2.55 was created in black leather, the color Chanel returned to again and again for its timeless elegance, and it was suitable for every occasion. The lambskin Chanel chose was originally used for glove making and therefore incredibly soft, although the bag was also offered in jersey and silk.

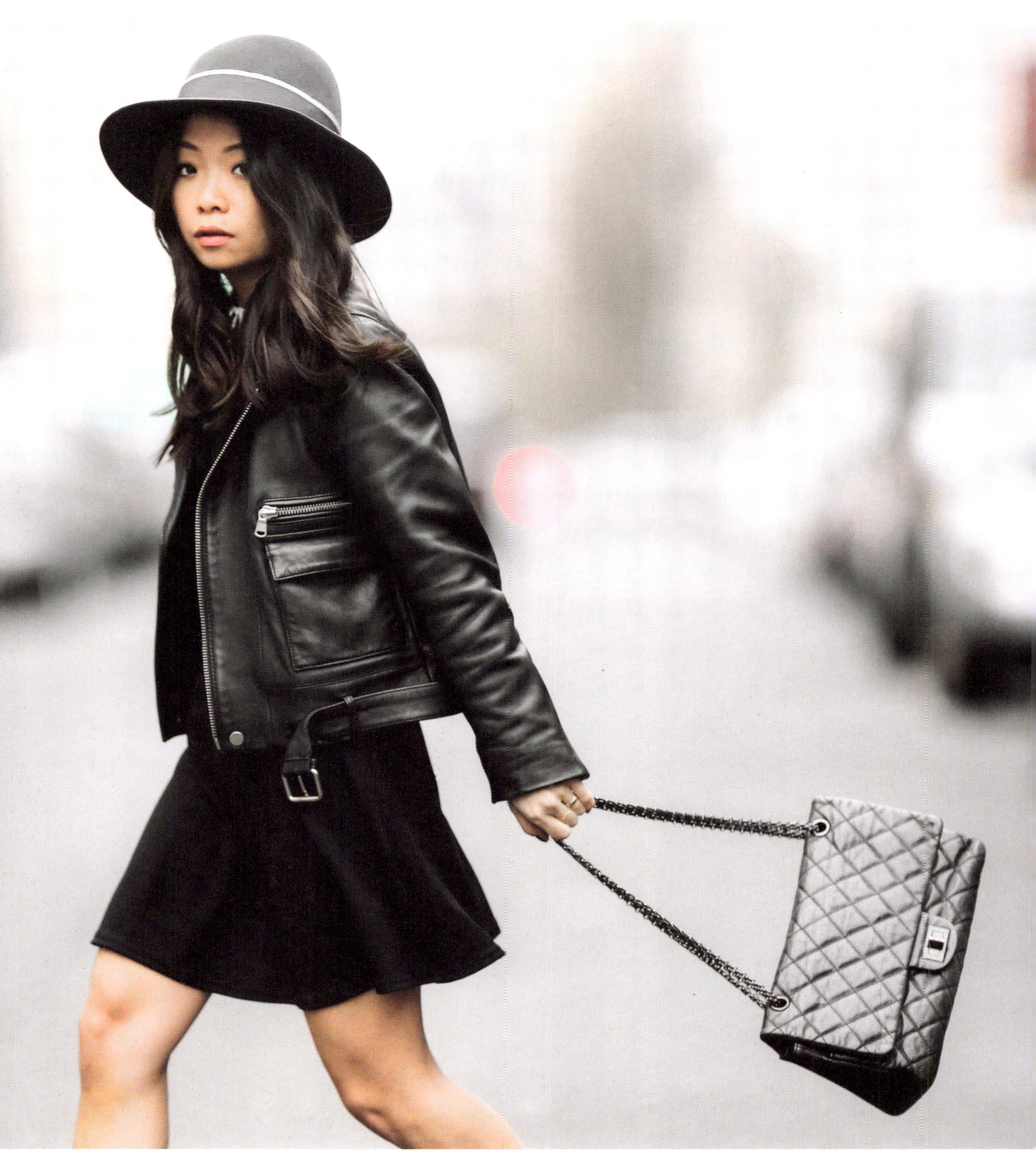

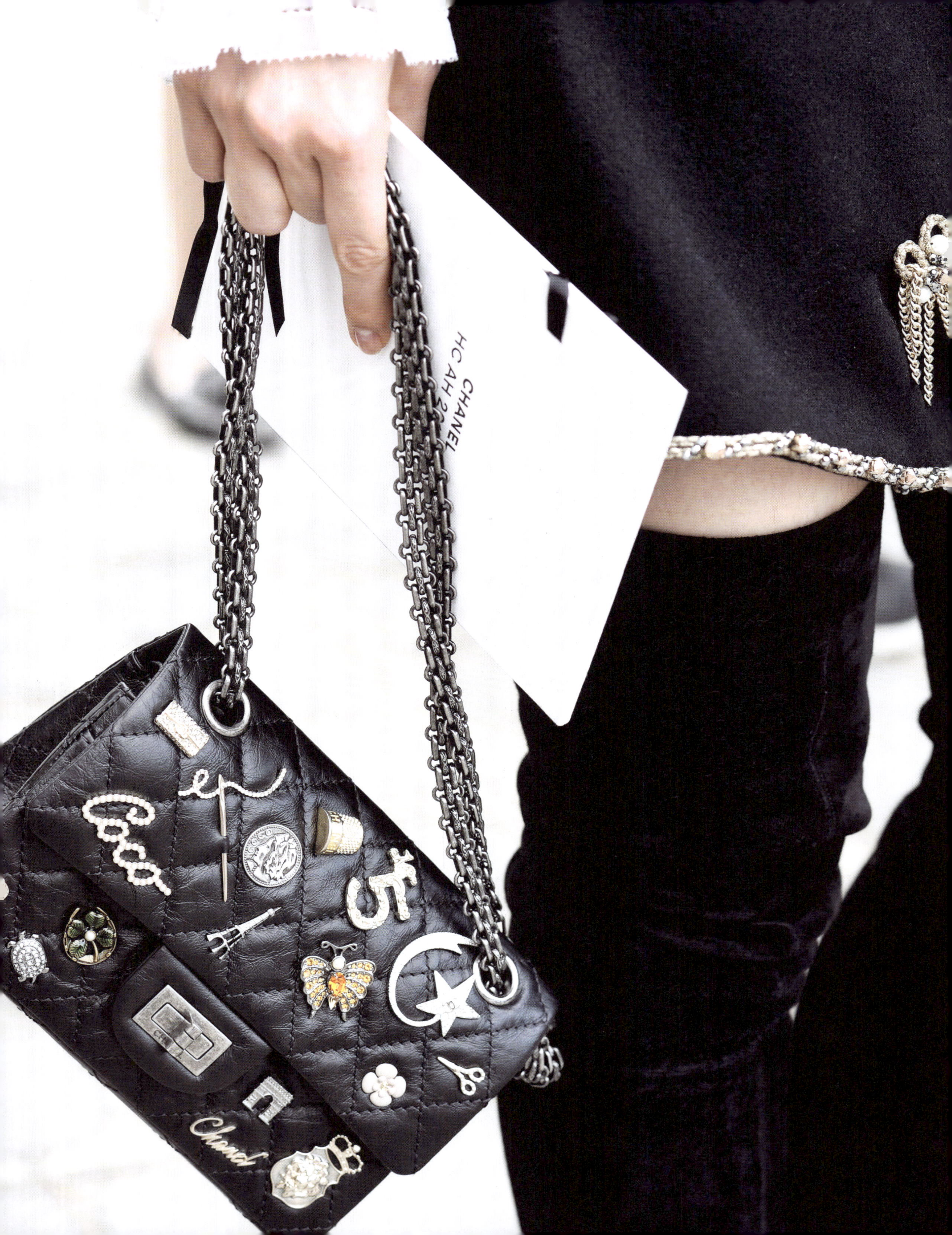
CHANEL
HC AH
Coco
Chanel

THE INSIDE MUST BE AS BEAUTIFUL AS THE OUTSIDE

Beyond the rectangular yet soft silhouette, the chain strap is an oft-used motif at Chanel, and chains are used inside the hems of tweed jackets to add weight and flattering drape to the fabric. For the 2.55, Chanel returned to her convent days, inspired by the chatelaine chains carried by the nuns to secure their keys. To begin with, the 2.55 had an all-chain strap which had a glamorous jewelry-like look, but the chains were woven with leather when materials reportedly became scarce. Whatever the composition, the long chain handle on the 2.55 is versatile because it can be worn long, across the body, or doubled-up to sit at shoulder bag height. Links can also be removed at Chanel stores to perfectly customize your 2.55.

The bag's burgundy lining was the same shade as Chanel's convent uniform, but the lighter interior also gives users a better view of their belongings. The seven clever pockets provide easy access. There is a large main compartment and two smaller pockets (ideal for a compact or mirror) bordering a round compartment for lipstick. On the inside of the flap, Chanel included a secret zippered section where legend says she stashed love letters, and 2.55 bags are classed as Double Flaps (excluding the mini size). The exterior pocket, where Chanel kept small bills and change for tipping, is nicknamed the Mona Lisa pocket because it curves upwards like a subtle smile. It was imperative to Chanel that "the inside must be as beautiful as the outside," and the individual elements of the bag are pieced together like a couture garment. Assembled using a reverse bridle stitch, a single bag takes 15 hours for artisans in Chanel's ateliers to create.

The 2.55 was definitely the world's first It Bag. Gabrielle Chanel herself popularized the style along with fashion icons such as Romy Schneider, Catherine Deneuve and Jackie Kennedy. Today, fans carrying the 2.55 reissue include Kate Moss, Claudia Schiffer and Taraji P. Henson.

While you might imagine a Chanel bag with a double CC logo fastening, the 2.55 bag has a Mademoiselle lock—a simple, minimal, rectangular clasp, named for the fact that Chanel never married. Initially, the lock was plain, but to celebrate the 2.55's 50th anniversary in 2005, Karl Lagerfeld released the 2.55 Reissue, an exact commemorative replica of Chanel's original bag with chain strap, double flap, secret pocket—and the addition of a Chanel stamp on the lock.

Beyond the selection of bags released in 2005, 2.55 reissues have become a catch-all description for any 2.55 style released since Lagerfeld's update. Even if a bag combines less traditional elements, it's often referred to as a 2.55, which can confuse an armchair aficionado. Leather 2.55 bags are often made from aged calfskin, but the style also comes in tweed or jersey versions, along with special editions that reflect each season's catwalk collection. If you are looking to invest in your own 2.55 reissue, the bags are often referred to by their size. There are six variations, from the Mini, Petit Sac 224, Sac 225, Grand Sac 226 (the most useful medium size), Maxi Sac 227 and 228. Although production of the 228 ended in 2008, there are vintage 228 sizes available.

Pages 22/23: Alexandra Lapp showcases a multicolored Classic Flap at Paris Fashion Week, March 2018

Page 25: Fashion blogger May Berthelot is spotted with a Chanel 2.55 reissue in Paris, 2017

Page 26: A "Lucky Charms" 2.55 reissue spotted in Paris, 2014

Next page: Alexandra Lapp is seen with a black tweed 2.55 Chanel bag during Berlin Fashion Week, 2019

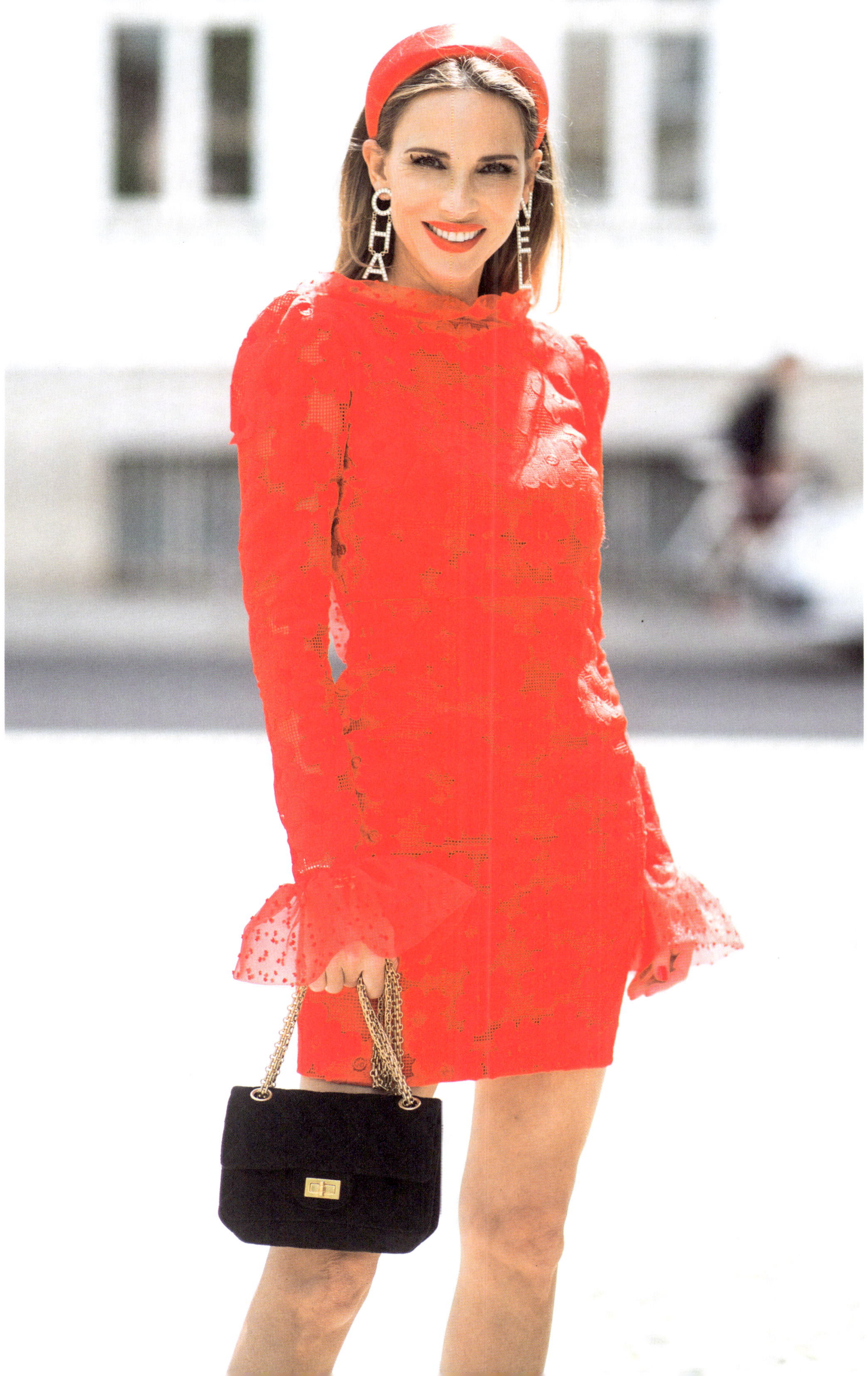
CHA

CLASSIC FLAP OR 11.12

With its double CC logo turnlock, signature quilting and chain strap interlaced with leather, the Classic Flap might be the bag that immediately comes to mind when you picture a Chanel handbag. Beyond the significance and history of the 2.55, the Classic Flap—also known as 11.12—has come to represent all things Chanel. However, it owes its existence not to Mlle Chanel herself, but rather to Karl Lagerfeld. Lagerfeld reworked the 2.55 and put his own spin on it to match the fashion mood of the 1980s. It's just as relevant today. The Classic Flap was launched in 1983 and is now known as the 11.12. The numerical name, which has been used exclusively since 2021, comes from the style code AO1112 found in every medium sized Classic Flap. Today, *any* size Classic Flap can be called the 11.12, and just as 2.55 bags created after the reissue run are still called 2.55 reissues, the Classic Flap and 11.12 names can be interchangeable.

So, how *did* Lagerfeld improve Chanel's original bag design? From being warned off the *maison* before he took the role of chief artistic director, Lagerfeld created a modern icon with the Classic Flap bag. "When I took over Chanel, everybody said to me, 'Don't touch it. It's dead. There's nothing you can do.' And I said to myself, 'I love that people think that. Now let's see.'" With a few simple tweaks, Lagerfeld ensured a new legend was born at the house of Chanel. Lagerfeld introduced the double CC logo turnlock fastening, which kickstarted the 1980s obsession with designer logos, along with the chain laced with leather, tweed or jersey, depending on what the specific bag is made from.

The Classic Flap is usually quilted, although there are chevron designs and a plain version as well, while the main finishes are either smooth lambskin or grained caviar leather. The technique used to create Chanel's signature diamond quilting is called *point droit de couturière*. Each season, the *maison* updates the 11.12 with catwalk-influenced motifs including versions made from clear PVC, sequins, tweed, denim, faux pearls, florals or styles encrusted with crystals.

Each bag takes over 180 steps and 15 hours of painstaking work to create. Chanel artisans use the *piqué retourné* technique, which translates as "stitch and turn." This means that as the bag is being constructed, it's turned inside out, and two bags—the interior and exterior—are sewn together for an immaculate finish. Sometimes the method is also described as "bag-in-a-bag," and the inside and outside bags are held together with *points de bride* stitches. The *piqué retourné* method is unique, as it gives every Chanel bag a plush, lifted and voluminous finish.

Next page: Irina Shayk carries a Classic Flap in gray leather at Milan Fashion Week, 2025

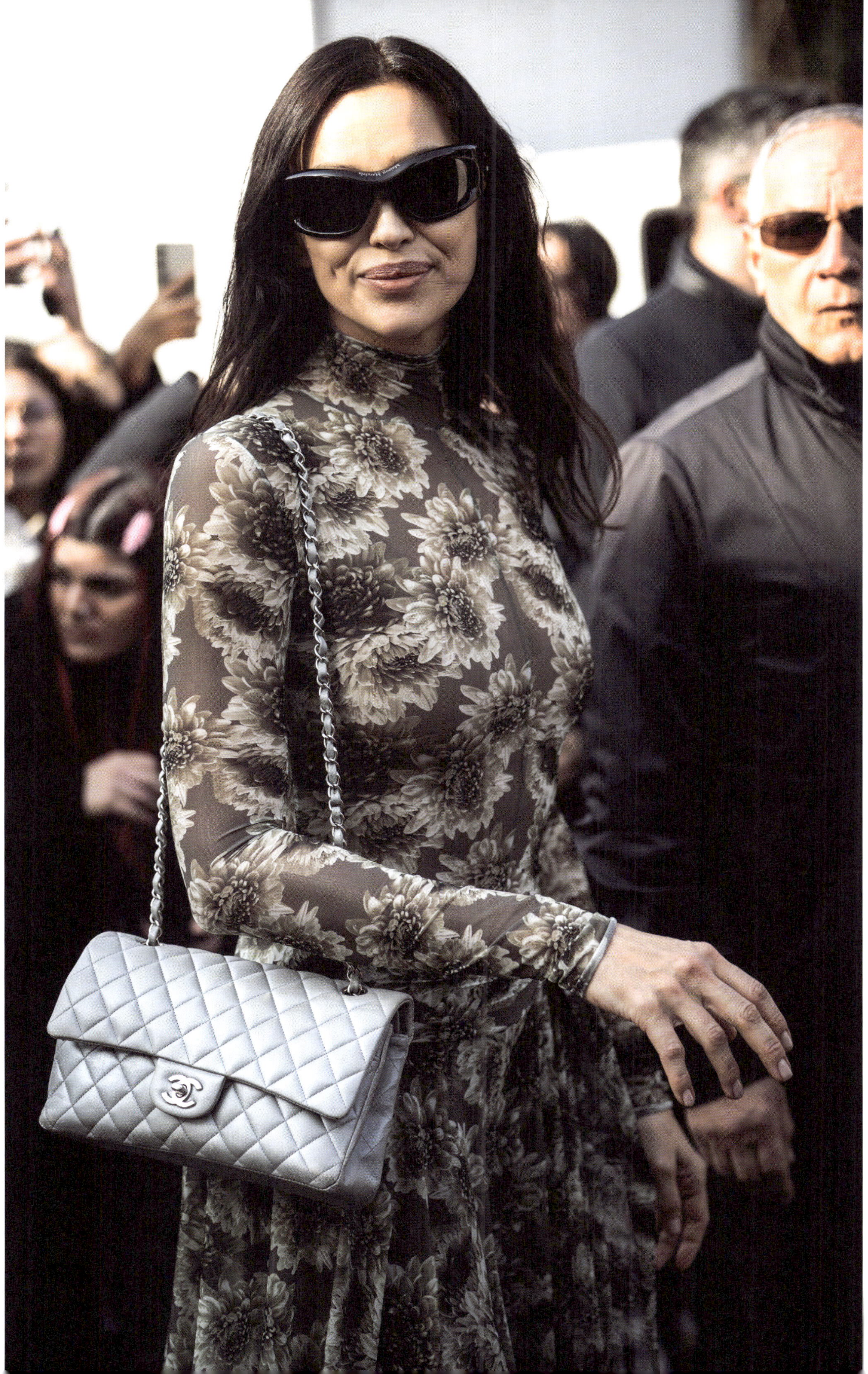

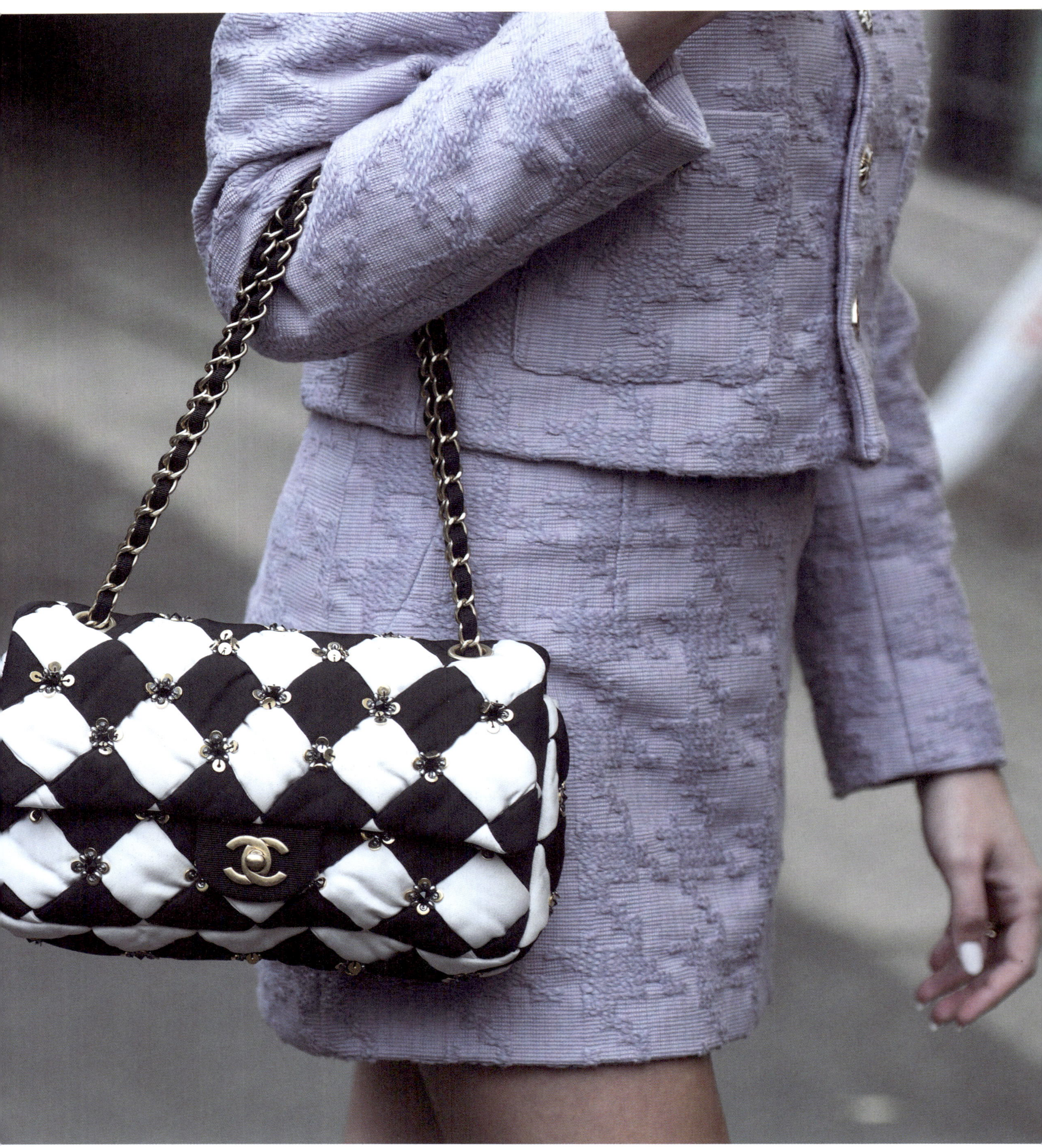

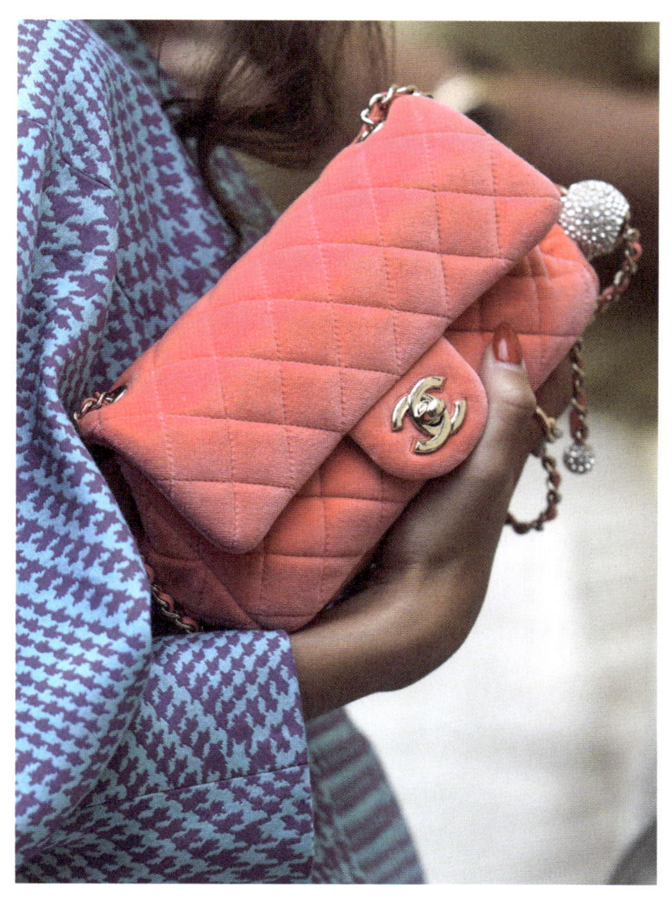

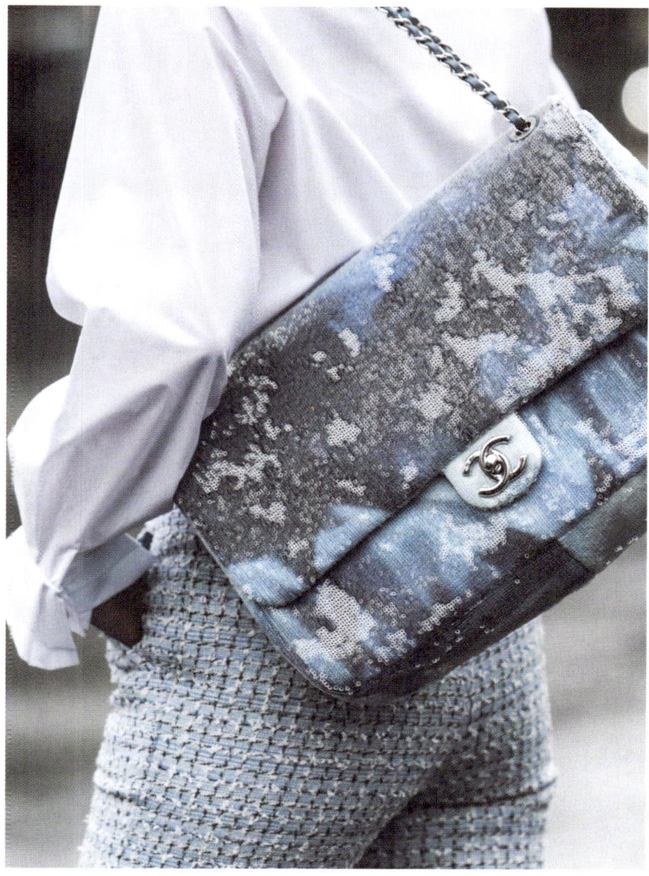

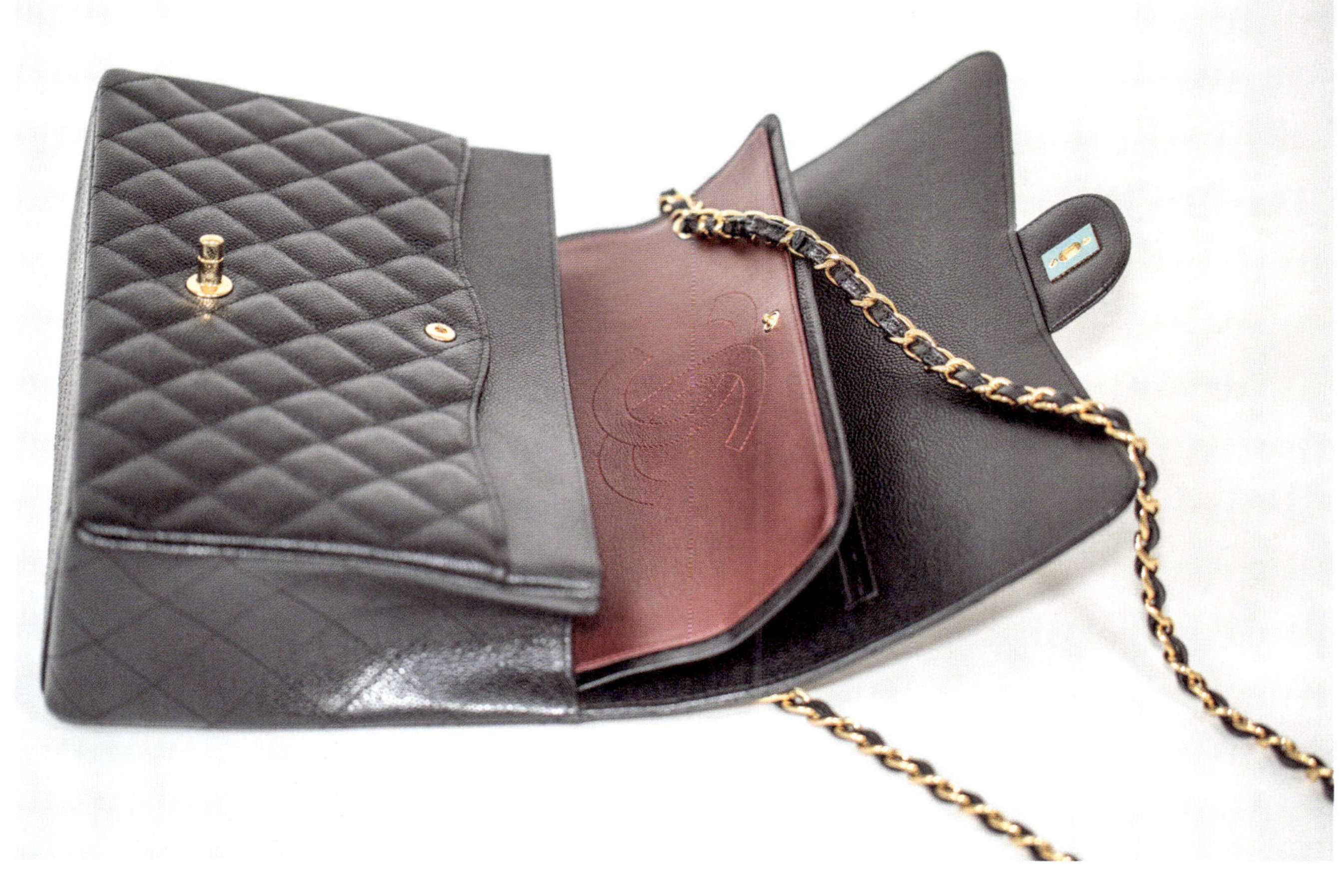

Despite Lagerfeld's updates, the 11.12 follows Mlle Chanel's signature seven-pocket design. All 11.12s are classed as double flap bags (except the mini size, which has a single flap), although single flap bags with just an exterior flap were produced sporadically since the initial launch. You can still find these to purchase through vintage outlets, although they aren't available in Chanel boutiques. The medium is the bestselling size because it is ideal for both day and evening use. The other sizes range from extra mini (which was discontinued in 2019 and now only available as pre-owned), mini square (17 × 13.5 × 8cm), mini rectangle, mini small, medium (which is sometimes described as 'medium/large,' as the former large style was discontinued), jumbo and maxi (34 × 23 × 10cm). Interestingly, on the resale market, the largest bags are not always the most expensive—medium (measuring 25.5 × 16 × 7.5cm) is the highest priced and seemingly most coveted. A Maxi Classic Flap bag in grained (caviar) calfskin leather currently retails for over £10,000 while a Classic 11.12 in lambskin leather is £8,850. A wool tweed version sells for £8,420.

If you're wondering about the properties of the different leathers, lambskin is famed for its luxurious feel. It is supple and soft, but vulnerable to accidental scuffs and scratches because the leather is so fine and fragile. Over time, the finish will also lose its plumpness and flatten out. Caviar leather, also known as grained calfskin, is definitely a more durable choice, which makes this finish perfect for everyday wear. Light marks aren't as noticeable due to the texture of the hide and the leather is a little stronger, meaning the bag will hold its shape brilliantly. Caviar leather bags also feature edge stitching. Patent leather is the flashiest option, beloved for its high-shine finish; however, fingerprints are very noticeable on the glossy leather. Scuffs and transfer

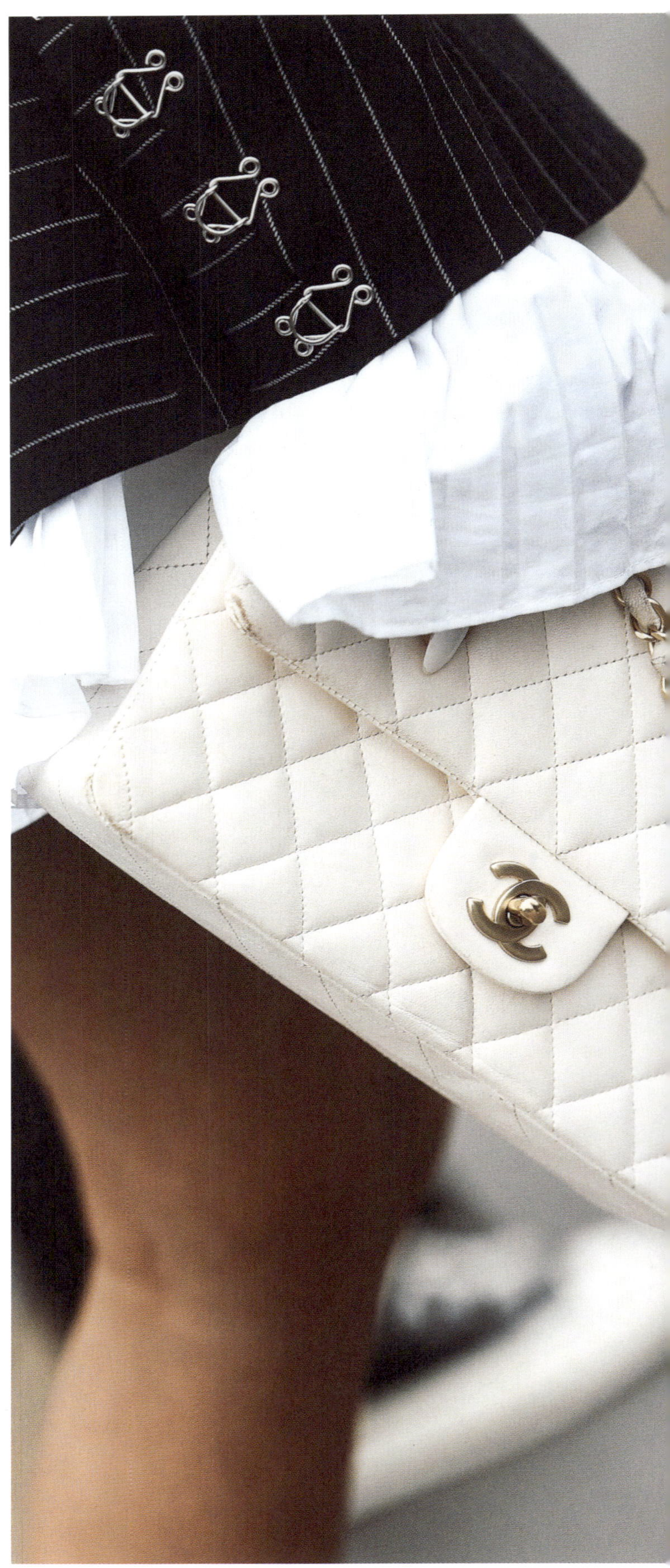

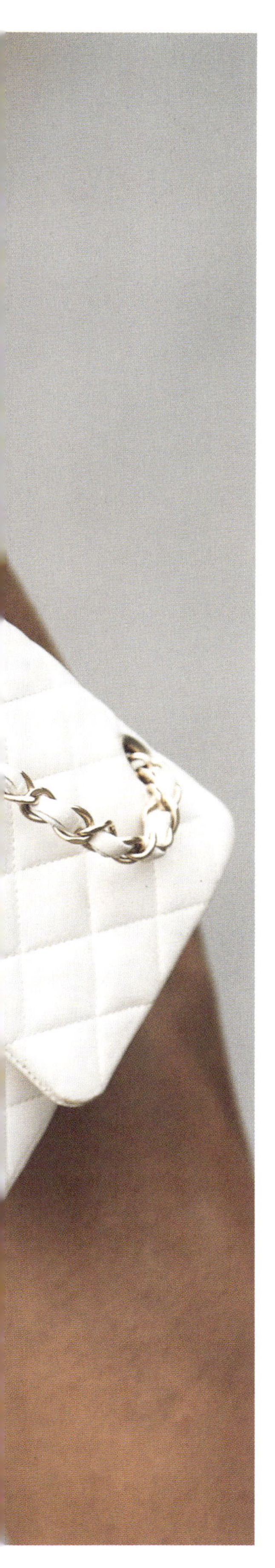

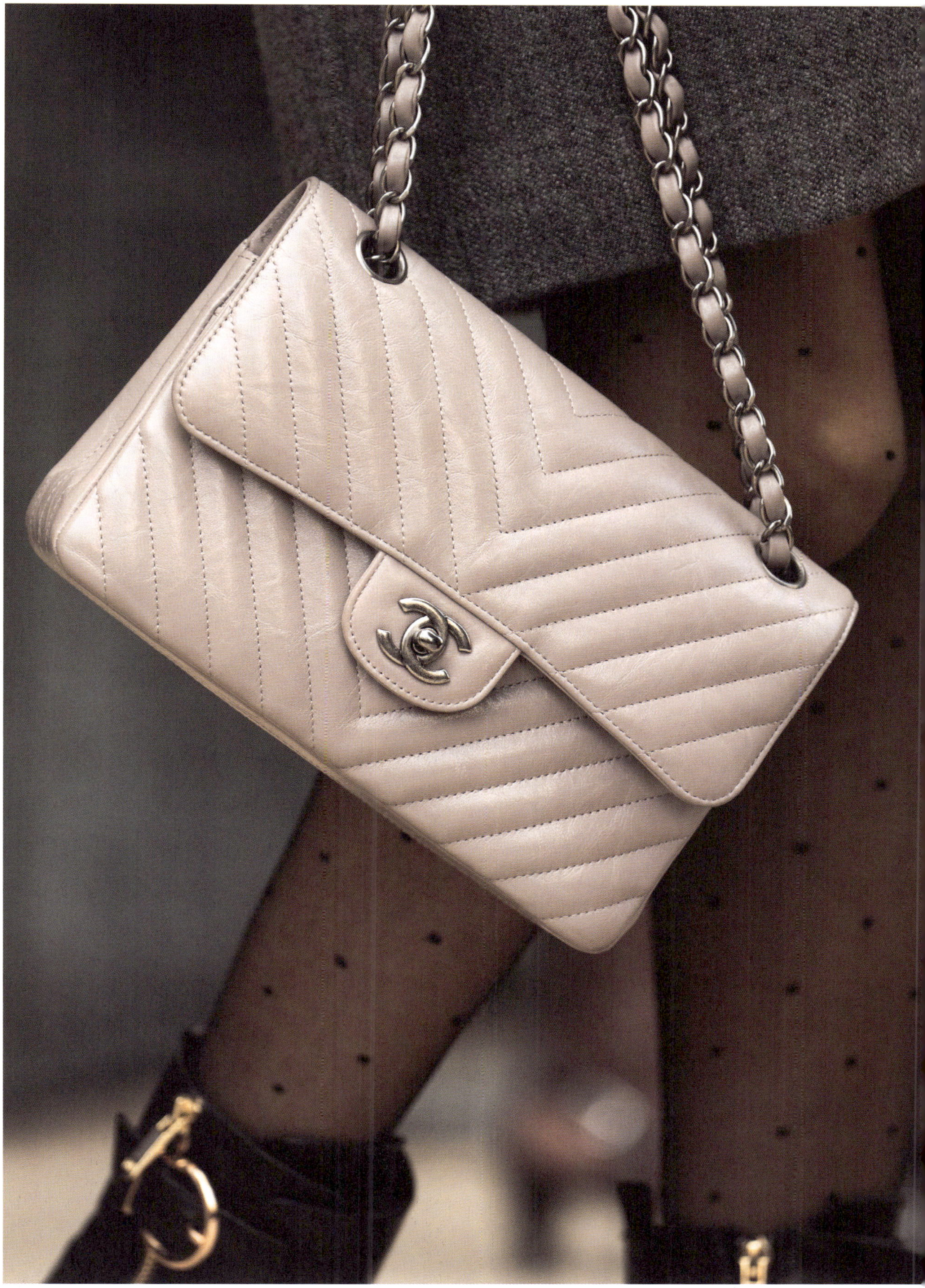

Page 32: Pre-Fall 2021 Métiers d'Art Checkerboard Embroidered Single Flap in satin observed in Milan, 2021

Page 33: (Top left) Pink velvet Pearl Crush mini Classic Flap, Milan, 2021; (Bottom) The iconic double flap; (Top right) A Paris Fashion Week attendee carries a Blue Waterfall Classic Flap from the Spring/Summer 2018 collection, Paris, 2019

Page 34: A Classic Flap in white leather, Paris, 2018

Page 35: A chevron Classic Flap showcased in Paris, 2024

Page 36 and 37: Alexandra Lapp is seen sporting a multicolored Mondrian Classic Flap (left) in Düsseldorf, 2021, and a black-and-white Garden of Versailles Classic Flap (right) in Berlin, 2017

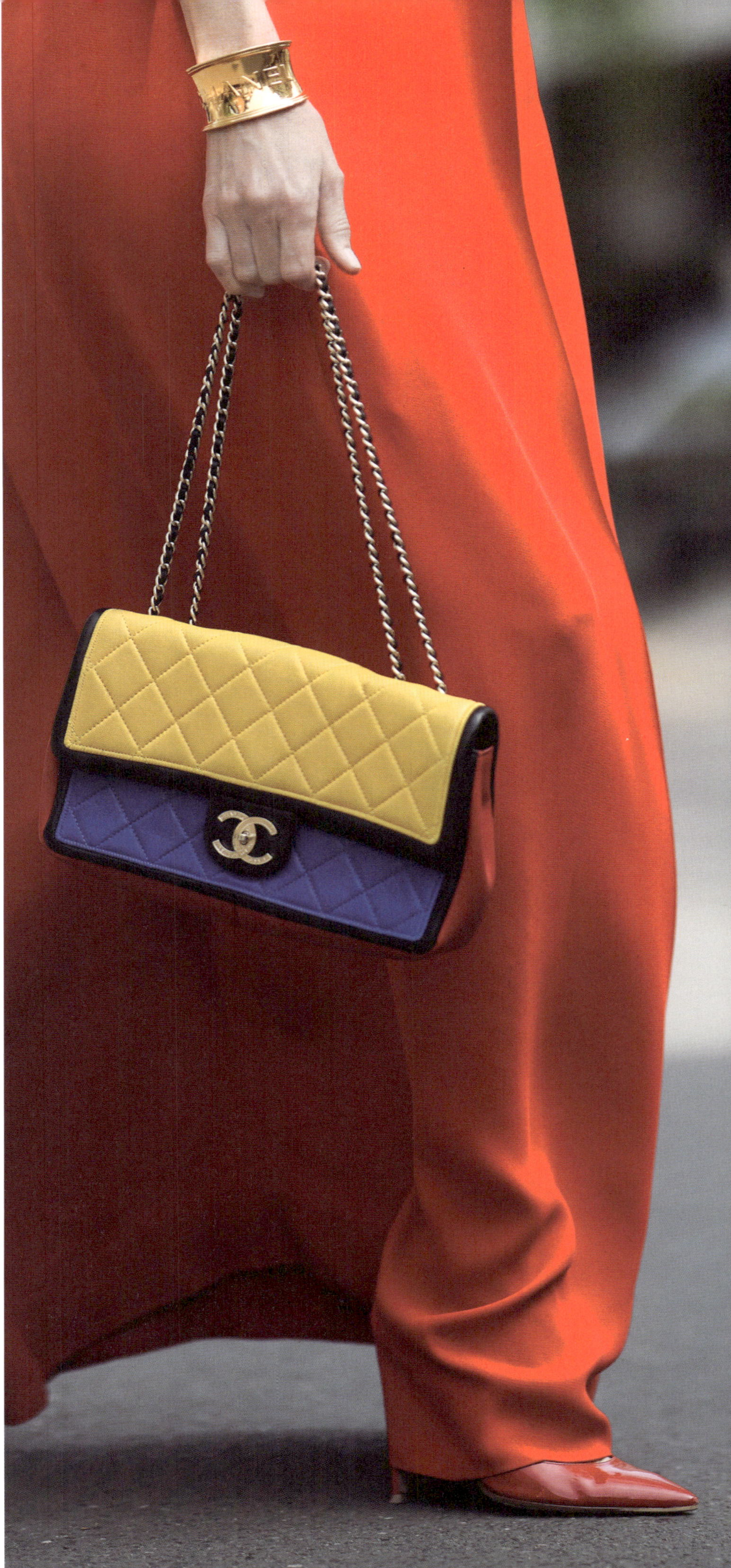

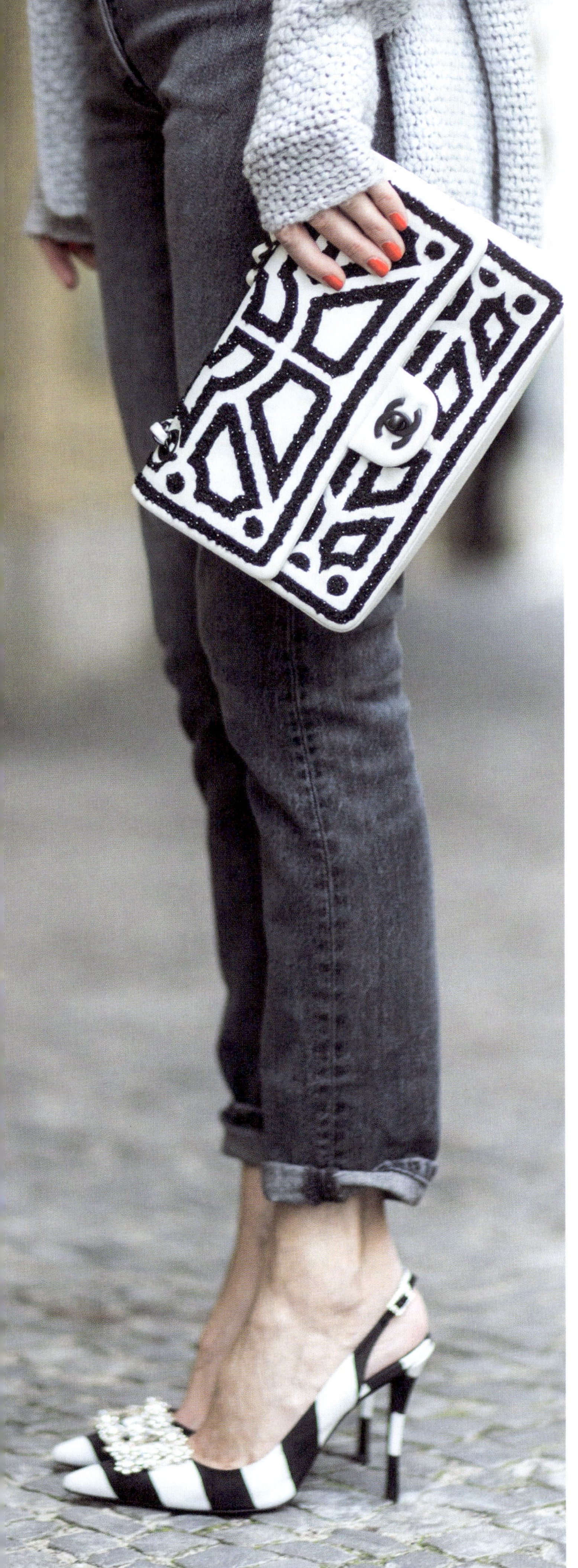

marks can also be much more noticeable on patent leather than on other finishes.

If you are searching for a vintage or pre-loved 11.12 bag, you should know that styles with a bijoux chain are some of the most coveted. Produced only in 2007 and 2008, these bags have wide-set chain links for their straps, instead of the interlaced versions on most Classic Flaps or the signature chains of the 2.55. Having been discontinued, a bag with a bijoux chain will be a rare find on the resale market, along with bags with an iridescent finish from the 2016 Cruise collection or the 18S emerald green colorway.

The hardware on bags made before 2008 has a deep yellow tone, reflecting the 24 carat gold-plated finish of that era. Bags made after 2008 use gold-toned metal, while silver hardware is often found on older styles. The rarest styles come with black hardware, as seen on the So Black Classic Flap, where all the hardware is black to complement a bag with a black body. Kim Kardashian has carried the style. Sometimes seasonal versions are produced with hardware in ruthenium, plexiglass, enamel, matte metal or metal with antique finishes. Chevron finishes aren't made every season (unlike the diamond quilting detail), so they are also a less common find.

In addition to Kardashian, Paris Hilton, Kerry Washington and Katie Holmes are all card-carrying Chanel Classic Flap fans. French actress Zoé Adjani, the star of the Spring 2021 ad campaign shot by Inez van Lamsweerde and Vinoodh Matadin, said, "It represents more than a bag: it's like carrying Paris on your shoulder." But far lighter.

BOY

So many iconic pieces from Chanel are interwoven with stories and anecdotes from Mlle Chanel's own life, even if they were created after her death. The Boy bag is one such piece. Launched as part of the Fall/Winter 2011 collection and designed by Karl Lagerfeld, the Boy stands out among the classics in Chanel's bag collection as an edgier, androgynous style that is perfect for city life. It's a favorite with younger Chanel fans, but its origins are rooted in history. Named after Chanel's lover, Arthur 'Boy' Capel, its design echoes Chanel's appreciation of country pursuits. Originally inspired by a cartridge bag, a working-style bag used by people at shooting parties, today's Boy bag is characterized by its rectangular shape with a wide top-stitched frame around the front.

So, who was the man who inspired one of Chanel's most iconic bags? Chanel met Capel in 1909 while she was still involved with Etienne Balsan, but their affair quickly eclipsed that relationship. Having spent the day riding together (but not exchanging a word), Chanel's first question to Capel was, apparently, to ask when his train was scheduled to depart. "The following day, I was at the station. I climbed onto the train," Chanel told her friend and memoirist Paul Morand. Entranced by Capel's looks, Chanel described him as "handsome, very tanned and attractive. More than handsome, he was magnificent. I admired his nonchalance, and his green eyes... I fell in love with him."

At a time when it was common for male artists, whether painters, sculptors or musicians, to have female muses, Chanel turned the status quo on its head yet again and found Capel to be her ultimate muse. Beyond his looks, Chanel was inspired by his sporting, shooting and polo-playing attire along with his loose blazers. The minimal silhouettes of Capel's jackets went on to influence Chanel's own womenswear designs. Capel and Chanel had a grand romance and Capel saw Chanel's obvious talent, helping to finance her early boutiques, although he was apparently never faithful. It was rumored that Capel proposed to Chanel, but she refused, saying she wanted to be financially independent before marrying. It is also said that Capel believed he needed to marry within aristocratic circles. In 1918, Capel wed Lady Diana Wyndham, daughter of Thomas Lister, 4th Baron Ribblesdale, meeting his requirements for an upper class union. However, Capel continued his trysts with Chanel until he died in a car accident in December 1919. The tire of his Rolls Royce was said to have exploded en route to meet Chanel for a Christmas reunion in the South of France. Chanel told a friend, "In losing Capel, I lost everything."

With such a romantic love story behind the bag, the Boy is surprisingly tough-looking, but its timelessness fits in effortlessly with the aesthetic of any decade. On the front of each Boy, there is a wide top-stitched border that physically frames the bag. Styles are quilted either diagonally or in chevron style on the main body, although some have plain bodies, while the framing

MORE THAN HANDSOME, HE WAS MAGNIFICENT ... I FELL IN LOVE WITH HIM.

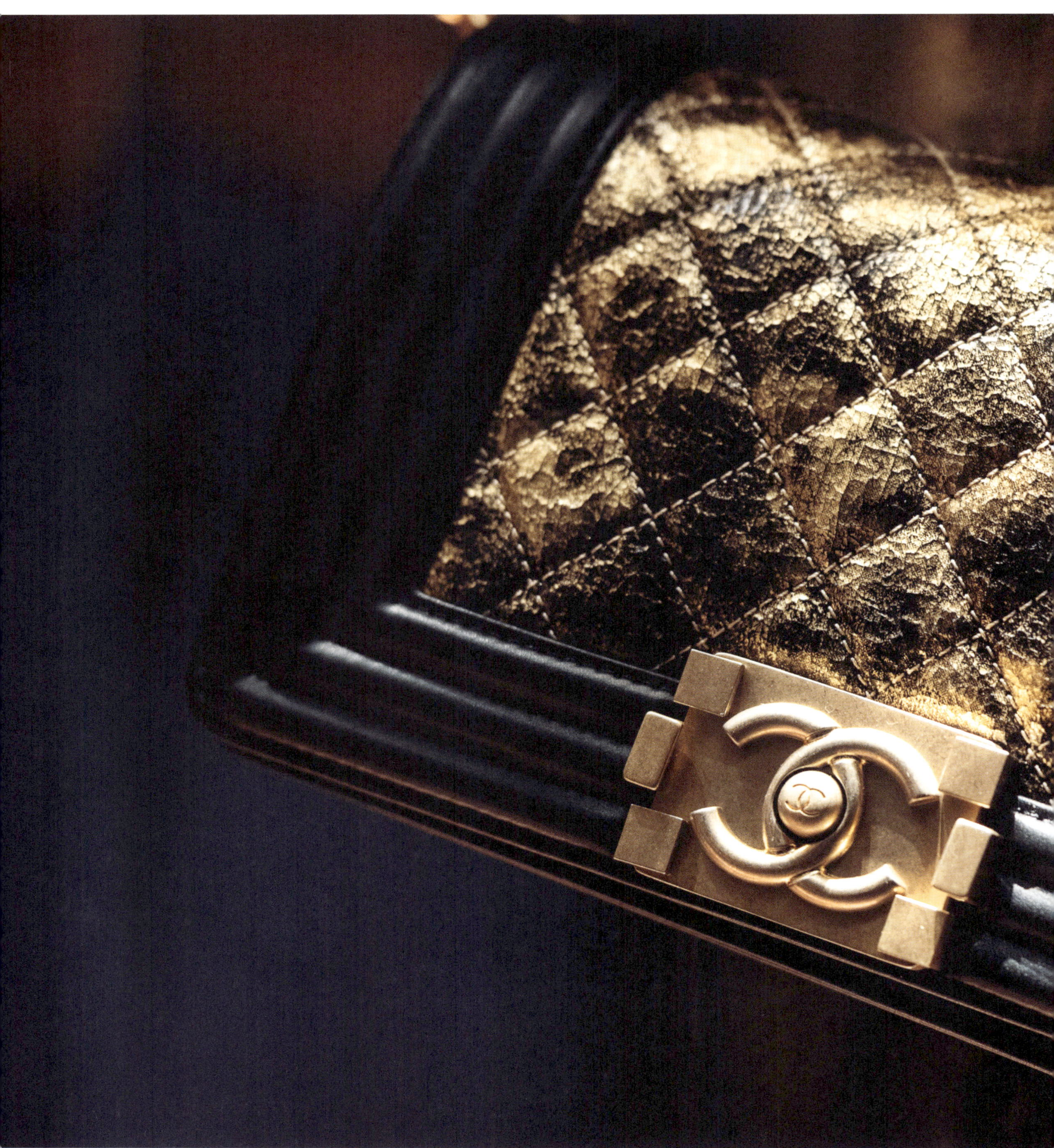

A Boy bag displayed in a store window in Milan, 2018

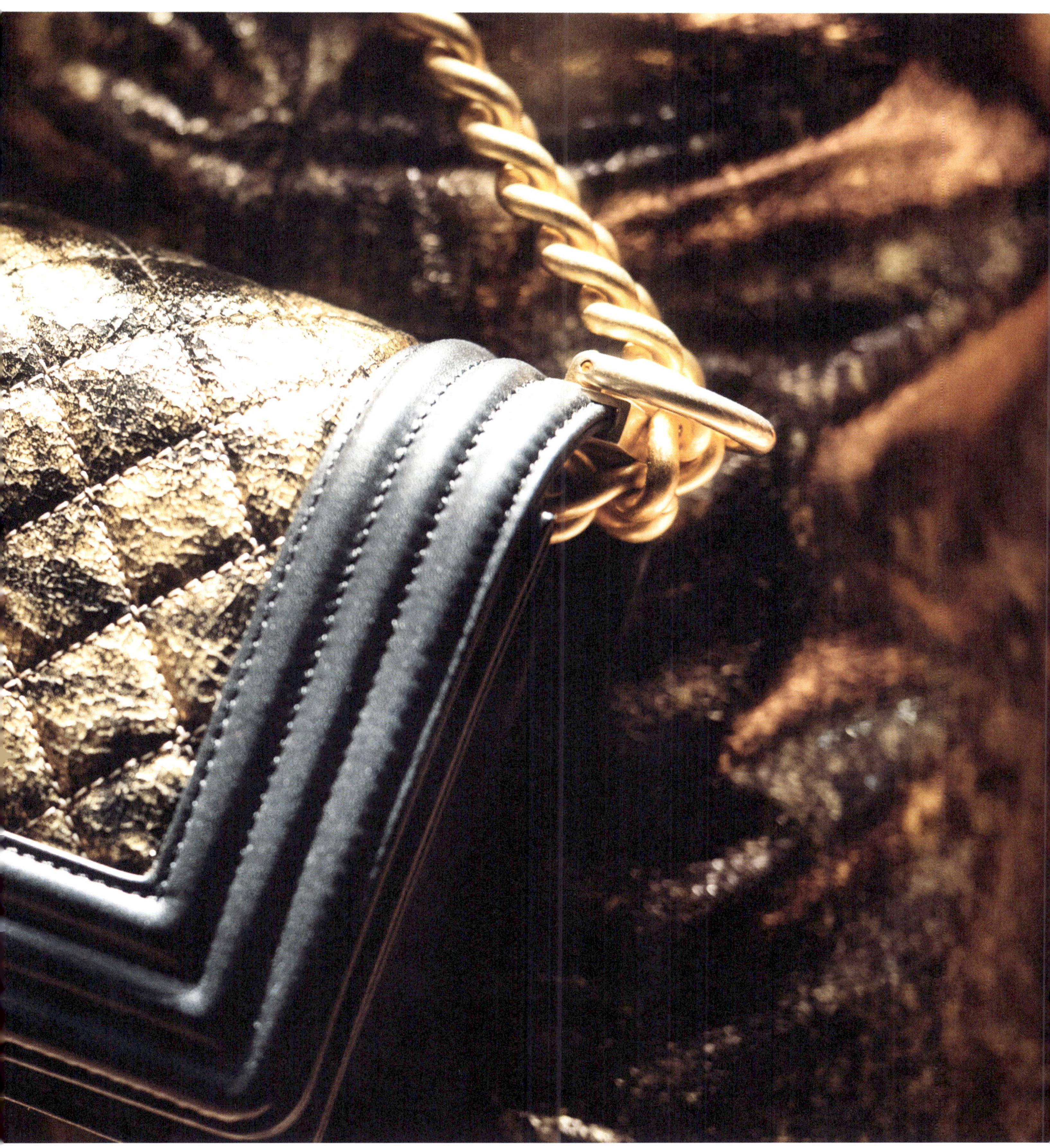

This page: Priya Jain is seen with a black chevron Boy bag at the Cannes Film Festival, 2023

Next page: Alexandra Lapp is captured with a bicolor Boy bag in Marrakech, 2018

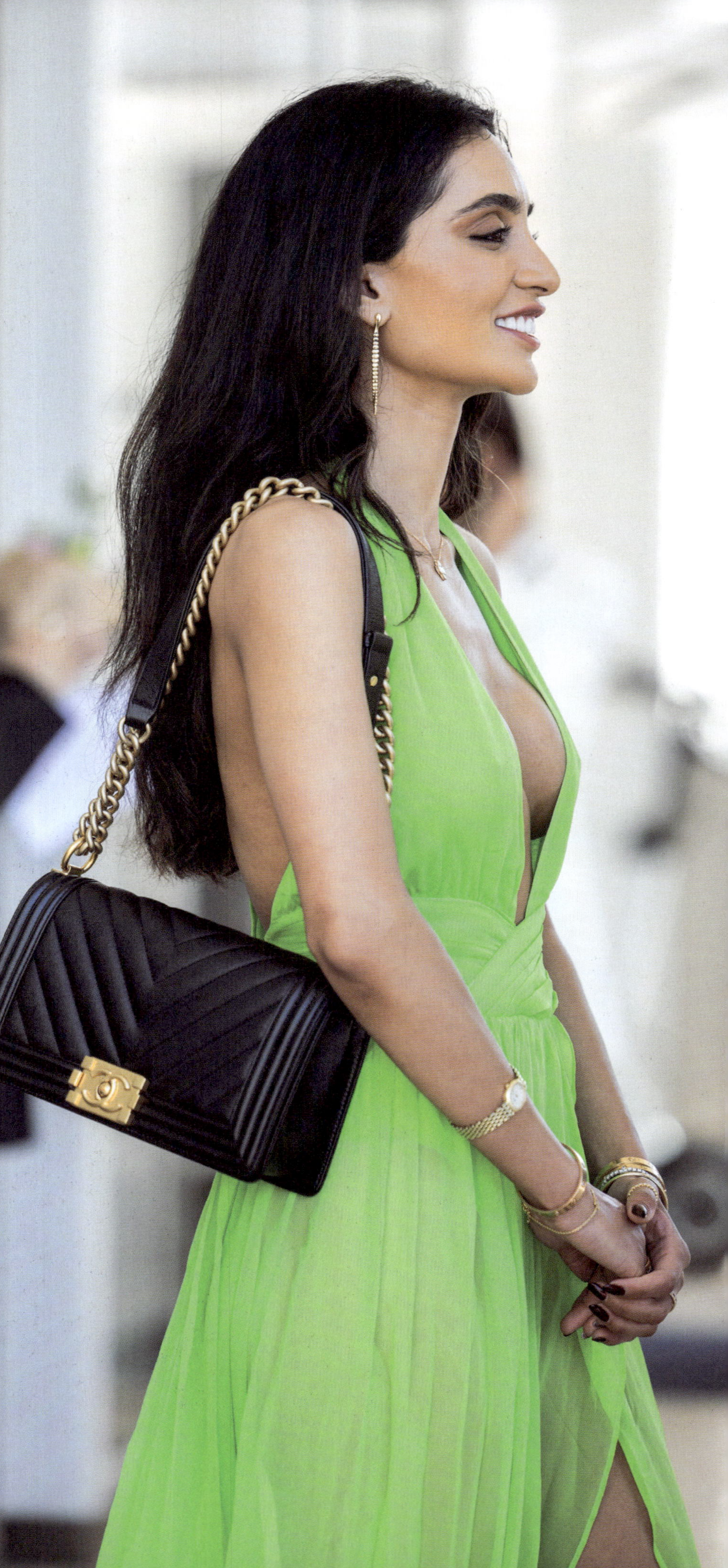

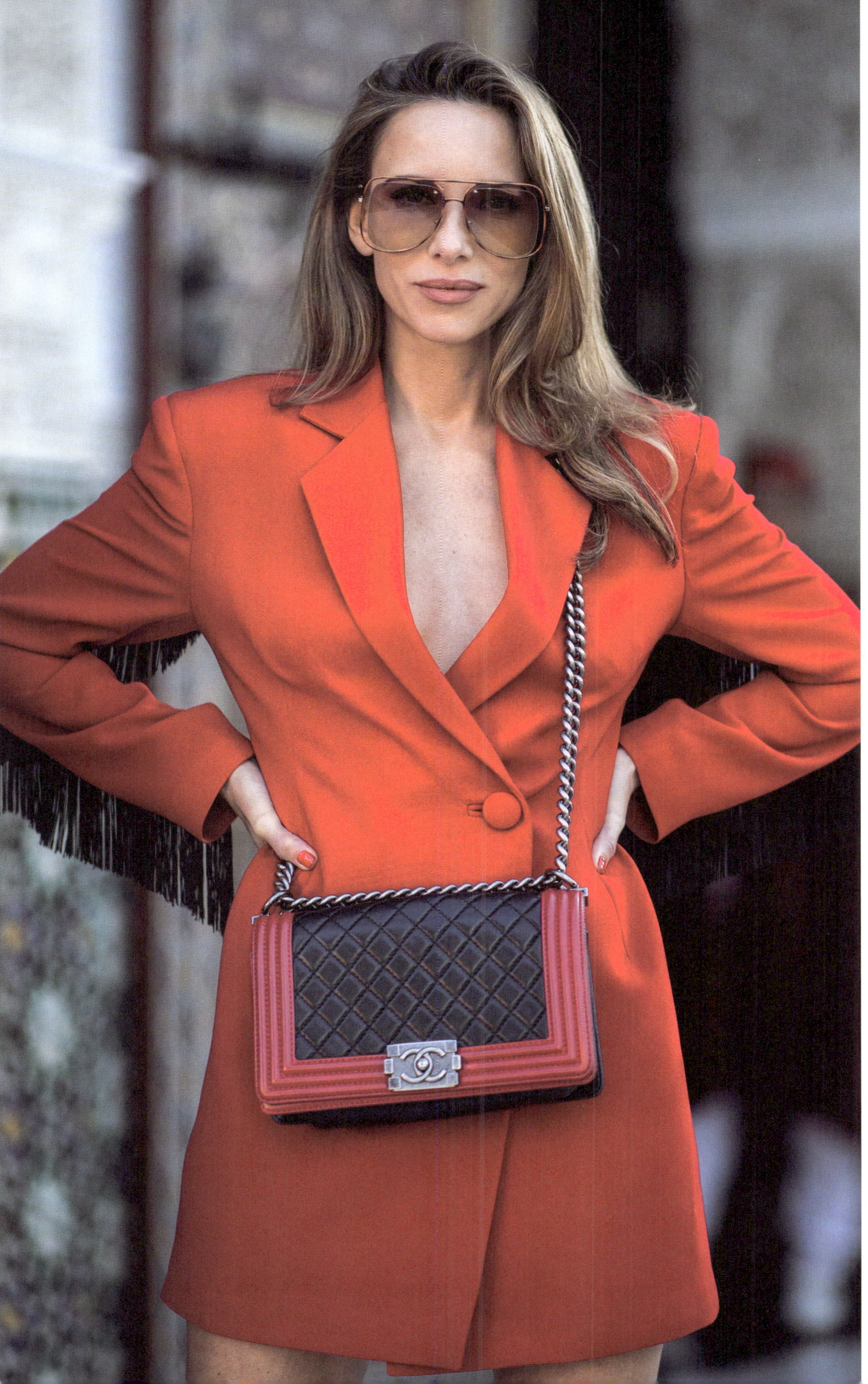

remains. Some bags reverse this detail with 'reverso quilting,' where the body is un-quilted and the border quilted.

Boy bags are usually made from grained caviar leather or classic lambskin, although there have been denim, ombré, iridescent, velvet, mosaic and tweed finishes and versions that are daubed with graffiti. A signature of the Boy bag is its long *gourmette* chain—a heavy linked curb chain with a definite masculine mood. Its length is versatile, allowing the bag to be worn cross-body or shoulder style as the wearer prefers. The similarly tough hardware echoes the chain and features a push-button closure with a double CC clasp designed specifically for the Boy style. In contrast with the heavy chain and exterior, the inside is fabric-lined, making the Boy light to carry.

Currently, a small sized Boy bag in black calfskin with ruthenium hardware retails for £5240, while a large grained calfskin with gold-tone metal sells for £6100. Sizes of the Boy bag have changed since its launch, but the small bag still measures 20.5 × 8.5 × 12cm: petite enough for an evening out, it's still big enough to hold the essentials. The medium bag is divided into 'old medium' and 'new medium' sizes. The old medium measures 25 × 9 x 15cm and the new medium, which was introduced in 2014, measures 28 × 9 x 18 cm. Large Boy bags measure 28 × 7.5 × 17.5cm and are a brilliant option for all day use, fitting all one's everyday necessities with ease. There are a legion of Boy fans including Jennie Kim, Ashley Graham, Nicki Minaj and Dua Lipa, who is the face of Chanel's newest bag, the 25. Lipa told *Vogue* about her first Chanel experiences. "When I first signed my record deal in 2014, I left my job in a restaurant, and when I got my first big check, I went to the Chanel store. The first thing I bought was a Boy bag; it was all the rage. I was so proud. Later, I went and got a leather backpack. I think just the idea of being able to do that for myself was such an empowering thing. Like, wow, I bought that Chanel bag with my *own* money. I felt really proud of myself. For me, it carried a lot of independence."

Now the Boy family has expanded to include a North-South Boy where, rather than the horizontal shape of the original, the bag follows a vertical silhouette. There are also tote bags and miniature wallet-on-chain styles. Lagerfeld also launched the Boy Brick "Lego" bag, a hard clutch often including plexiglass with square edging details. A red carpet favorite, rare models of these *minaudière* can fetch up to $20,000 at auction.

Next page: (Top left) A Paris Fashion Week attendee carries a silver quilted leather North South Boy bag, 2019; (Top right) Close-up of a Pearl Boy Brick clutch in Paris, 2017; (Bottom left) Alexandra Lapp carries a black and white Bar Code Boy Brick in Paris, 2017; (Bottom right) A visitor flaunts a white North South Boy at Paris Fashion Week, March 2017

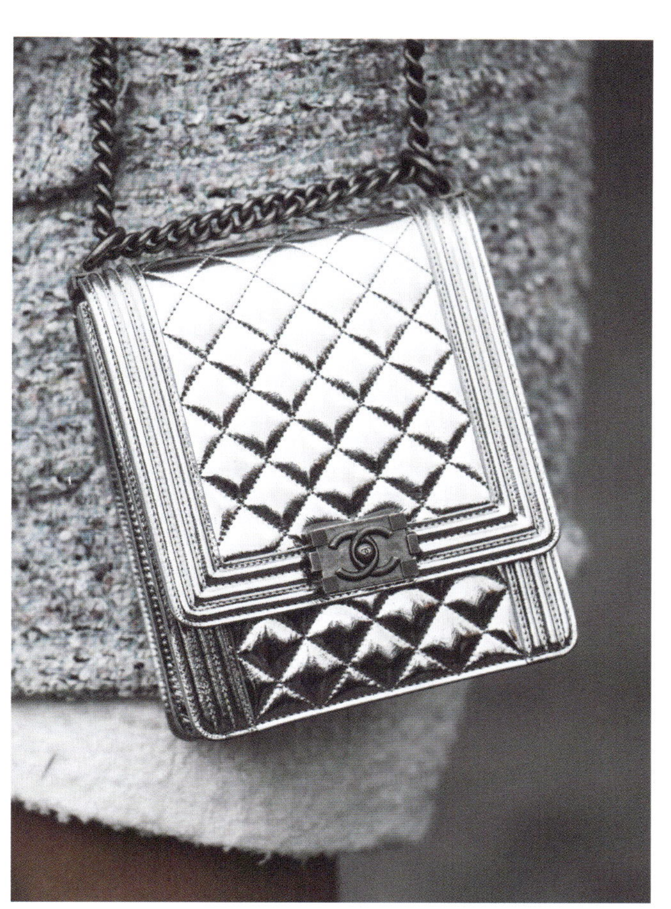

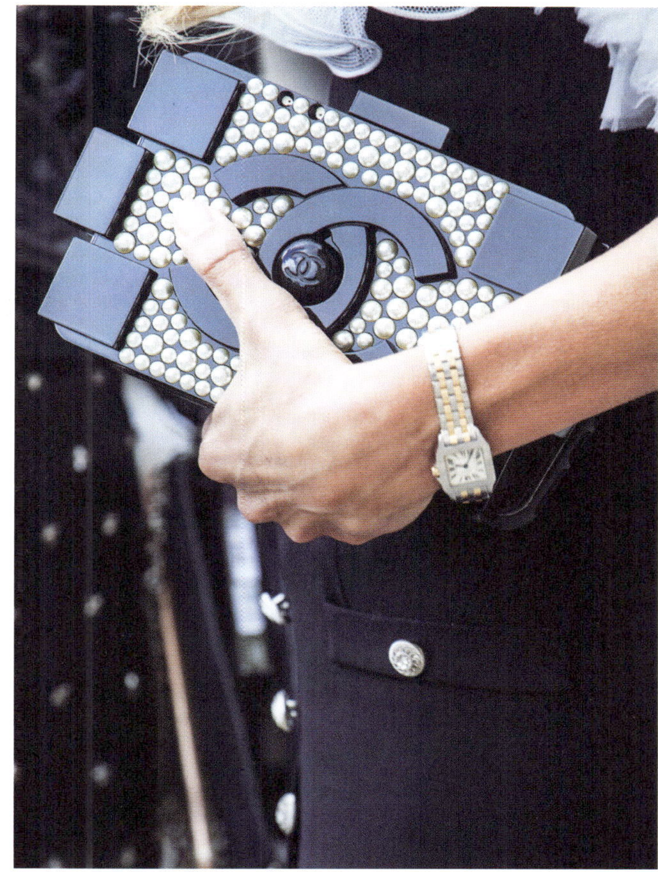

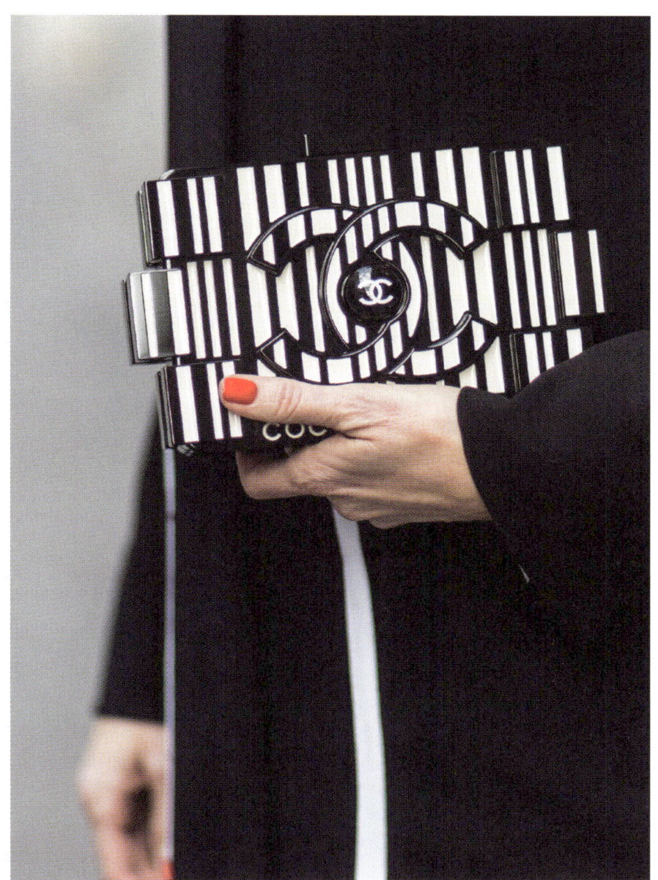

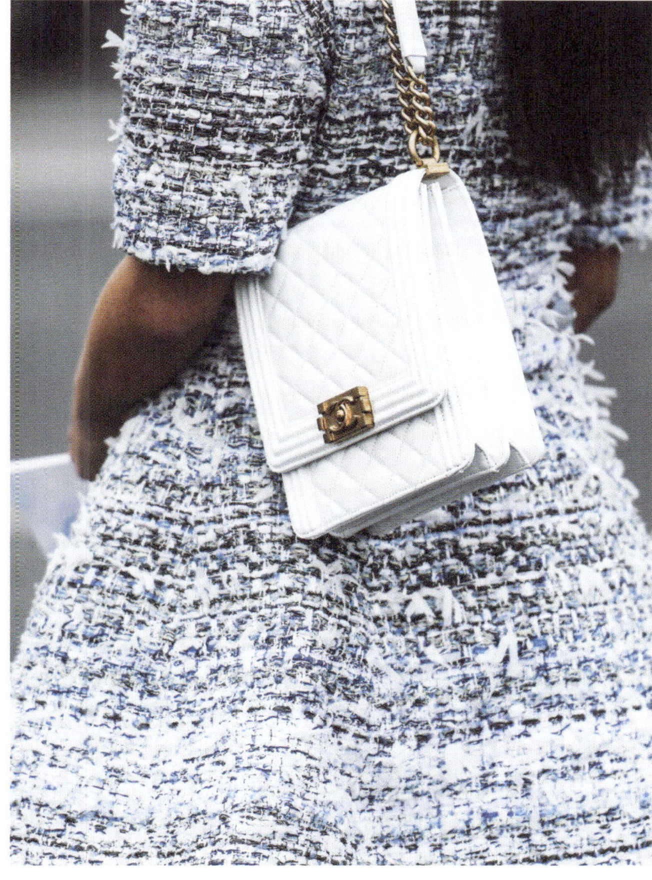

This page: Alexandra Lapp elegantly combines a gold Boy bag with a blue metallic pleated skirt from ROQA and So Kate 120 Stripy Glitter suede pumps by Christian Louboutin, observed during Paris Fashion Week, February 2019

Pages 48/49: Close-up of a tweed Chanel bag, Paris, 2024

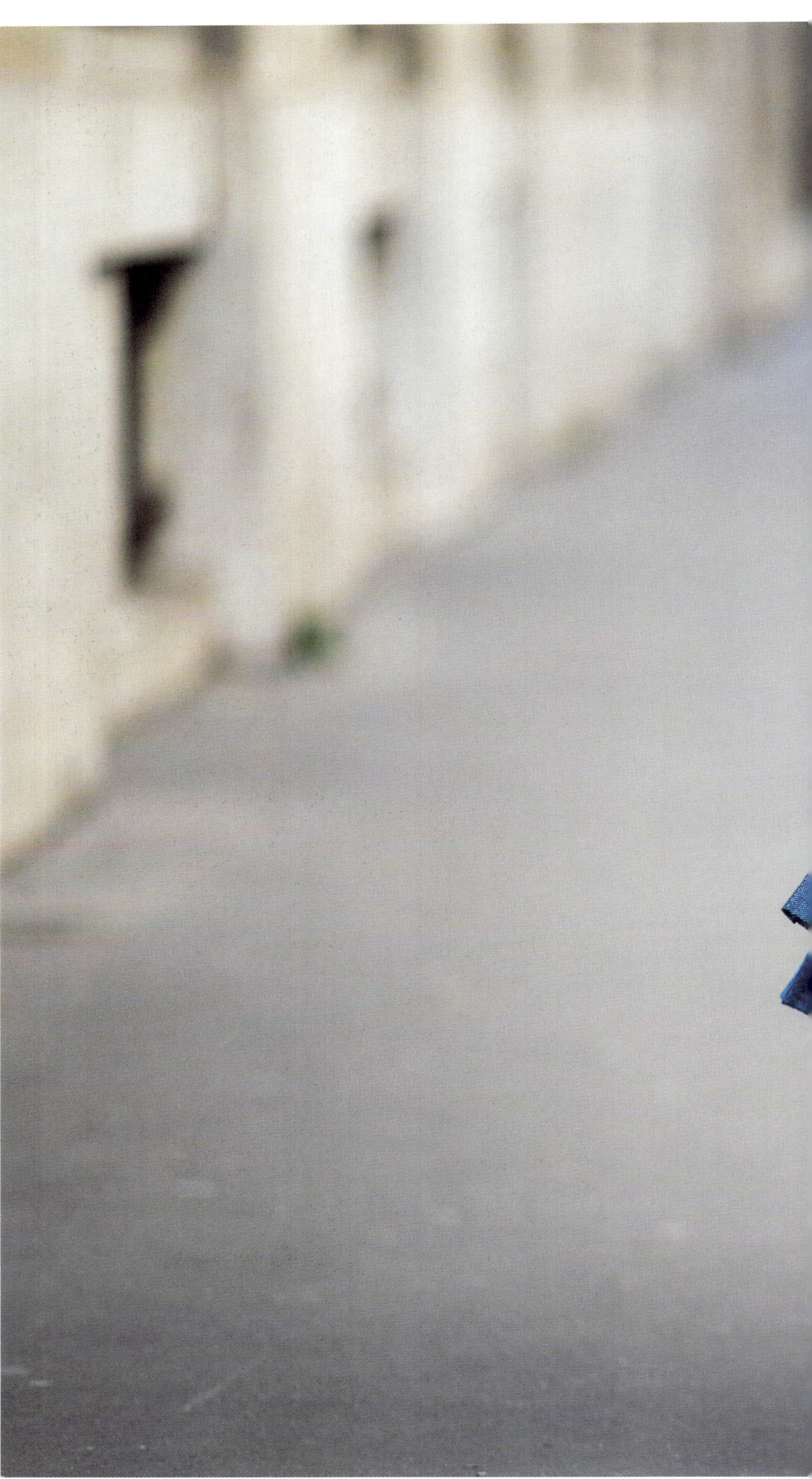

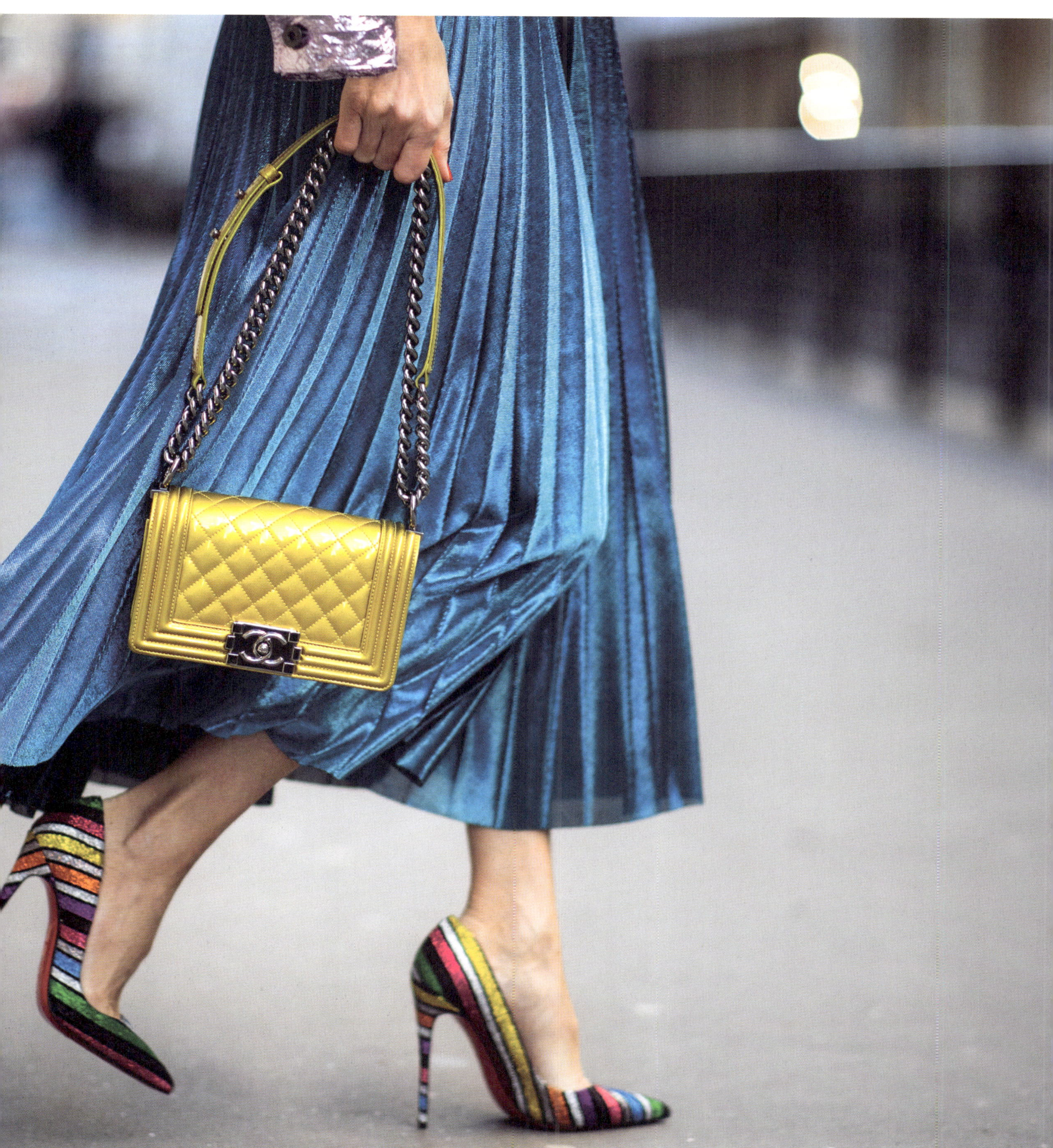

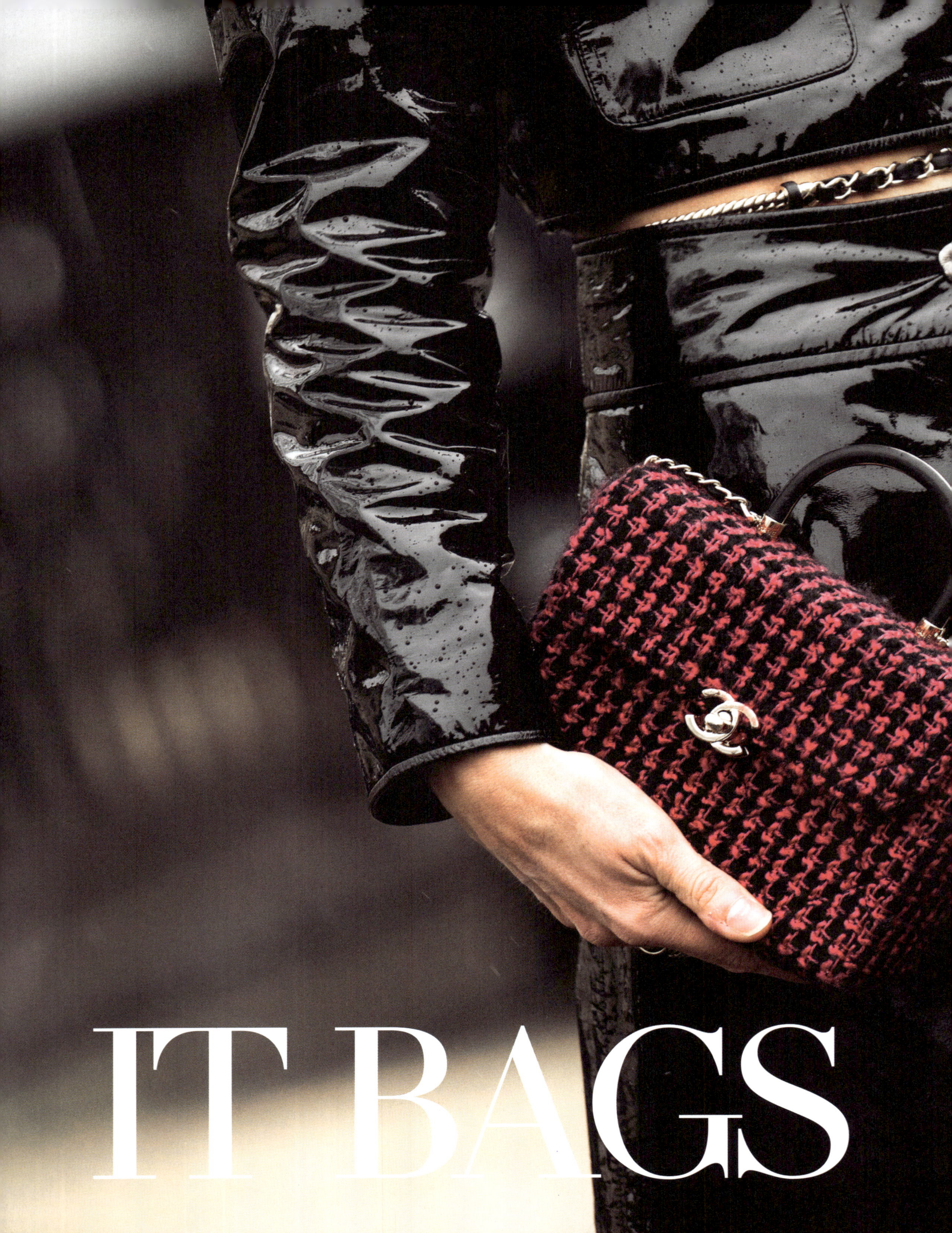

IT BAGS

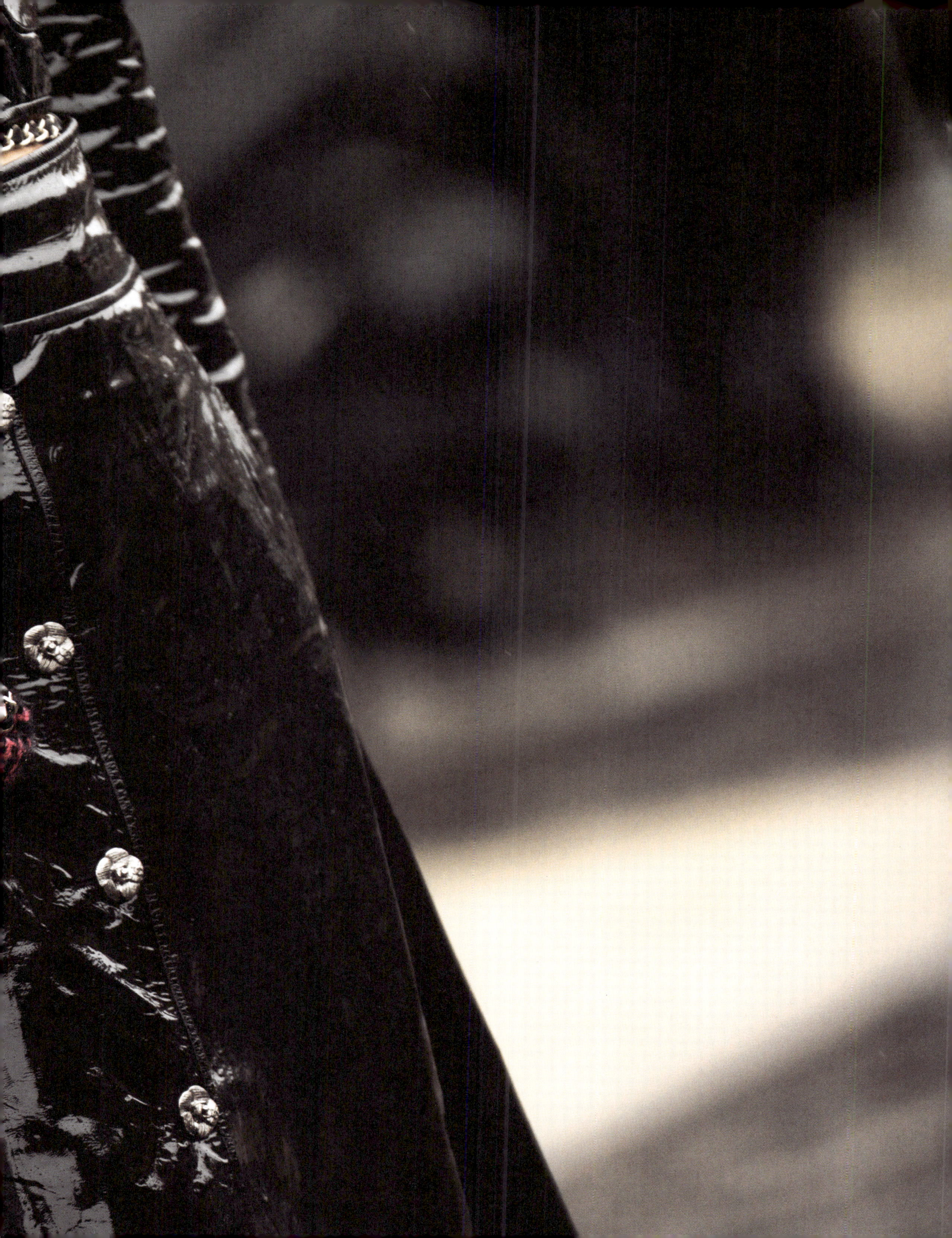

GABRIELLE

Taking the name of Chanel's founder, Gabrielle was the next bag to be launched after the Boy, making its catwalk debut during the Spring/Summer 2017 show in Paris. Gabrielle was the first bag that the house described as gender-neutral, which has cemented its It bag status. Pharrell Williams was part of the bag's launch marketing, along with Kristen Stewart, Cara Delevigne and Caroline de Maigret. Chanel declared 2017 to be the "year of Gabrielle," with a perfume launch and four-part film to complement the bag's debut. However, to the horror of many fans (including Meghan Markle), Chanel announced the Gabrielle would be discontinued in 2023.

Gabrielle bags have a hobo silhouette, meaning the fabric-lined interior is capacious and practical. A shopper tote, drawstring bag and backpack were also part of the family, which gave a contemporary update to the Chanel catalog. Compared to the 2.55, 11.12 or Boy, Gabrielle is less instantly recognisable as Chanel, but honors Chanel's own love of menswear styles. Lagerfeld was reportedly influenced by VR glasses and binoculars while designing the style.

Each bag has a rigid base, often in smooth thermo-formed leather, with a quilted upper. The strong base gives the bag stability, while the upper is supple. This contrast in structure makes Gabrielle light to carry while allowing easy access. The unique double chain is available in mixed gold and silver toned metals and comes interlaced with leather. Zipped to fasten, the chain strap is adjustable, so Gabrielle can be worn over the shoulder, cross-body or together in a V shape for clever weight distribution.

There are several possible reasons why Gabrielle was cancelled, including a decline in demand, a renewed focus on the classics and upcoming launches. Now pre-loved versions of bags in the Gabrielle family can be found on the resale market and are competitively priced, compared to pre-loved 11.12 bags.

Next page: A model walks the runway showcasing a Gabrielle bag during the Chanel Womenswear Spring/Summer 2018 show, Paris Fashion Week, October 3, 2017

Page 52: Gabriella Berdugo is seen with a black shiny leather Gabrielle handbag during a street style photo session in Paris, 2022

Page 54: A tweed and leather "Gabrielle Coco" Gabrielle bag featured at Paris Fashion Week, 2019

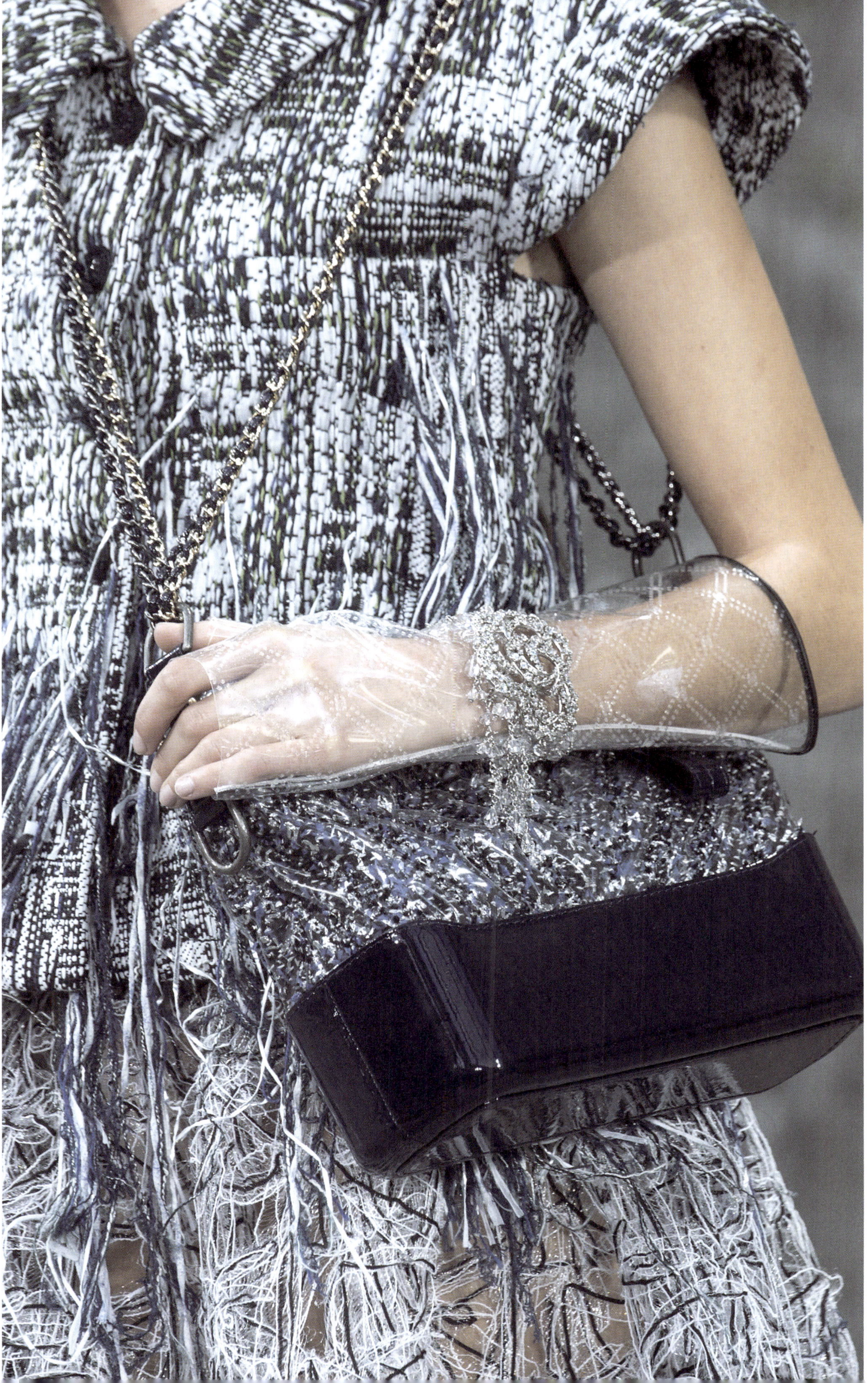

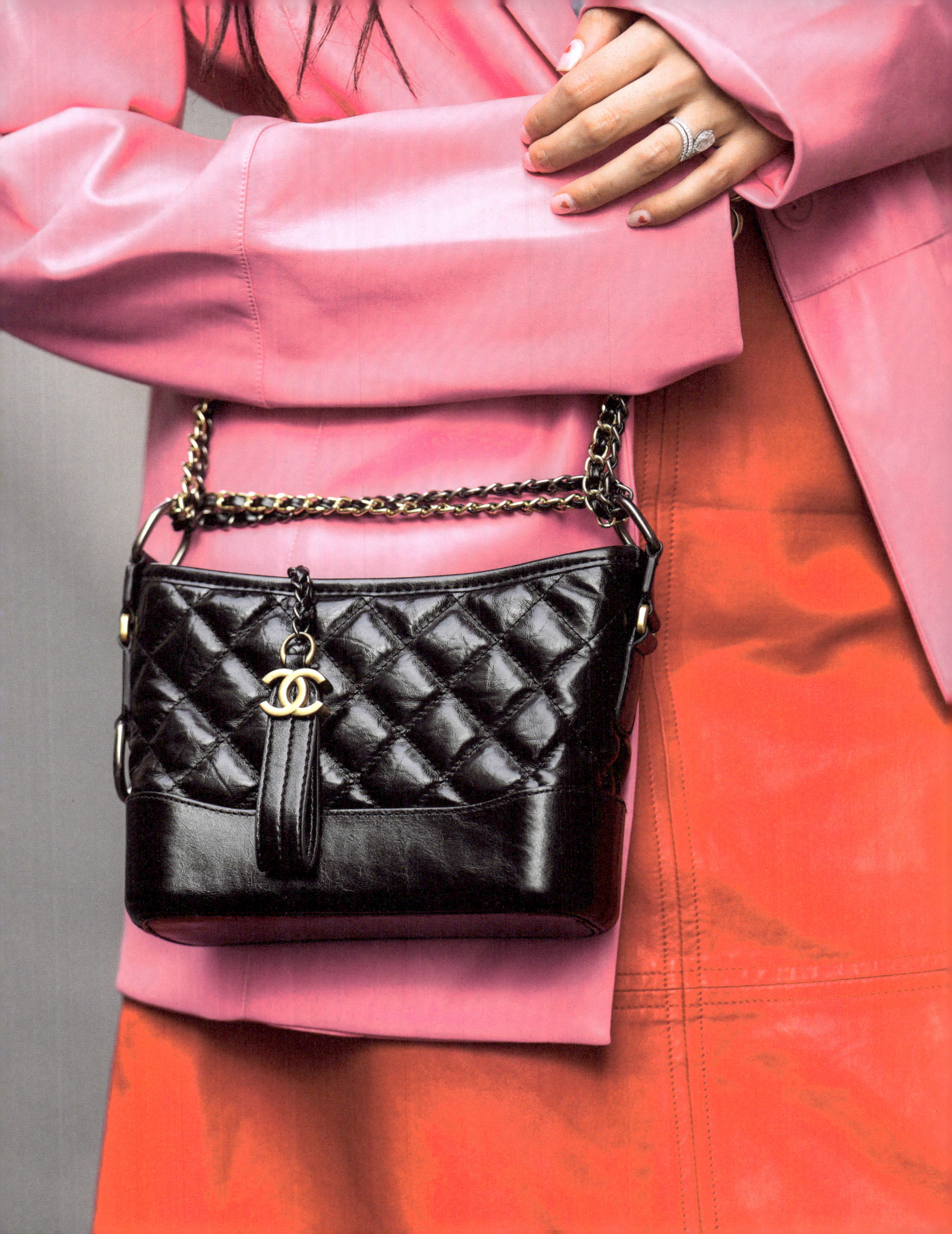

GABRIELLE BAGS HAVE A HOBO SILHOUETTE, MEANING THE INTERIOR IS CAPACIOUS AND PRACTICAL.

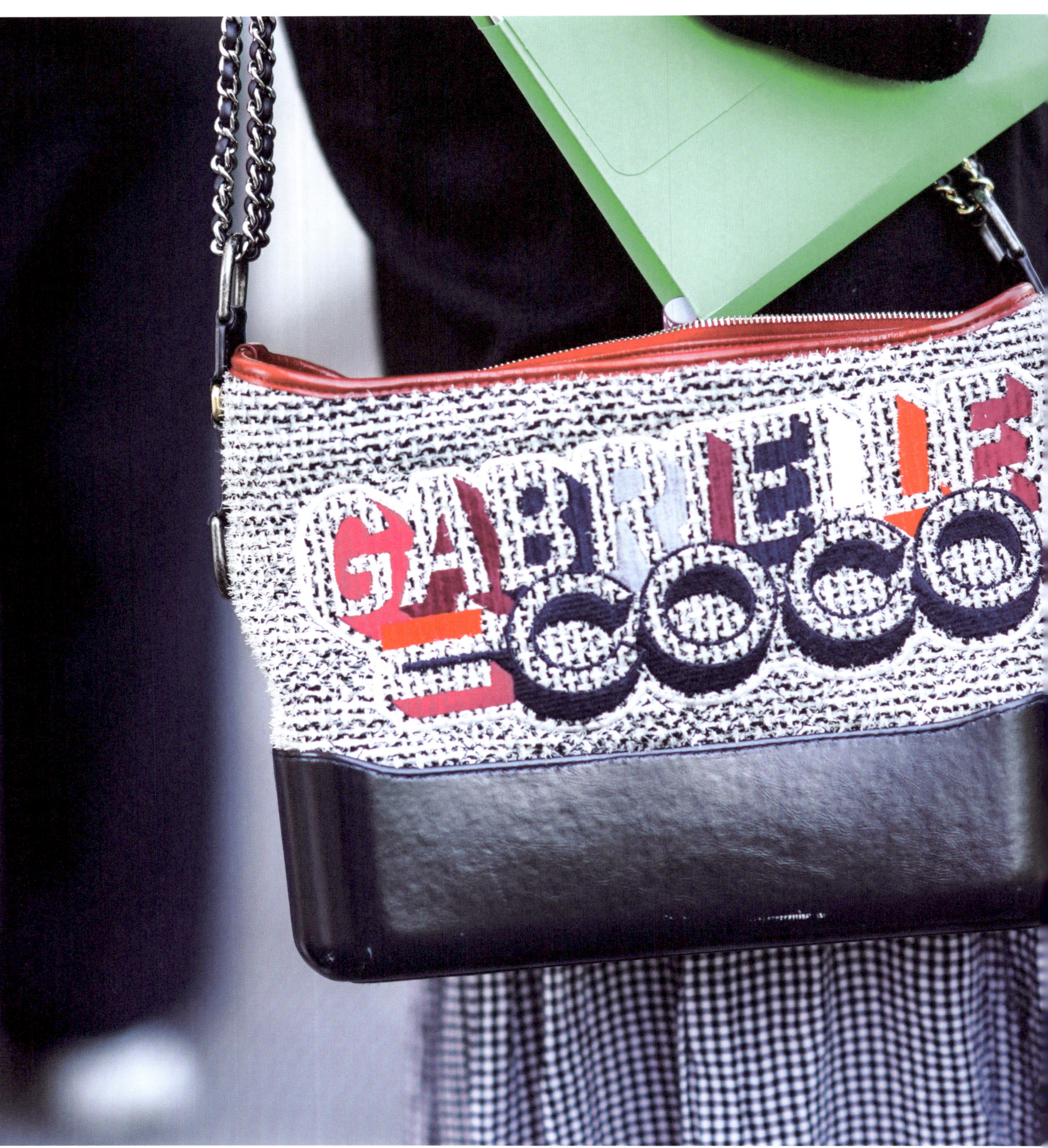
COCO

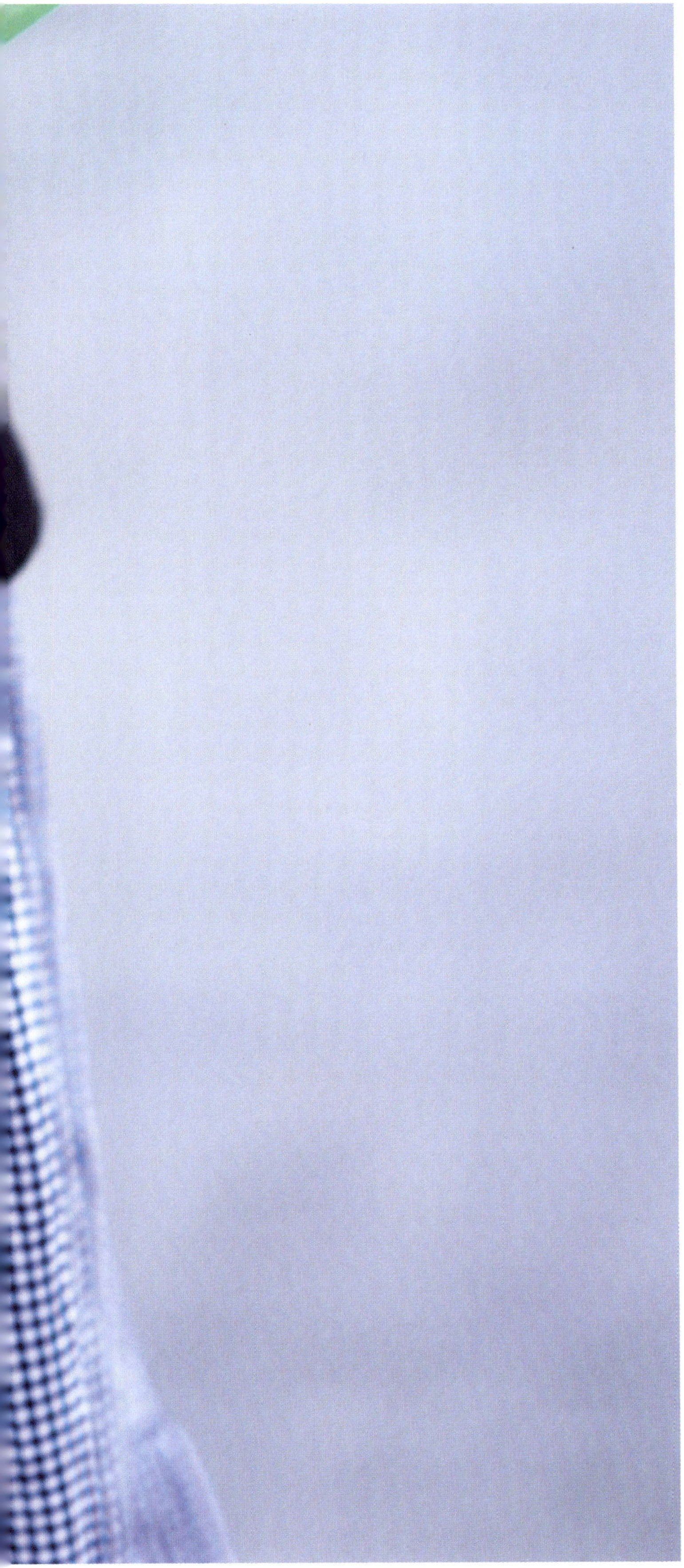

19

As the last bag Karl Lagerfeld designed before his death in 2019, the Chanel 19 is heavily influenced by Chanel's house codes while remaining contemporary. Taking inspiration from the 2.55 and 11.12 in silhouette and flap shape, the 19 is inherently more relaxed. The name recalls the year of the bag's launch and legendary perfume No.19 as well as Chanel's own birth date: the 19th of August.

Instead of the small quilted stitching seen on other bags, the 19 has exaggerated diamond quilting, producing a squashy, slouchy shape. When the bag debuted on the catwalk in March 2019 as part of the *maison*'s Fall/Winter 2019 collection, models clutched their bags like teddy bears or wore them around their waists. Just as Gabrielle Chanel created the shoulder strap on the 2.55 to offer women freedom, the 19 echoes that sentiment with an array of sizes and carrying options. The waist bag, in particular, echoes the practicality of Chanel's own vision, as it allows wearers to go handsfree.

The key elements of the 19 include a chunky top handle *gourmette* chain with three types of interwoven hardware. Silver, aged gold and ruthenium (a precious metal similar to platinum) combine to make a tricolor chain, although some limited editions have been created with single-color hardware. The logo clasp has an interlocking oversized double CC motif laced with leather. The 19's casual vibe ties in with a phenomenon multi-brand e-tailer NET-A-PORTER.COM called the "casualization" of fashion, where traditional, stricter dress codes are easing and athleisure and loungewear are acceptable everyday options.

The 19 family includes the waist bag, flap bag, large flap and maxi flap bag, as well as the option of a wallet-on-chain and flap wallet—all in an array of tempting finishes and fabrics: everything from classic black goatskin leather to denim, tweed, sequin, silk and jersey.

THE LOGO CLASP HAS AN INTERLOCKING OVERSIZED DOUBLE CC MOTIF, LACED WITH LEATHER.

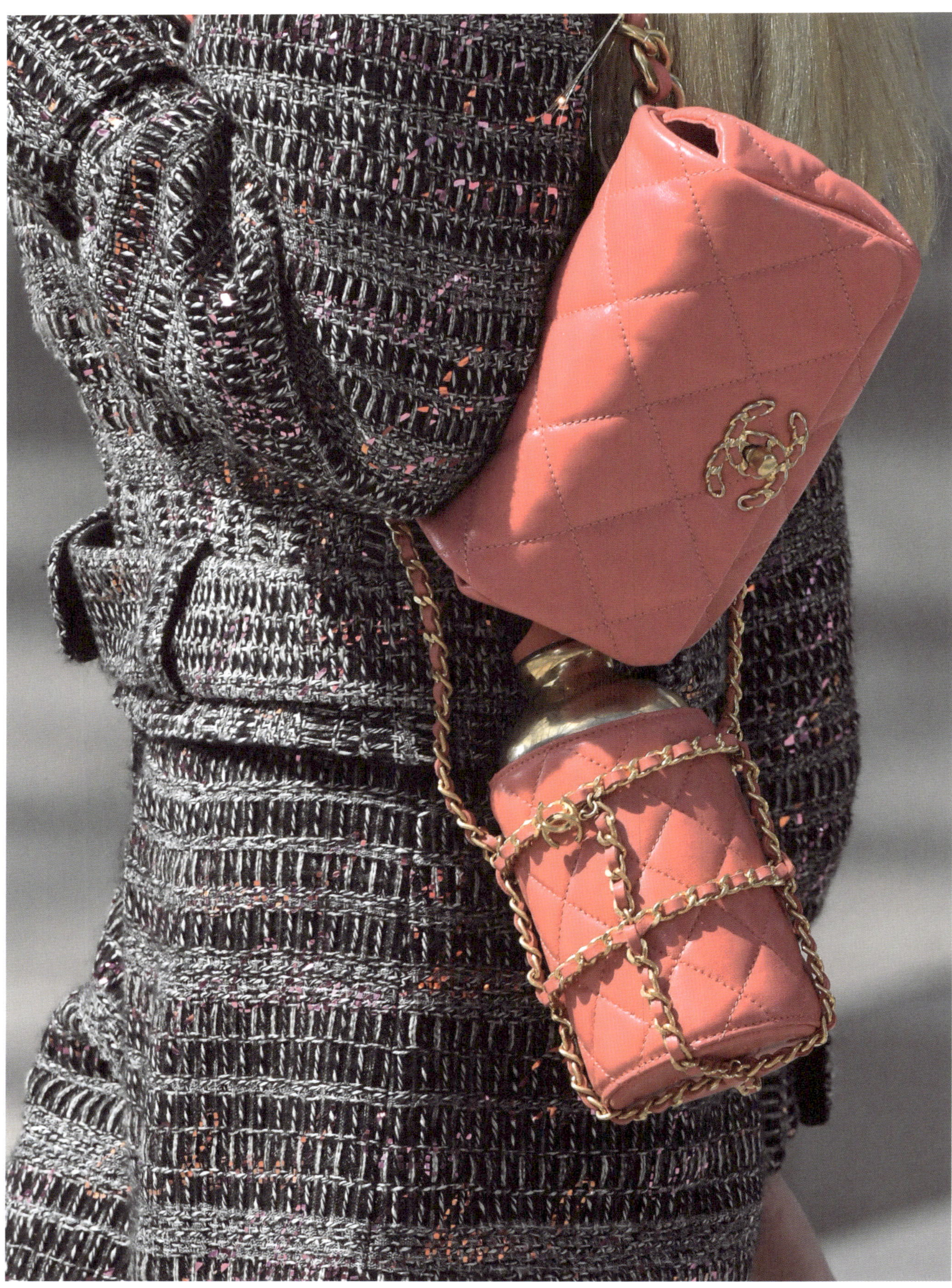

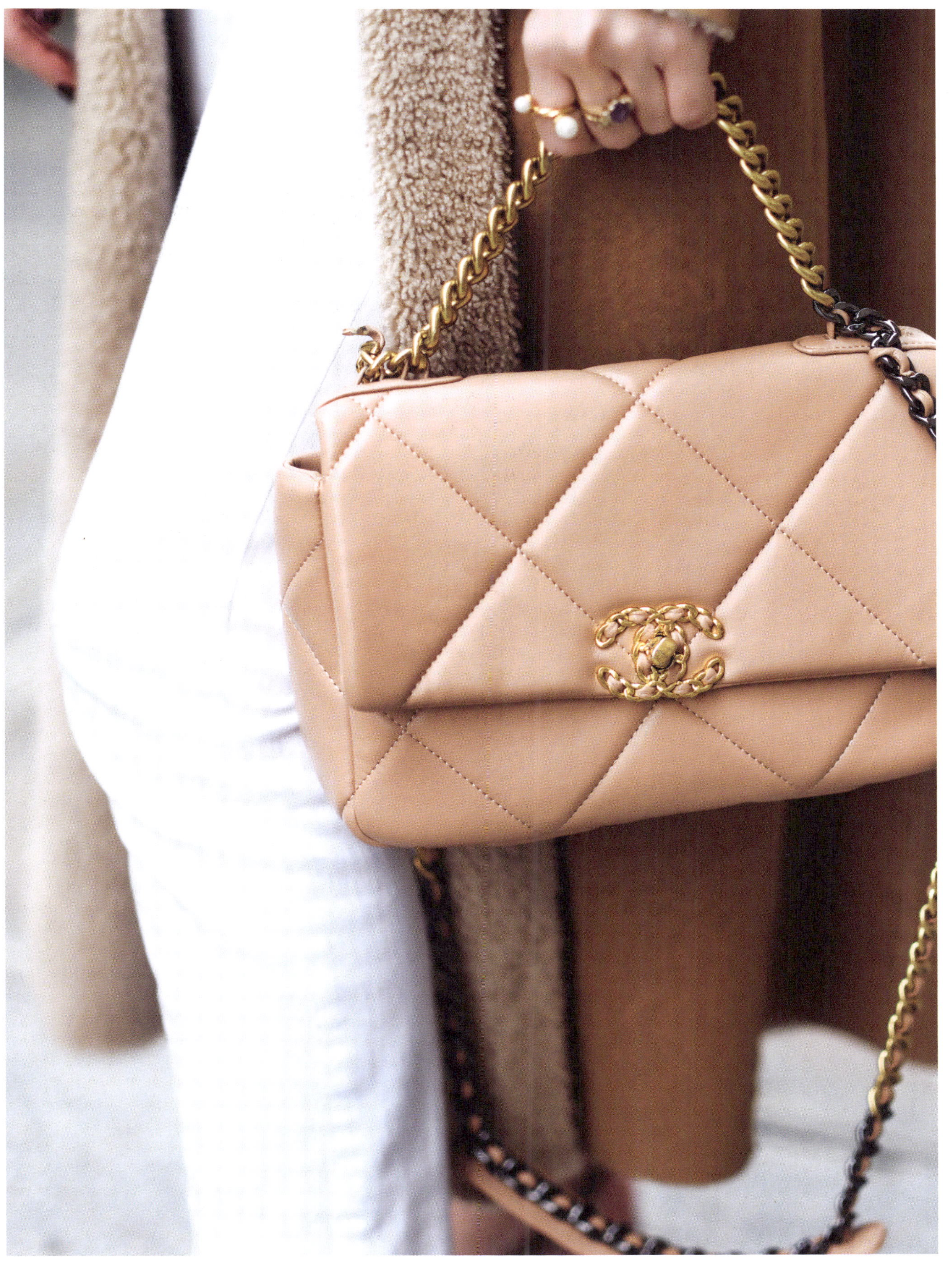

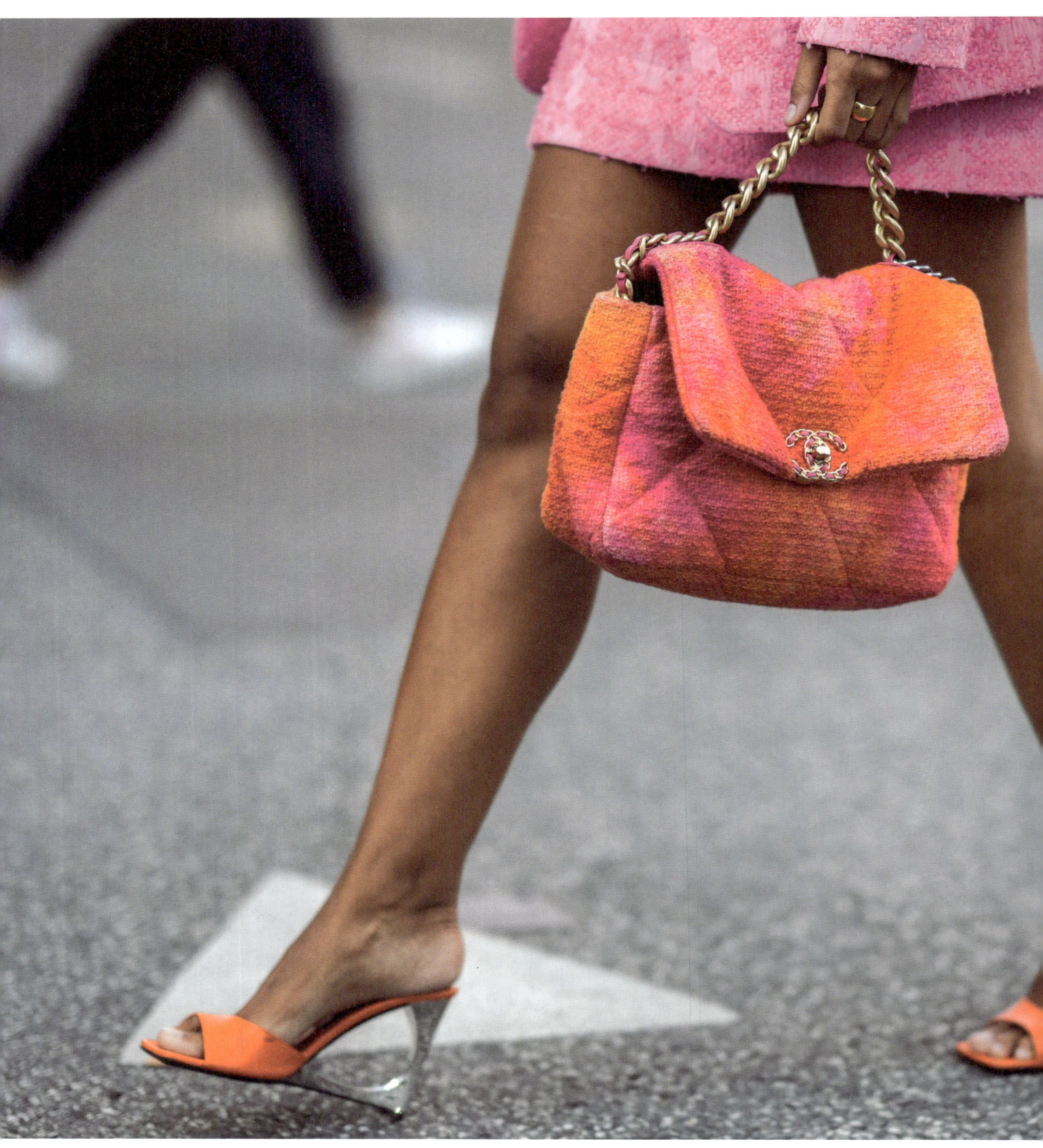

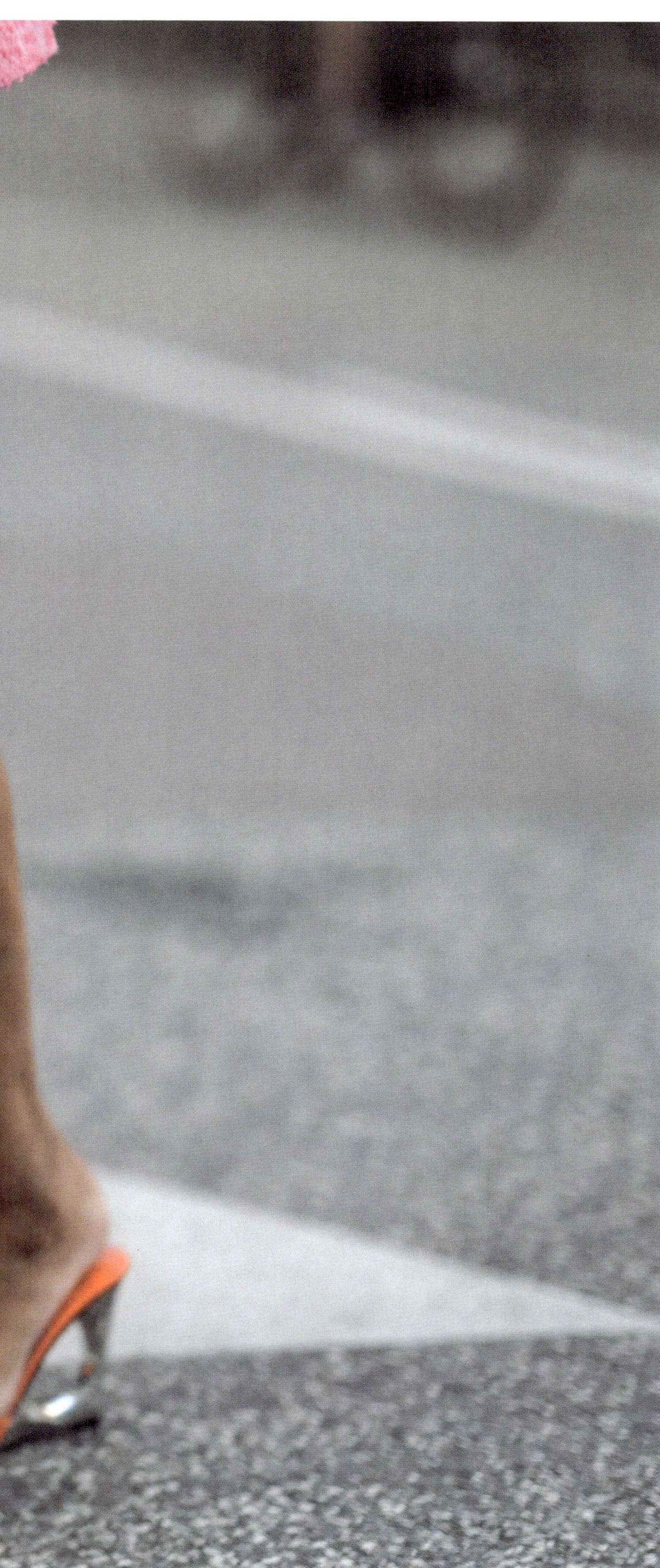

Page 58: A model walks the runway presenting a 19 bag alongside a gold water bottle with a quilted sleeve during the Chanel Cruise Collection 2020 show at Grand Palais, Paris, May 3, 2019

Page 59: Alba Garavito Torre styles a beige Chanel 19 bag during a street style photo session in Paris, 2023

This page: A visitor at Copenhagen Fashion Week Spring/Summer 2023 dons a pale pink and white braided tweed short skirt paired with a neon orange and pink tie-dye printed tweed 19 handbag

22

In step with the relaxed, comfortable everyday wear to suit the mood of the 21st century, the 22 bag is another soft, hobo-shaped style which reflects the needs of women today while honoring Chanel's history. Again, the name echoes the name of a fragrance. Perfume No. 22 was launched in 1922 and created by Ernest Beaux.

First revealed on the catwalk in October 2021 as part of the preview of the Spring/Summer 2022 collection, the 22 bag family is part of Virginie Viard's legacy at Chanel and was designed by the former artistic director. Launched with Lily-Rose Depp, Margaret Qualley and Whitney Peak as the faces of the 22, the advertising campaign was shot by Dutch-American photography duo Inez Van Lamsweerde and Vinoodh Matadin in Los Angeles, Palm Springs and New York, giving the bag global appeal.

Simply designed in a square shape with a drawstring closure, the 22 is a flexible style with regard to both texture and finishes. Checking all the house code boxes, the bag has an interlocking double CC medallion, but its soft, supple body echoes the lightweight ease of a cotton tote rather than the formality of the 11.12 or 2.55. The bag comes in an oversized quilted design, although there are different variations available each season, from pastel metallics to embellished denim.

Available in four sizes, the 22 mini measures approximately 20 × 19 × 6cm; a small 22 is 35 × 37 × 7cm, while the regular size is 36 × 42 × 8cm. If you choose the large size, it will measure 45 × 48 × 10cm. All bags come with a detachable internal pouch and a versatile chain strap. There is also a backpack in the 22 family, which measures a practical 29 × 34 × 7.5cm. Both the large and backpack versions can fit a 13-inch laptop inside. As the 22 is a relatively new design, there are fewer bags available on the resale market, making it a rare find.

Next page: Close-up of a black 22 mini bag featuring a pearl chain detail, Paris Fashion Week

Page 64: A black tweed 22 bag adorned with white streaks and multicolored Chanel letters, Paris, 2024

Page 65: A white leather 22 bag observed in Japan

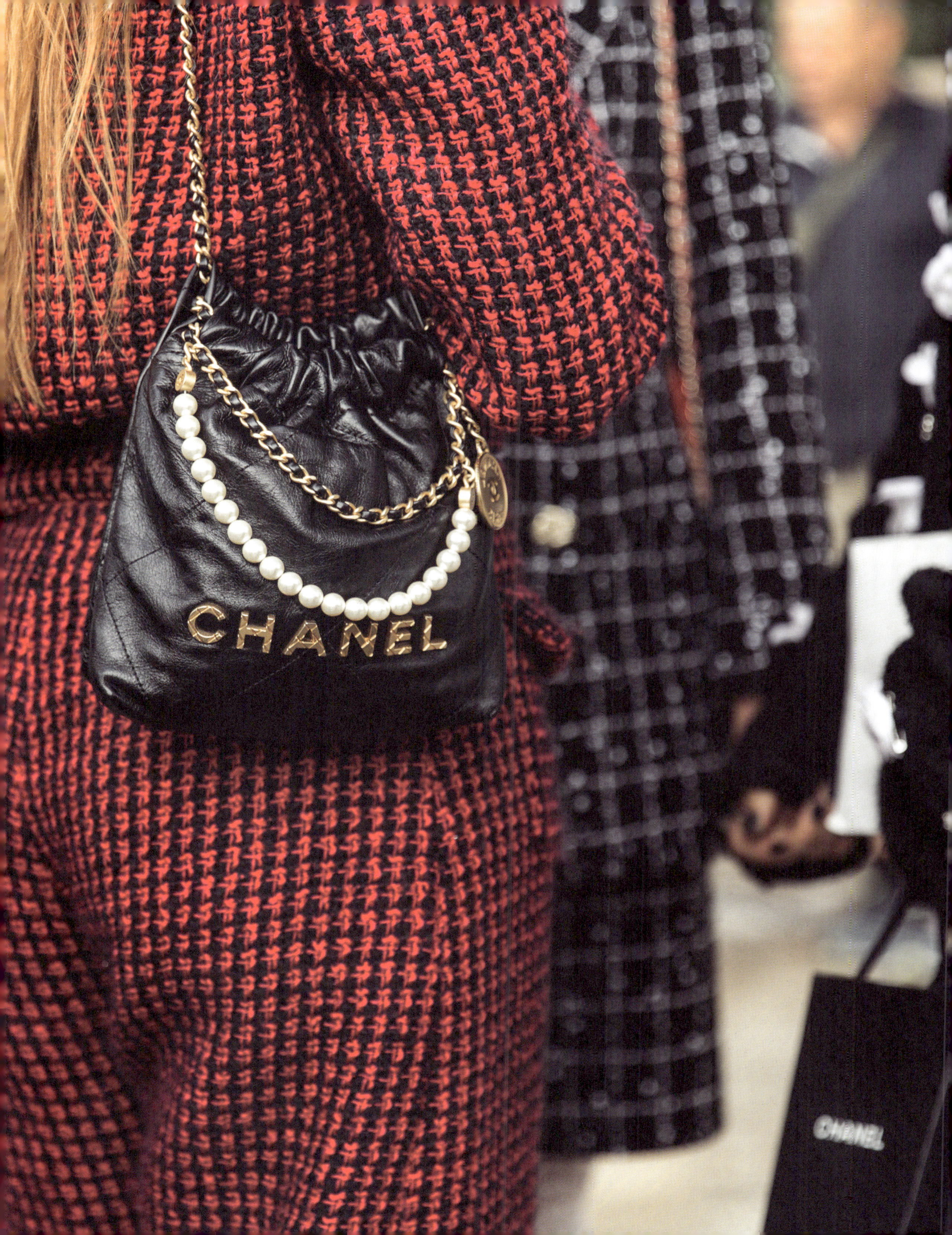
CHANEL
CHANEL

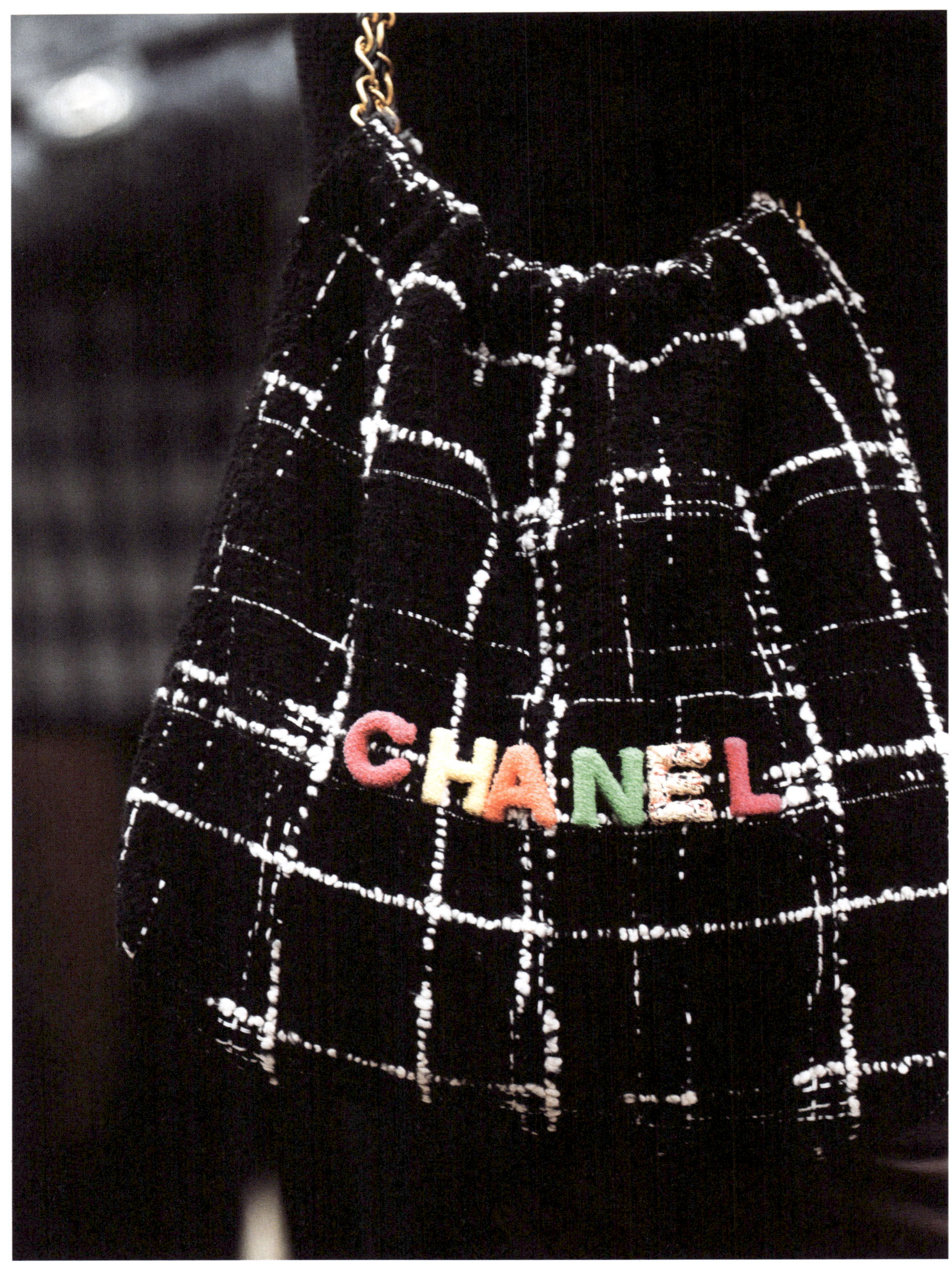
CHANEL

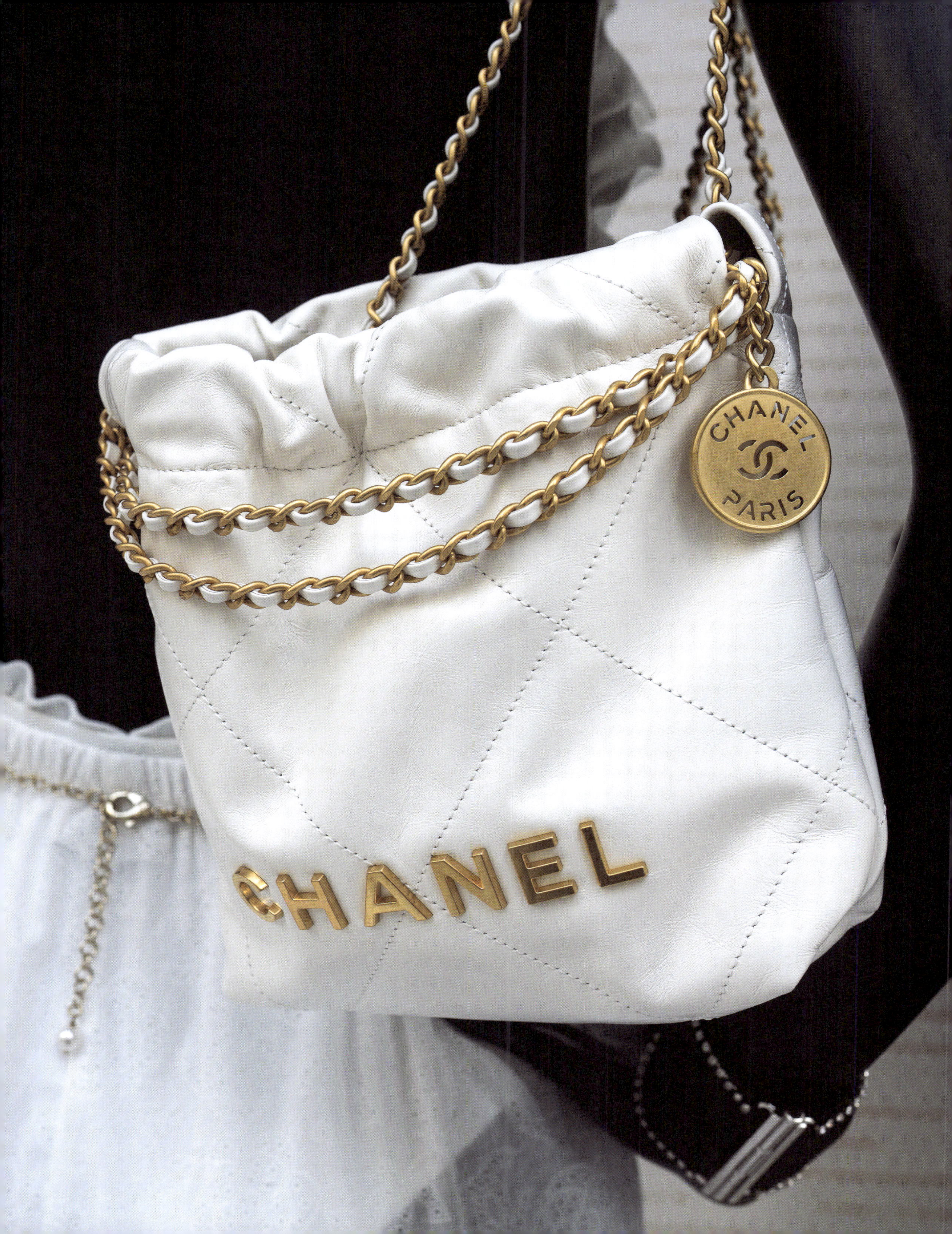
CHANEL
PARIS
CHANEL

25

The newest bag to join the ranks of Chanel's It bags is the 25. Launched 25 years into the new millennium, it continues the *maison's* use of numbers significant to Chanel. Gabrielle Chanel considered '5' to be her lucky number. She was born under the fifth sign of the zodiac (Leo) and the number was a repeated motif in her life.

With the 25, all of Chanel's intrinsic house DNA is on display. One can see the quilted exterior, chunky interlaced chain and useful pockets—on the exterior, in this case—that make the 25 a functional bag, just as Chanel would have liked. Three sizes are offered to cater to women "living life in the fast lane," and the bag has a trapezoid hobo shape. It's closed with a drawstring chain and adorned with an interlocking double CC logo; each side pocket is also secured with a double CC fastening.

First revealed as part of the Cruise 2024/25 collection, the 25 is available in three sizes. The launch color palette includes classics such as black, white and beige along with pastel pink and gray denim for Spring/Summer 2025. At the moment the 25 comes with gold-toned hardware. The small version measures 30 × 26 × 14cm; the medium bag comes in at 40 × 30 × 15cm, while the largest bag is 42 × 36 × 15cm and easily fits a 13-inch MacBook. Chanel describes the bag as lightweight and flexible.

The launch campaign was shot by *Vogue* contributor David Sims and stars Dua Lipa, who says, "I'm obsessed with this bag… because it's got these great pockets for all my favorite things. There's a place for my books, a place for my sunglasses, maybe a notebook or two, and even a place for my crystals." In March 2025, the *maison* also announced that South Korean singer Jennie Kim would join Dua as the face of the Chanel 25 handbag.

Next page: A model walks the runway presenting a pale pink 25 handbag during the Chanel Womenswear Spring/Summer 2025 show in Paris, 2024

Page 68: Dua Lipa showcases a black 25 bag at the Chanel Haute Couture Spring/Summer 2025 fashion show in Paris, January 2025

Page 69: Hollie Mercedes Peters is seen in a white shirt, an off-white crop coat with tassels, a black bonnet, and a black Chanel 25 bag outside the MKDT Fall/Winter 2025 fashion show during Copenhagen Fashion Week, 2025

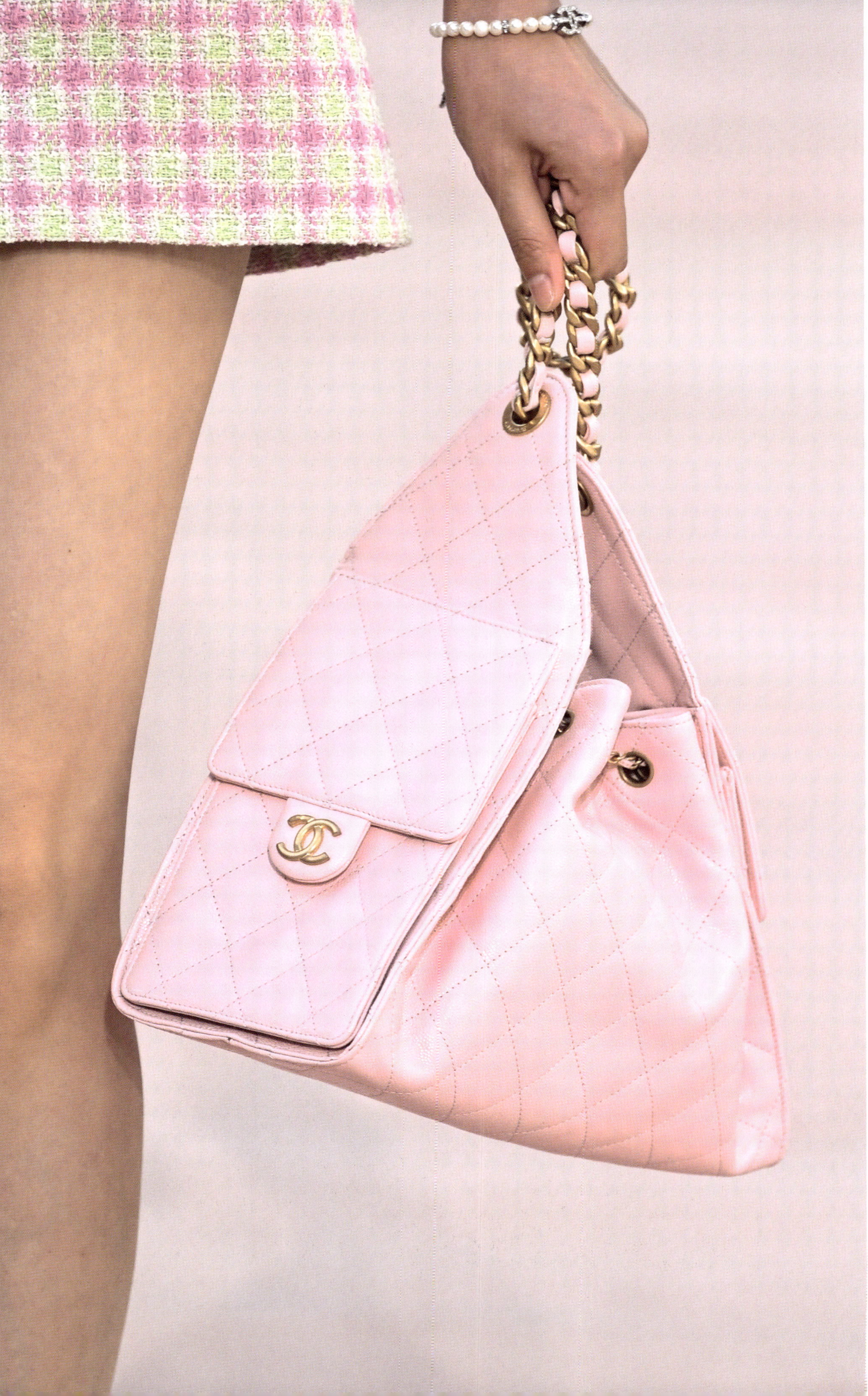

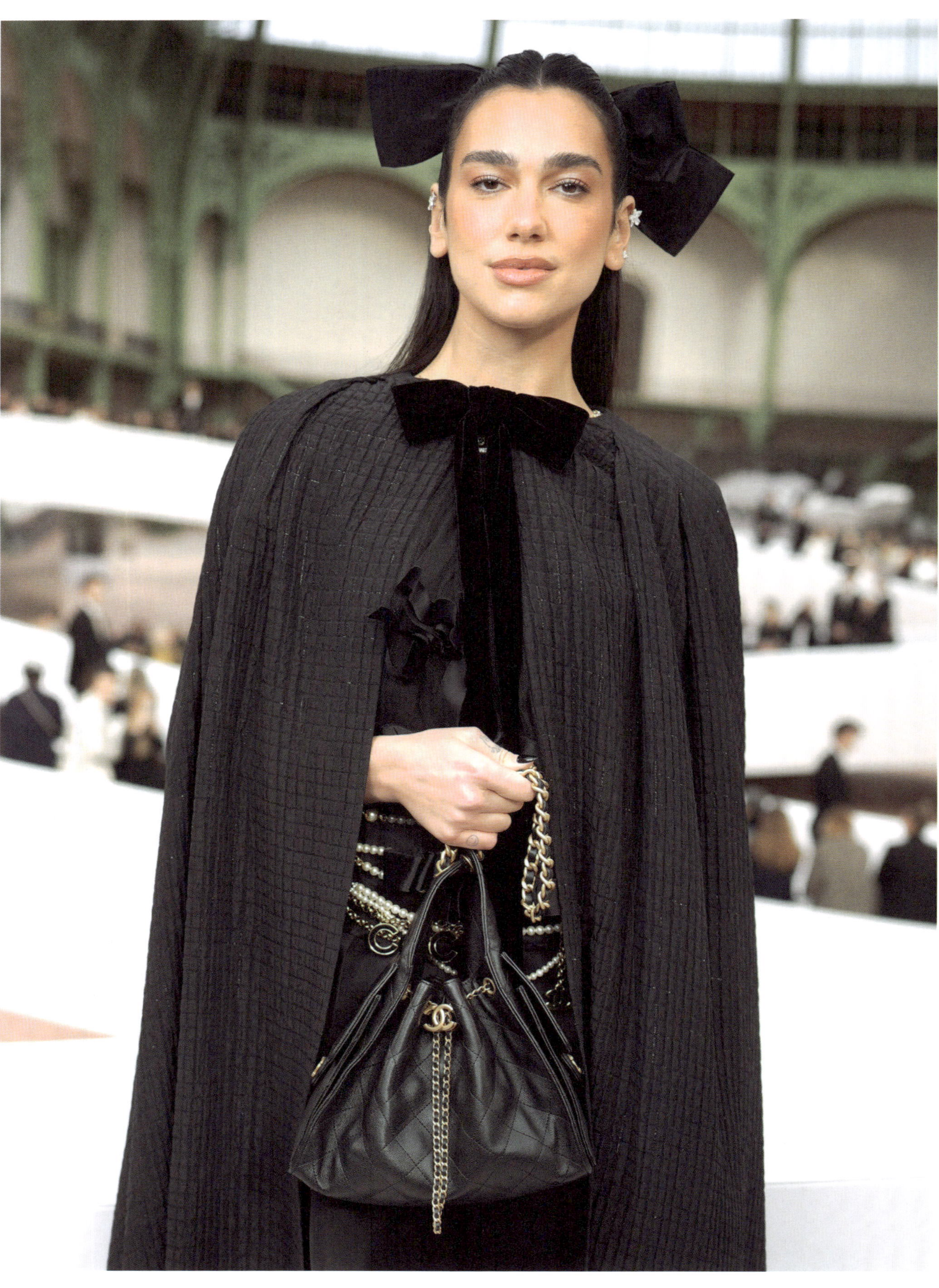

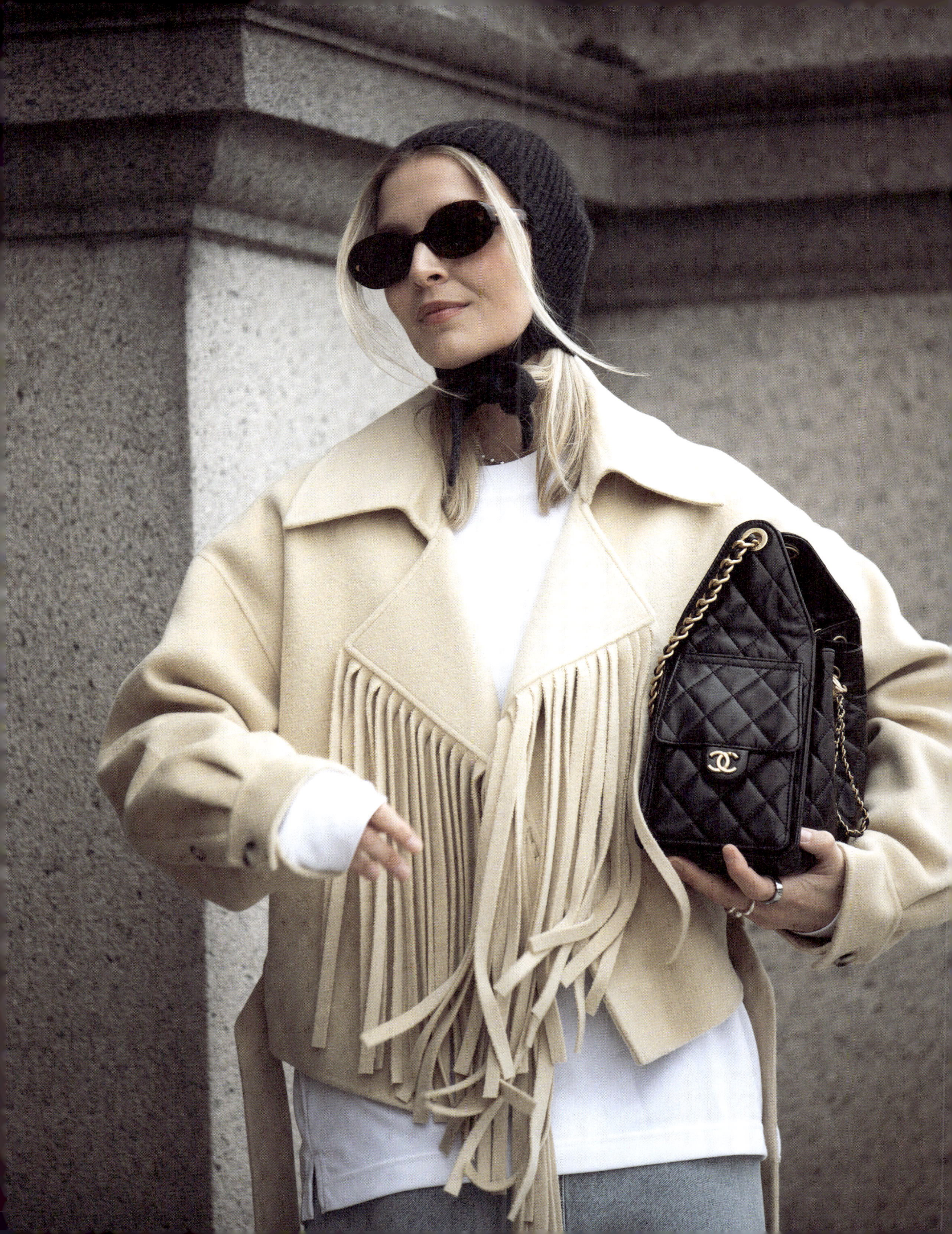

31

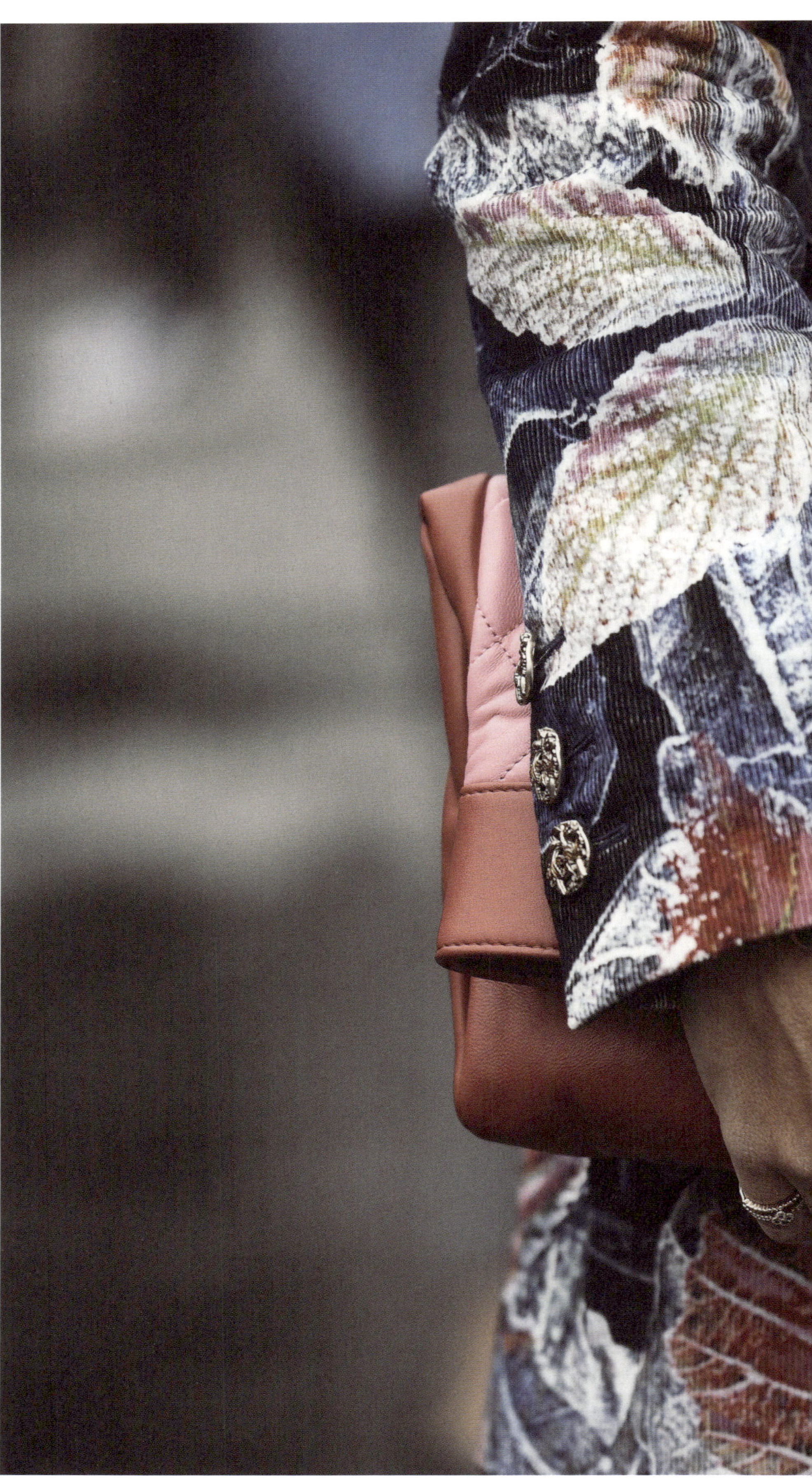

First introduced in 2018, the 31 bag offers versatility, allowing it to be styled as a tote, worn over the shoulder (in larger sizes), or folded over as a clutch, as seen in Paris, 2018

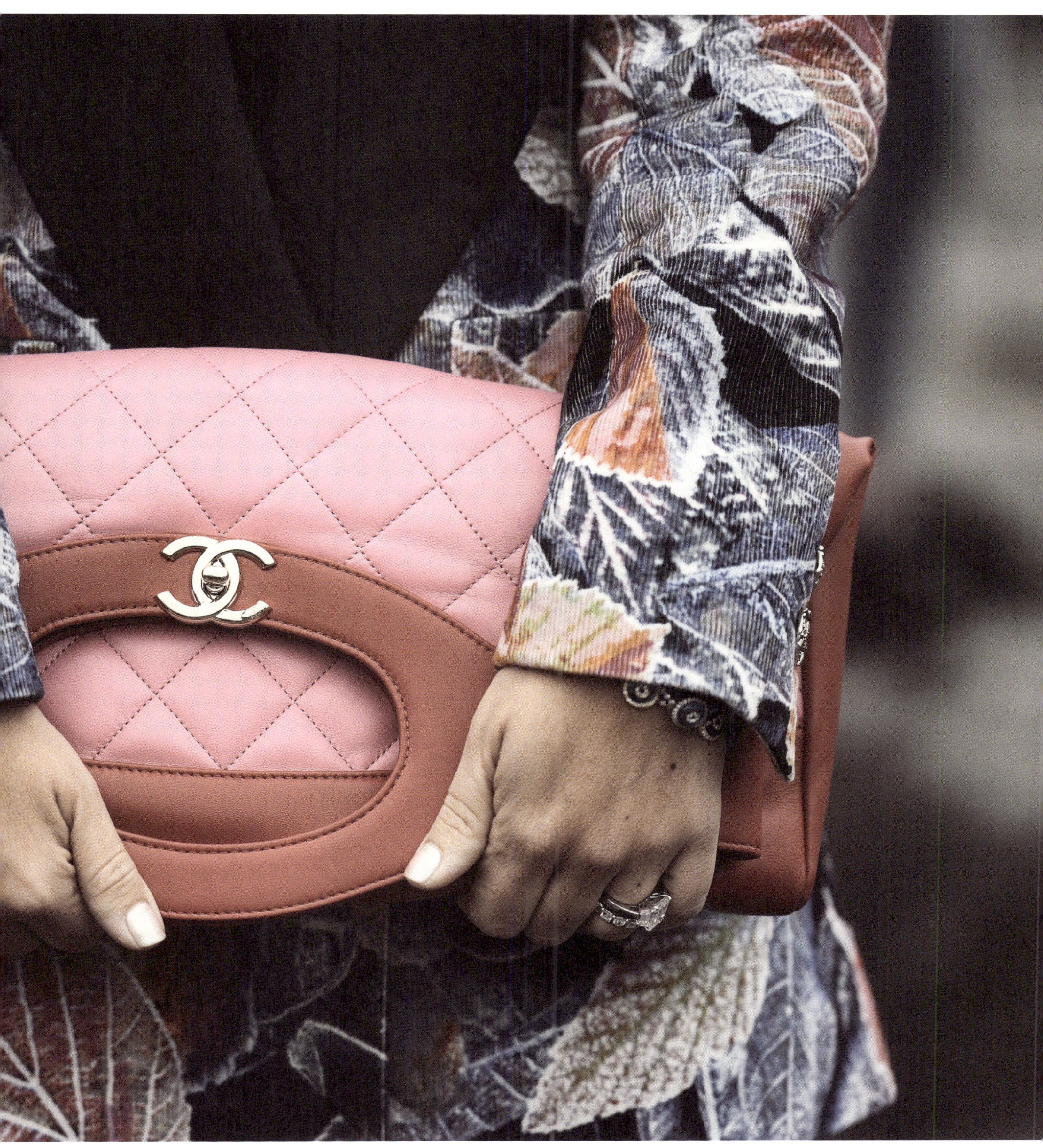

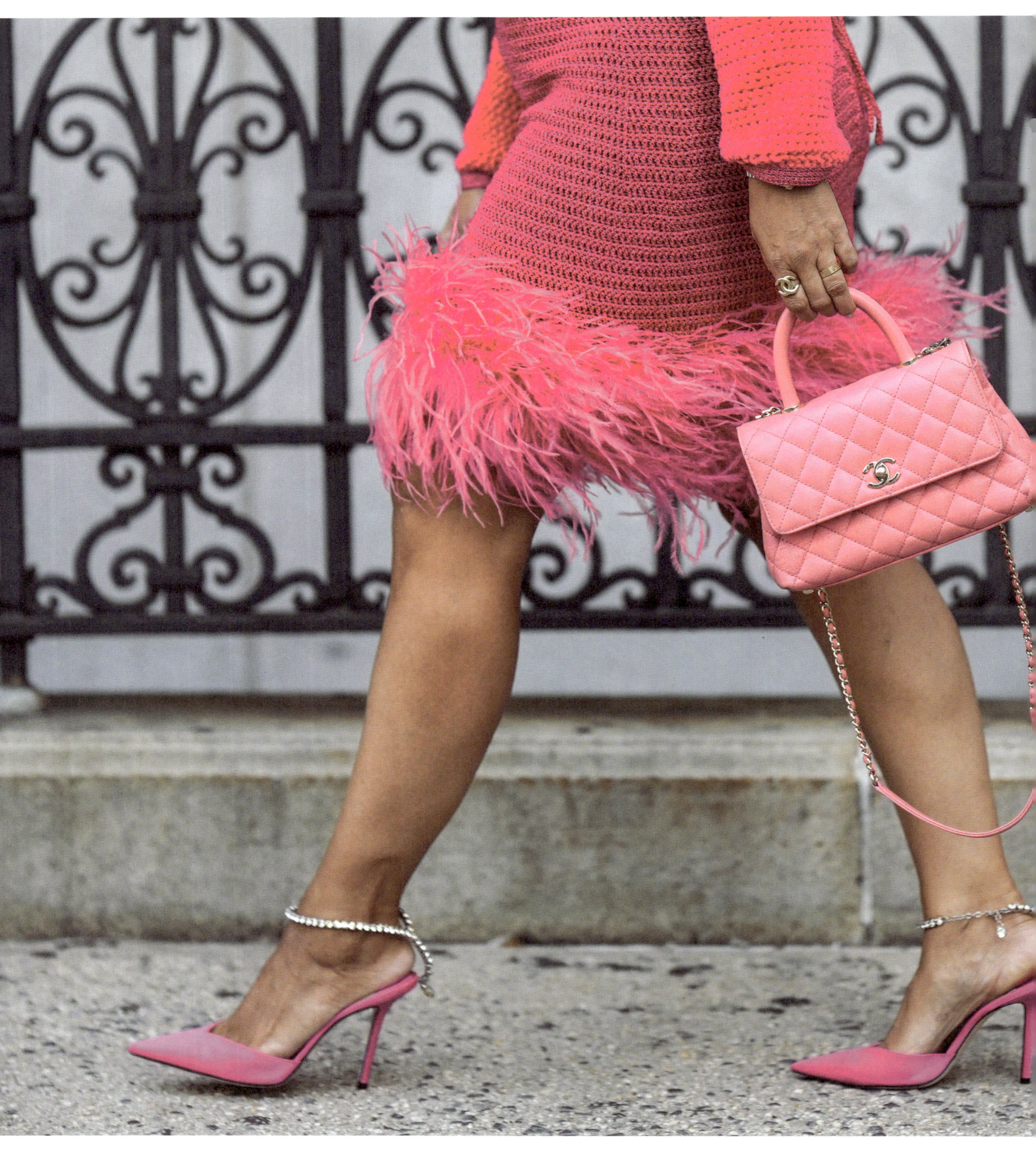

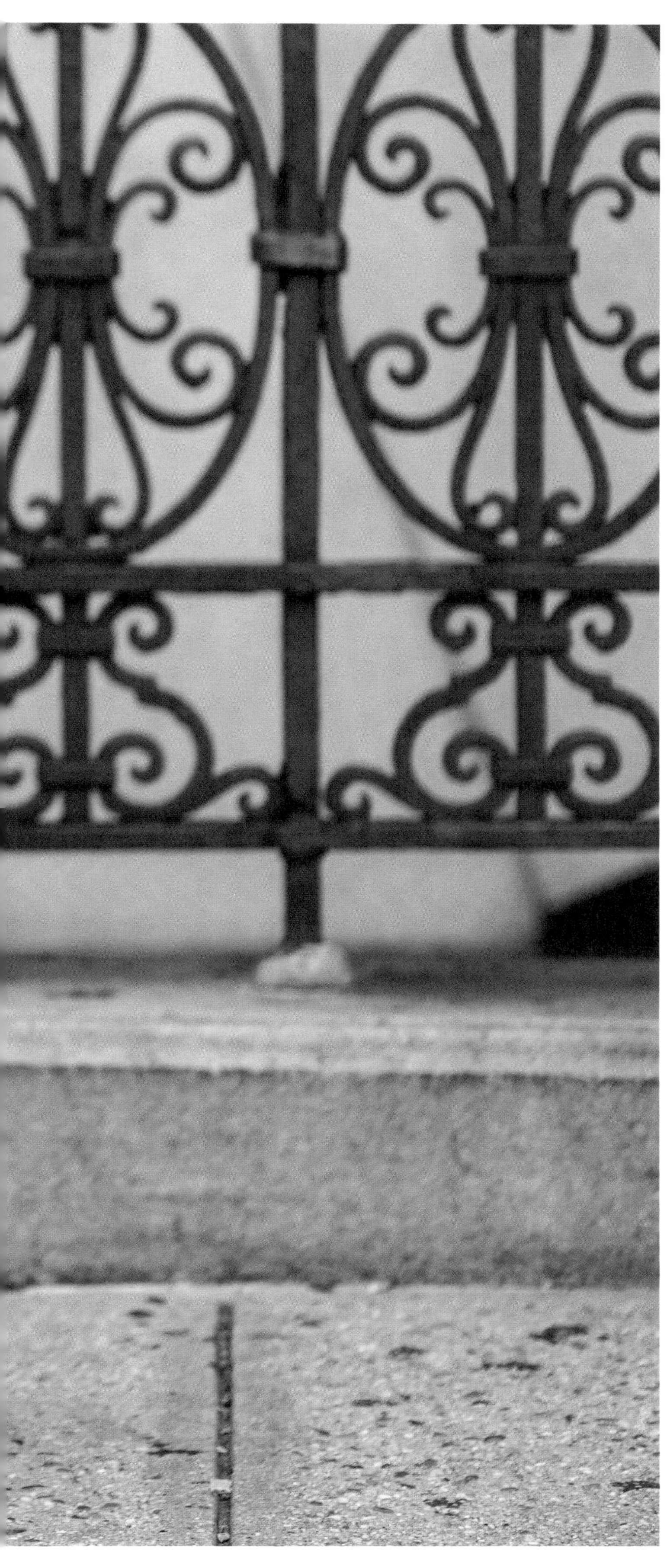

COCO HANDLE

A visitor showcases a neon pink skirt with feathers paired with a pink shiny leather Coco Handle handbag from Chanel during New York Fashion Week, September 2022

CAMERA CASES

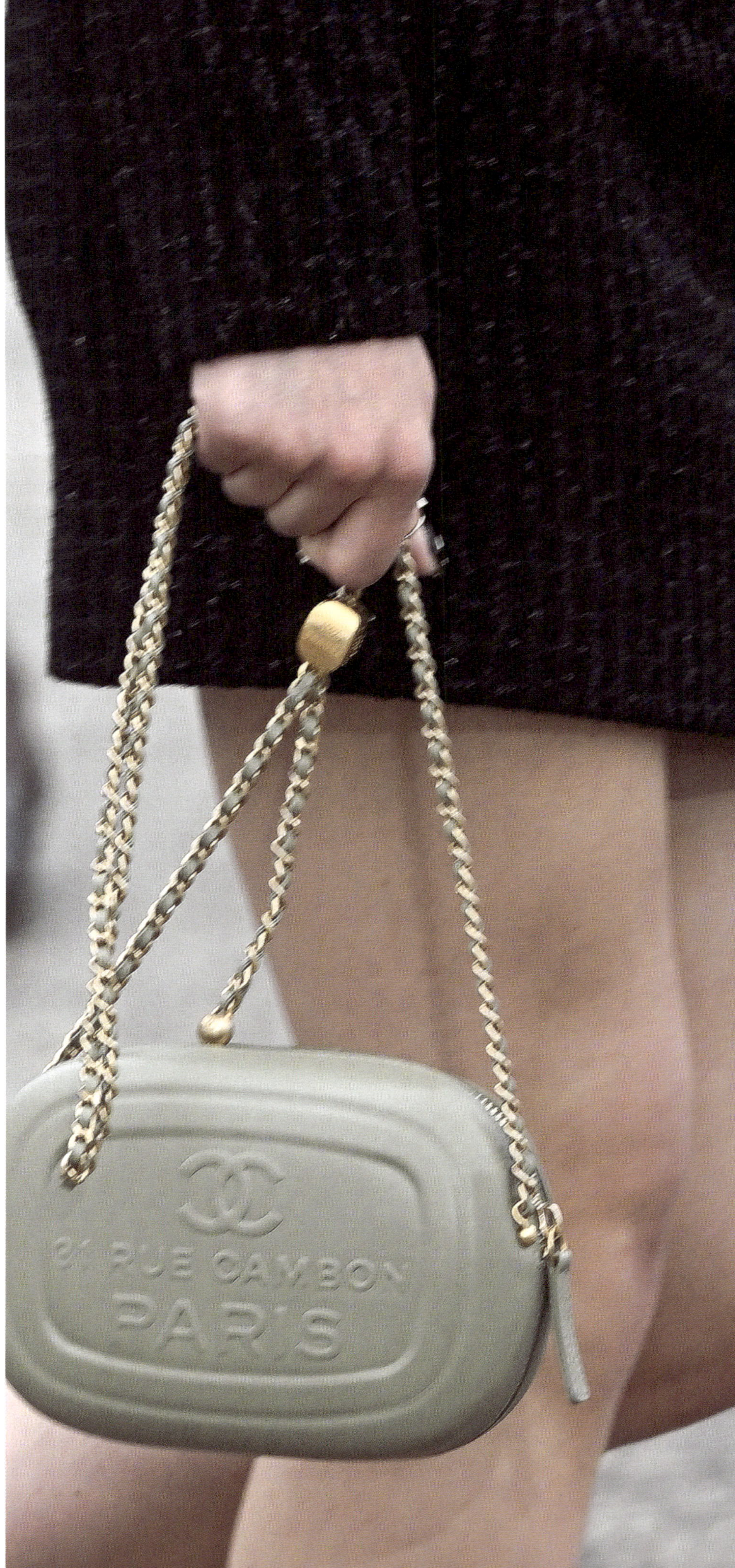

Pages 74/75: Camera case bags are available in various shapes, styles, and materials. The mini camera case bag on the left features Chanel's first address and was presented on the runway during the Cruise 2024/2025 fashion show on May 2, 2024, in Marseille. The white quilted lambskin camera bag on the right conceals a mirror behind the "lens," Paris.

Pages 76/77: Similar to camera cases, vanity cases come in diverse shapes and materials. Some resemble jewelry boxes, while others mimic miniature luggage. The round multicolored tweed and lambskin CC Mania Mini Vanity Case bag (page 76) originates from 2019, Paris, 2019.

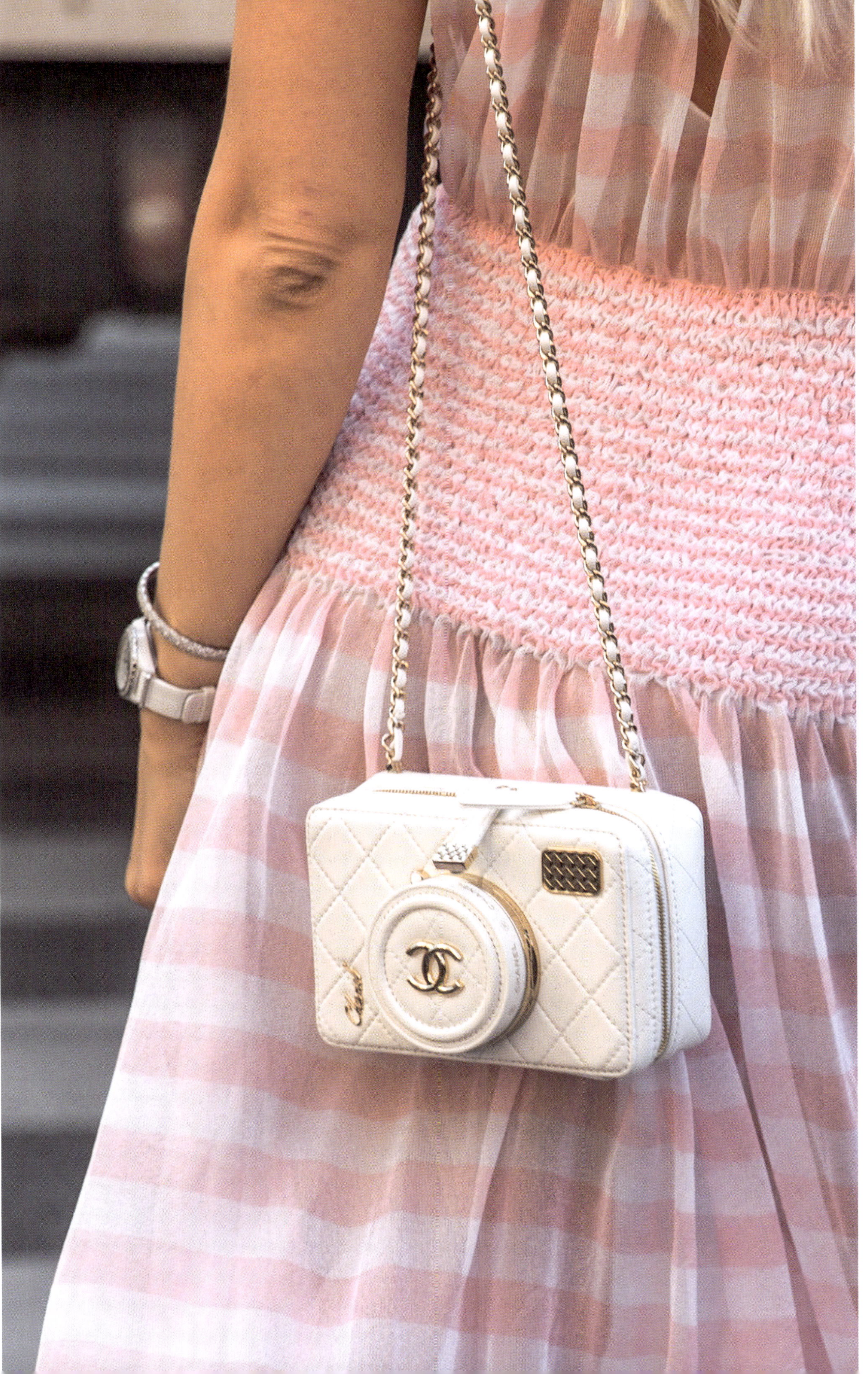
CHANEL

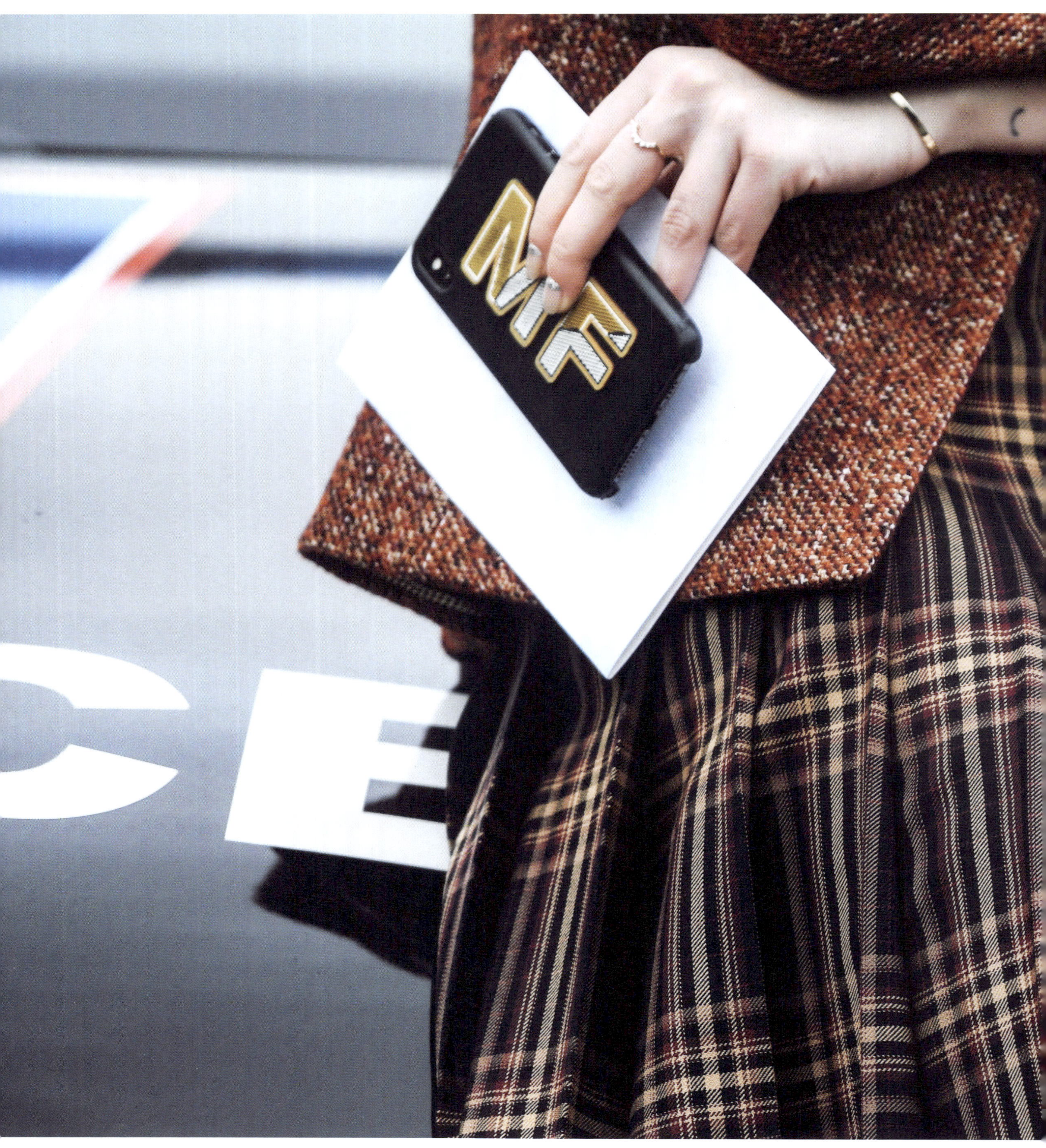
MF
CE

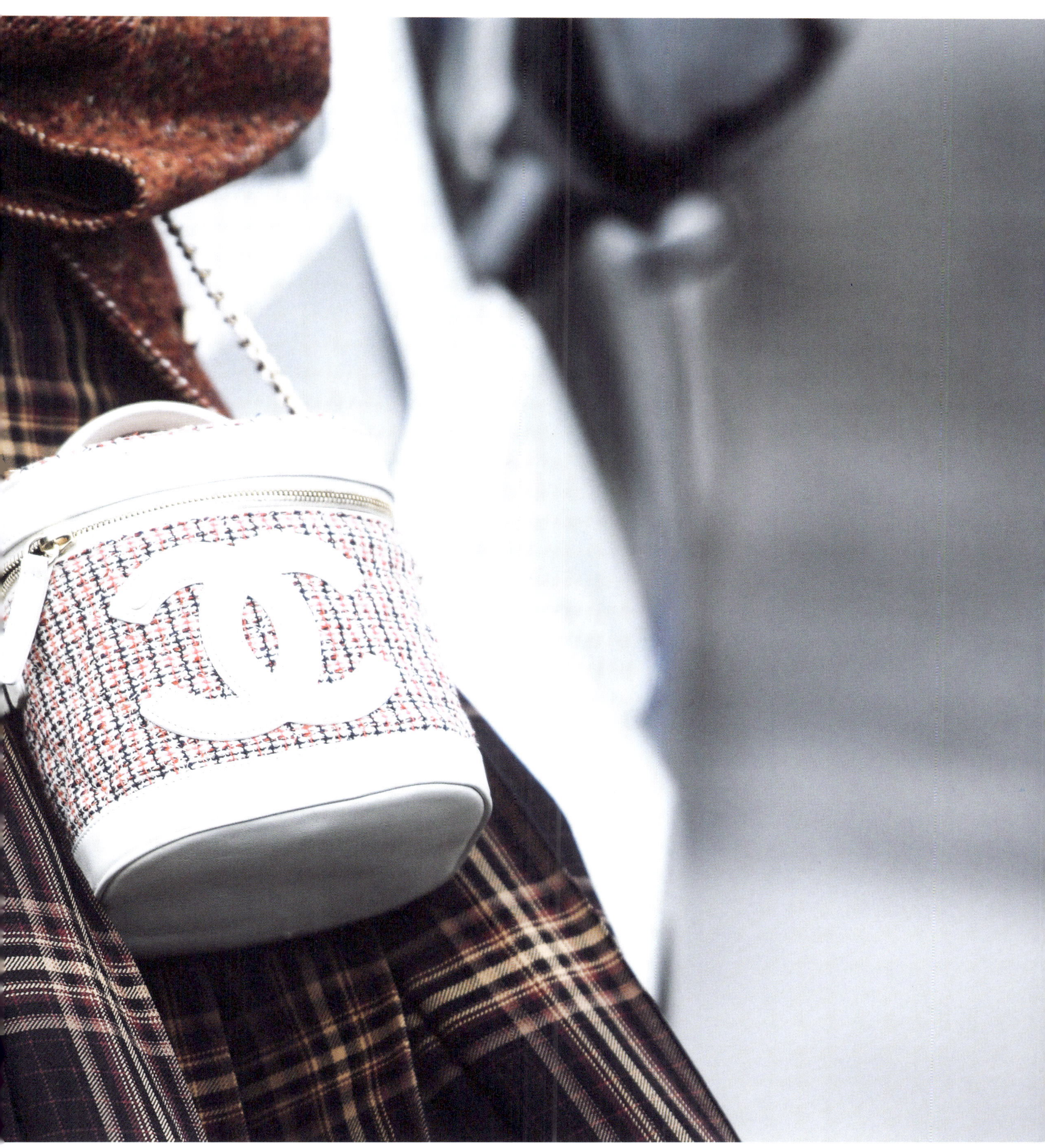

VANITY CASES

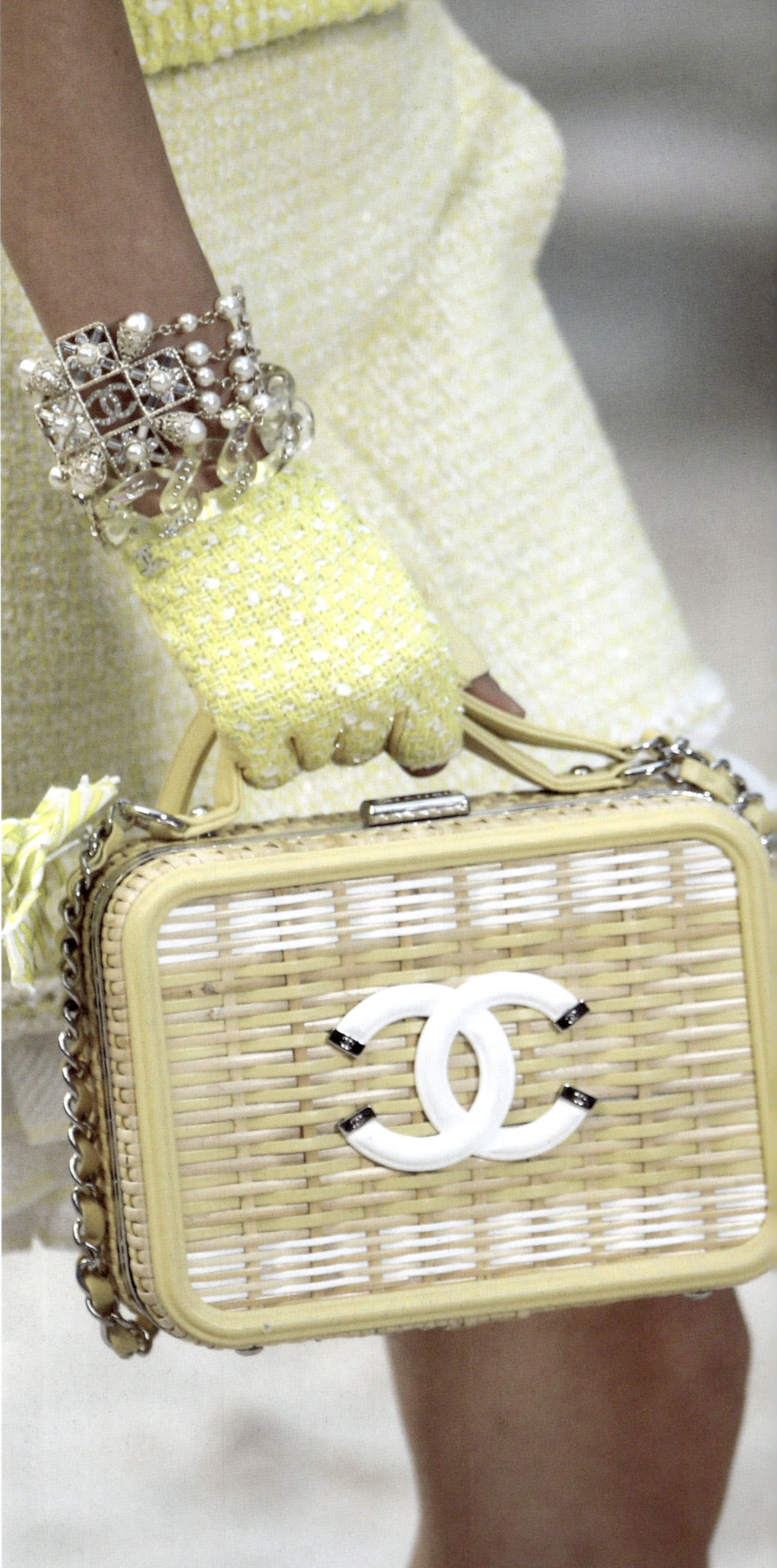

The yellow wicker CC Filigree Vanity Case bag (left) was showcased at the Spring/Summer 2019 fashion show on October 2, 2018. A black and white leather CC Filigree Vanity Case (right) as seen at Paris Fashion Week in March 2019.

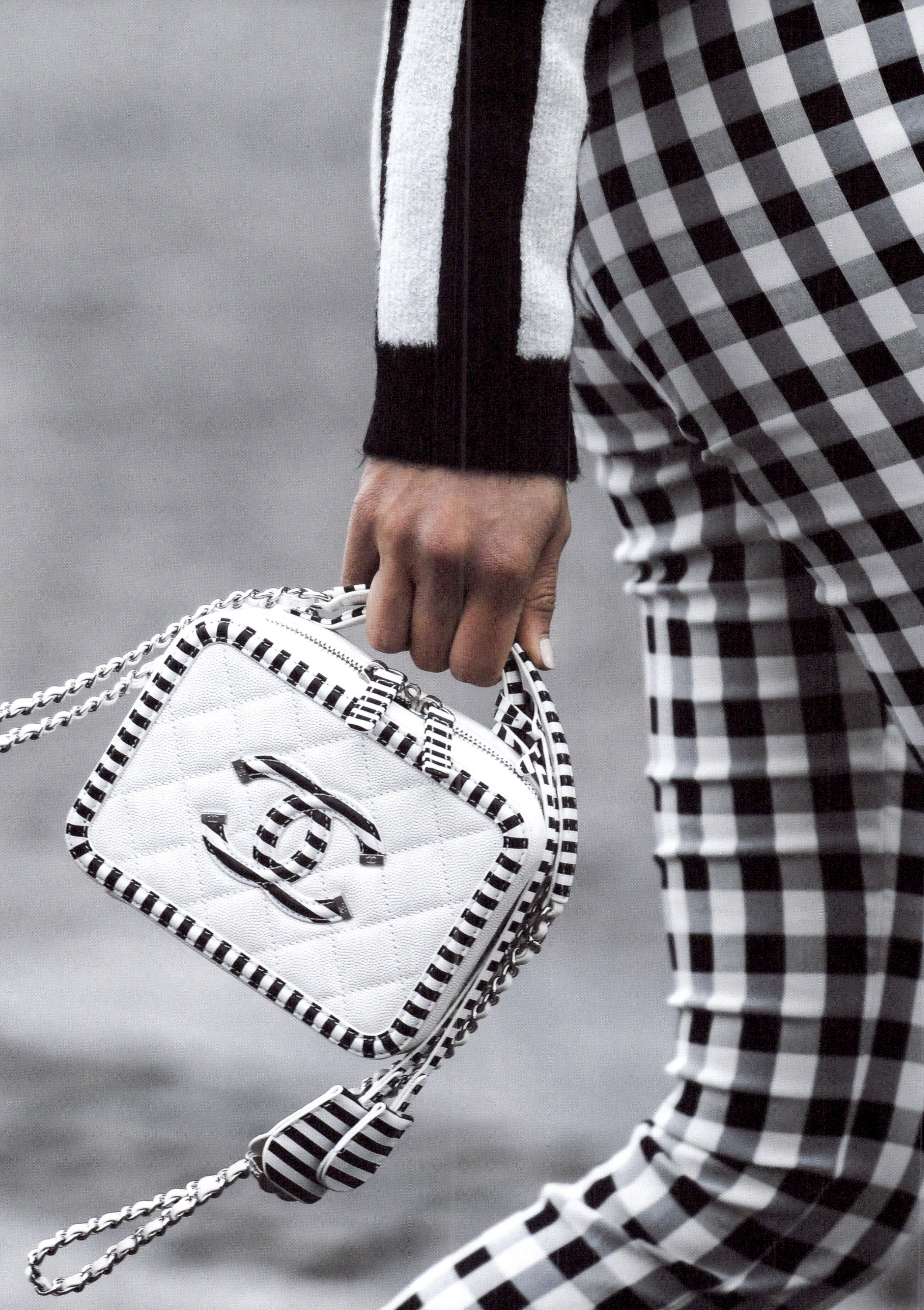

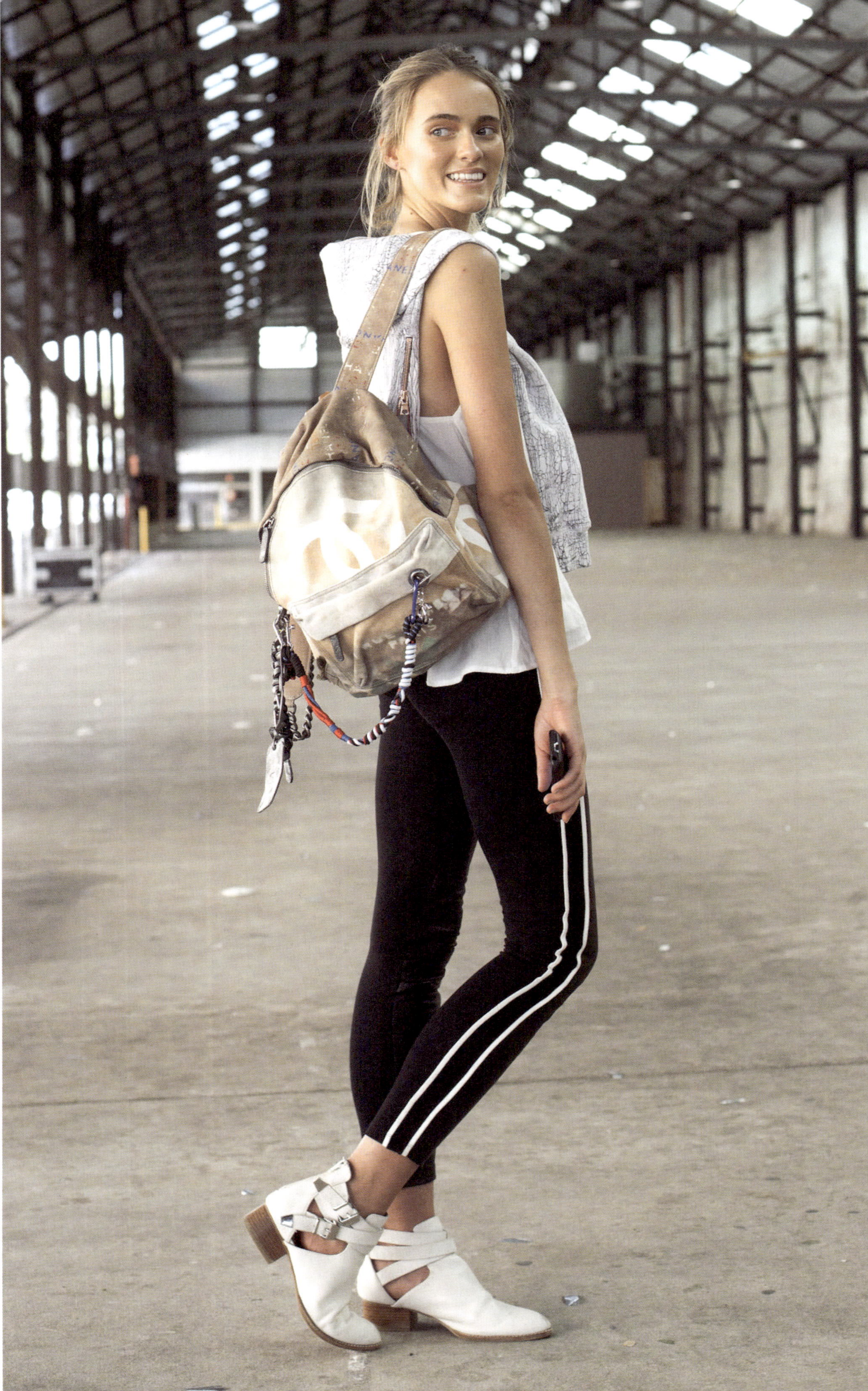

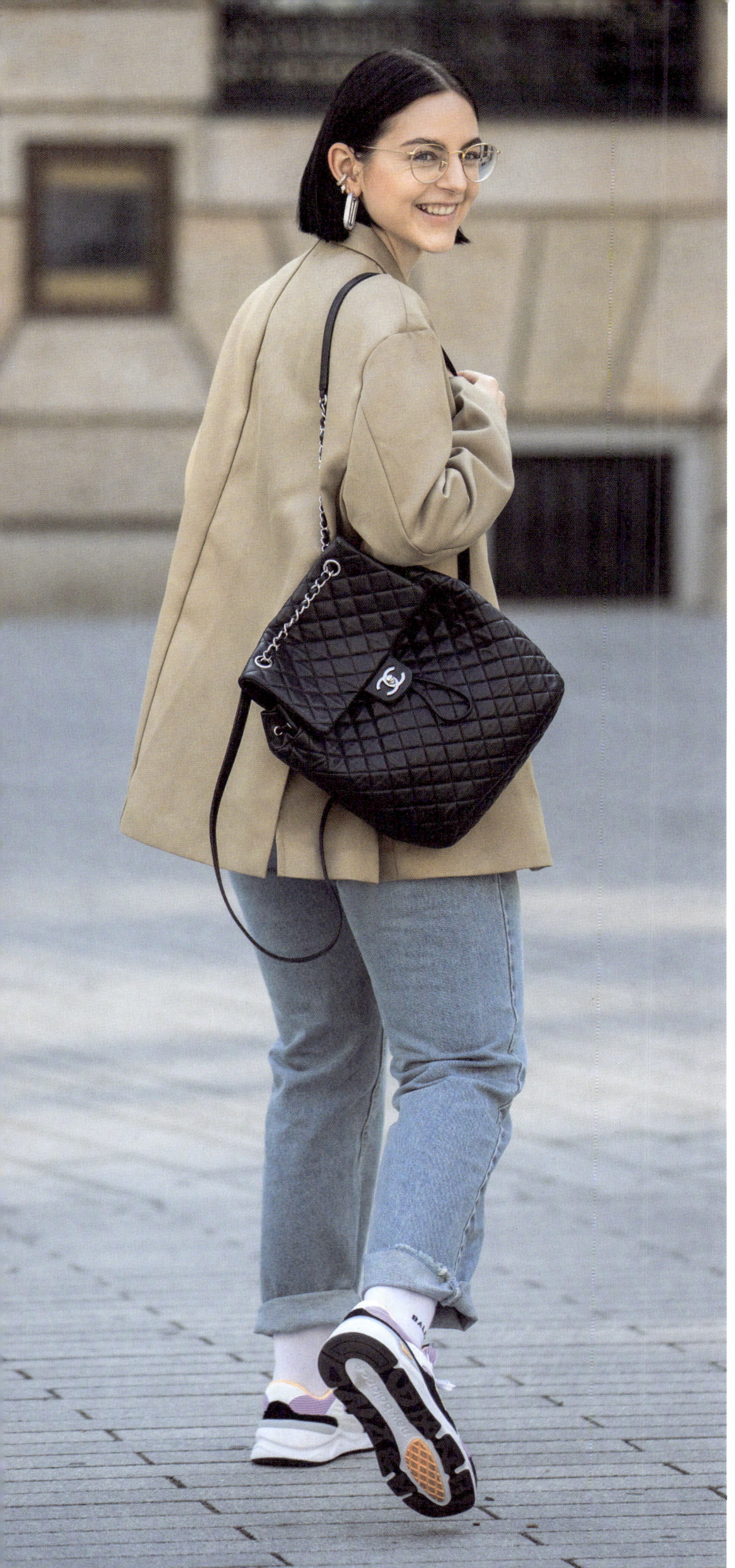

BACKPACKS

Previous page: Model Florence Fahmy displays a Chanel Graffiti backpack at Mercedes-Benz Fashion Week Australia 2015 in Sydney. The "Graffiti" collection debuted in Spring/Summer 2015, and the backpack quickly gained popularity with celebrities, including Miley Cyrus, Lily Allen, and the Kardashians.

This page: Maria Barteczko is seen with a classic black leather Chanel backpack in Düsseldorf, 2019

Page 82: Alexandra Lapp is spotted with a white Chanel Classic Flap and a tweed backpack from the Spring/Summer 2016 "Airport" collection in Düsseldorf, 2021

Page 83: Romina Meier sports a bicolor Gabrielle backpack in Düsseldorf, 2020

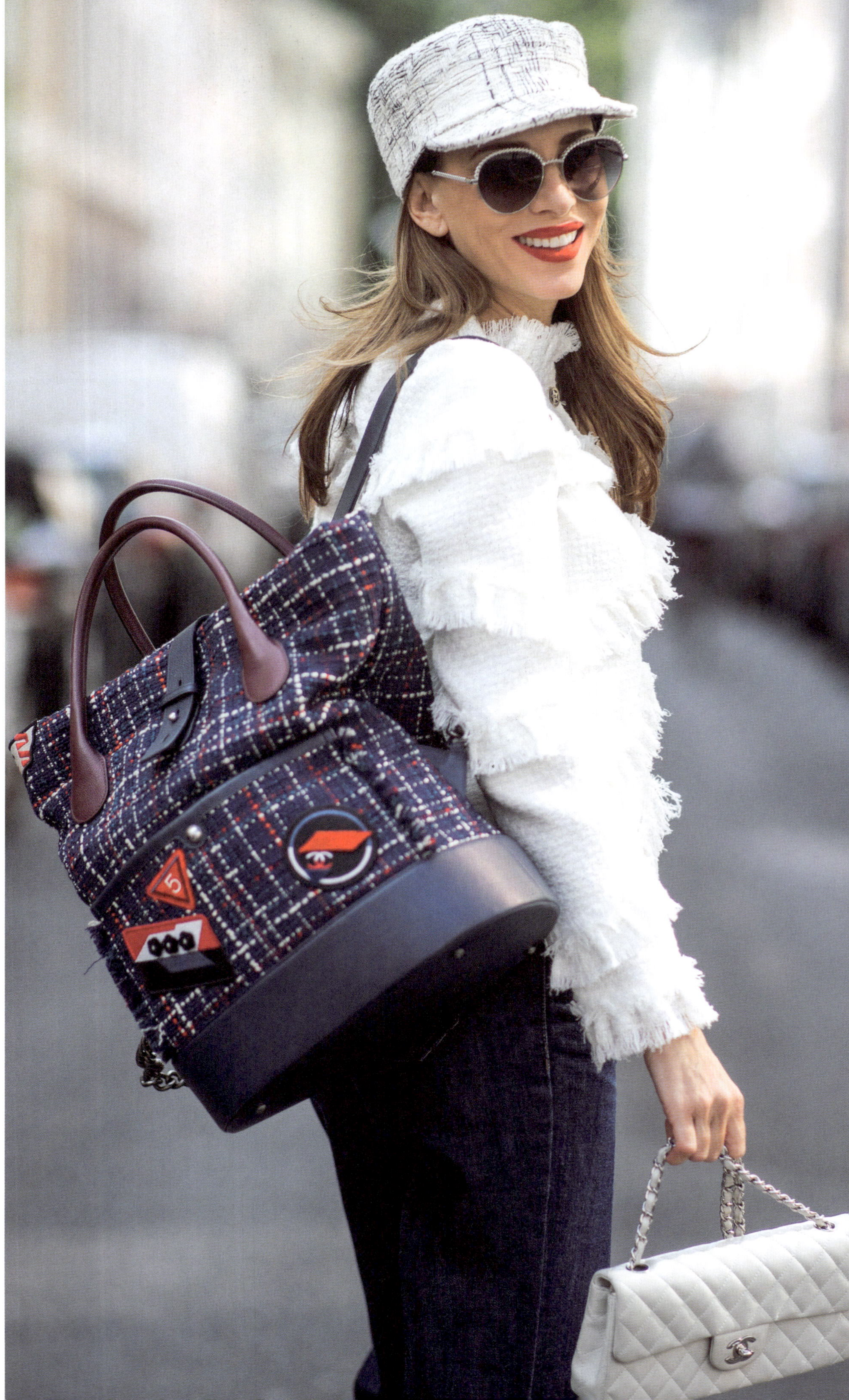
5

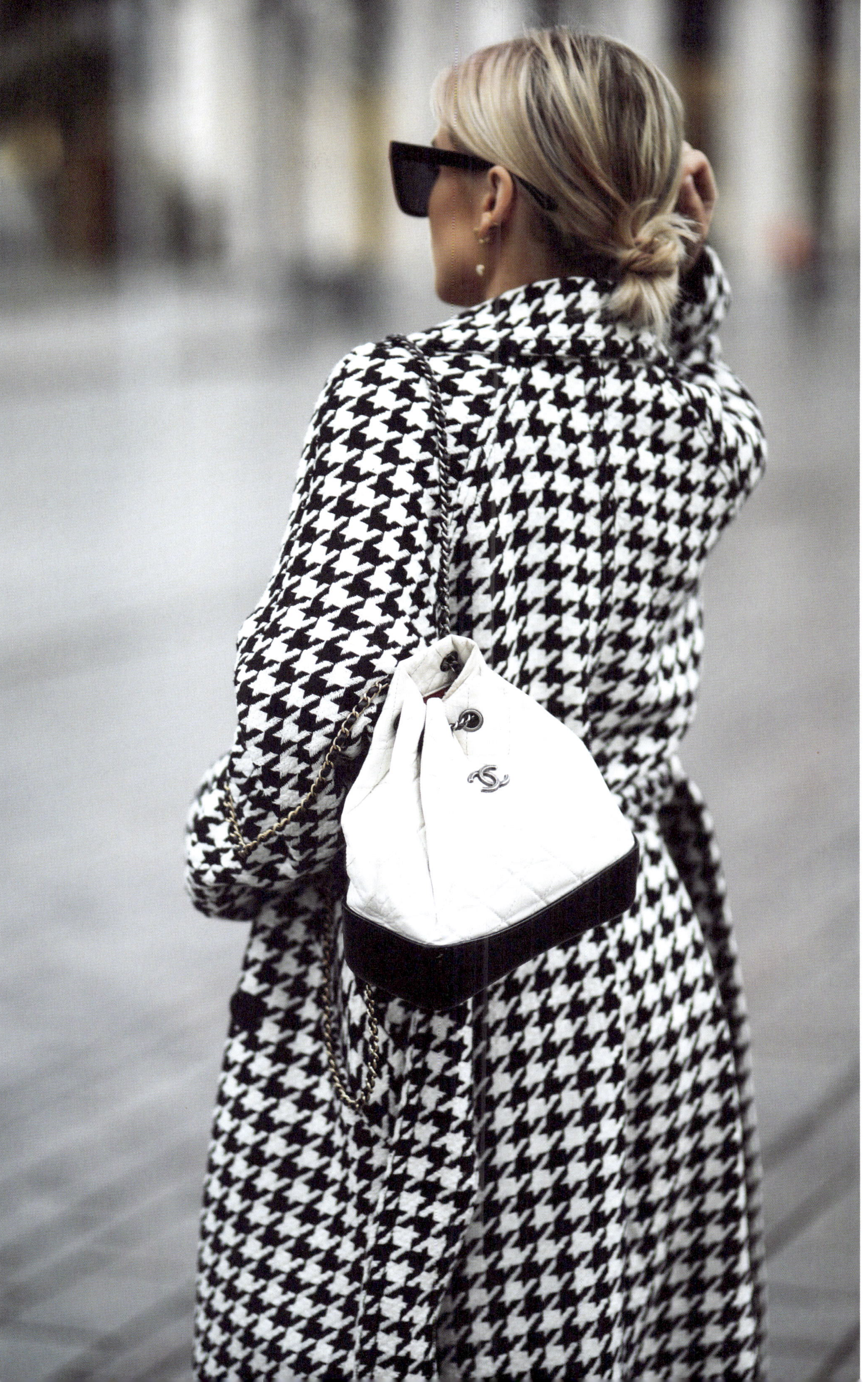

TOTE BAGS

Chanel may be closely associated with shoulder bags, but the tote bags created by the *maison* are equally impactful. Totes are often part of each style's family, but the first bigger bag launched under Karl Lagerfeld's direction was the Grand Shopping Tote, affectionately abbreviated to GST.

Most often created in the sturdiest finish of caviar leather, the supersized fabric interior had multiple pockets and signature chain straps and became an instant favorite. A more delicate lambskin option is lined with leather. The exterior featured beautiful quilted stitching and a stitched interlocking double CC logo. The GST measured a practical 33 × 25.5 × 13.5 cm. Each season, the bag would be reinvented with the colors and finishes of the season. It was joined by a Petite Shopping Tote, Petite Timeless Tote and XL sizes, but it was unfortunately discontinued in 2015. Now described as a unicorn bag due to its rarity, finding a GST is only possible through pre-loved retailers.

Another short-lived tote that has reached iconic status on the vintage market is the Medallion tote. Available for less than a decade, the bag follows a shopper silhouette, but was lined in leather and had leather straps instead of a chain. Named after the medallion zip closure, the bag had a moment in the spotlight when it was gifted to reality show star Lauren Conrad in *The Hills* by her then-boyfriend. Along with classic Chanel colorways like black and beige, a diamond-encrusted Medallion bag was released with a price tag of $26,000. Although discontinued in 2013, the rarity of the style now adds to its appeal. The thrill of not knowing when Chanel might cancel a bag—or raise its prices—has built up the myth of the *maison*.

Right now, the most in-demand Chanel tote is the Deauville style, described simply as a "shopping bag." As the seaside location of Chanel's first multi-item boutique, it makes a divine beach bag or first class carry-on due to the lightweight canvas structure and capacious interior.

Launched as part of the Spring/Summer 2012 collection, renowned architect Zaha Hadid created a set dotted with giant coral, seashell and seaweed structures for the models to walk around. The original bags were made from canvas jacquard in a small array of classic colors, including ecru and denim, but now have expanded to include a metallic gold style and luxurious shearling lambskin option (£7650).

On the exterior, the interlocking double CC logo is accompanied by the text "31 rue Cambon," and the bags have intertwined chain and leather straps. Inside is a key clasp, small pouch and zippered pocket for organization. A magnetic snap closure keeps all your belongings secure. The Deauville is available in small, medium, large and extra large versions.

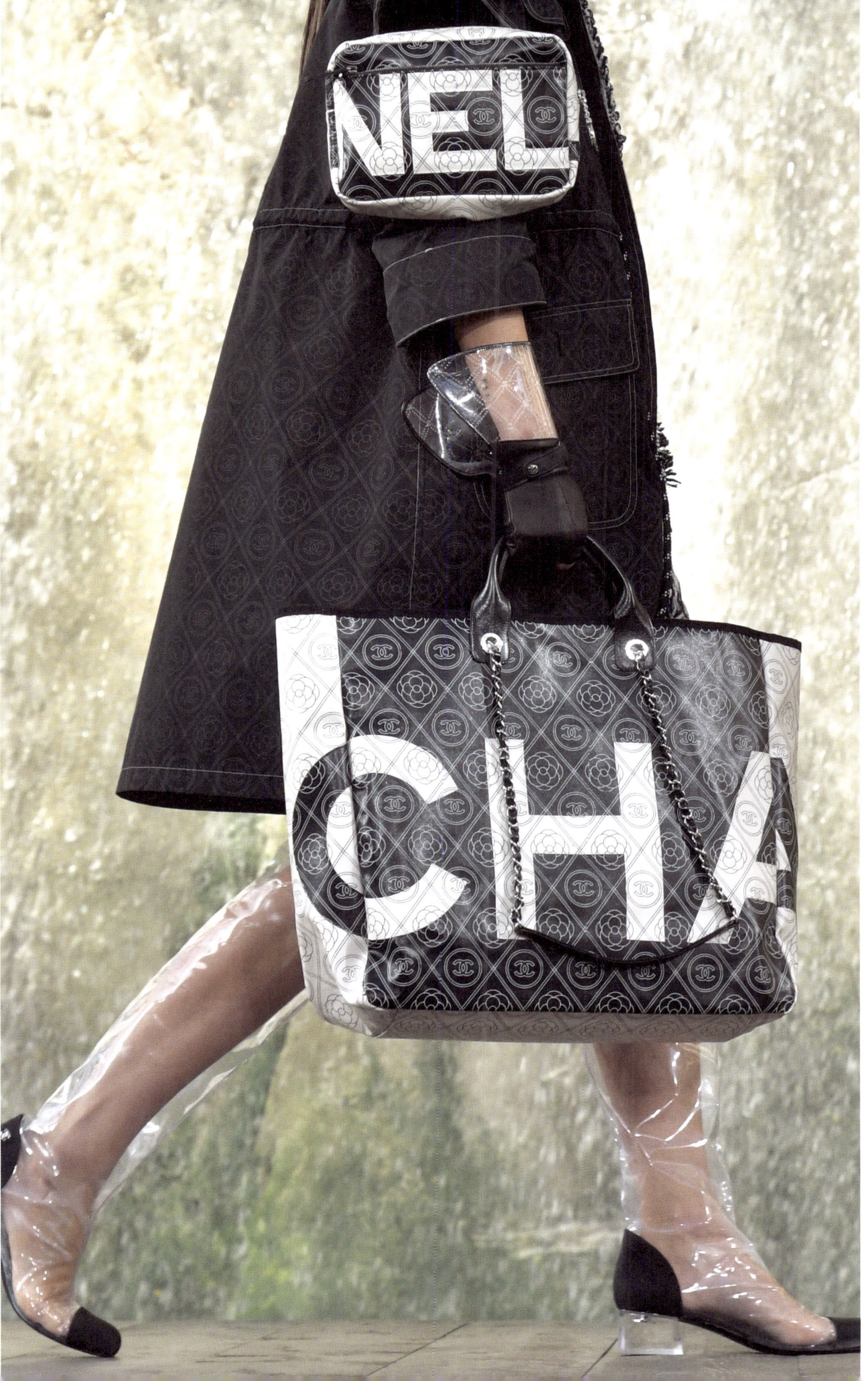
NEL
CHA

Previous page: A large shopping bag presented at Chanel's Spring/Summer 2018 show in Paris, October 2017

This page: Paris Hilton is photographed with her Medallion bag in Beverly Hills

Next page: Myleene Klass carries a Grand Shopping Tote (GST) through London, 2013

Page 88: A model walks the runway showcasing a Deauville tote bag with shearling trim during the Chanel Womenswear Fall/Winter 2024 show, Paris, 2024

Pages 90/91: A canvas Deauville bag featured in Paris, 2020

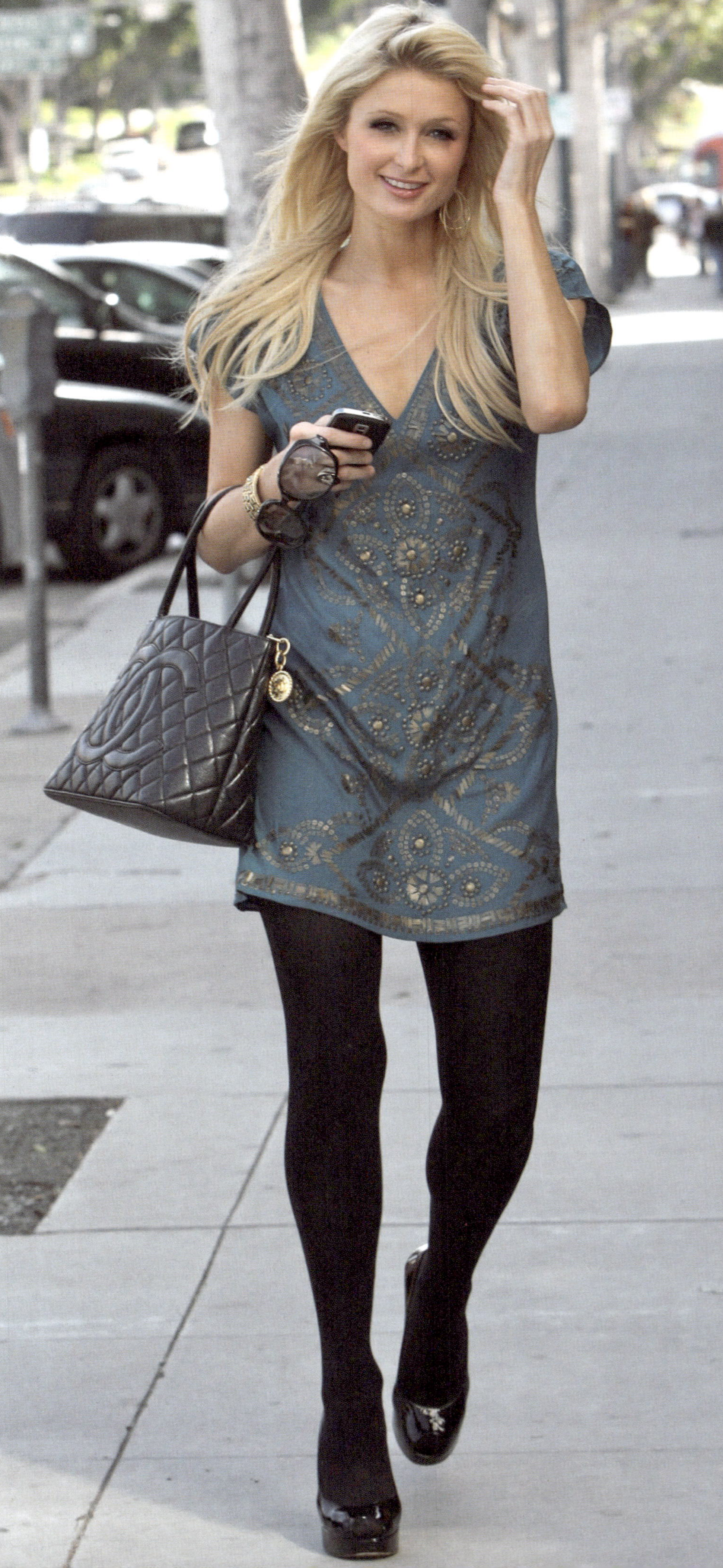

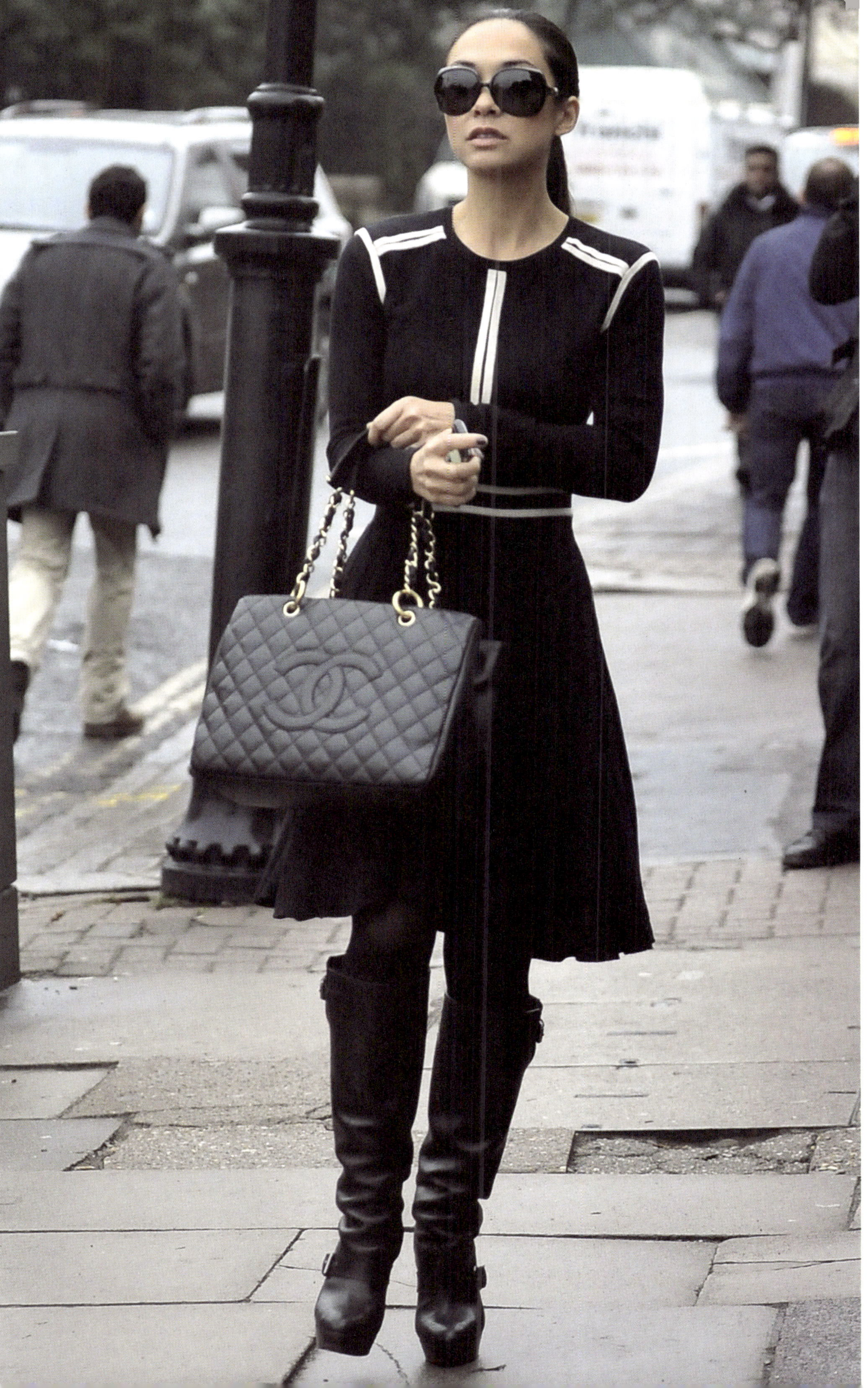

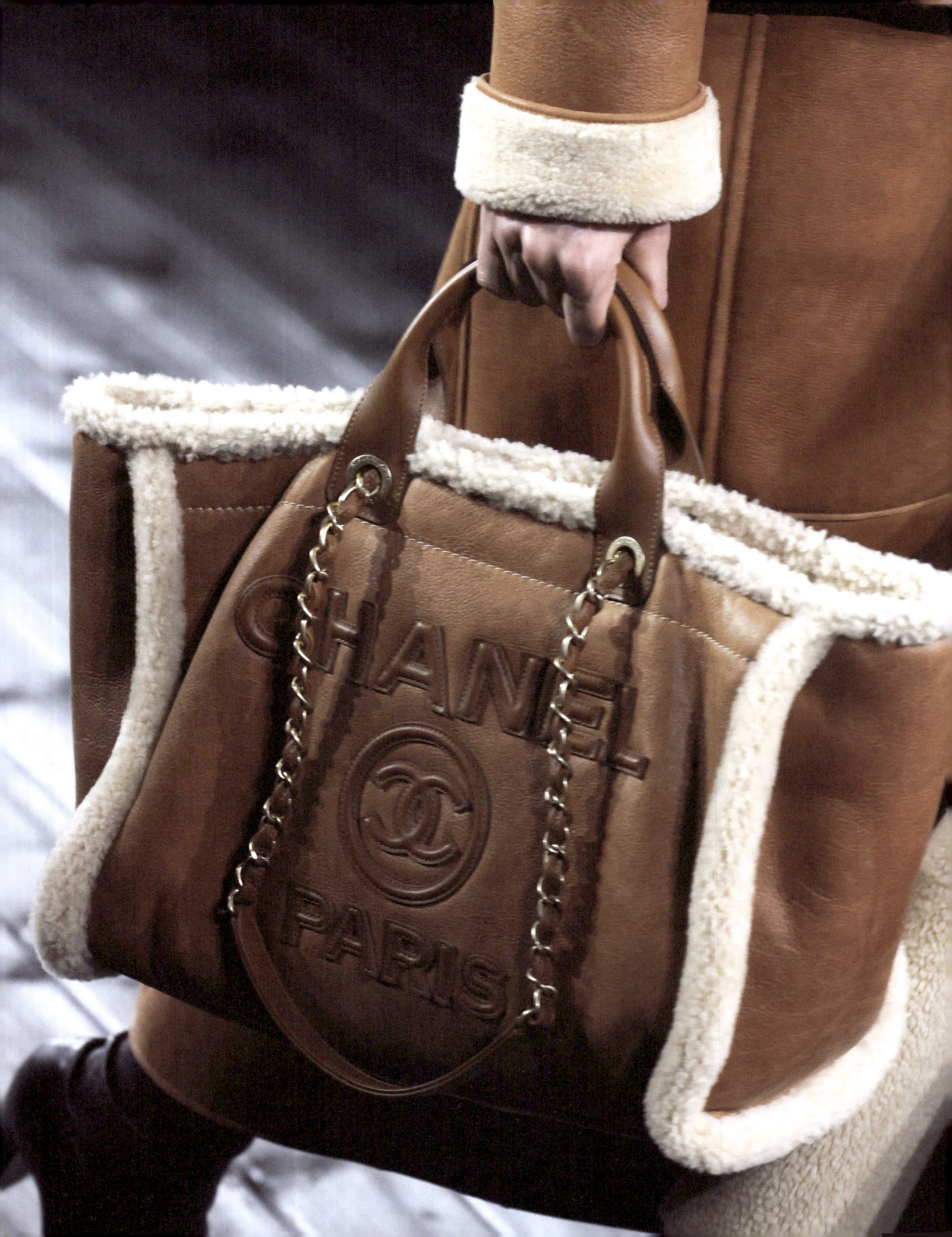
CHANEL
PARIS

CHANEL MAY BE CLOSELY ASSOCIATED WITH SHOULDER BAGS, BUT THE TOTE BAGS ARE EQUALLY IMPACTFUL.

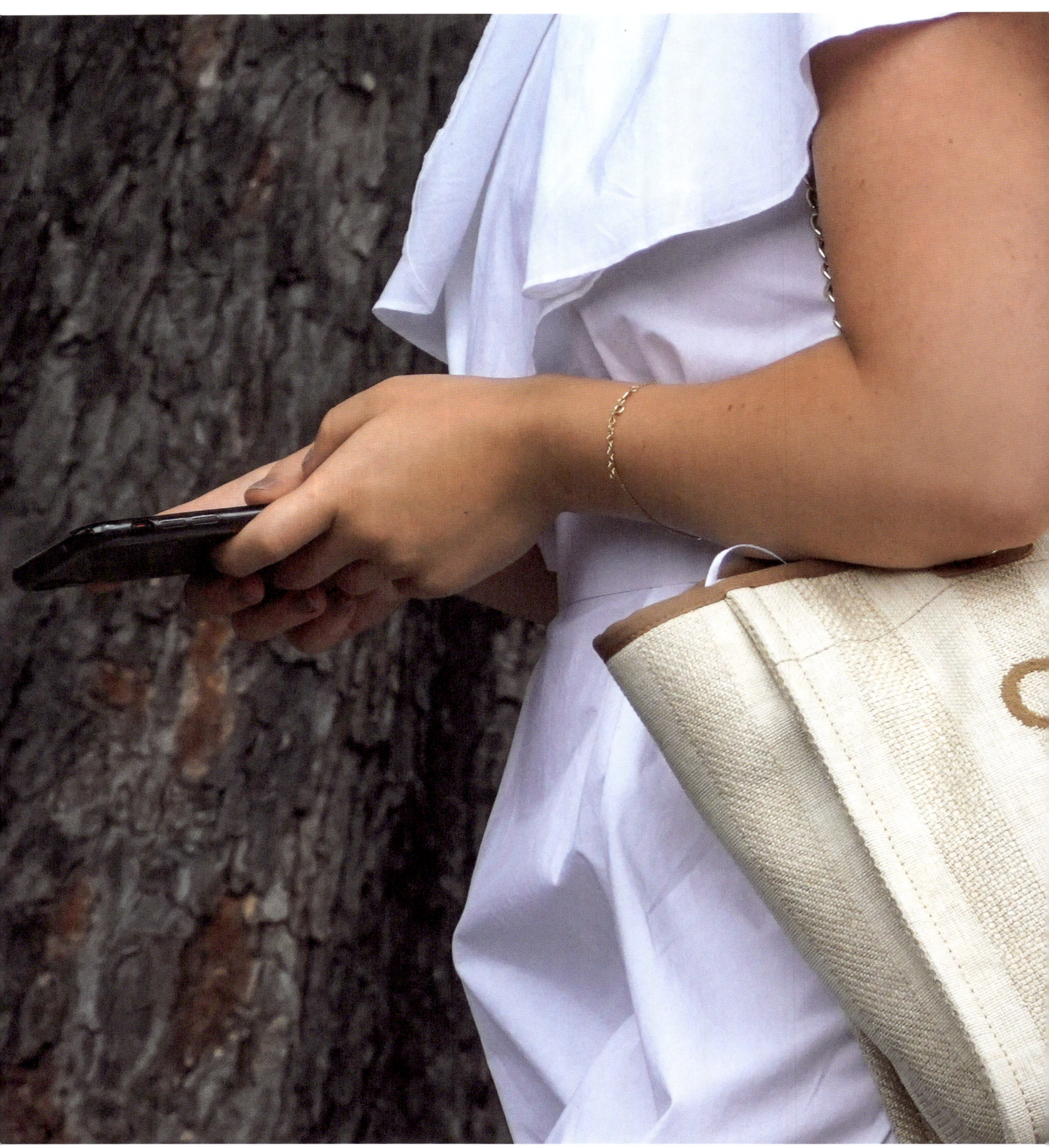

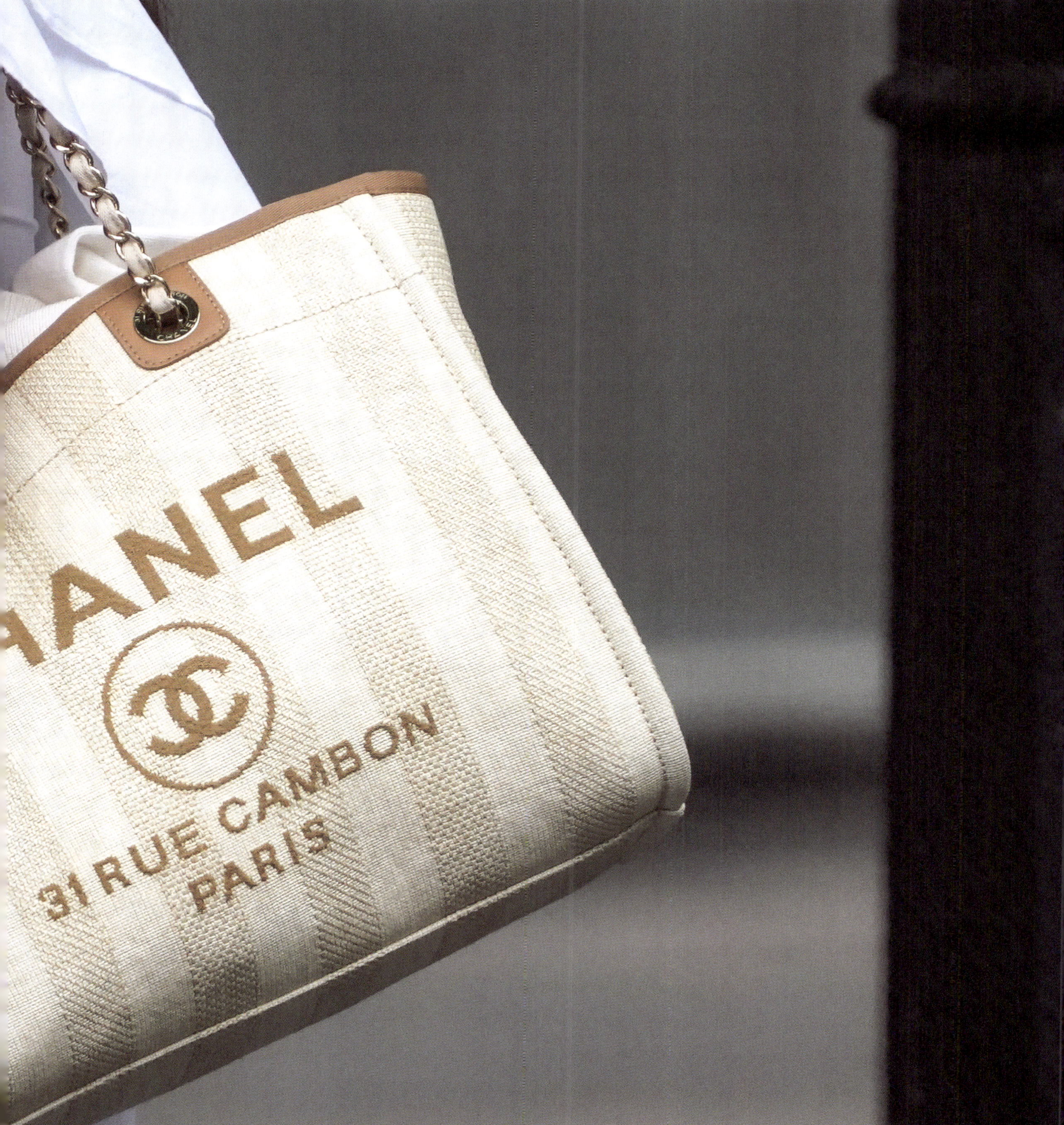
HANEL
31 RUE CAMBON
PARIS

WALLET ON CHAIN

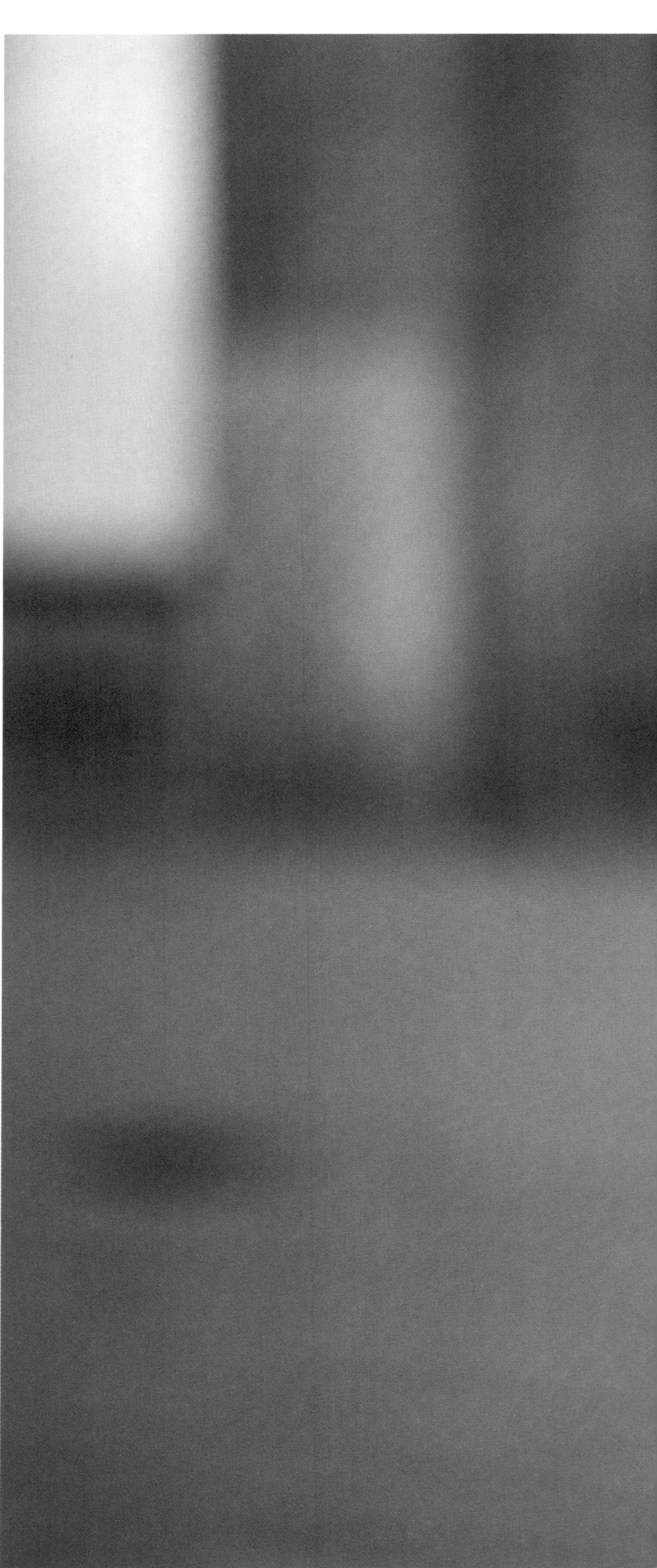

While affordability is subjective, the collection of Wallet On Chain designs, or WOC, come at a far more accessible price point than other Chanel bags, as they fall within the category of "small leather goods" rather than handbags. The simple addition of a 24-inch chain to a wallet was a genius move, and the WOC has consistently been one of the most in-demand styles for the *maison*.

Launched in 1997, the Wallet on Chain offers all the signature details of a larger Chanel bag with pared-back functionality, which is ideal for more minimally-minded fashion fans. Carrying a Wallet On Chain is liberating. The small size allows the wearer to take only the essentials with them. Inside the WOC you will find 6 card slots, an open compartment and a zippered pocket—depending on the model—while each WOC measures approximately 19 × 12 × 3.5cm. There are multiple versions of the WOC reflecting the different bag families; for example, the 19 or the 11.12 have both had WOC as part of their designs. As the WOC has been available for almost 30 years, there are a myriad of finishes, fabrics, colors and styles available on the resale market.

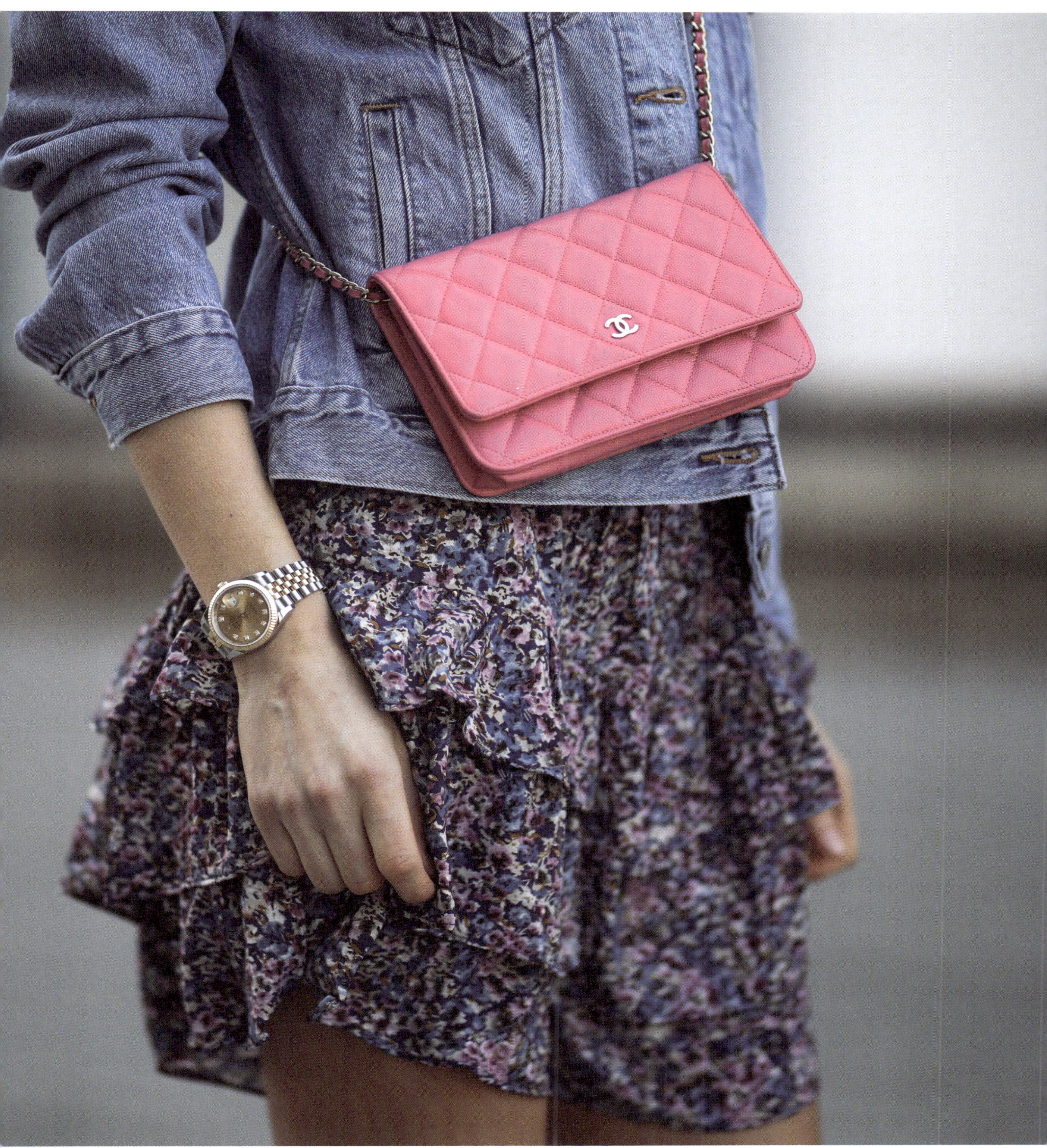

Page 93: Scarlett Gartmann is seen wearing a Neo Noir flower mini dress, a pink Chanel Wallet on Chain bag, and a blue Levi's jeans jacket in Düsseldorf, 2021

This page: Kaitlyn Dever, presenting a white WOC with black trim, attends a Chanel dinner celebrating the 90th Anniversary of Gabrielle Chanel's 1932 High Jewelry Collection in West Hollywood, 2022

Next page: Close-up of a black Wallet on Chain, Paris, 2024

Page 96: Julia Comil sported white lace tights, a yellow dress, a beige trench leather coat, and a blue Chanel Wallet on Chain outside the Marie Adam-Leenaerdt Fall/Winter 2025 fashion show in Paris

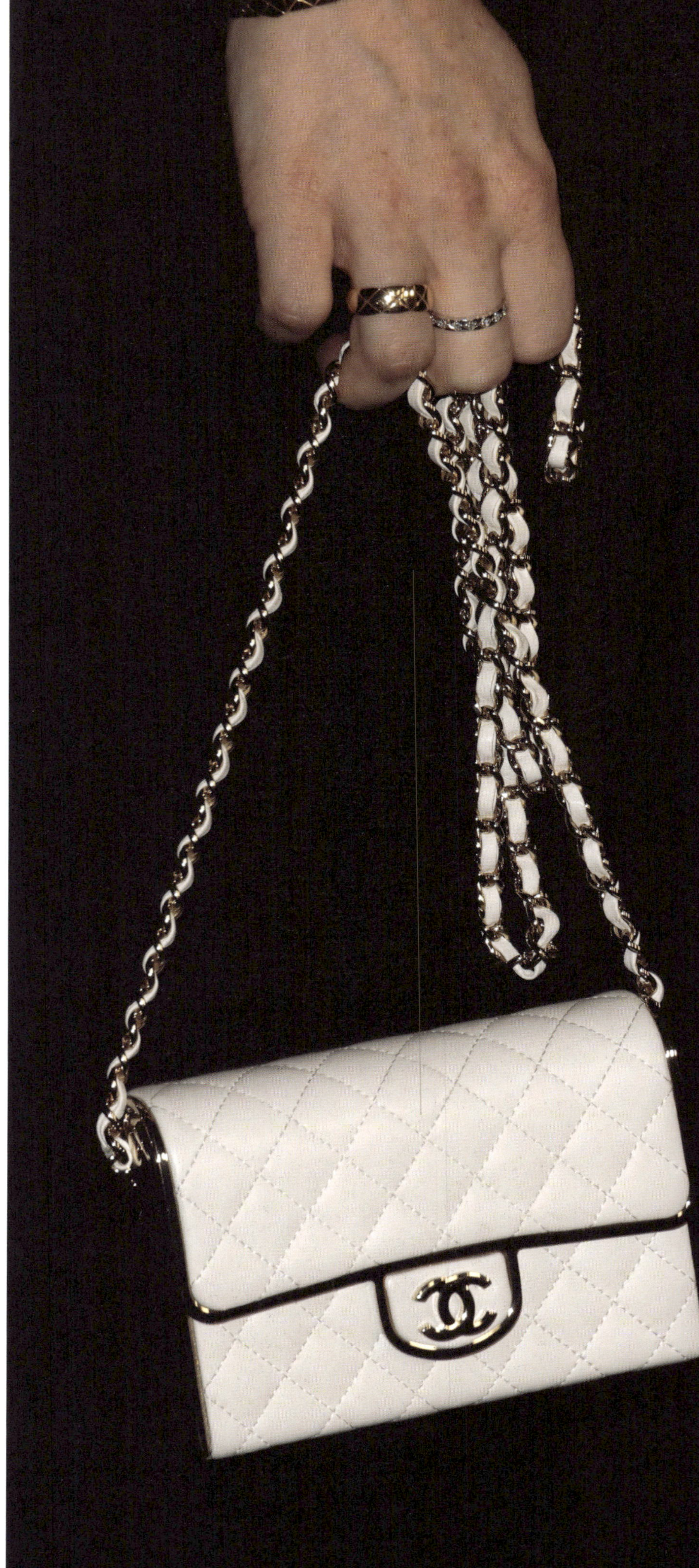

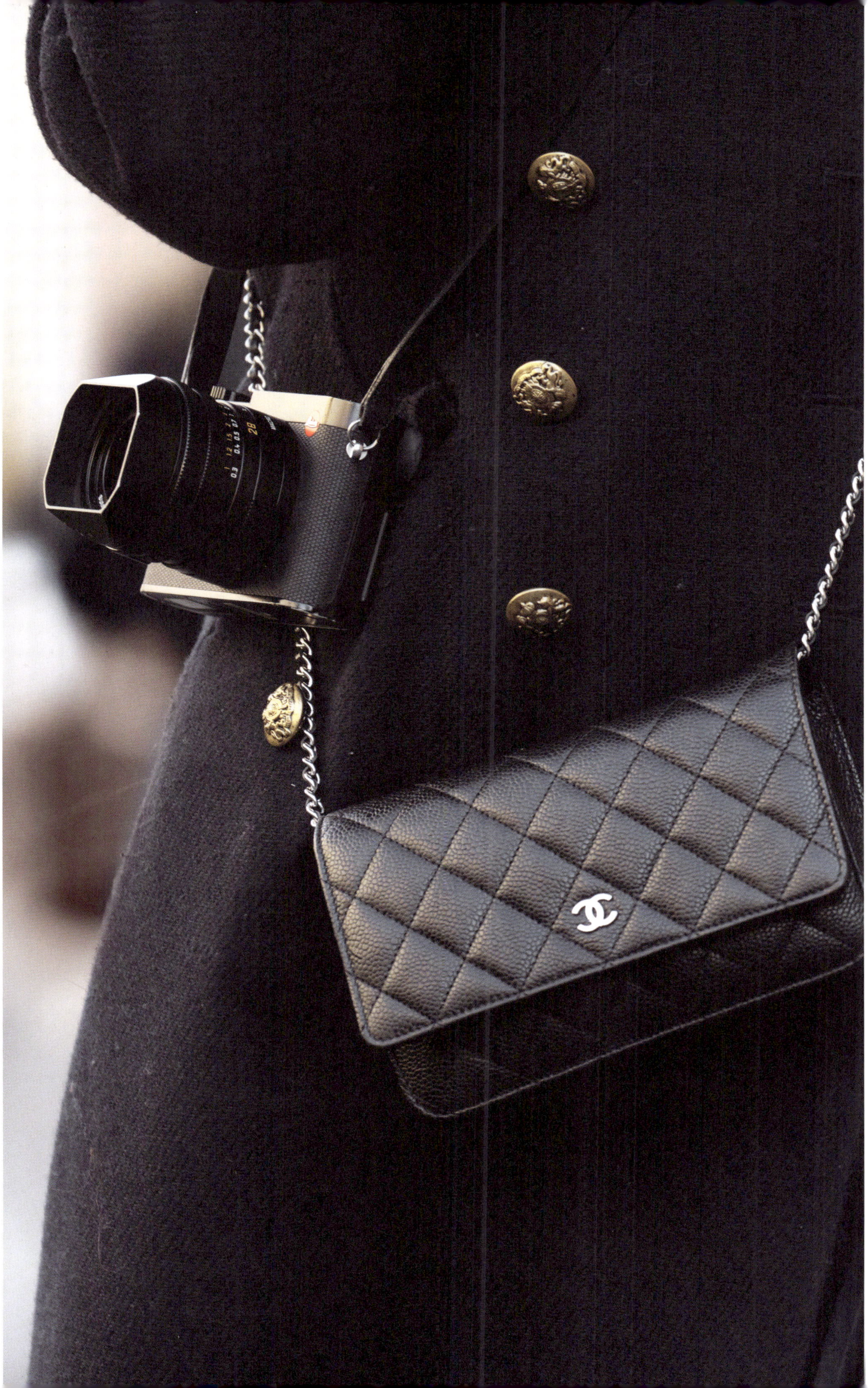

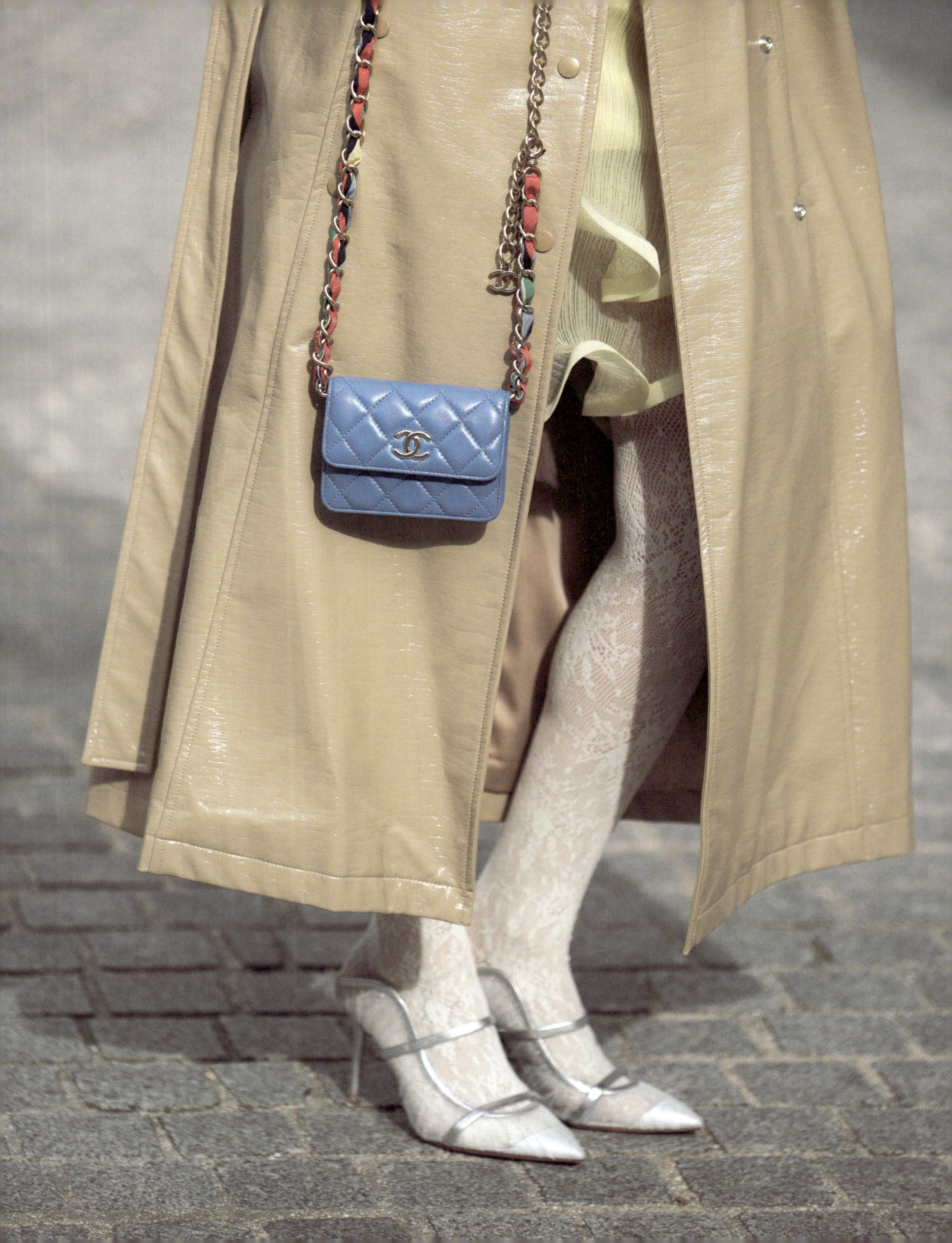

THE SIMPLE ADDITION OF A 24 INCH CHAIN TO A WALLET WAS A GENIUS MOVE

GIRL

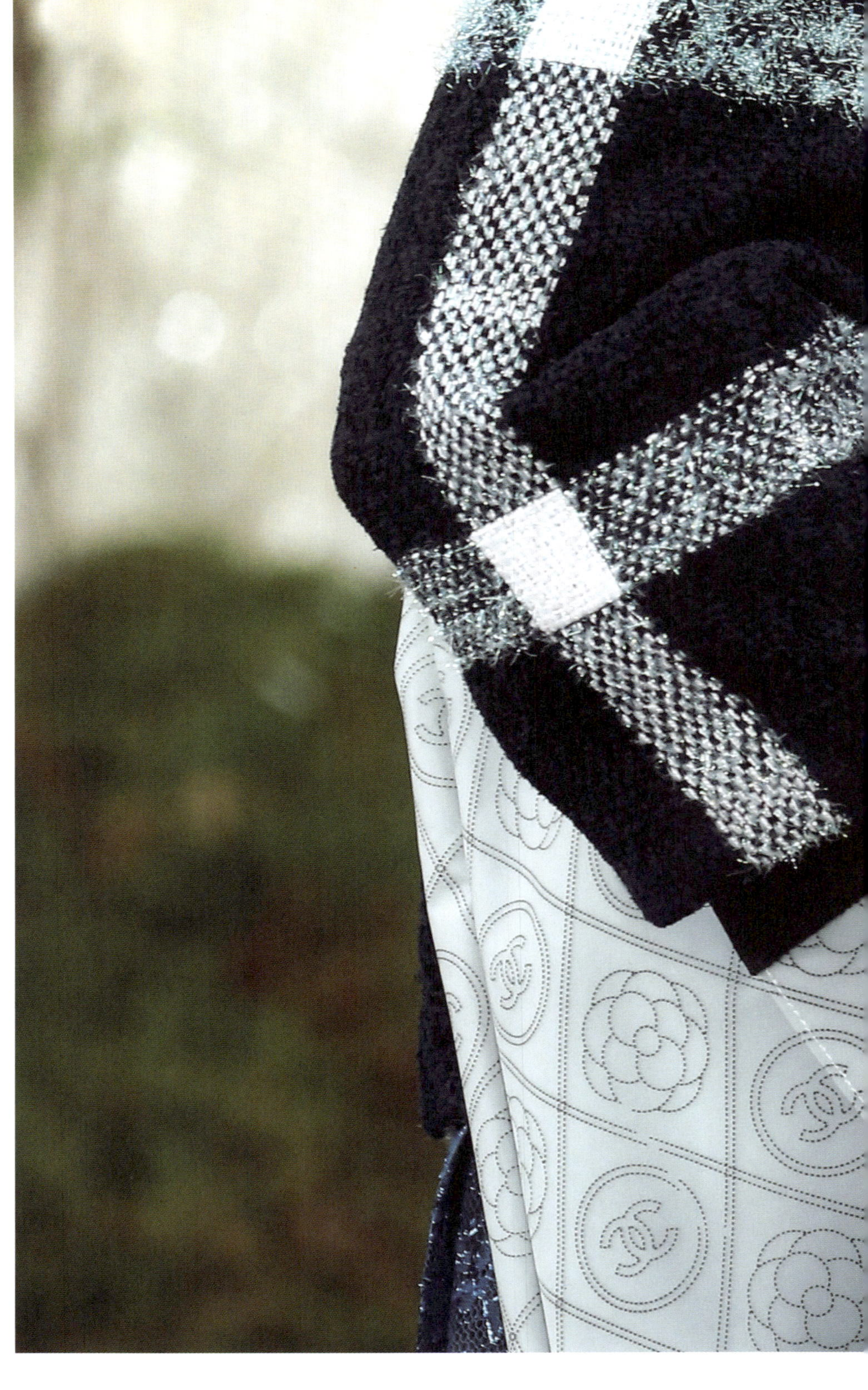

A model showcases a Girl bag during the Spring/Summer 2018 Chanel fashion show in Paris, October 2017. Designed by Karl Lagerfeld and launched in 2015, the Girl bag resembles a suit jacket, complete with pockets, buttons, and trim.

Page 100: Bella Hadid carries a Bowling bag in New York City, 2017

Pages 102/103: A limited edition Perfume Bottle *minaudière* from 2017, Paris, 2019

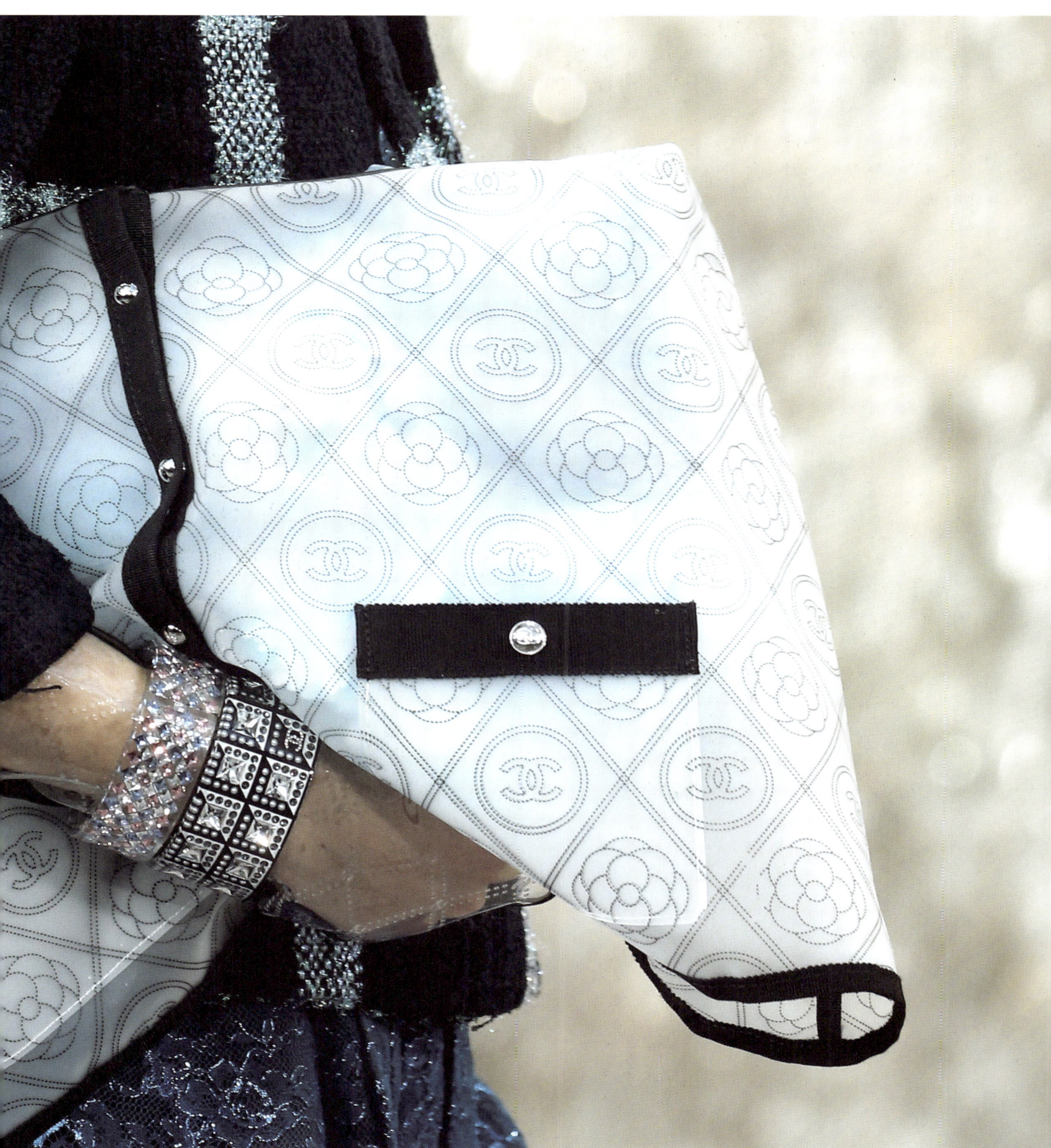

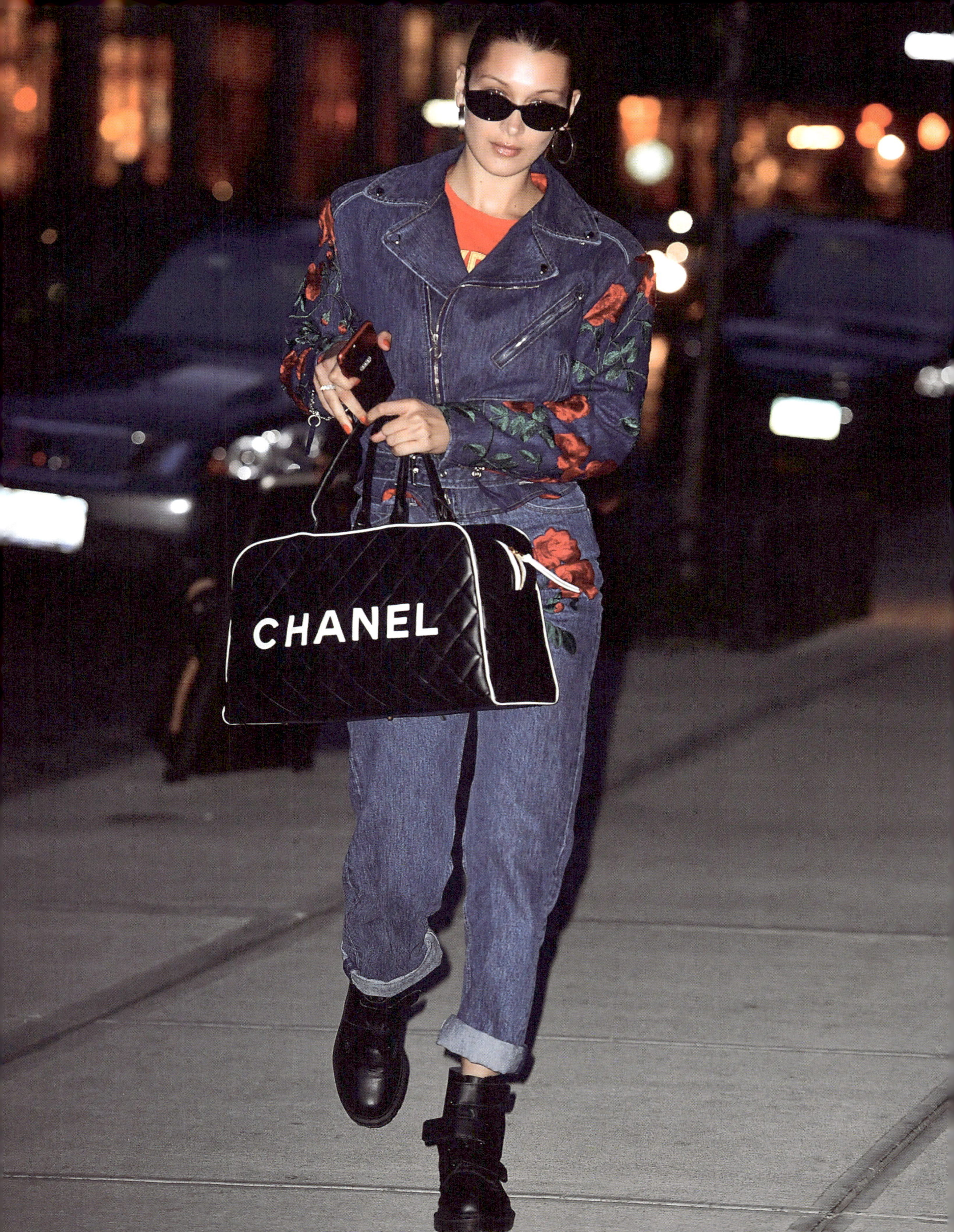
CHANEL

THE 90s NOSTALGIA REVIVED THE BOWLING BAG AS WELL.

SPECIAL BAGS

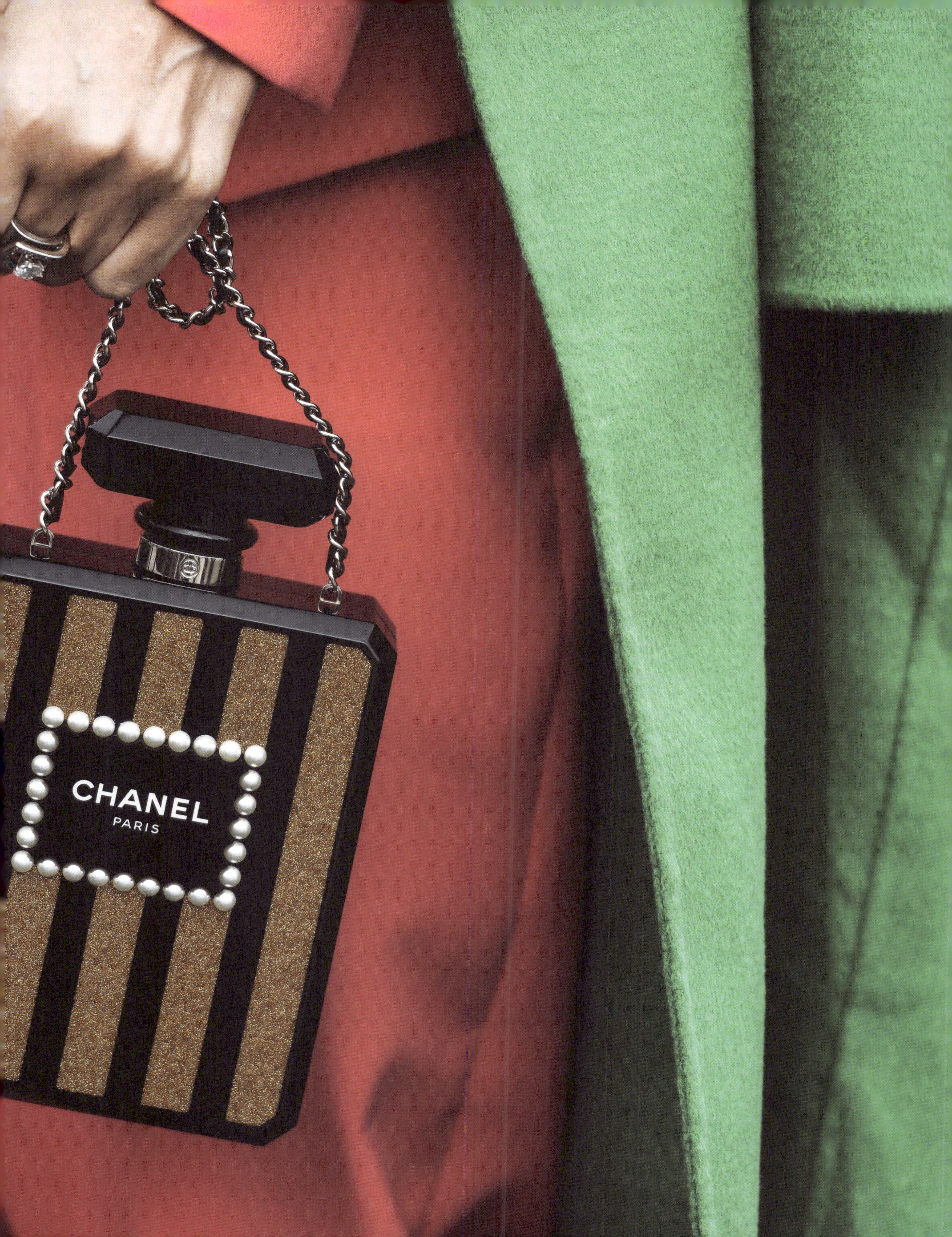
CHANEL
PARIS

MINAUDIÈRES

Each Chanel collection, from Karl Lagerfeld's tenure onwards, features an array of incredible novelty bags that echo the theme of each show. Only available in extremely limited editions and with elevated price tags, these tiny yet mighty *minaudière* are some of the most coveted Chanel bags ever created. To secure a piece, one must have an established relationship as a VIP Chanel client.

Minaudière translates into English from French as meaning something flirtatious. These bags' origin is linked to the emergence of flapper style in the 1920s, when small metal evening bags were essential for the emancipated woman in the Jazz Age. Created to hold cosmetics and decorated with intricate, filigree-like elements, *minaudière* were a mix between bag and jewelry but faded from fashion until Lagerfeld reintroduced the style in the early 2000s.

At Chanel, each collection presents a unique inspiration, whether that's space (for Fall/Winter 2017, the show saw a rocket launched from the Grand Palais); supermarket shopping (the show space was transformed into the chicest supermarket ever with real produce) or Spring/Summer 2012, when an "under the sea" theme saw Florence + The Machine perform inside a seashell. A freshwater pearl-covered seashell from this collection retailed for $48,000.

Other memorable *minaudière* include the Chanel Perfume bottle bag from Cruise 2014; the Lait de Coco milk carton from Fall/Winter 2014; and the Ski Gondola from Fall/Winter 2019. As part of Lagerfeld's last collection, the tiny lacquered and crystallized lucite clutch looks like a real ski lift with incredible attention to detail, featuring miniature skis and a realistically fogged-up window. Some of the most highly sought after *minaudière* are the Boy Brick "Lego" pieces, which can reach prices of over $20,000 at auction, along with styles from the annual Métiers d'Art collections. These presentations showcase the different couture-level craftsmanship the house employs through specialist workshops that are owned by Chanel, including embroidery, millinery and beading. Handcrafted with impeccable care, *minaudière* are often created from a plexiglass base which allows Chanel's artisans freedom to create the most ornamented—and desirable—designs.

Next page: A Lait de Coco milk carton *minaudière* from the Fall/Winter 2014 collection

Page 106: The Scarab *minaudière*, part of the Egypt-inspired Métiers d'Art collection 2019

Pages 108/109: Kristin Ducote is seen with a Chanel No. 5 Crystal *minaudière* from the Fall/Winter 2015 collection at Paris Fashion Week, 2015

Page 110: The Casino Monaco Slot Machine *minaudière* hails from Chanel's Resort 2023 collection

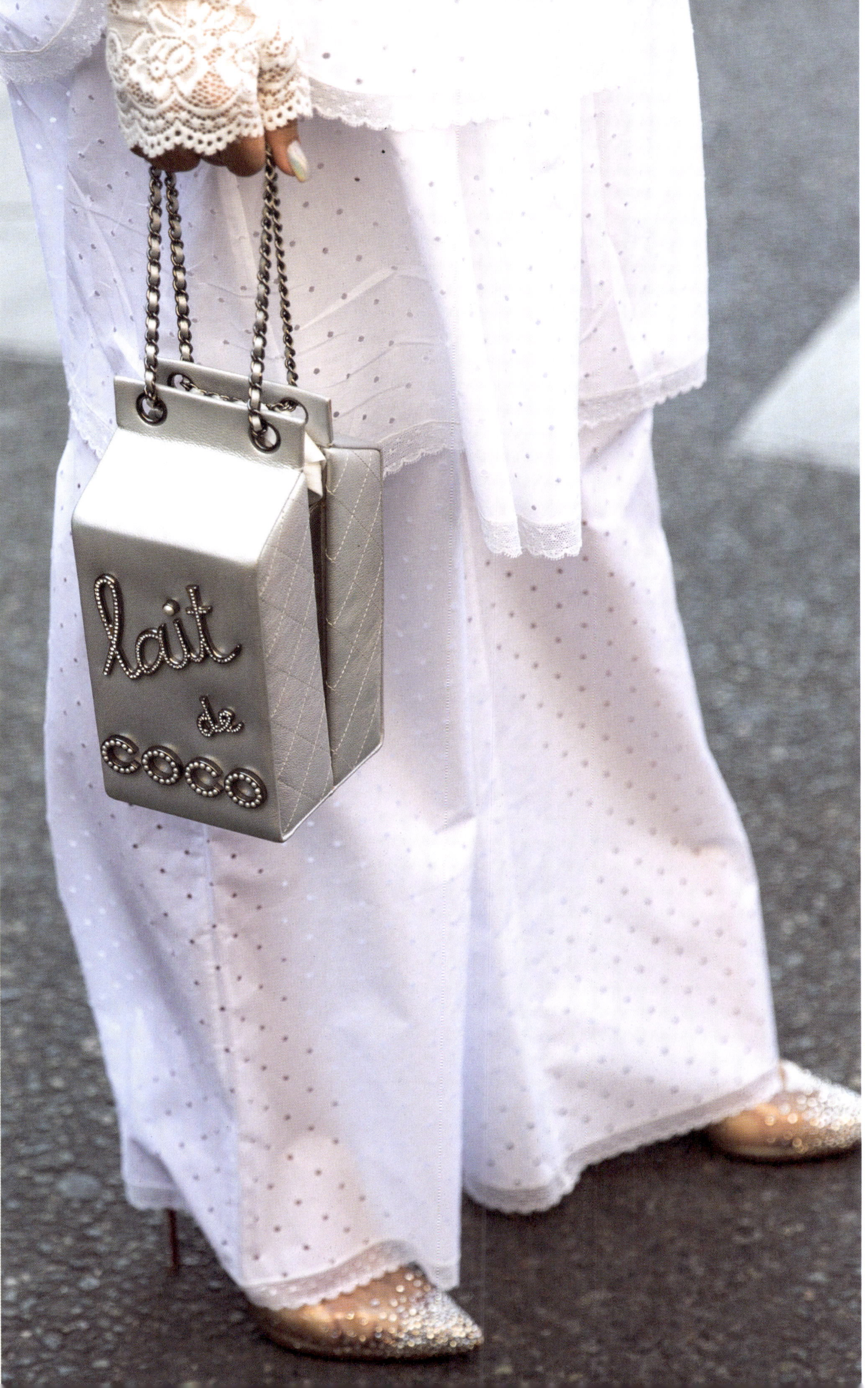
lait
de
coco

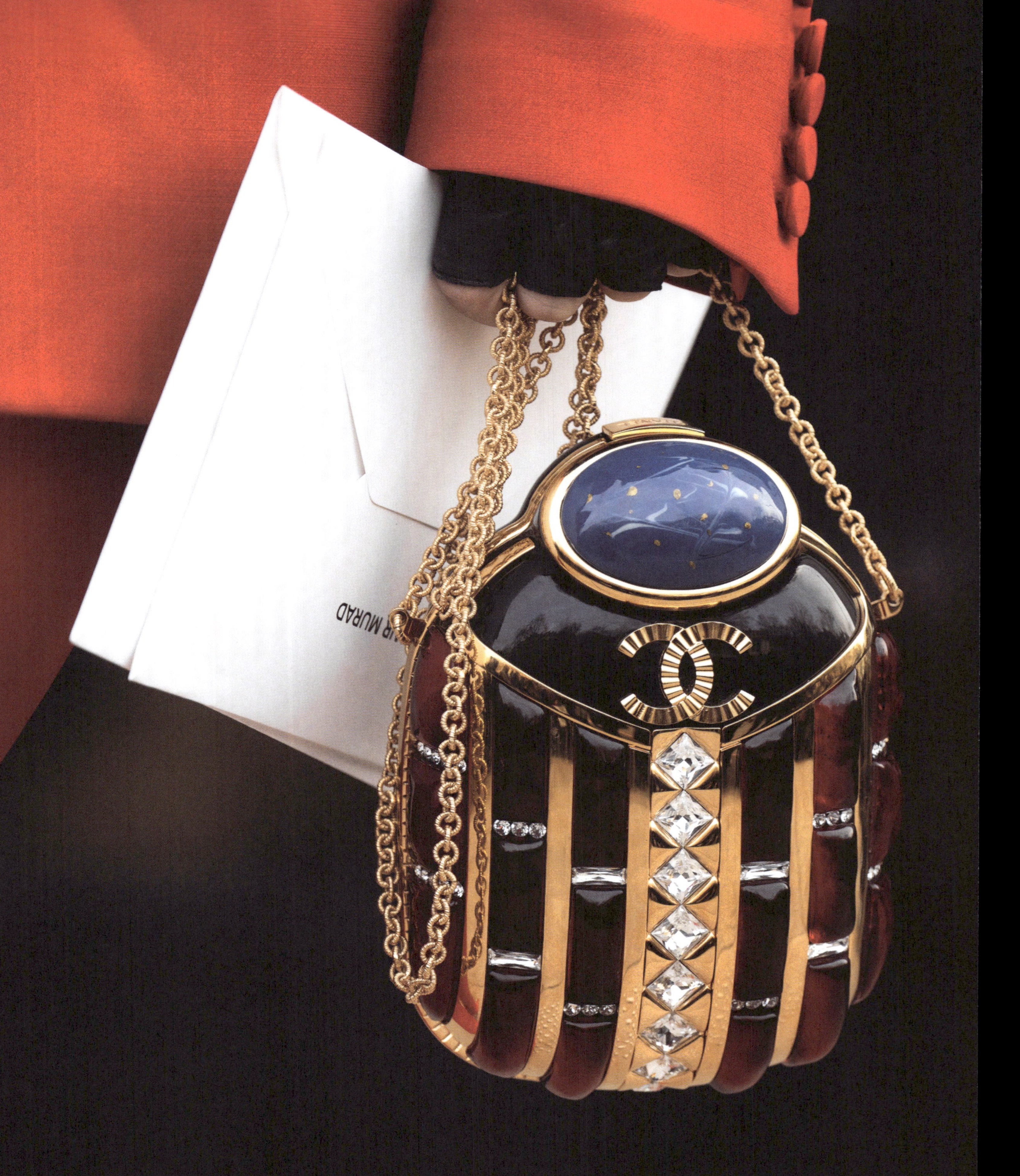

EACH CHANEL COLLECTION FEATURES AN ARRAY OF INCREDIBLE NOVELTY BAGS

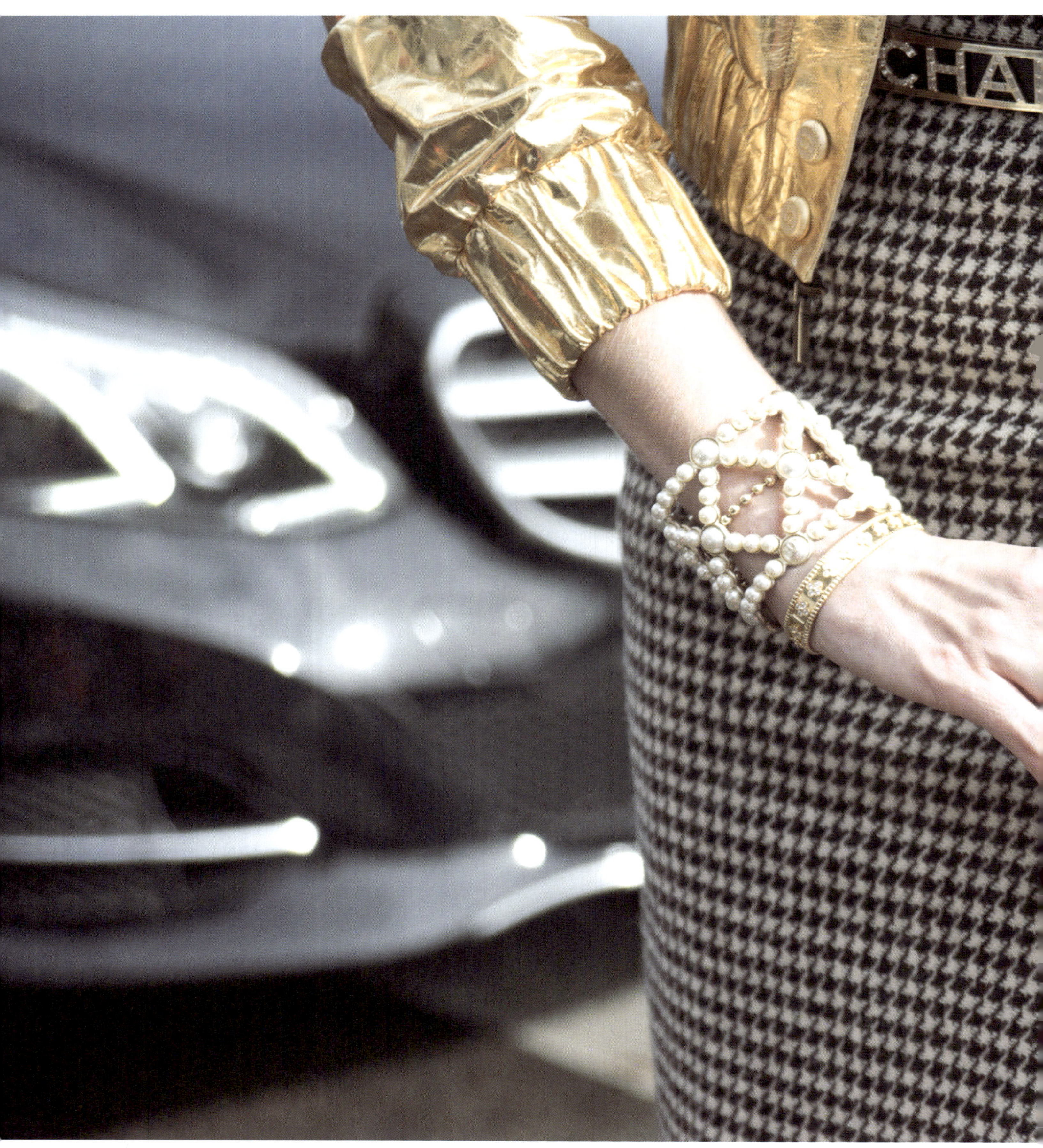
CHA

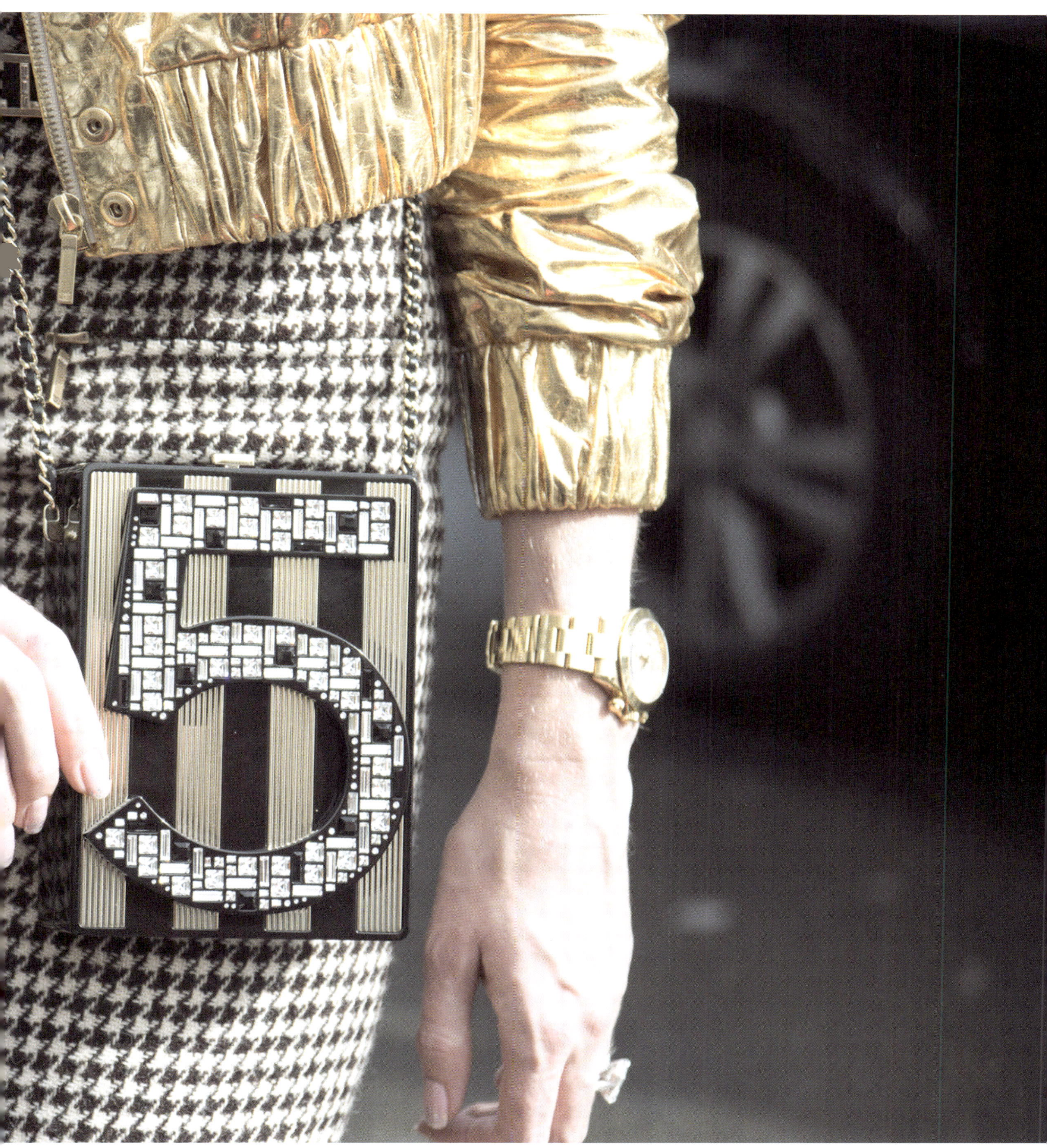

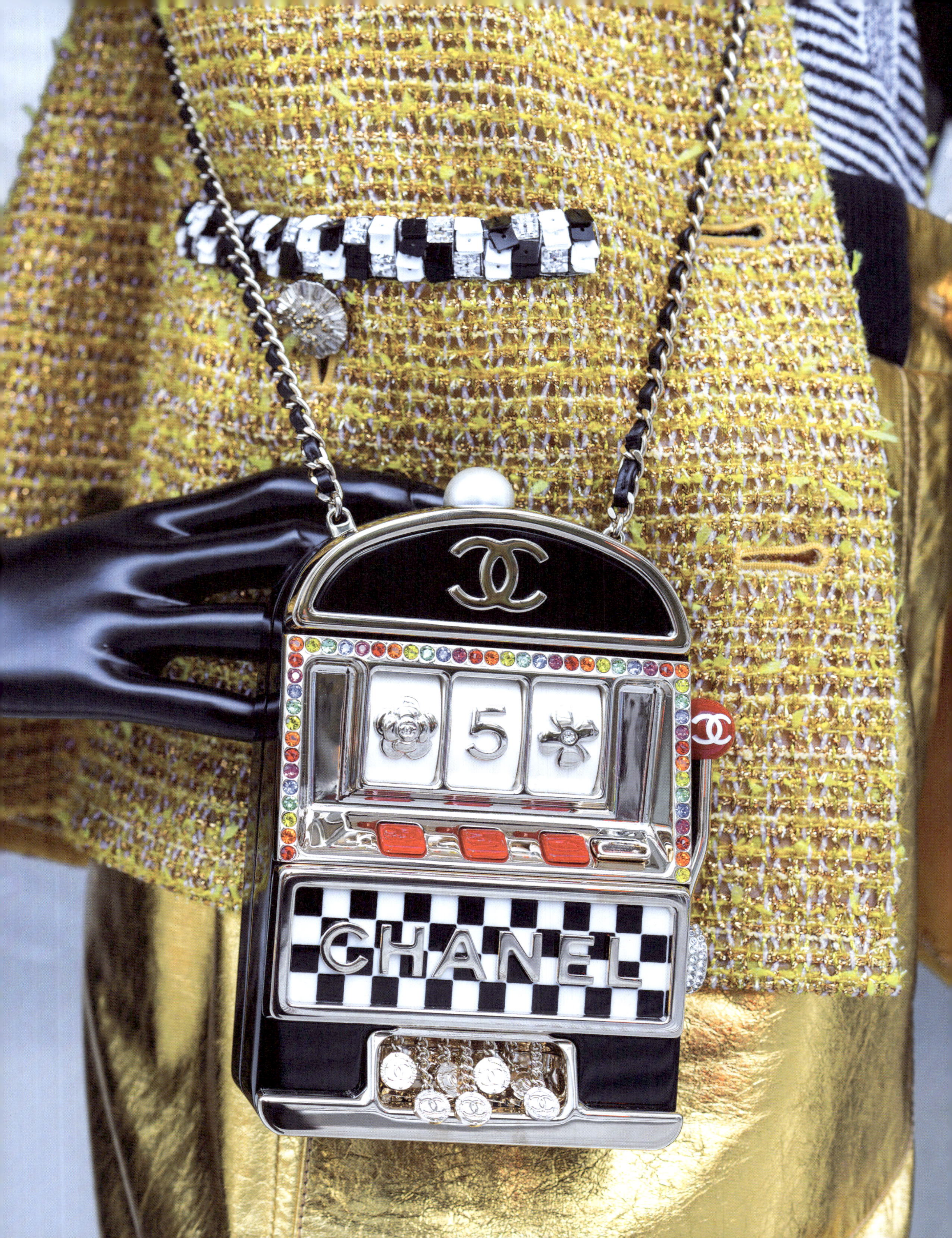
5
CHANEL

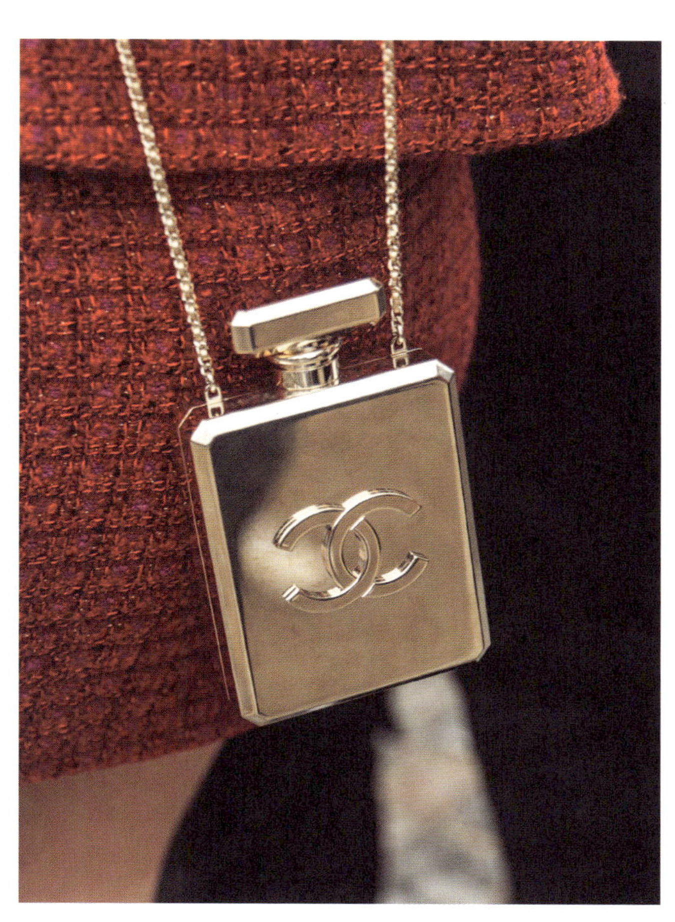

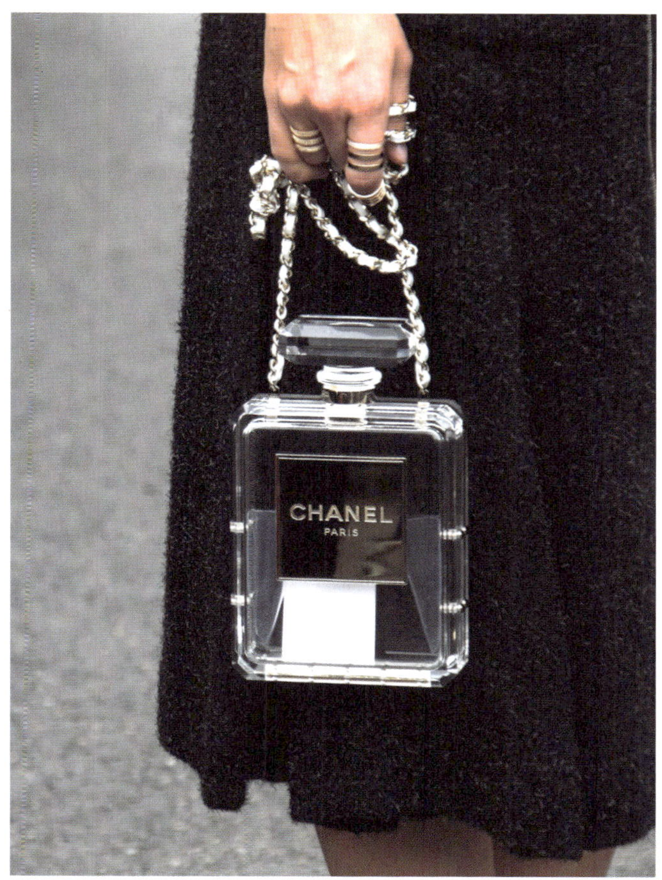
CHANEL
PARIS

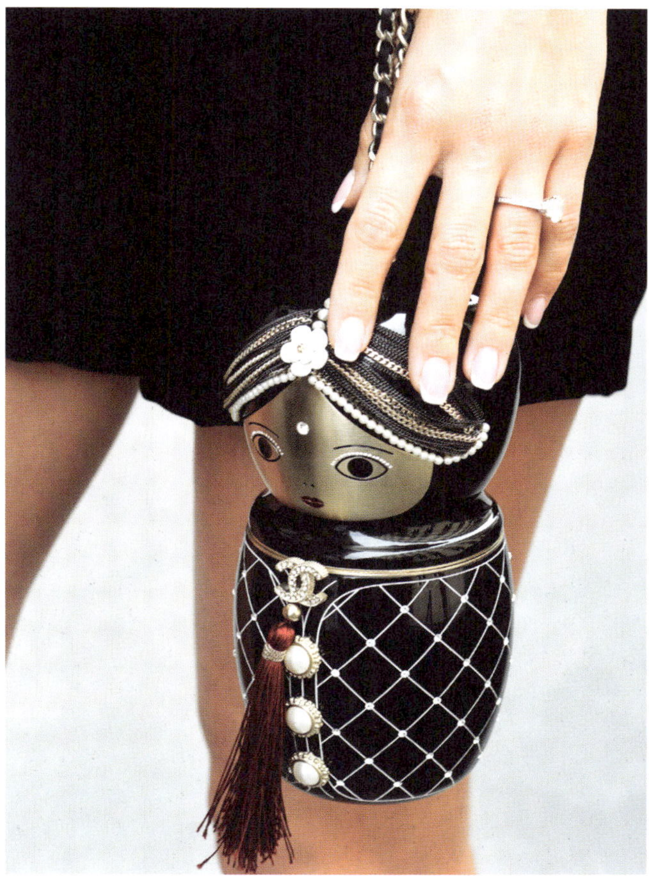

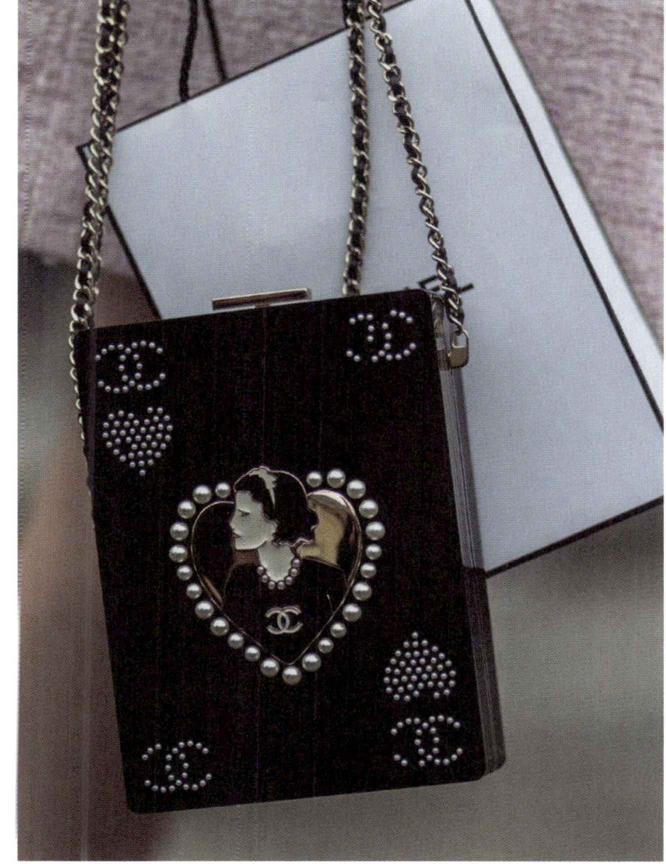

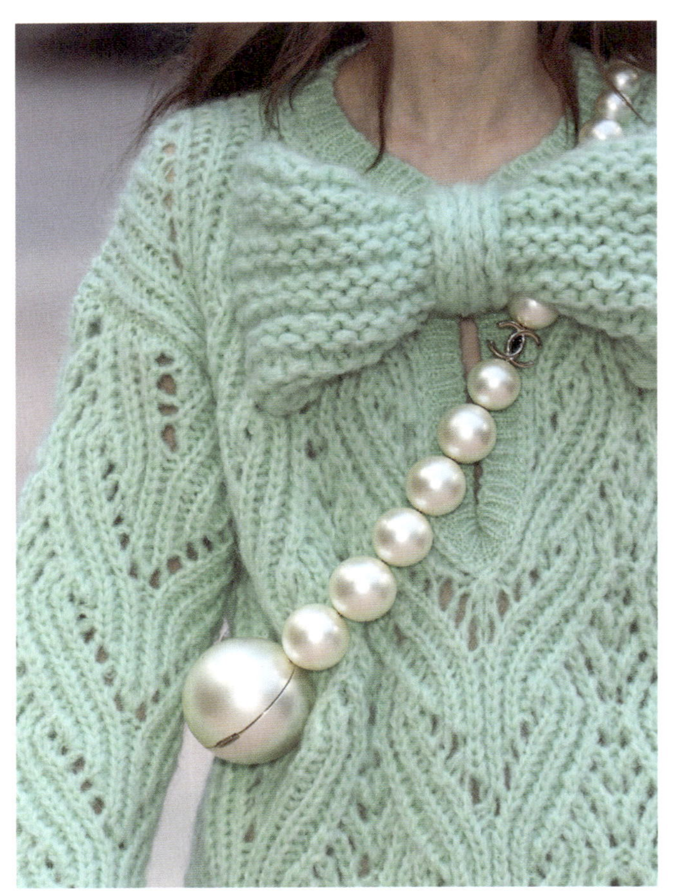

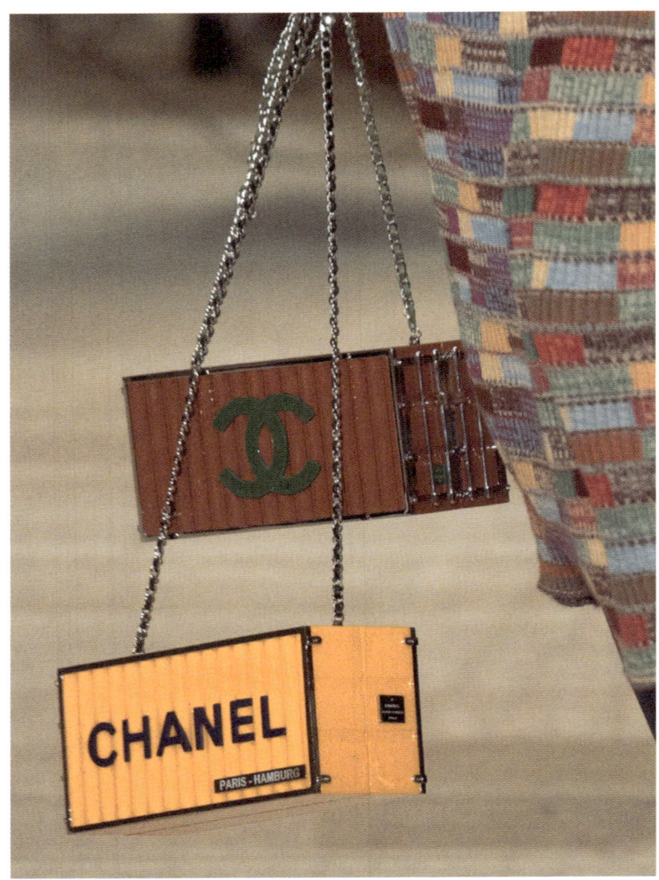
CHANEL
PARIS - HAMBURG

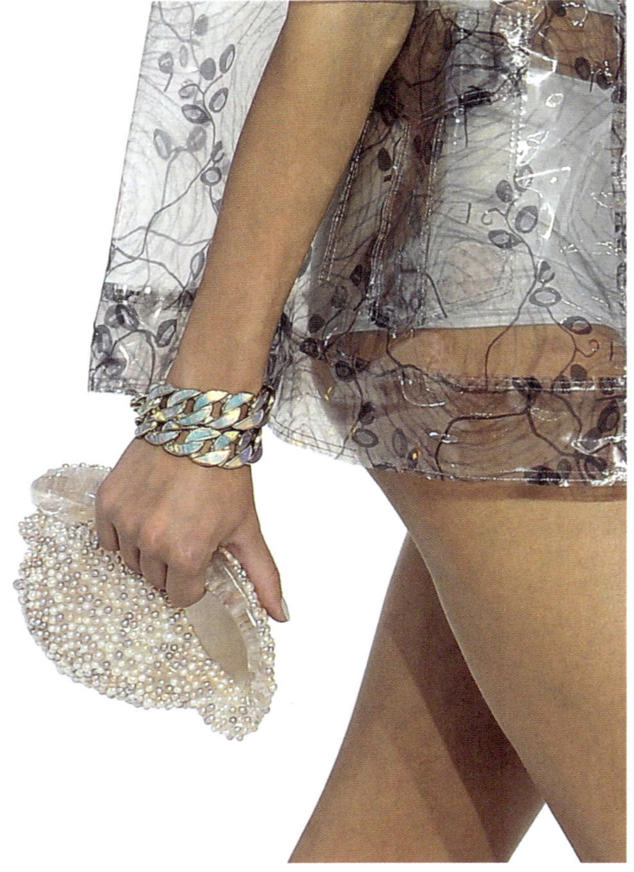

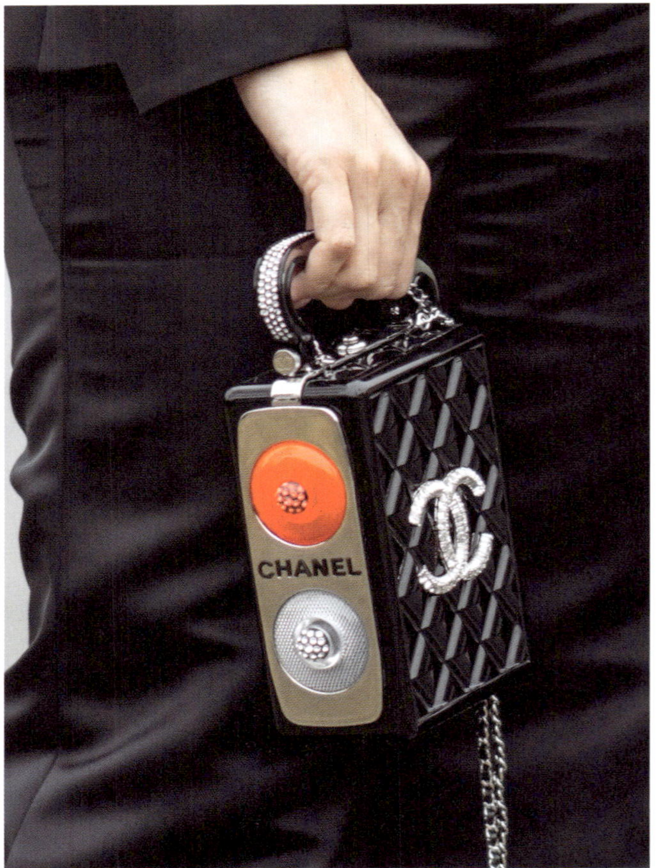
CHANEL

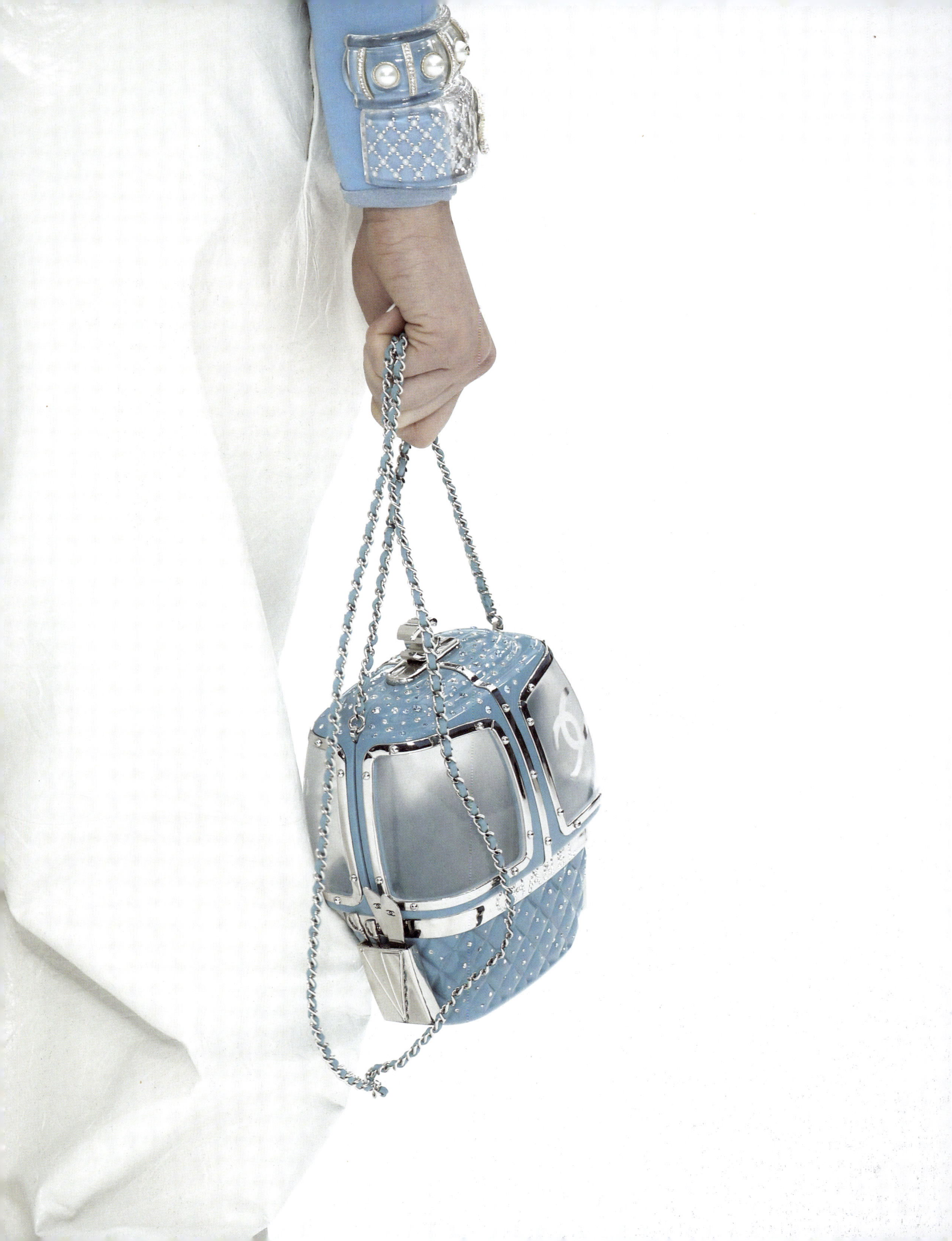

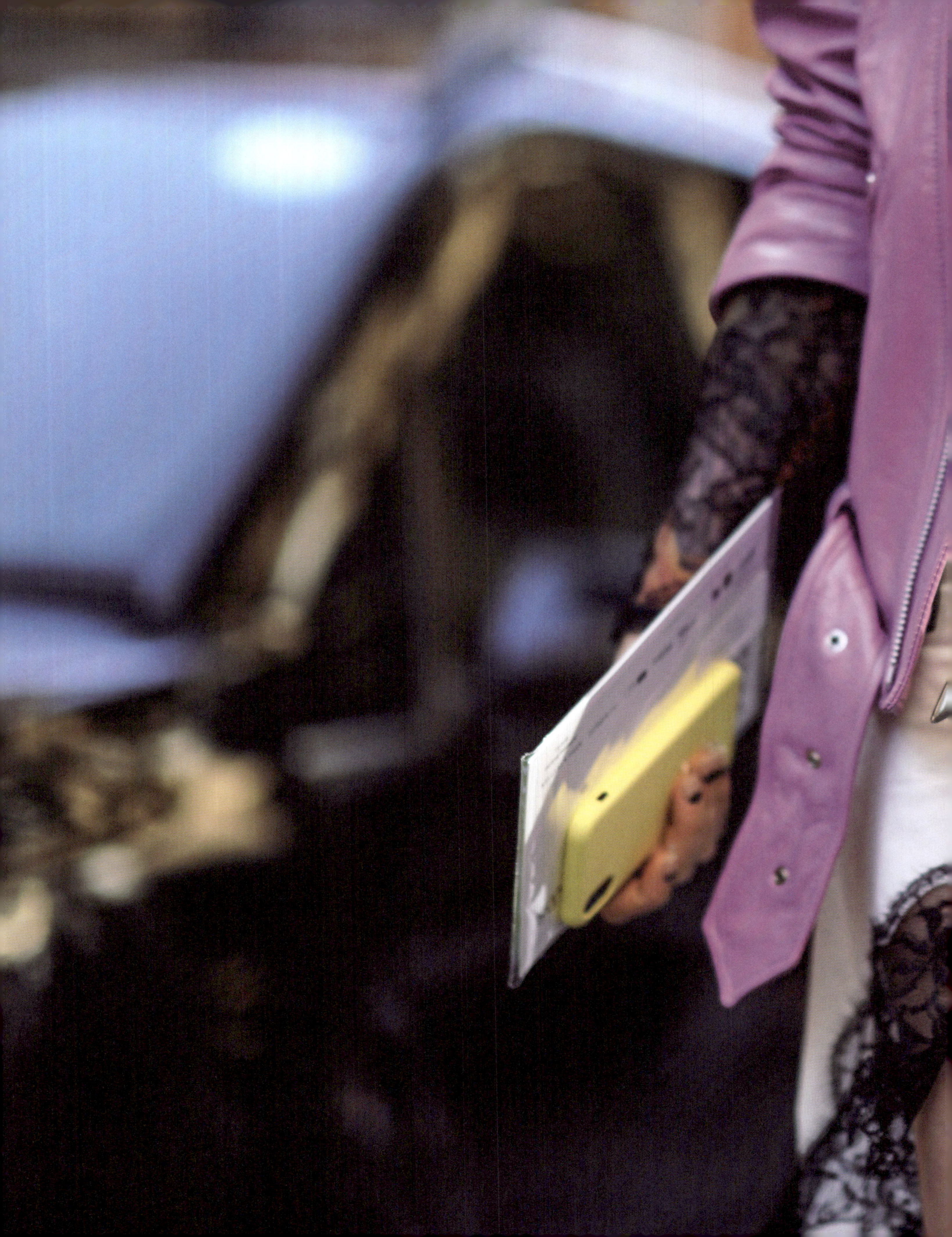

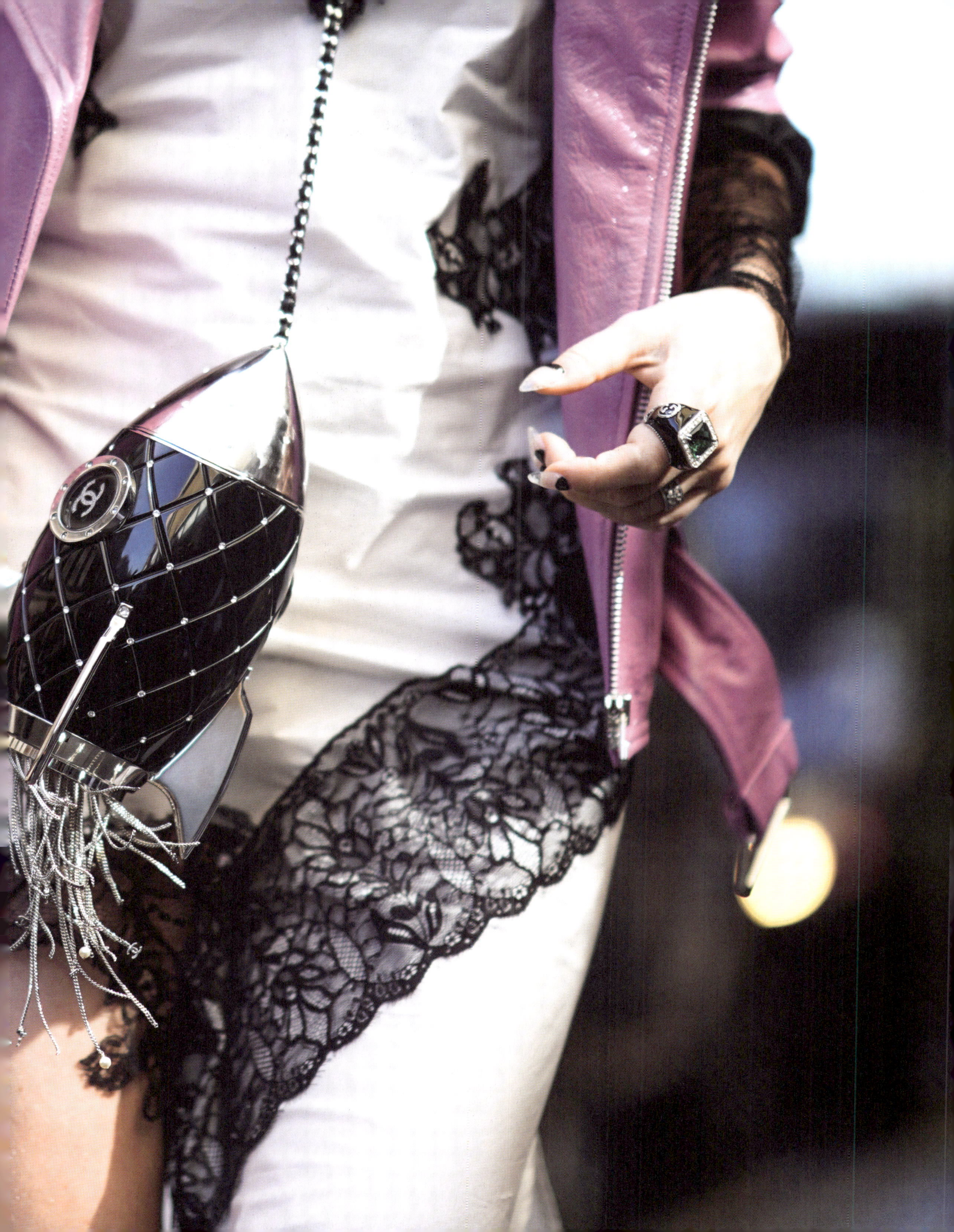

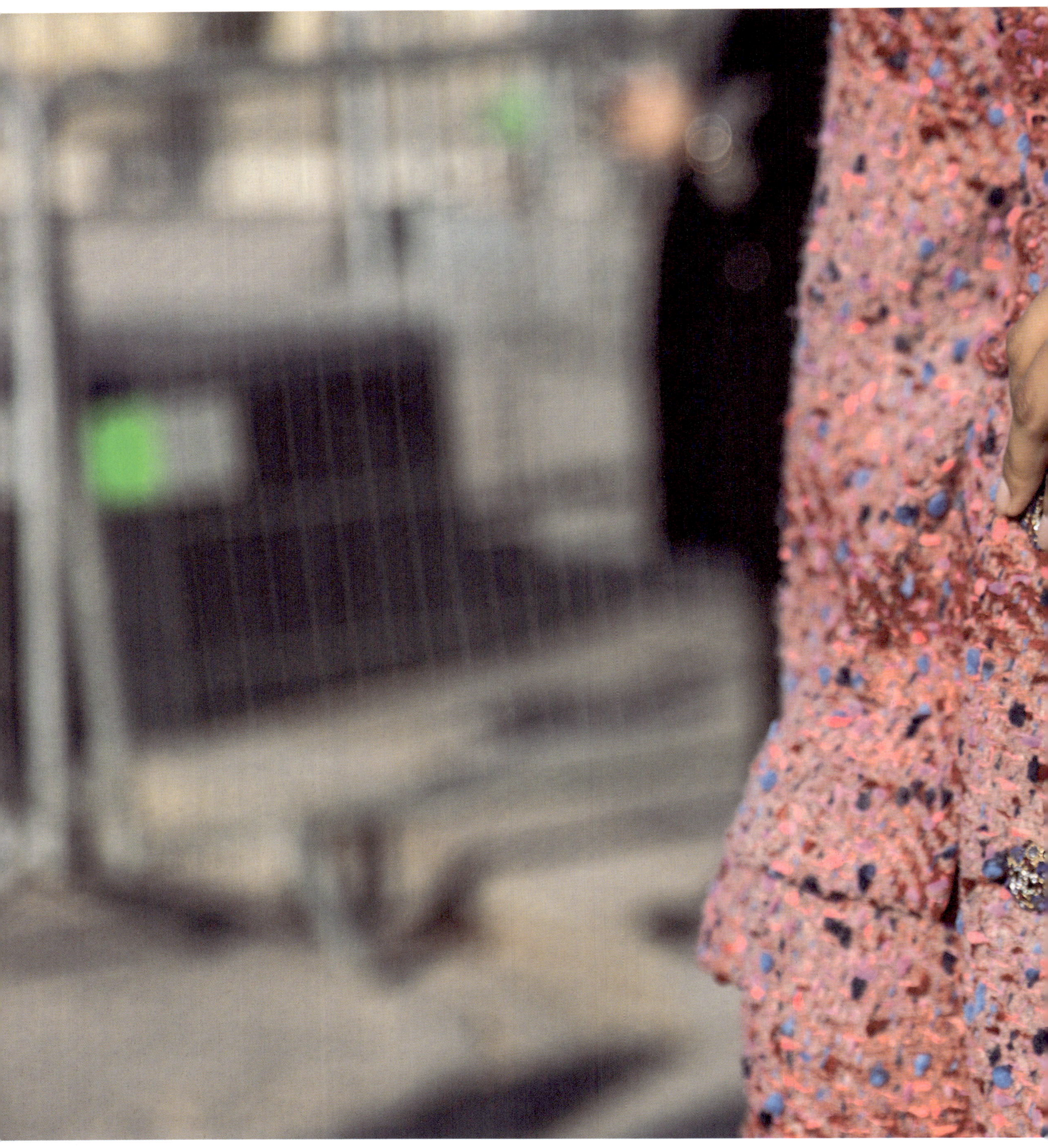

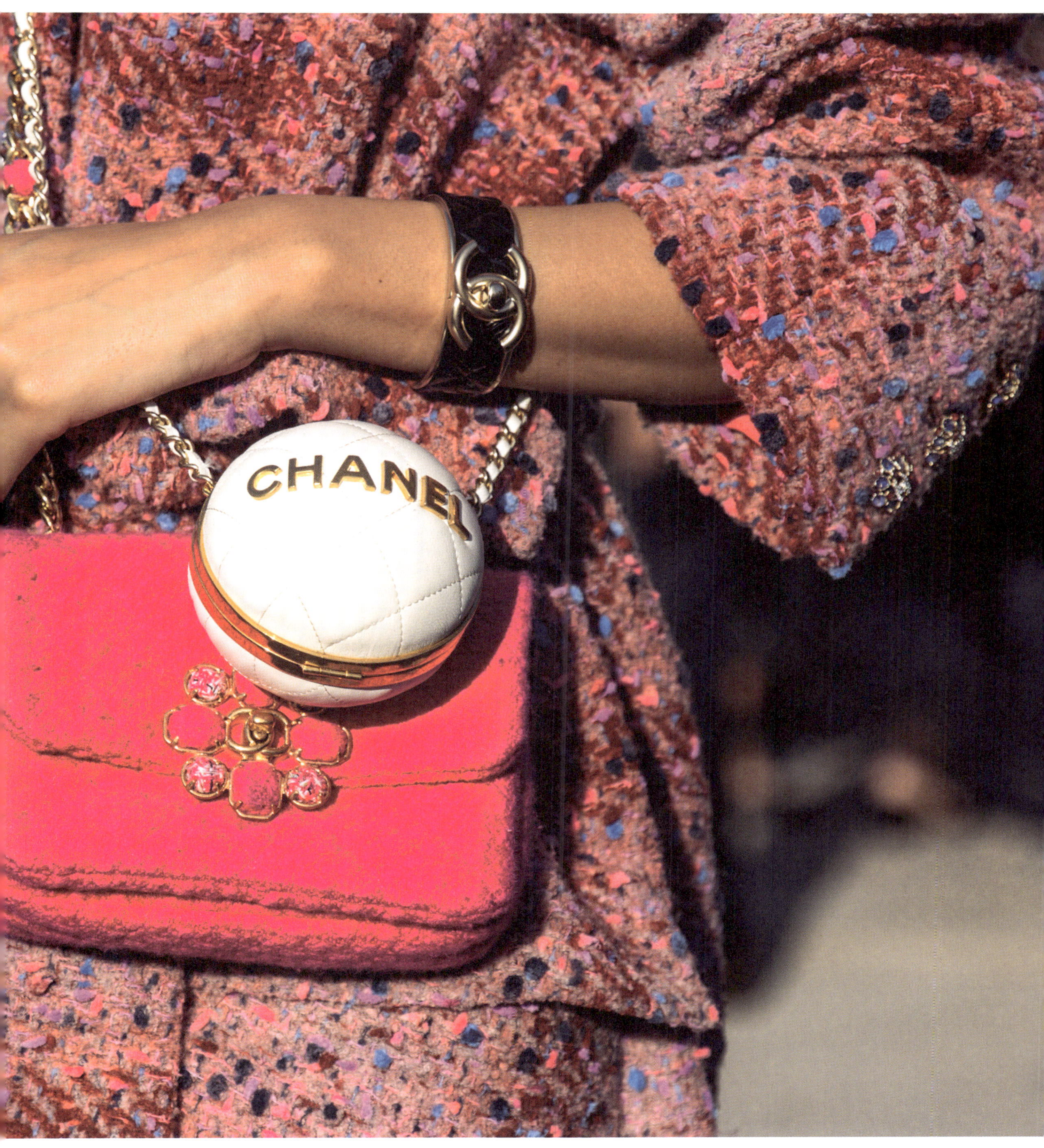
CHANEL

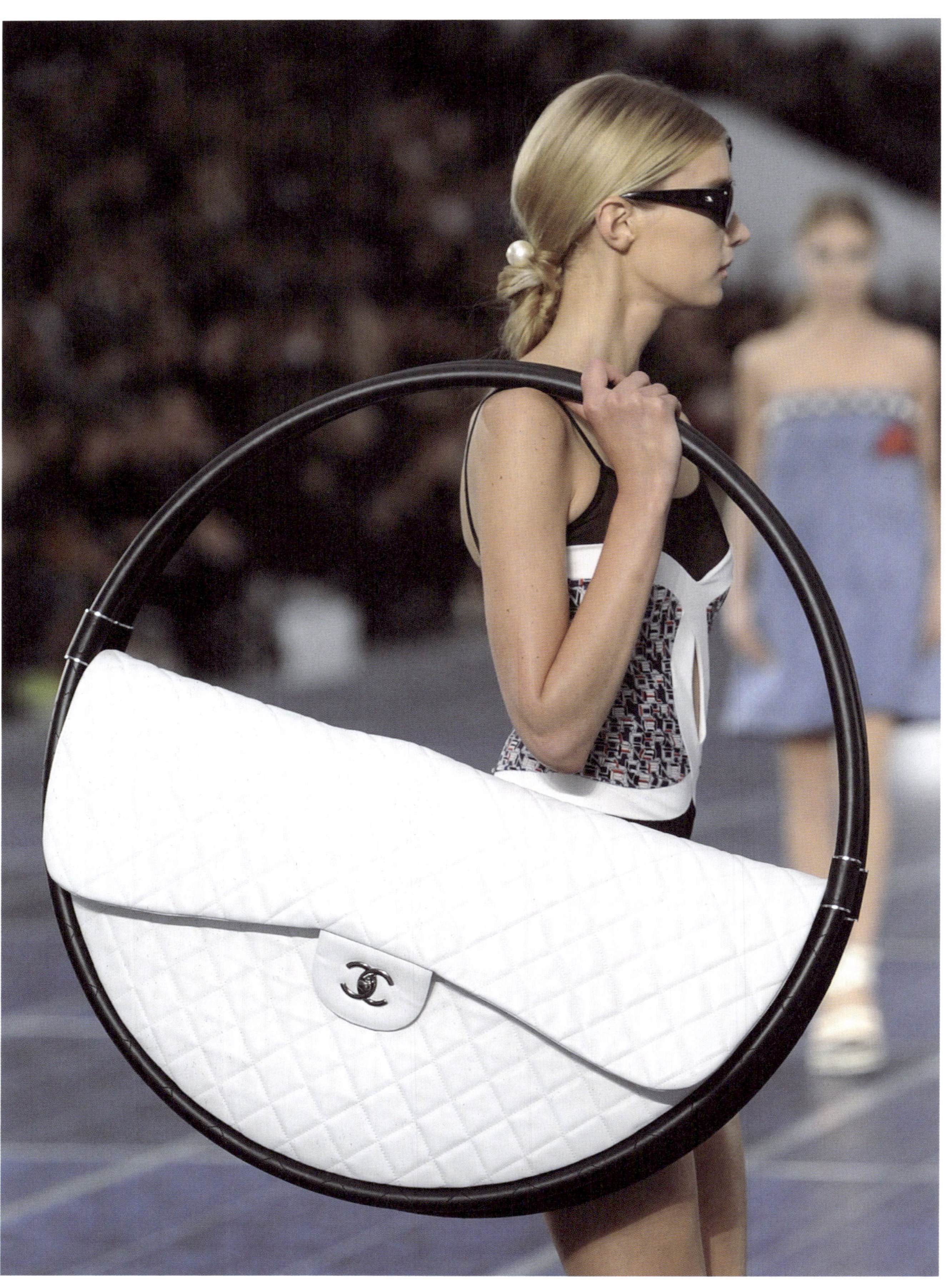

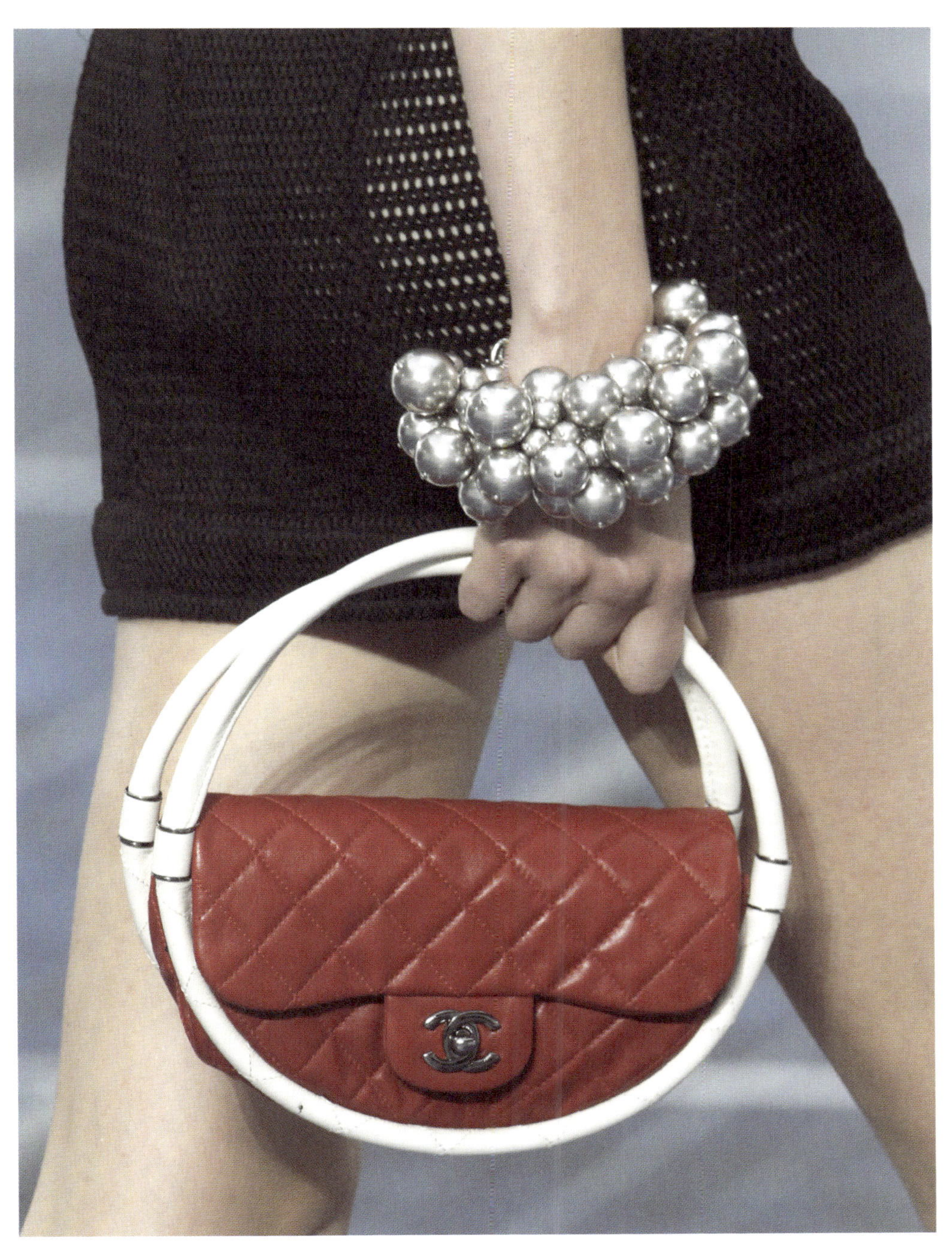

Page 111: (Top) Two Perfume Bottle *minaudières* in gold and plexiglass capture Paris street style; (Bottom left) The Chanel Matryoshka *minaudière* from the Métiers d'Art Paris-Bombay 2012 collection; (Bottom right) A Chanel Playing Card *minaudière* is seen outside the Chanel Haute Couture show in Paris, July 2016

Page 112: (Bottom left) A model showcases a pearl-covered Shell *minaudière* during the Chanel ready-to-wear Spring/Summer 2012 show at Grand Palais, Paris, 2011; (Top left) A Pearl bag is introduced during the Chanel Womenswear Fall/Winter 2025 show in Paris, March 2025; (Top right) A model presents a Paris-Hamburg Shipping Container *minaudière* on the runway at the Chanel Métiers d'Art Paris-Hamburg fashion show at the Elbphilharmonie in Hamburg, 2017; (Bottom right) A Traffic Light *minaudière* from the Cruise 2020 collection

Page 113: Close-up of a Ski Gondola *minaudière* featured in the Fall/Winter 2019 fashion show in Paris

Pages 114/115: The Rocket Ship *minaudière* debuted in the Fall 2017 collection and is worn during London Fashion Week, 2019

Pages 116/117: A woman wears a white quilted lambskin Sphere *minaudière* at Paris Fashion Week, October 2022

Pages 118/119: Models showcase an oversized and a small Hula Hoop bag during the Spring/Summer 2013 show at the Grand Palais in Paris

Pages 120/121: The Spring/Summer 2018 ready-to-wear collection creates a stir with hobo and shopping bags crafted from PVC, Paris

Pages 122/123: The double-bag trend is celebrated on the runway during Chanel's Womenswear Spring/Summer 2019 fashion show in Paris, October 2018

Pages 124/125: Close-up of a Resin Crystal Rescue Wheel *minaudière*, Paris

Page 126: A visitor at Paris Fashion Week showcases a black leather and gold metal Camellia round clutch with a chain strap slung over her shoulder

Page 127: Close-up of a black and white En Vogue round bag, Paris, 2019

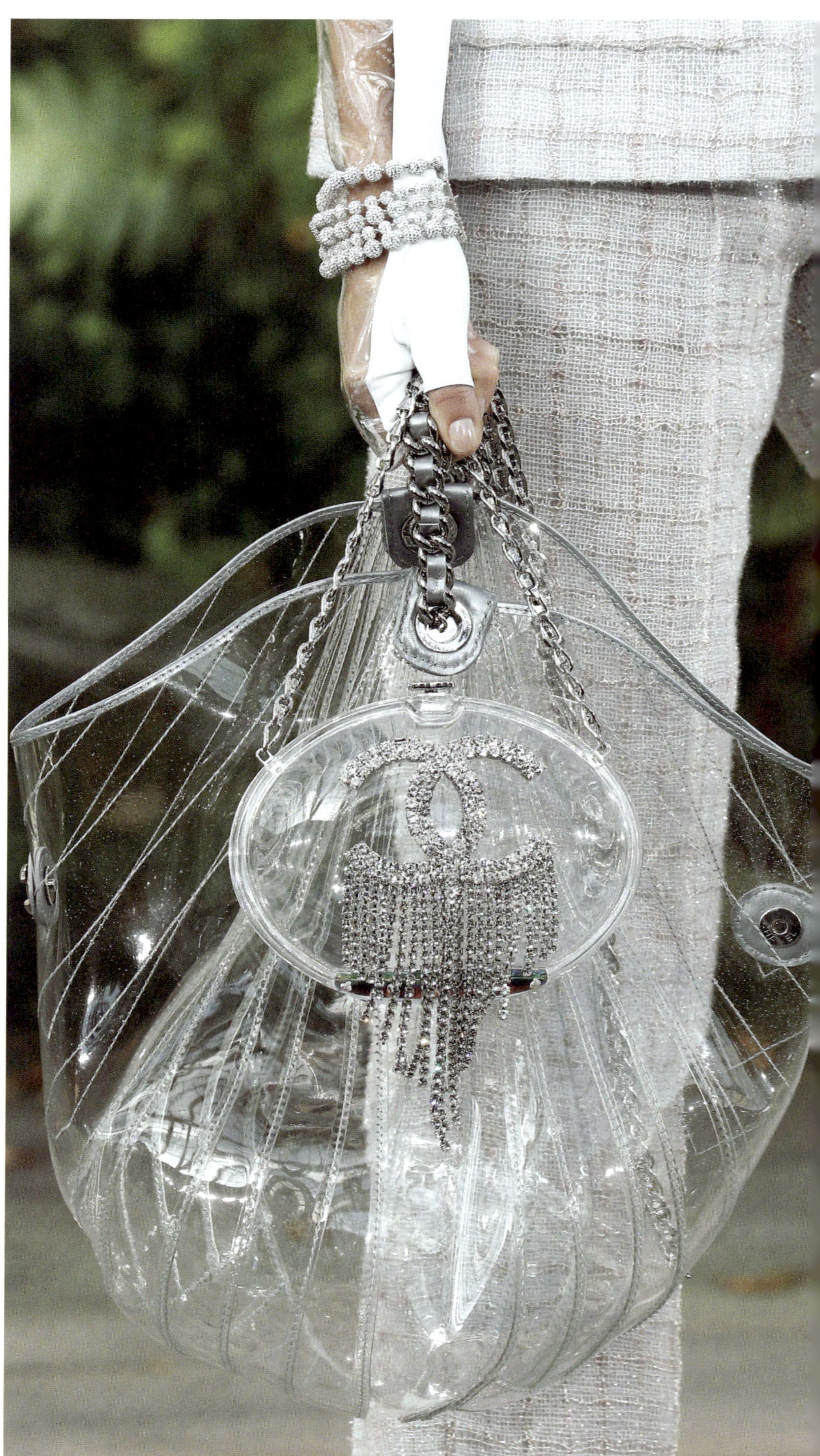

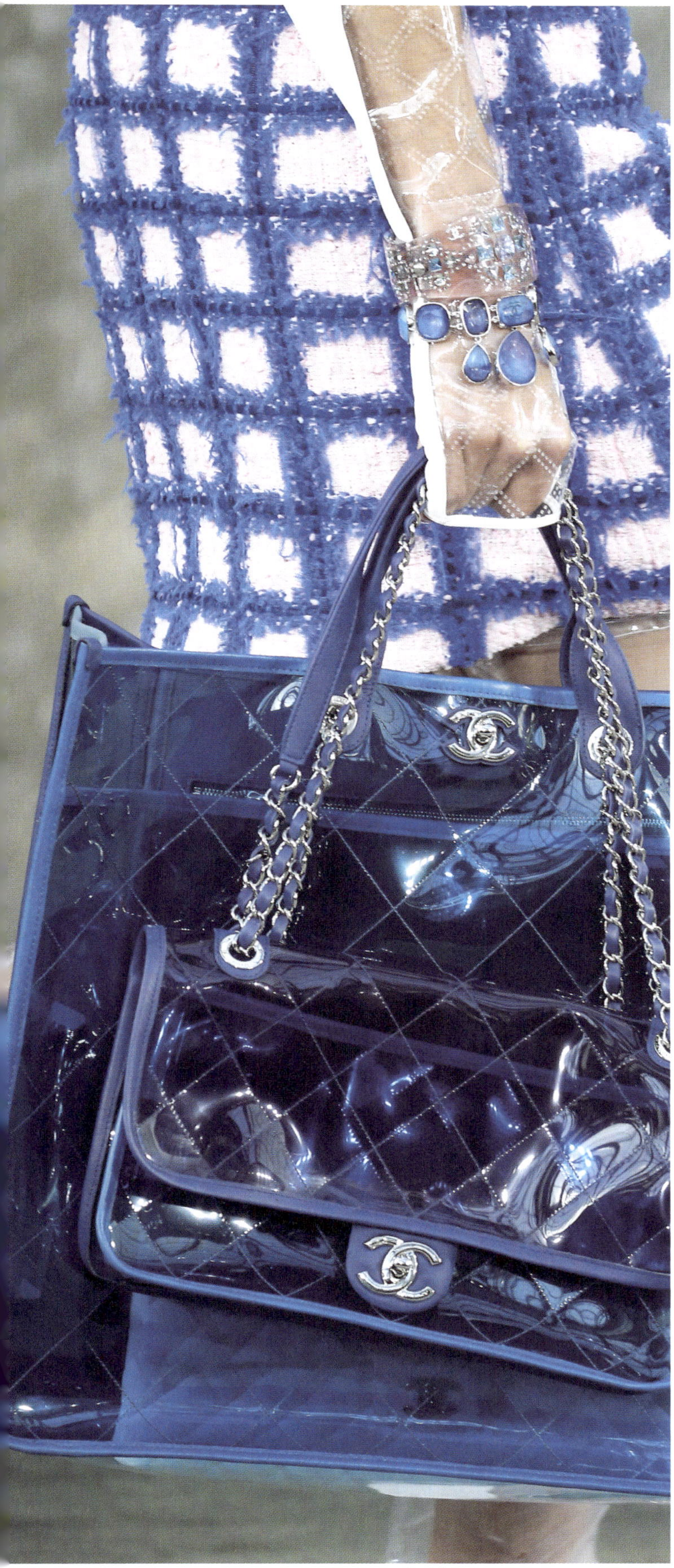

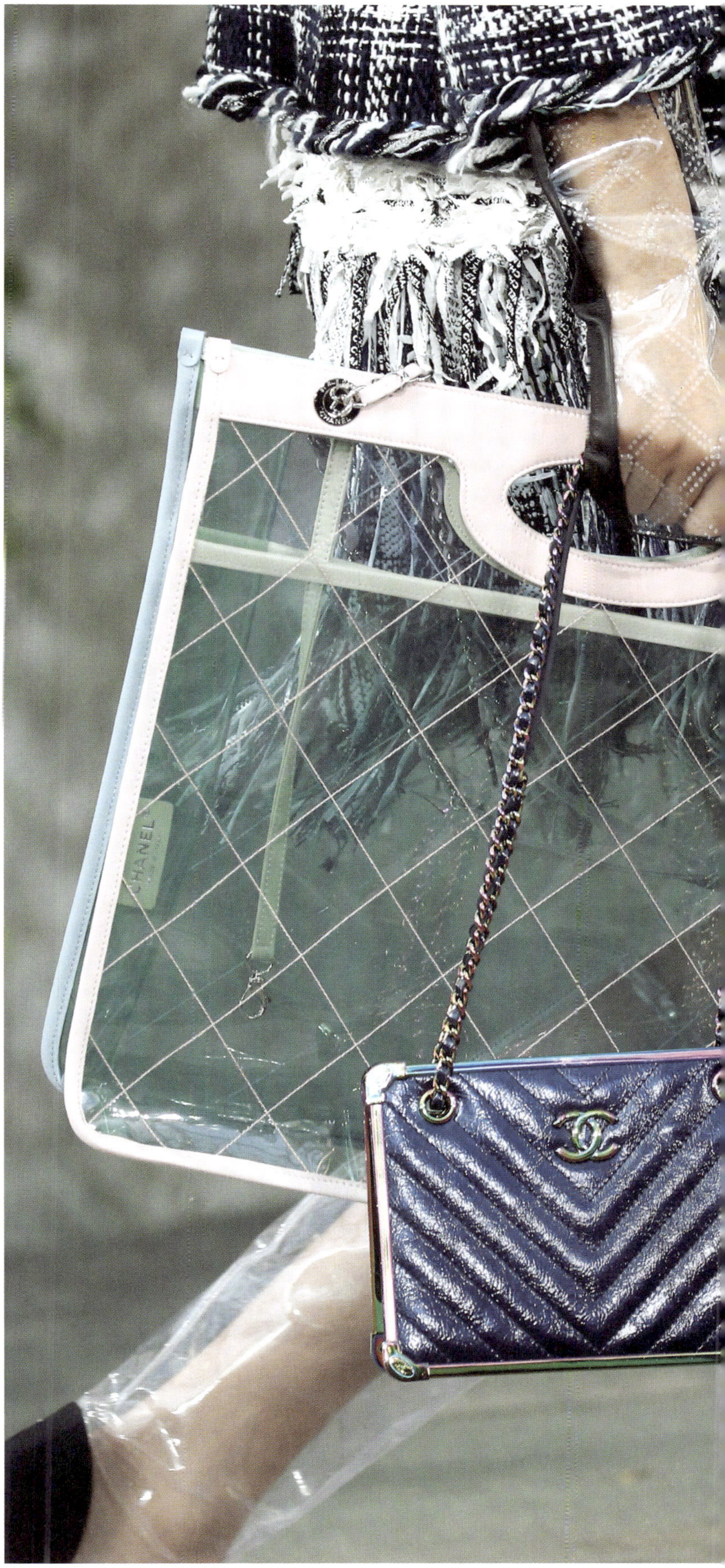

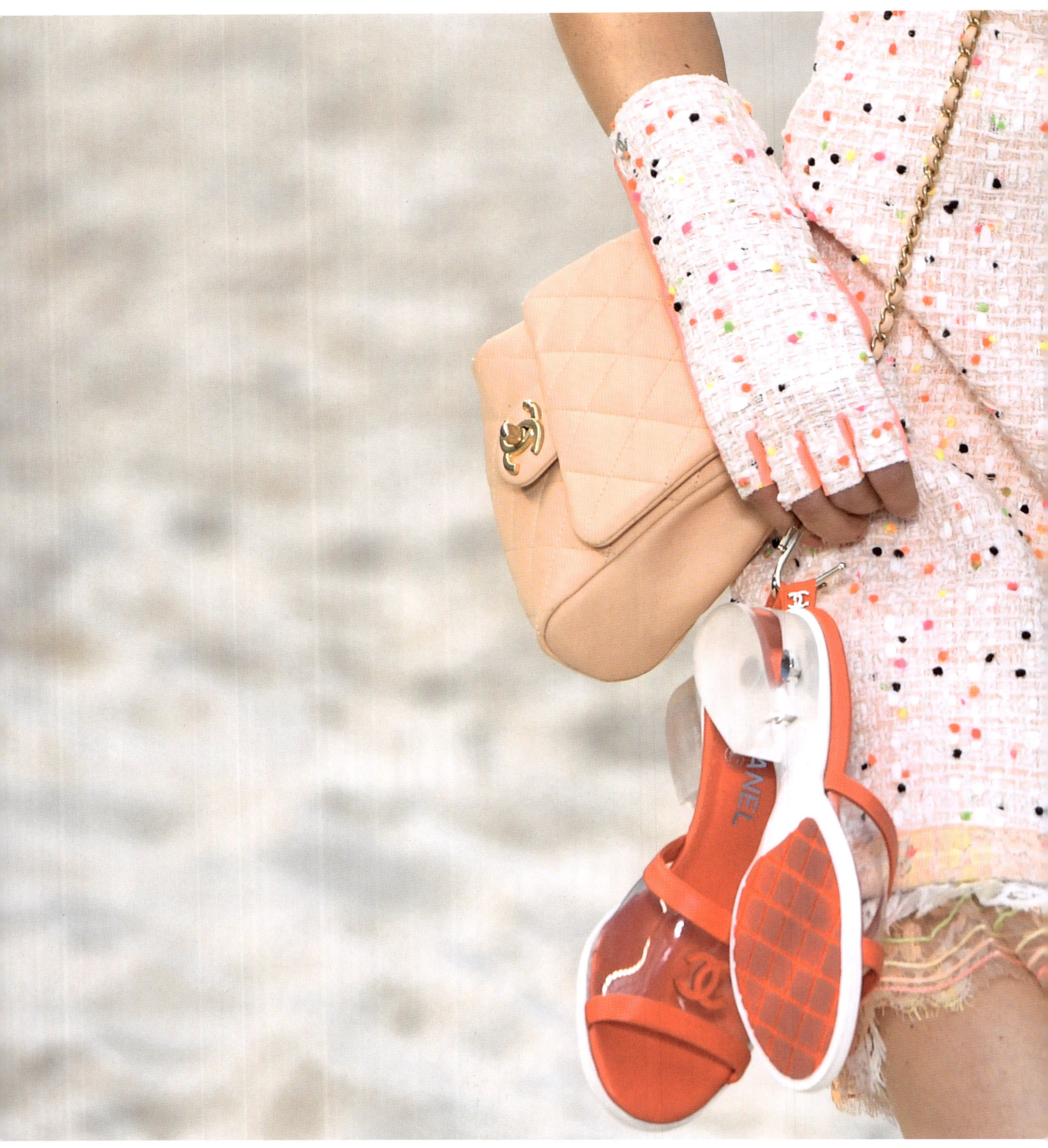

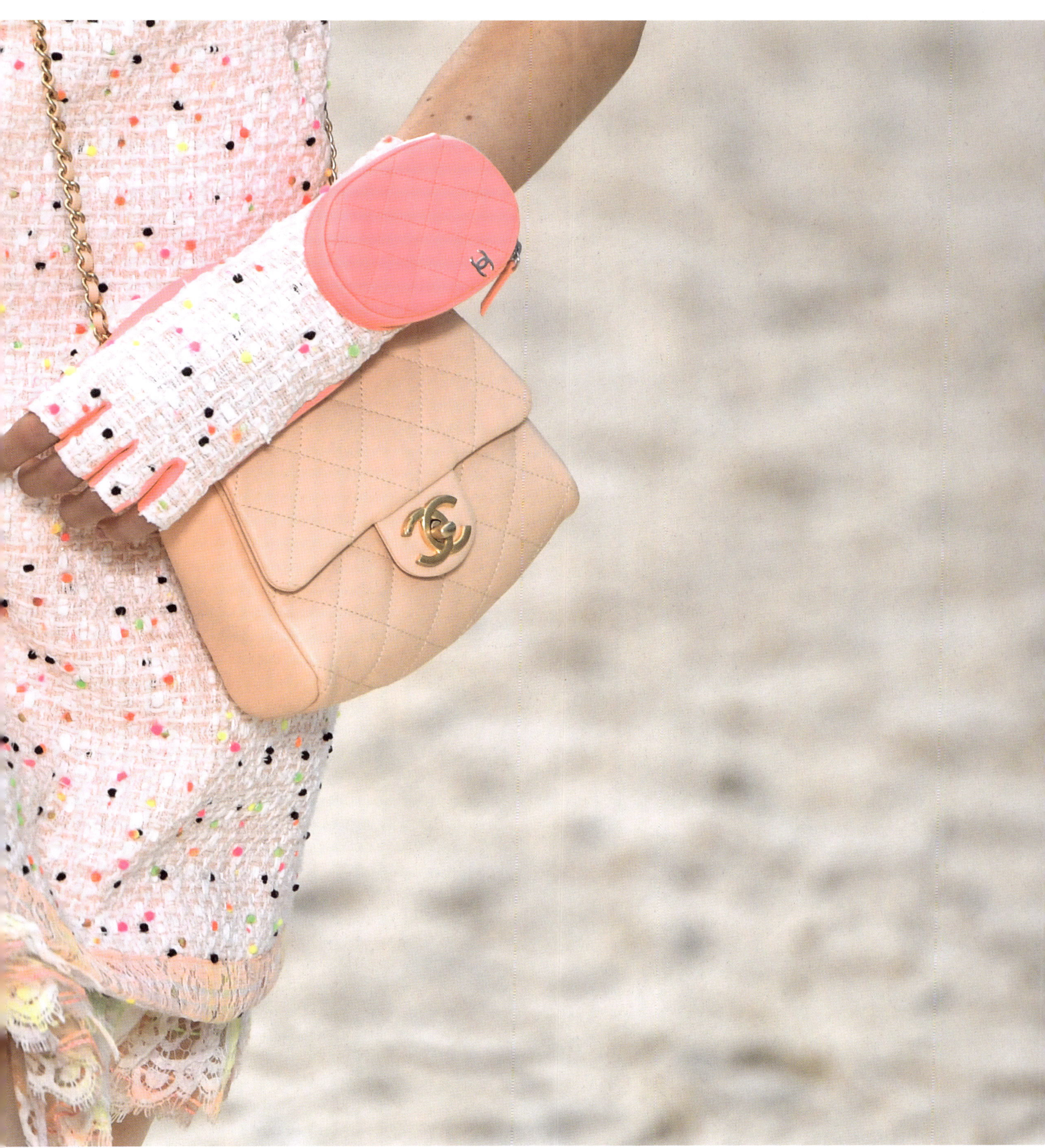

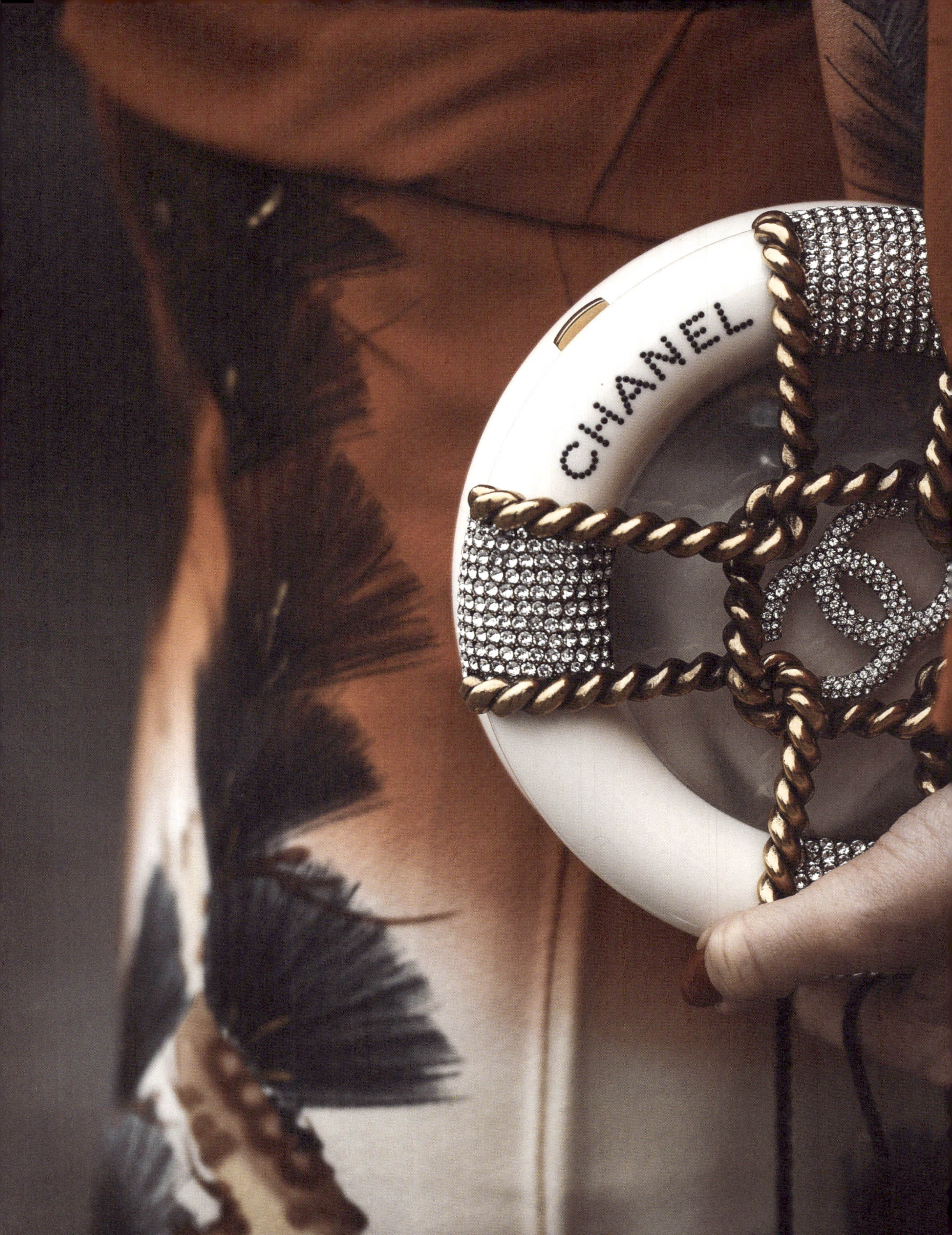
CHANEL

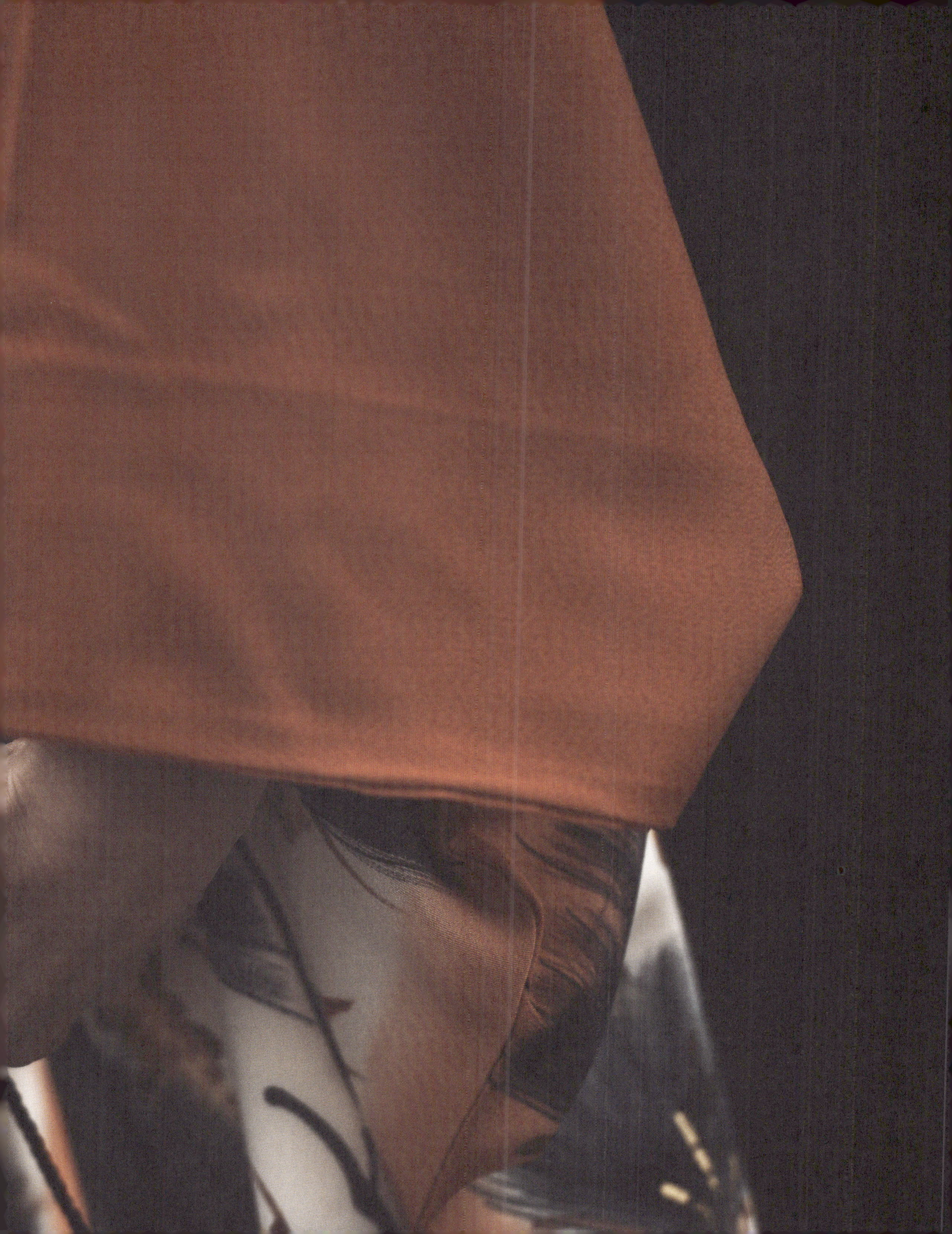

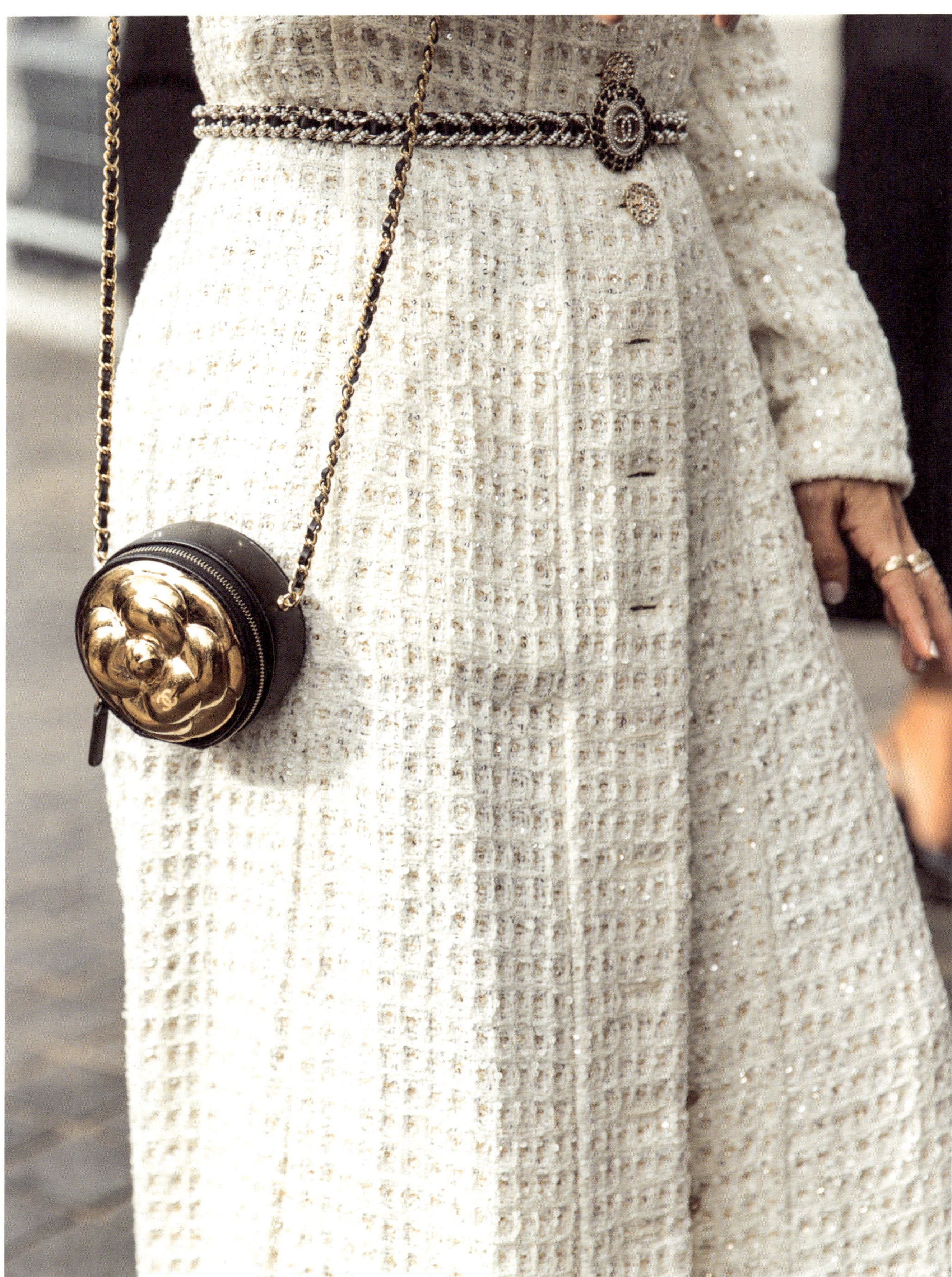

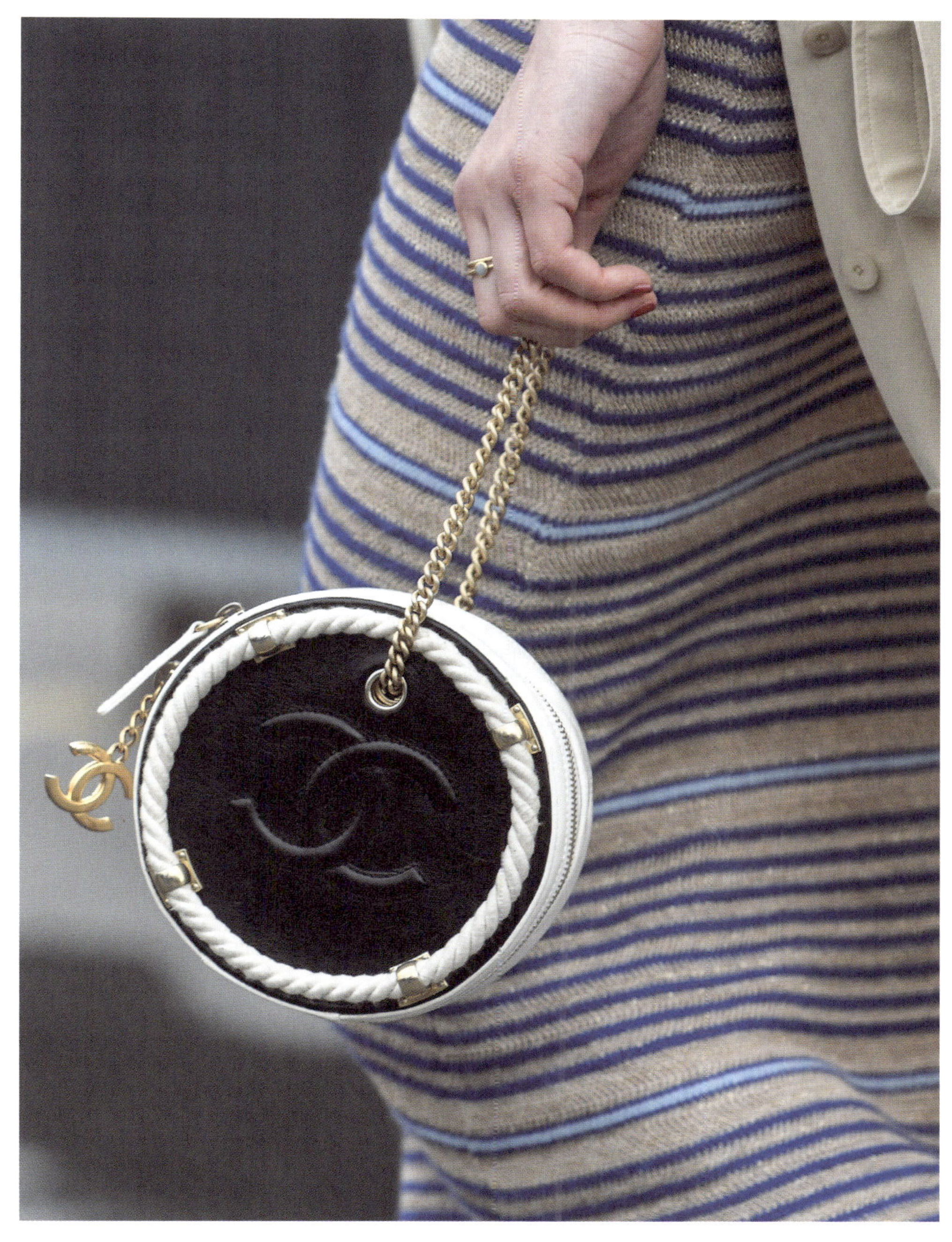

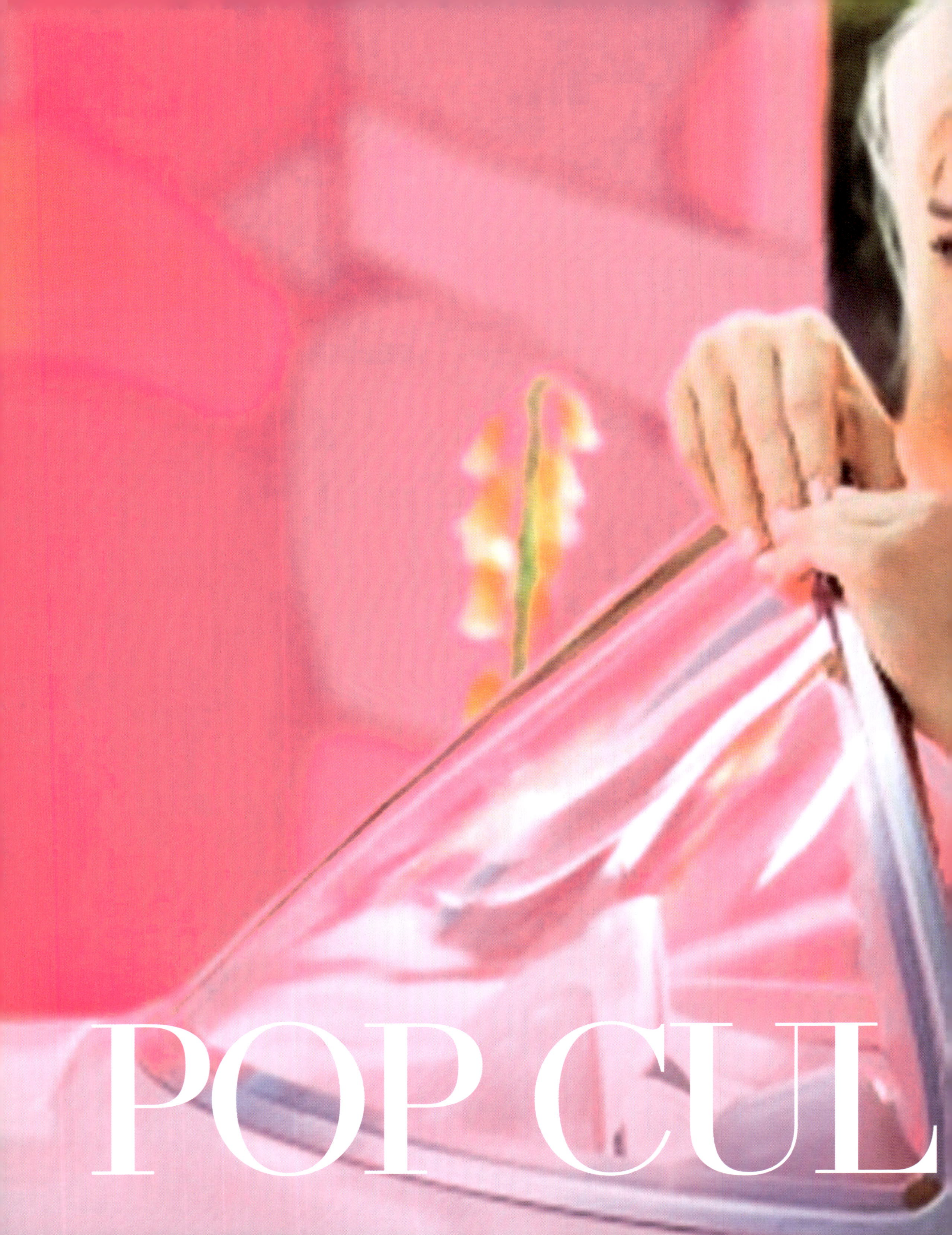

POP CUL

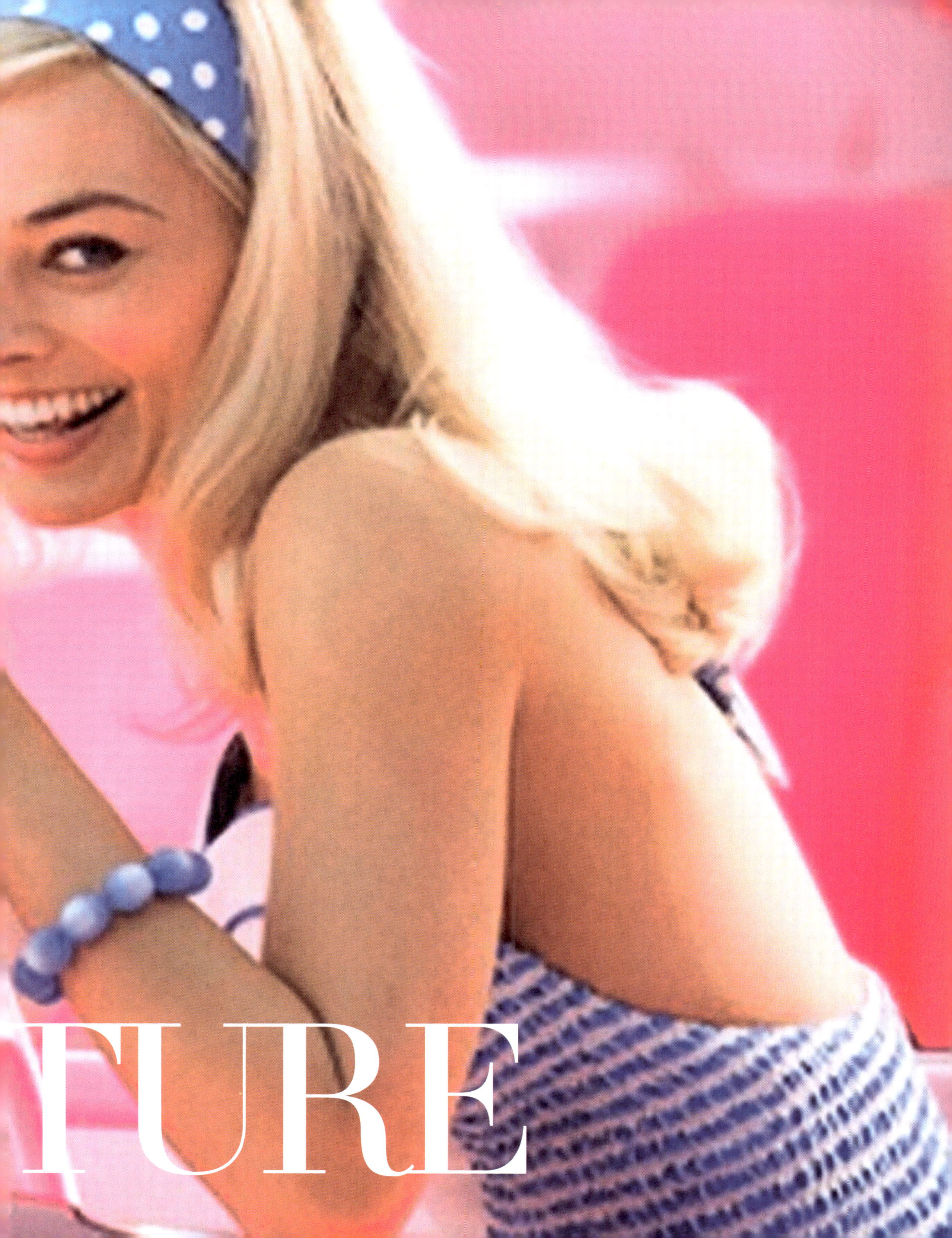
TURE

BEYOND THE CATWALK

"Baby girl was draped in Chanel," rapped LL Cool J in 1997, propelling the French *couturier* to another level of appreciation and aspiration in popular culture, during the era of MTV, supermodels and hip hop.

However, just like the interlocking double CC logo, Chanel has *always* been intertwined with music, film and the art world. Gabrielle Chanel mused that "Fashion is not something that exists in dresses only. Fashion is in the sky, in the street, fashion has to do with ideas, the way we live, what is happening." Beyond her atelier, Chanel understood the importance of aligning her creations with other art forms. Her own fame helped to cement Chanel's reputation as a house with creativity at its heart, a legacy that lives on today.

Chanel's collaborations began with dance. After watching Igor Stravinsky's controversial ballet *The Rites of Spring* in 1913, she began funding the Ballets Russes dance company and went on to create costumes for several productions, including a wool one-piece bathing suit in cyclamen pink for *Le Train Bleu* (1924), which ballet historian Cyril Beaumont described as "uninteresting." Chanel also worked with Stravinsky and Ballets Russes on *Apollon Musagète* (1929) and *Bacchanale* (1939), where she worked alongside surrealist artist Salvador Dalí.

The *maison's* connection to dance continued into the 21st century, when Virginie Viard worked on costumes for the principal dancers at Paris Opera in 2019. Tulle skirts were embellished with exquisite cornflower, wisteria and rose motifs and met with critical acclaim in a performance of Serge Lifer's *Variations*.

The serendipity of Chanel's social connections helped the designer create cross-platform fame. Chanel met film producer Samuel Goldwyn in Monte Carlo, where she received a million-dollar invitation to create costumes for Goldwyn's studio in Hollywood twice a year. With inflation, Chanel's rate would be worth around $20 million today.

Chanel designed costumes for Gloria Swanson in *Tonight or Never* (1931) and Ina Claire in *The Greeks Had A Word For Them* (1931), but found the greatest synergy between her work and French films. Chanel described Hollywood as "the capital of bad taste," and The New Yorker magazine alleged that the film industry didn't find her dresses "sensational" enough, prompting her to return to Europe. This did not deter Chanel's private clients, including Greta Garbo and Marlene Dietrich. Brigitte Bardot, Catherine Deneuve, Elizabeth Taylor, Jackie Kennedy Onassis and Jane Fonda all became fans of the *maison,* while Audrey Hepburn's character, Holly Golightly, carried a Chanel bag in *Breakfast at Tiffany's* (1961). Being aligned with icons of cinema ensured Chanel's appearance on multiple magazine covers too, continuing to cement the house's celebrity.

With Karl Lagerfeld at the helm, film collaborations continued. Victoria Abril's character in *High Heels* (1992),

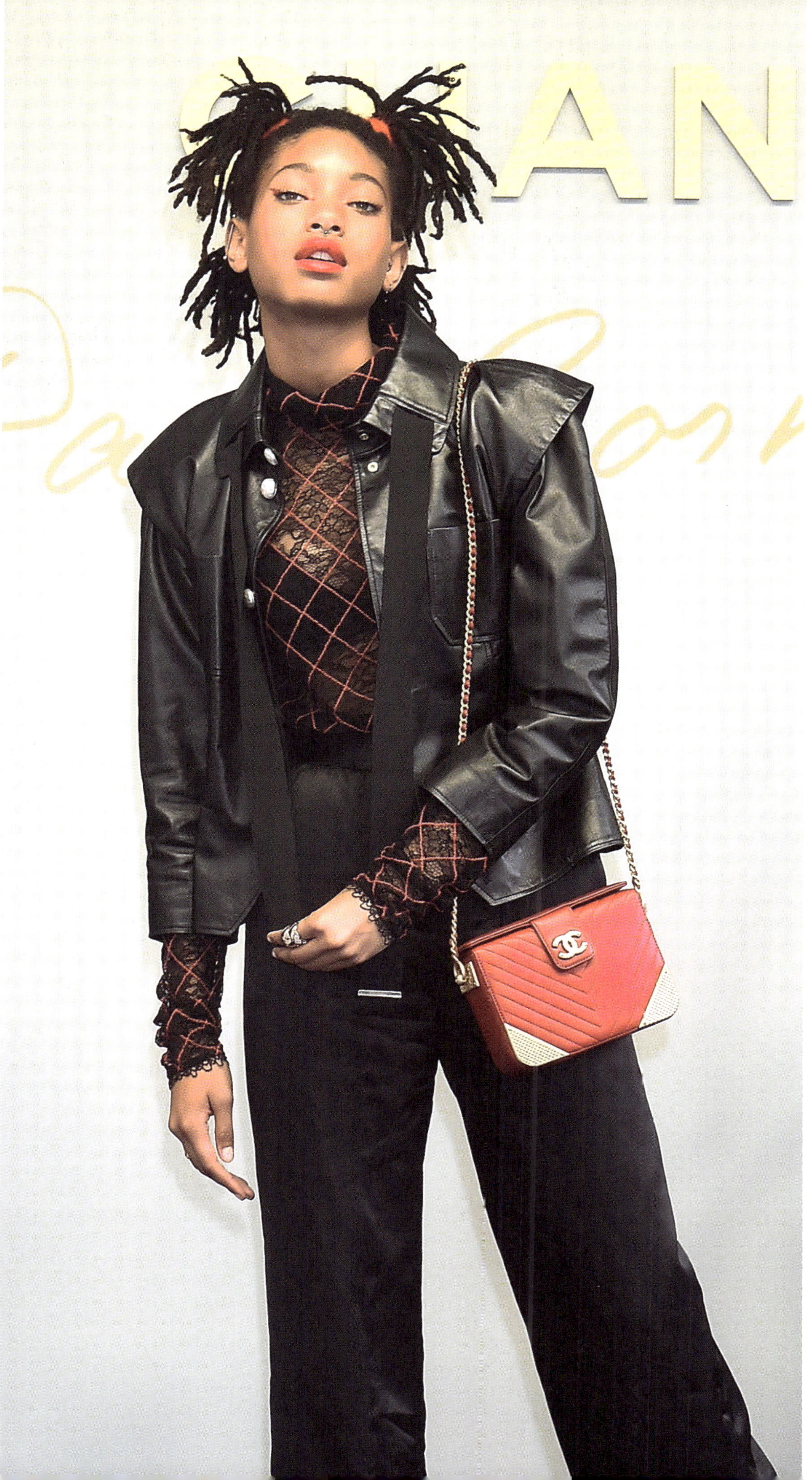

Pages 128/129: Margot Robbie portrayed Barbie in the 2023 Warner Bros. Pictures film, where Chanel fashion and bags played a prominent role

Page 131: Chanel brand ambassador Willow Smith attends the Chanel "Paris Cosmopolite" Métiers d'Art Collection show in Tokyo, 2017

Page 132: Blake Lively owns a diverse collection of Chanel bags; here, she carries a square flap denim backpack in New York City, 2023

Page 133: Mother and daughter duo Lily Rose Depp and Vanessa Paradis have close ties to the *maison*. Both have appeared in Chanel bag advertisements. Vanessa Paradis was the face of an advertising campaign for the Cambon Ligne range in the early 2000s, while Lily-Rose Depp has promoted the 22. Here they attend the Chanel Cruise Collection 2020 in Paris, May 2019.

Page 134: Charlotte Casiraghi, daughter of Princess Caroline of Monaco, carries a classic Chanel bag

Page 135: Princess Caroline of Monaco and designer Karl Lagerfeld in Monaco, 2006

Page 136: Diana, Princess of Wales, showcases the bag that bears her name in Chicago

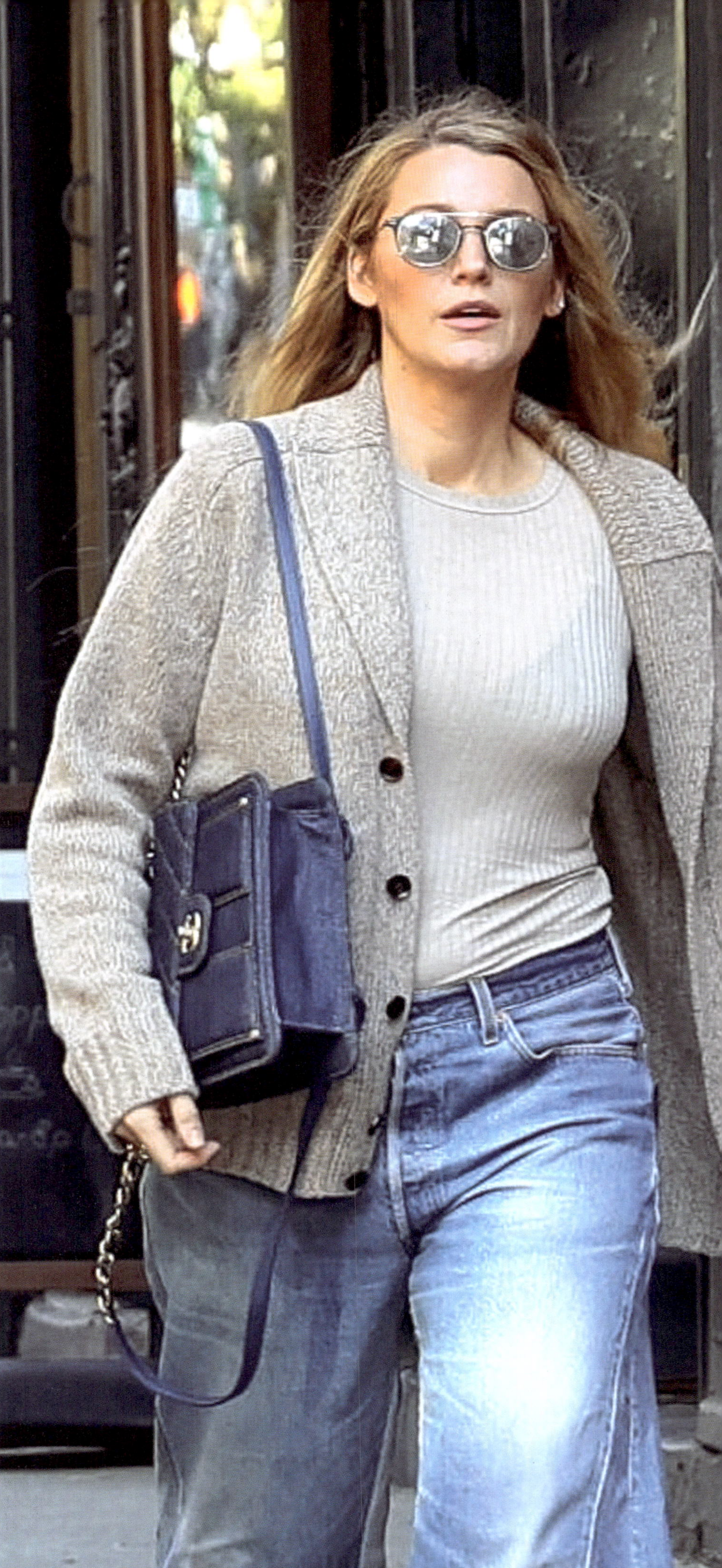

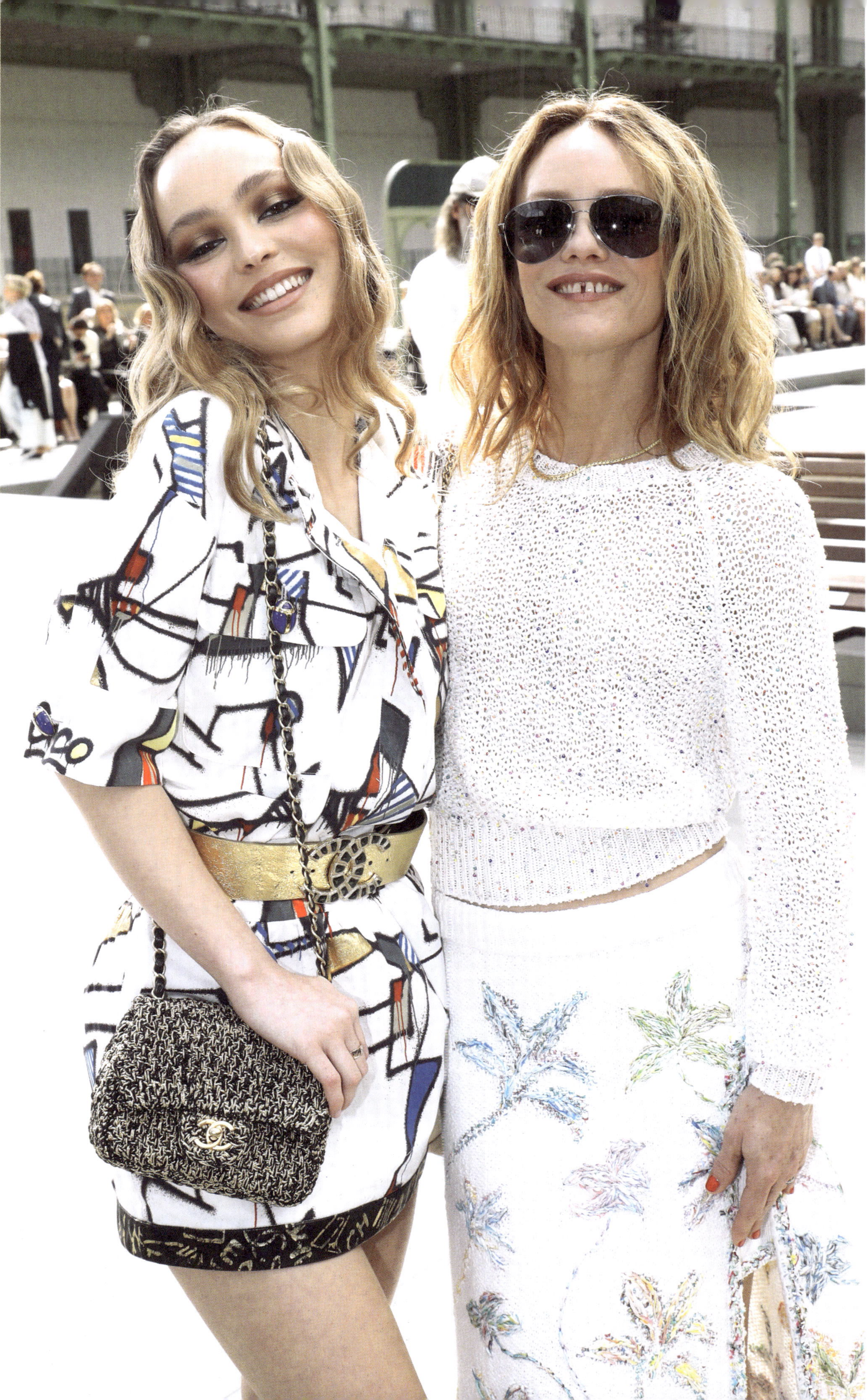

directed by Pedro Almodovar, wore Chanel throughout. Lagerfeld also created all the costumes for Maria Callas, played by Fanny Ardant, in *Callas Forever* (2002). You can spot Chanel fine jewelry on Kristin Scott-Thomas in *Gosford Park* (2002), and one of the most memorable scenes in *The Devil Wears Prada* (2006) focuses on the transformation of Anne Hathaway's character, Andy Sachs, into a fashion maven when her astounded colleague asks what she's wearing. "Are you wearing the..." gasps Emily Blunt's character Emily Charlton. "The Chanel boots? Yeah, I am," retorts Sachs in a much-memed mic drop moment.

Cate Blanchett, Kristen Stewart and Blake Lively all wore Chanel for their roles in Woody Allen's *Cafe Society (*2016), including archive pieces uncovered by costume designer Suzy Benzinger. Chanel took a supporting role in *Atonement* (2008), as seen on Keira Knightley, and Margot Robbie carried a classic 2.55 bag for her portrayal of Sharon Tate in *Once Upon A Time In Hollywood* (2019).

Chanel ambassador Kristen Stewart played Diana in the biopic *Spencer* (2021), which charted the life of The Princess of Wales. The Classic Flap Jumbo was a notable inclusion, and Chanel provided financial backing and archival access for the film.

More recently, Margot Robbie portrayed the most famous doll in the world in Greta Gerwig's *Barbie* (2023). Costume designer Jacqueline Durran told *Vogue*, "If Margot wears anything that we didn't make, it's pretty much [all] Chanel." Appearing in a pink tweed skirt suit from the Spring/Summer 1995 collection originally modelled by Claudia Schiffer, Barbie also carries a heart-shaped hot pink bag from the same season and has a camellia-print tote bag from Spring/Summer

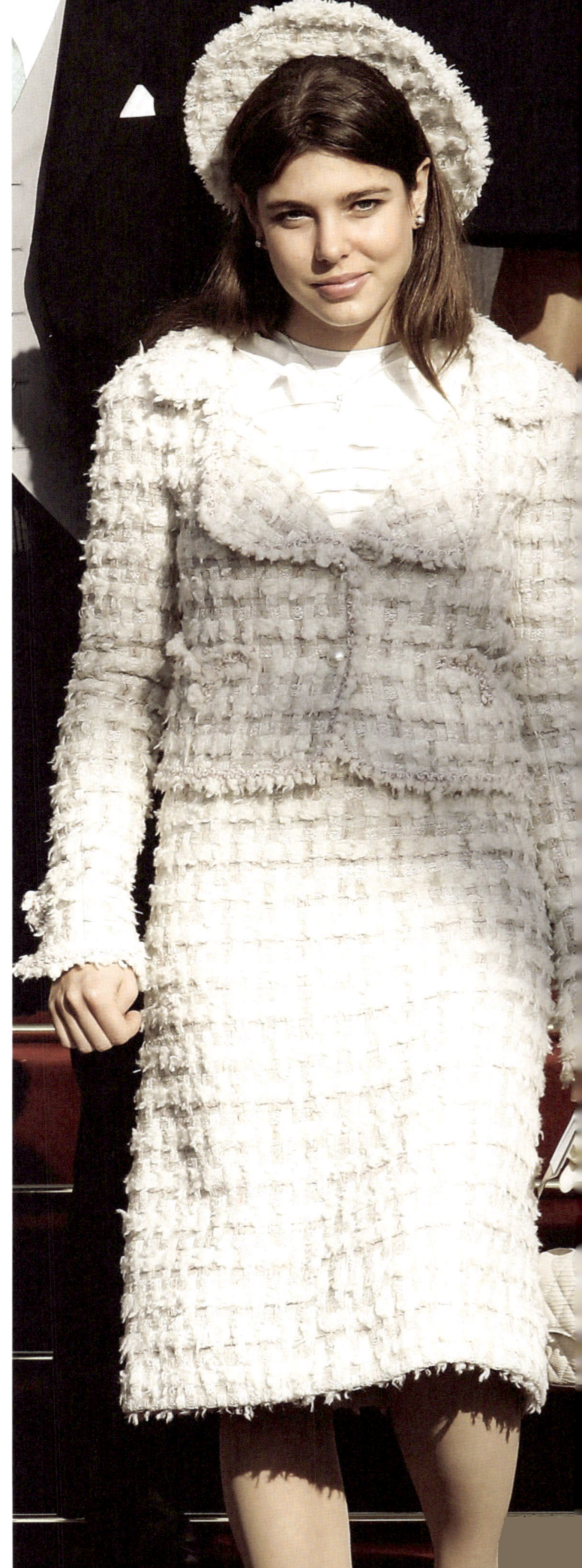

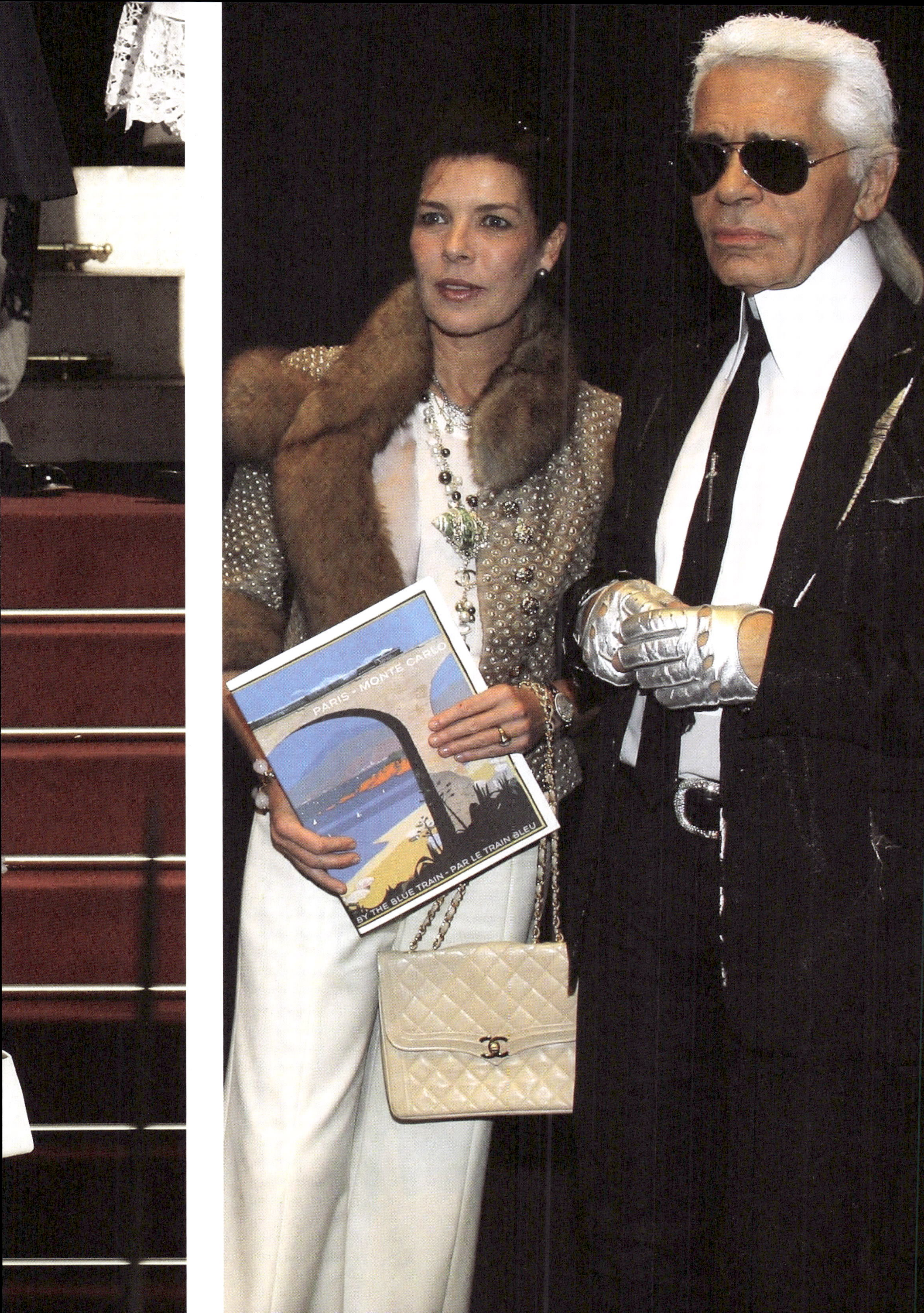
PARIS - MONTE CARLO
BY THE BLUE TRAIN - PAR LE TRAIN BLEU

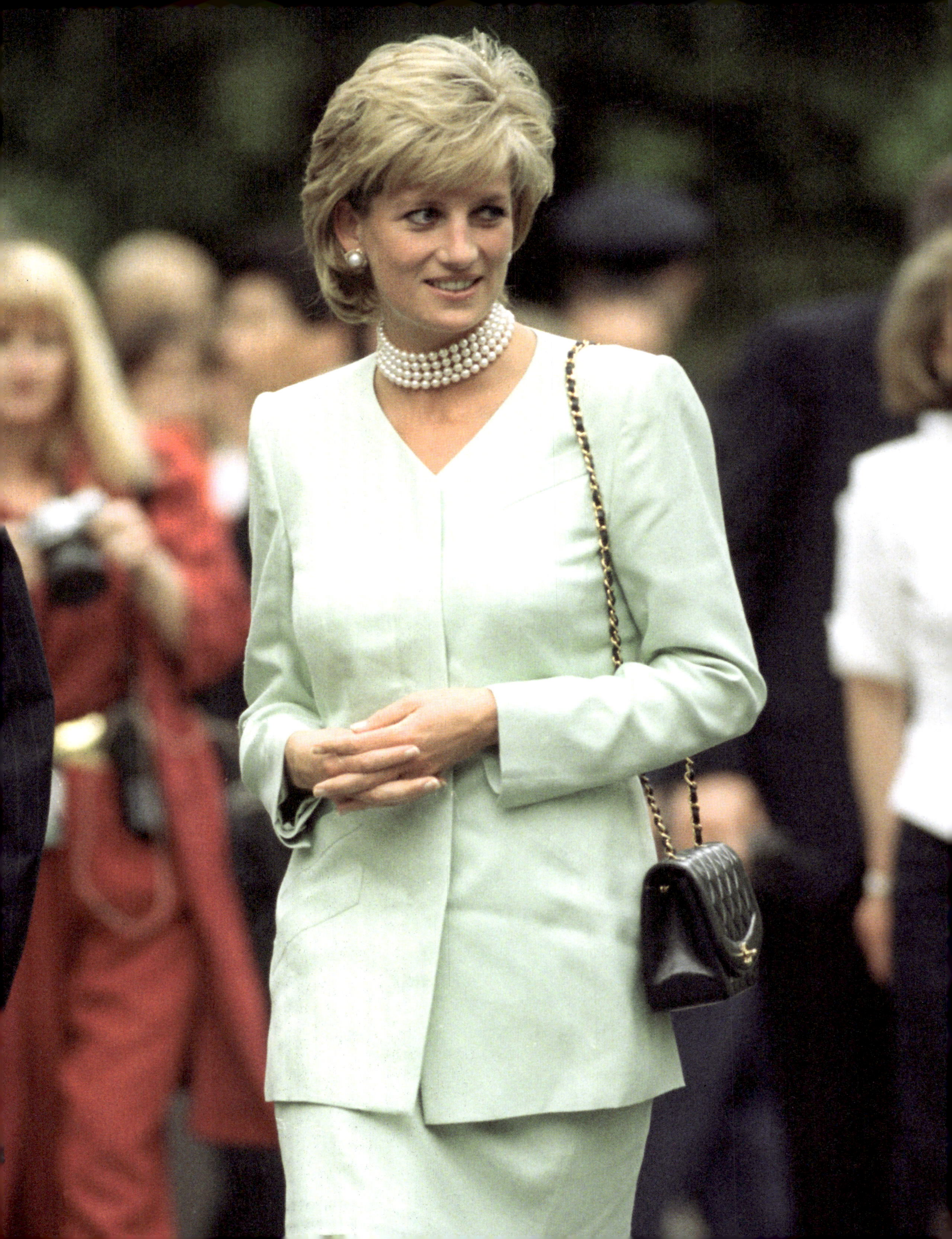

KARL LAGERFELD CREATED THE DIANA BAG IN 1989.

137

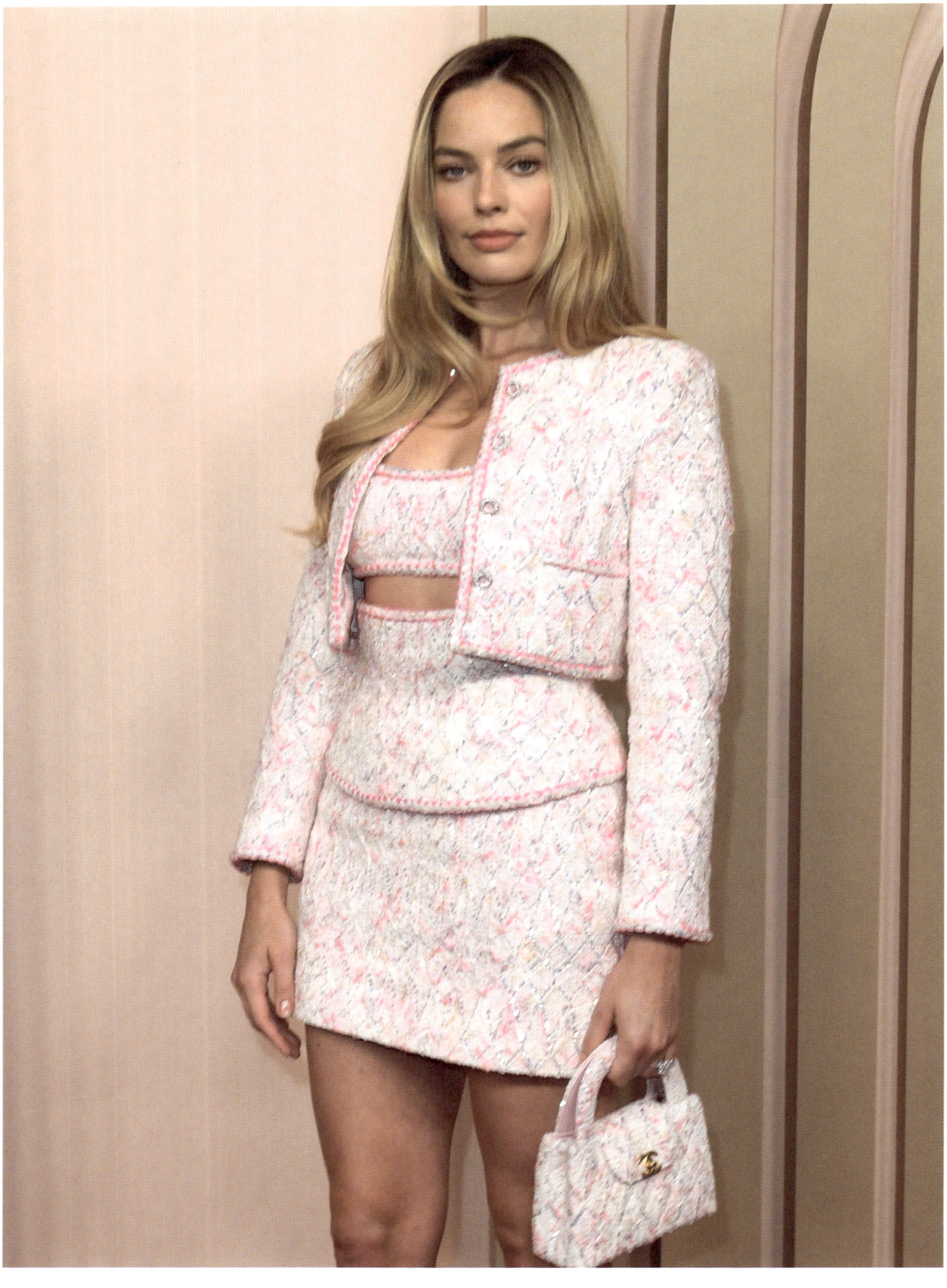

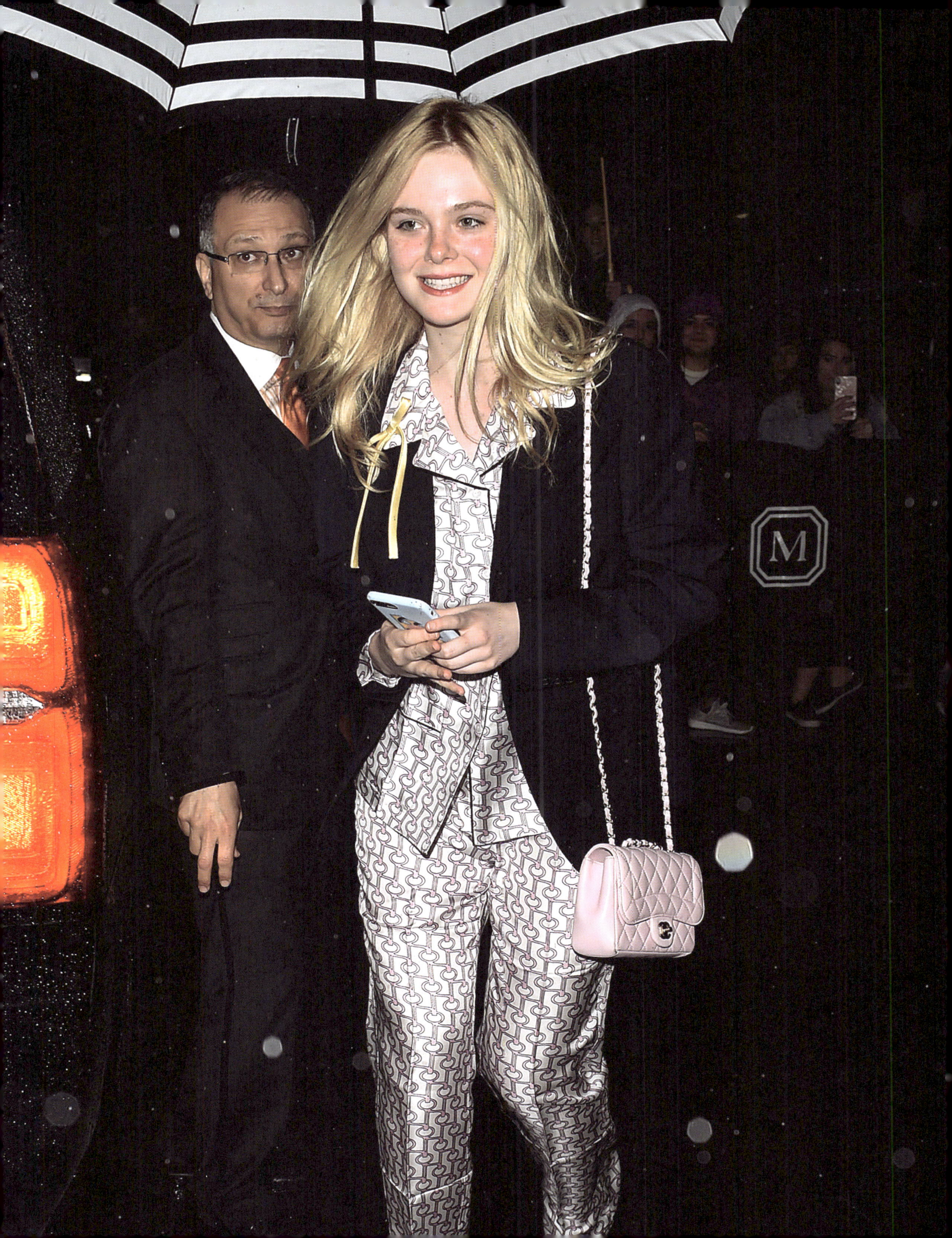
M

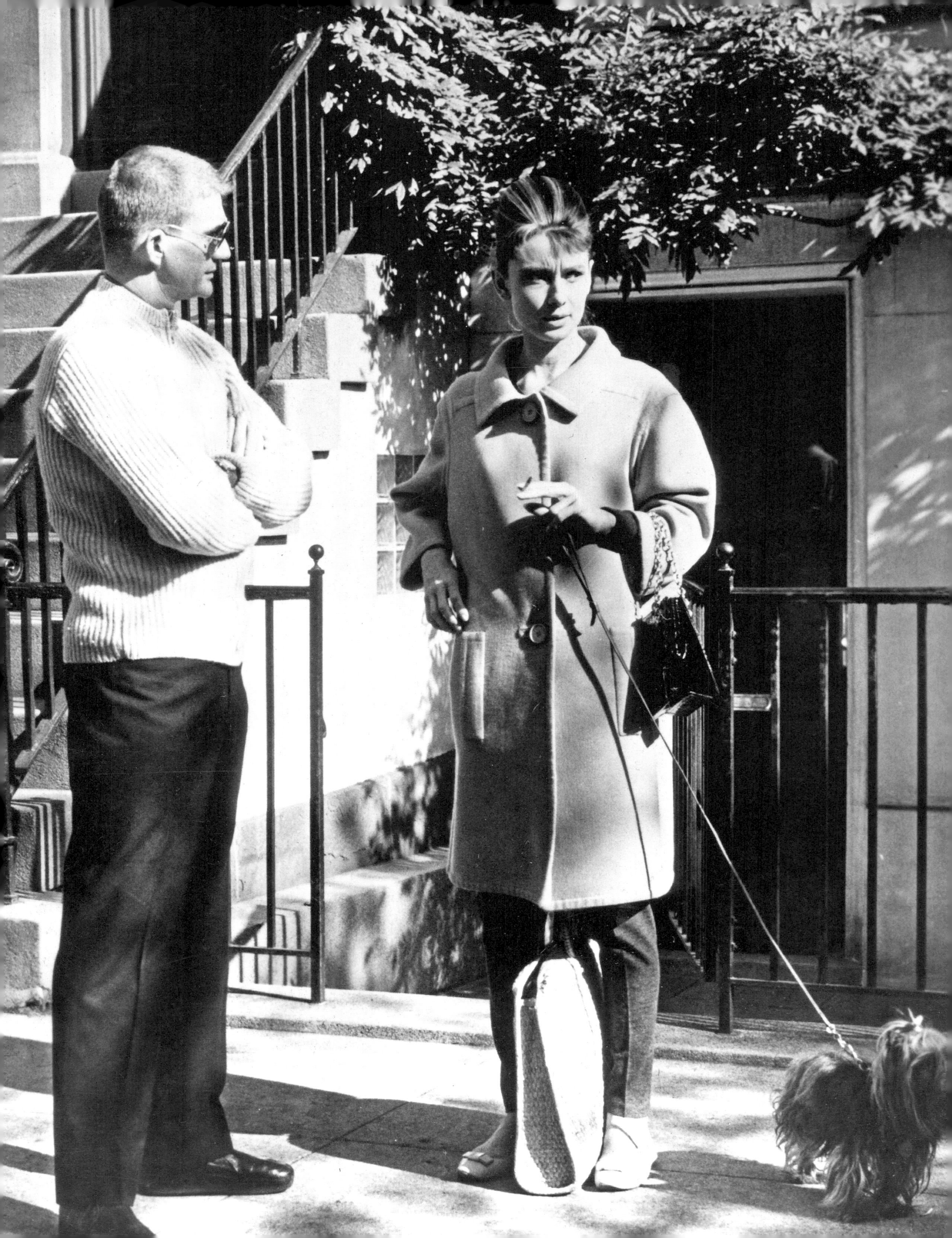

1997 hanging in her Dreamhouse closet. The iconic doll also carries a pink 19 bag, and throughout the press tour, Robbie and her stylist Andrew Mukamal followed the method dressing formula. Robbie appeared in a carousel of Barbie-worthy looks, wearing vintage Chanel on the Australian leg of the tour.

Beyond the cameos from Chanel pieces in film, the life of Mlle Chanel provides rich inspiration for the silver screen, too. *Chanel Solitaire* (1981) focused on the designer's influences and relationships, while the made-for-TV movie *Coco Chanel* (2008) starred Shirley MacLaine as Chanel. *Coco avant Chanel* (2009) spotlit the early life of Chanel, with star Audrey Tatou navigating the tough formative years. *Coco Chanel and Igor Stravinsky* (2009) centered Chanel's short yet passionate relationship with the composer (which the estate of Stravinsky denies), with Anna Mouglalis playing the title role.

On television, the most important characters need significant costumes—and bags—to cement their status. Fans of *Sex and the City* (1998-2004) tuned in for the fashion moments as much as the relationship dramas. As Samantha Jones, Kim Cattrall carried a white quilt-printed tote bag and often was seen with a Classic Flap. Carrie Bradshaw, played by Sarah Jessica Parker, also had a hot pink Classic Flap, and Cynthia Nixon's character Miranda Hobbes tucked a vintage black clutch under her arm. In the sequel series, *And Just Like That*, it's Kristin Davis as Charlotte York who gets to carry the most Chanel bags, including a gold crossbody camera bag and the My Own Frame Bag in pink tweed from 2022.

Teen drama *Gossip Girl* (2008-2012) follows the lives of rich kids in Manhattan, all of whom naturally carried the most fashionable bags of the moment. Blake Lively, as Serena van der Woodsen, owned a Cerf Tote, a royal blue patent Puzzle bag, several 2.55 reissues (in purple and embellished black) *and* an 11.12, which co-star Leighton Meester (Blair Waldorf) also owned, in addition to several mini totes and a Mademoiselle bowling bag in scarlet patent leather.

In *The Mindy Project* (2012-2017), Dr. Mindy Lahari (Mindy Kaling) carries Chanel 11.12 bags in almost every episode of the sitcom, with pink, black, white, blue and orange options in her character's closet.

Emily Cooper, the heroine of *Emily in Paris* (played by Lily Collins) is also a major Chanel bag collector. A rare and limited edition oversized pearl *minaudière* is in Cooper's possession, along with a shearling double CC logo bag, a slouchy pink 19 and a hoop handle Evening By The Sea bag in deep blue. Making a cameo in the series (which debuted in 2020 and is still running) is a Pearl Flap Bag from Spring/Summer 2019, which exemplifies Chanel's own belief that "pearls are perfect for every occasion." The costumes in *Emily in Paris* were designed by Patricia Field, who also worked on *Sex and the City* and received an Oscar nomination for Best Costume Design for *The Devil Wears Prada*.

The proliferation of reality TV has seen an explosion of Chanel on the small screen: *The Hills*, *The Real Housewives* franchise and *Keeping Up With The Kardashians* all have cast members flaunting Chanel on screen. Kim Kardashian has a 30,000 piece fashion archive, yet was moved to tears when her mother Kris Jenner was gifted a rare Chanel Lego clutch. On *The Late Late Show* with James Corden, Kardashian told viewers she was expecting to be given a bag on her first shoot with Karl Lagerfeld, in 2013, while she was 8 months pregnant with daughter North West. But when the designer met Jen-

Page 138: Australian actress Margot Robbie attends the Oscar Nominees Luncheon at the Beverly Hilton in Beverly Hills, wearing a Chanel tweed ensemble and a matching Chanel Kelly bag, 2024

Page 139: Elle Fanning is spotted carrying a pale pink Classic Flap in New York City, 2019.

Page 140: Audrey Hepburn with a classic Chanel bag on the set of *Breakfast at Tiffany's*, USA, 1961

This page: Catherine Deneuve showcases a 2.55 Chanel handbag in Paris, 1961

Page 144: Jackie Kennedy carries her Chanel bag at an event in London, 1962

Page 145: Catherine Deneuve and Roger Vadim, 1963

Page 146: Liz Taylor, with a 2.55, and Eddie Fisher leave Moscow's Sovetskaya Hotel on July 17, 1961

Page 147: Romy Schneider on the set of *Le Combat dans L'Ile*, 1962

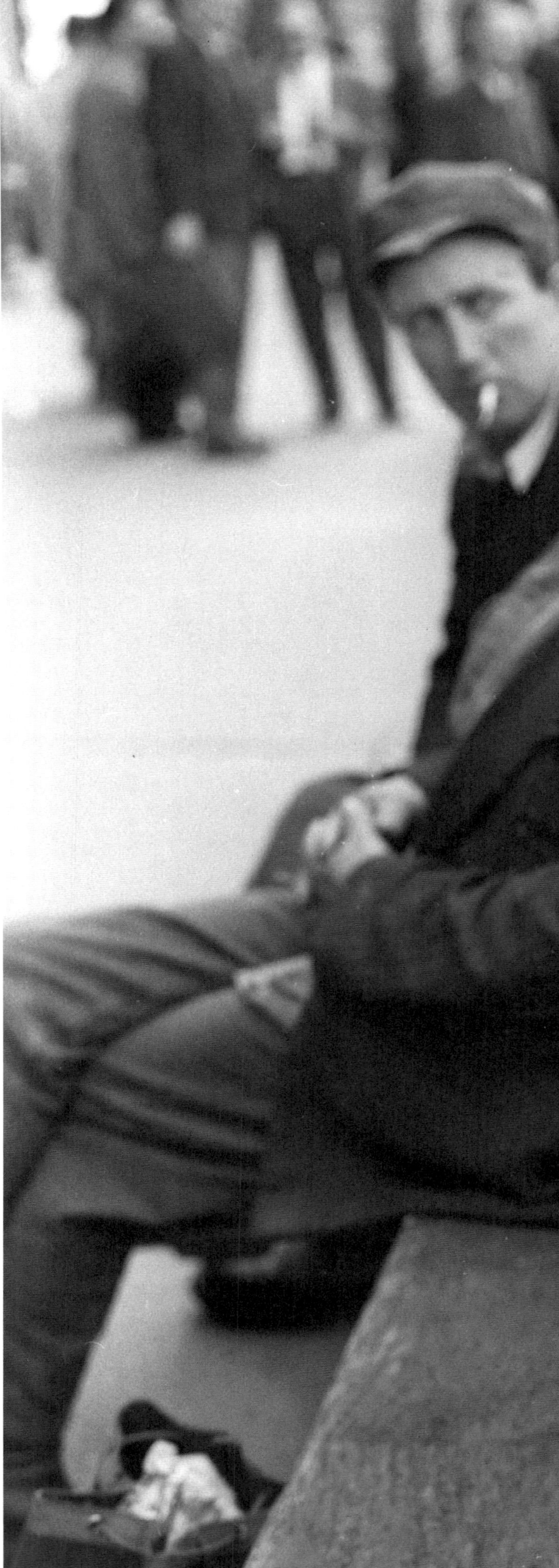

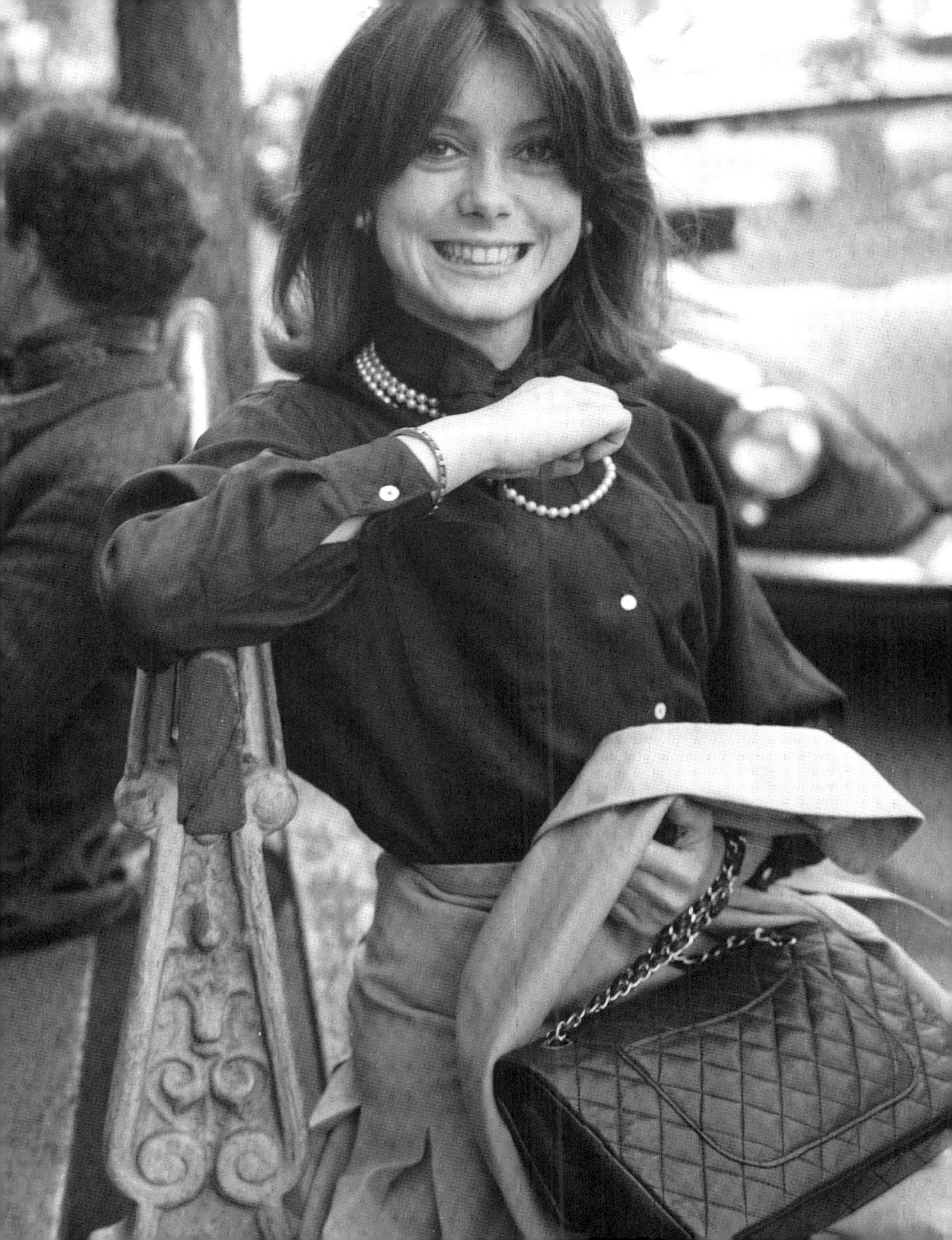

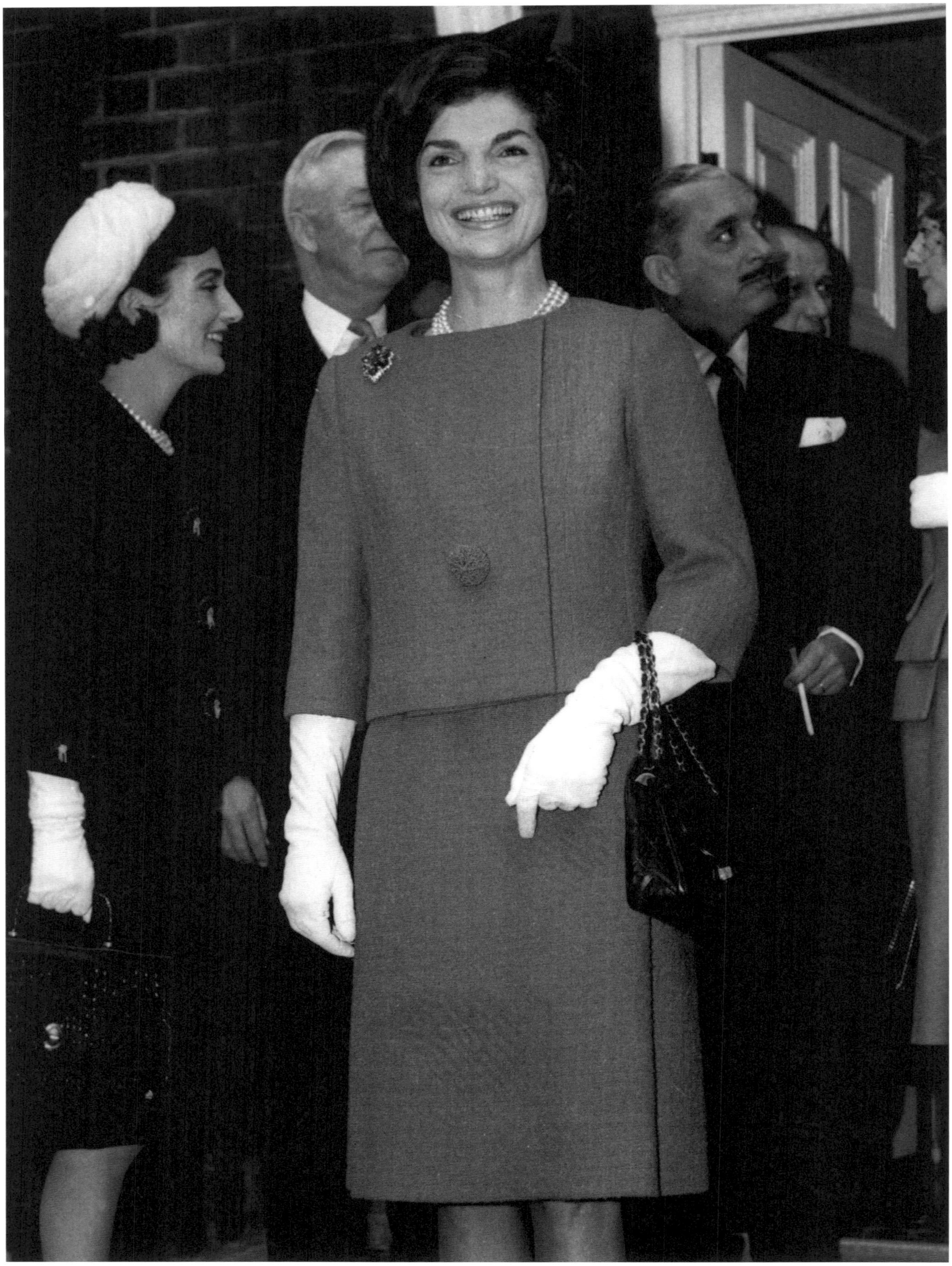

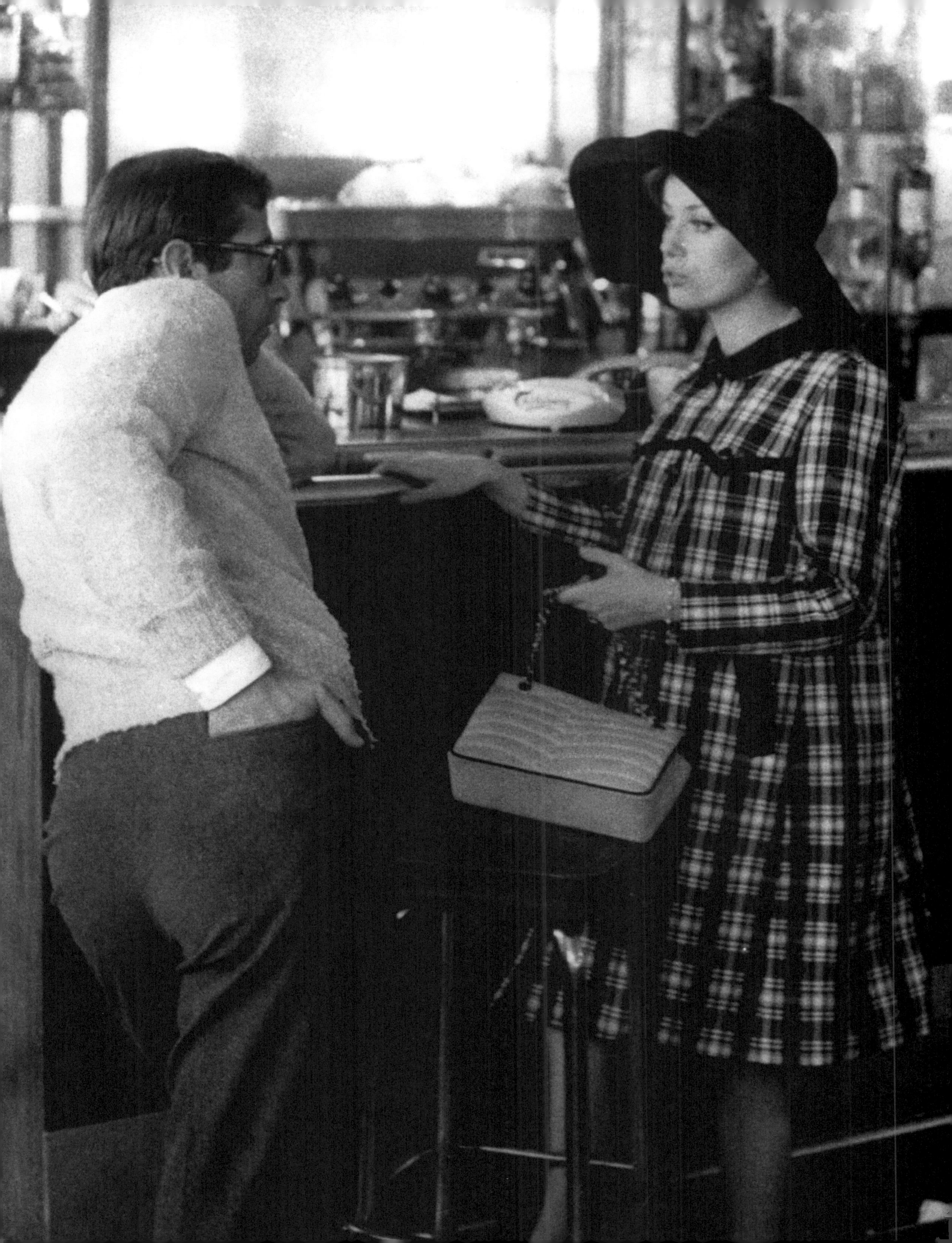

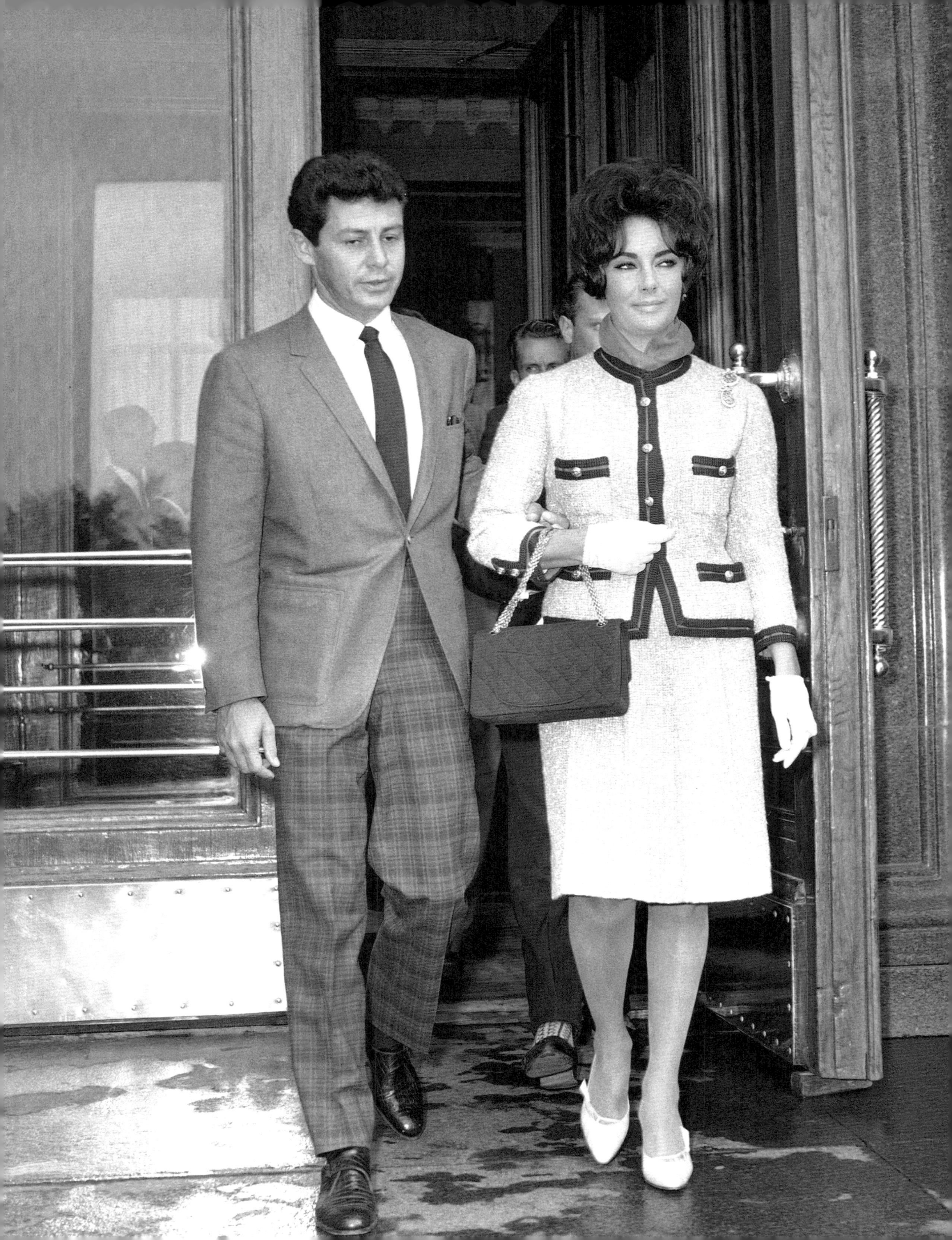

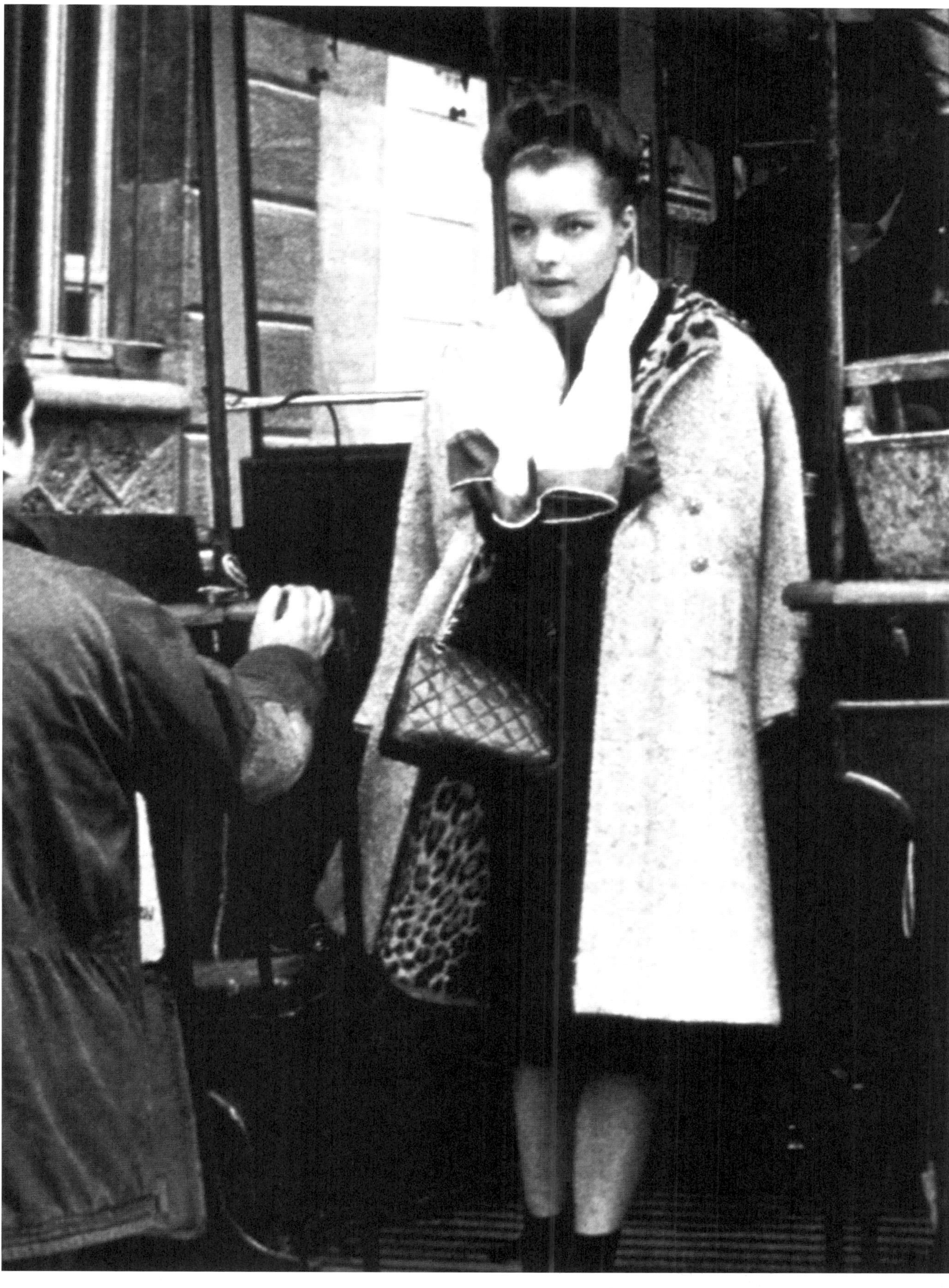

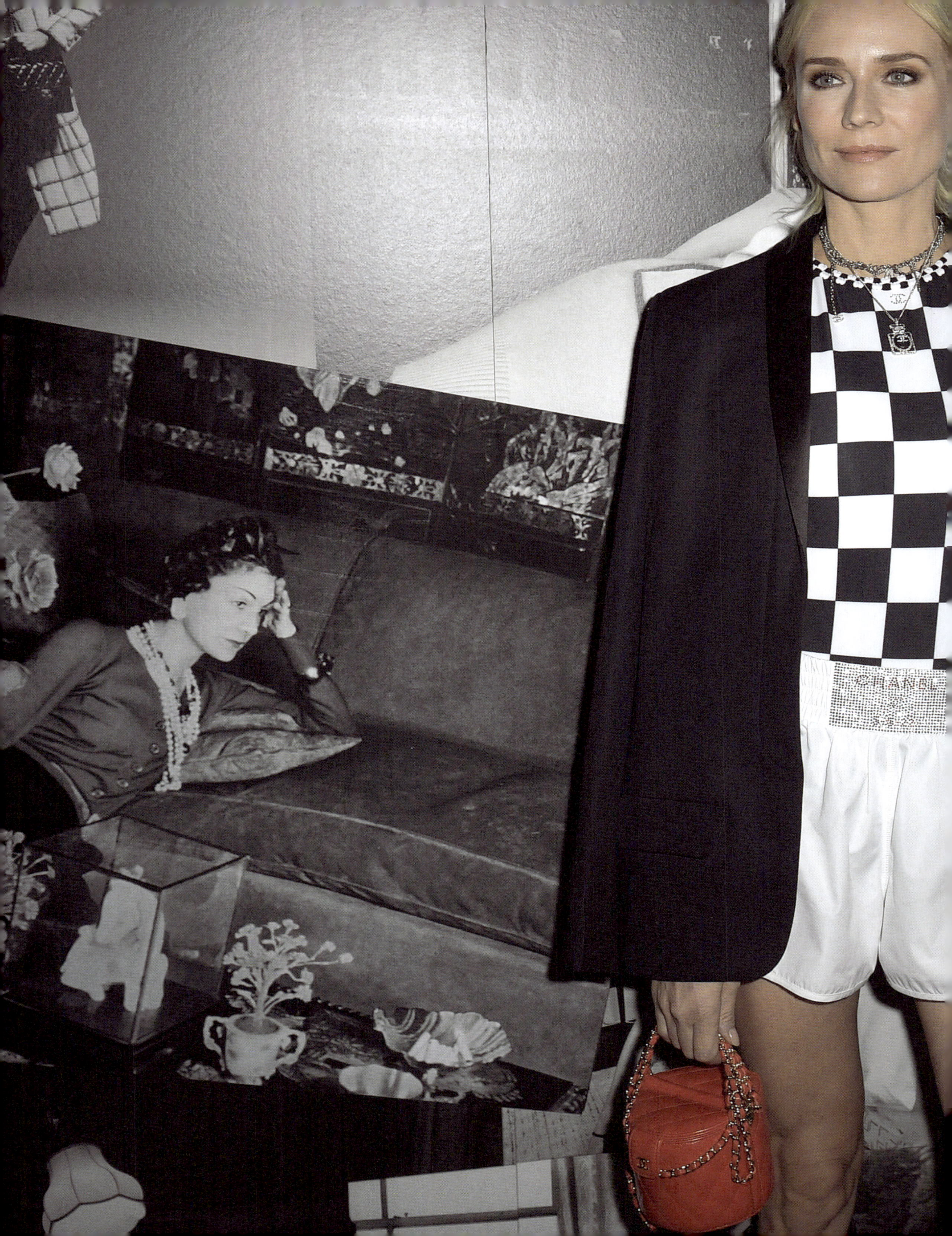
CHANEL

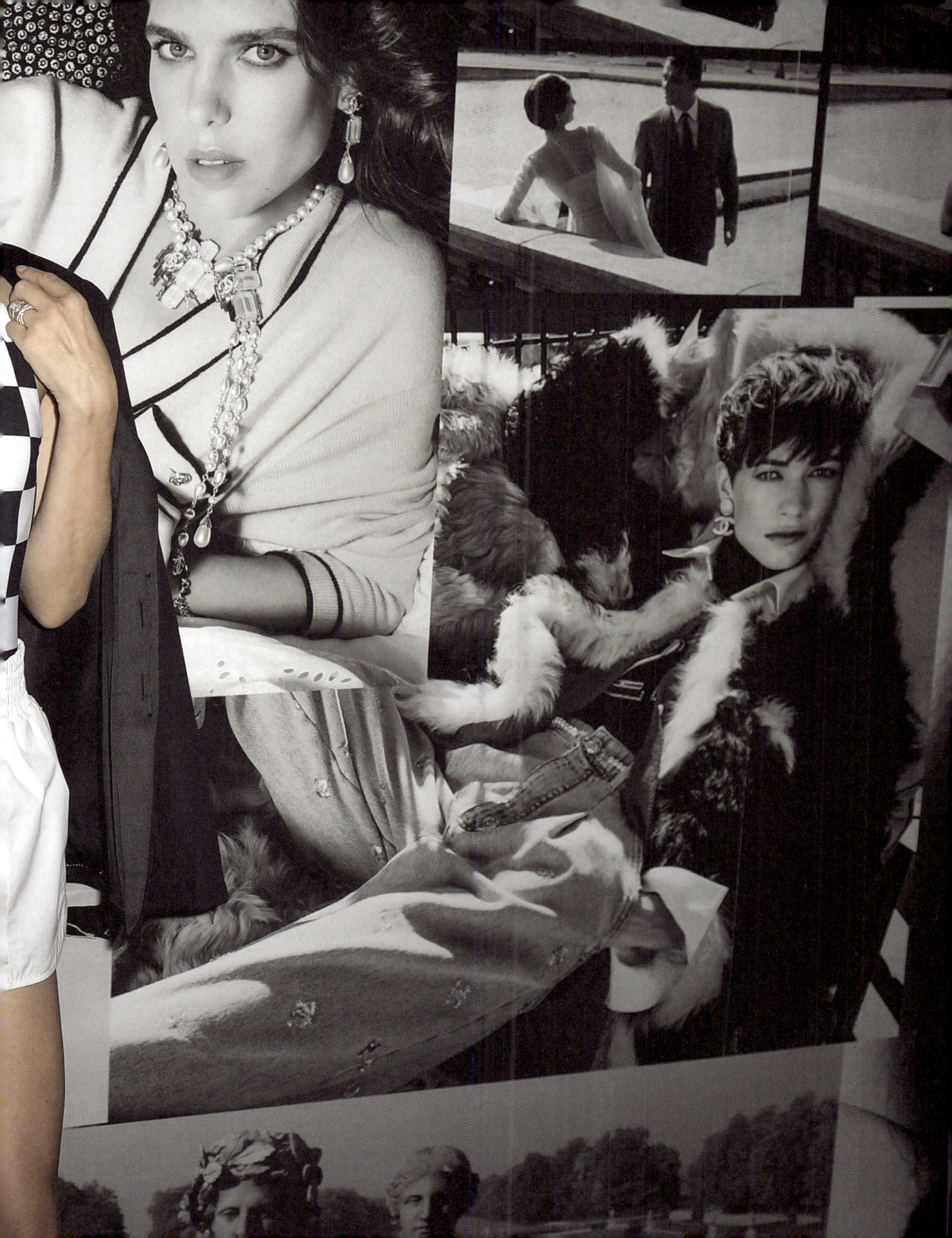

Pages 148/149: Diane Kruger attends the Chanel Womenswear Spring/Summer 2023 show carrying a red vanity case, Paris, October 2022

This page: Kim Kardashian is spotted with a black vanity case on September 15, 2023, in Los Angeles

Next page: Leighton Meester and Blake Lively on the set of *Gossip Girl*. Lively's character, Serena van der Woodsen, carries a royal blue patent Puzzle bag in Port Washington, 2008

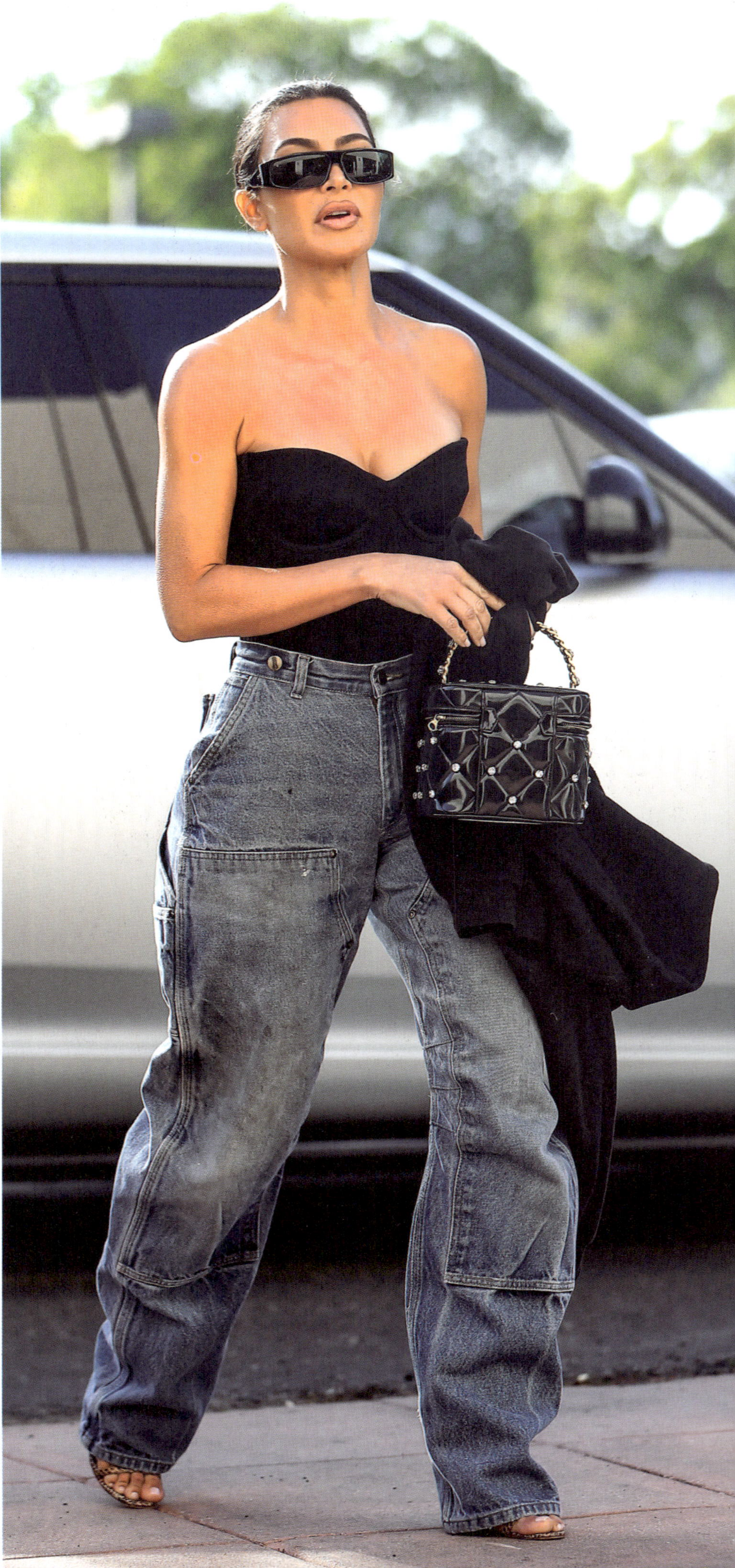

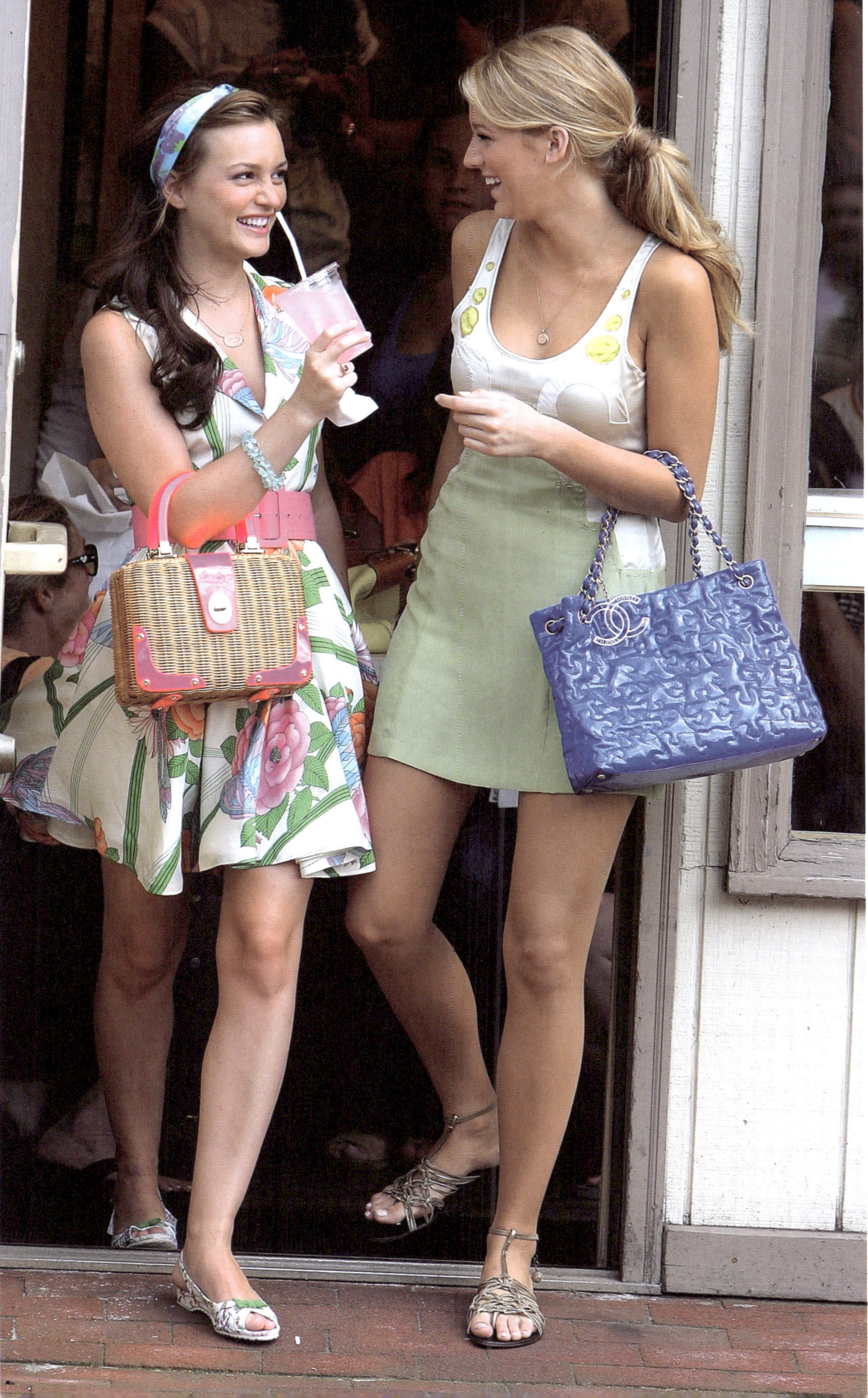

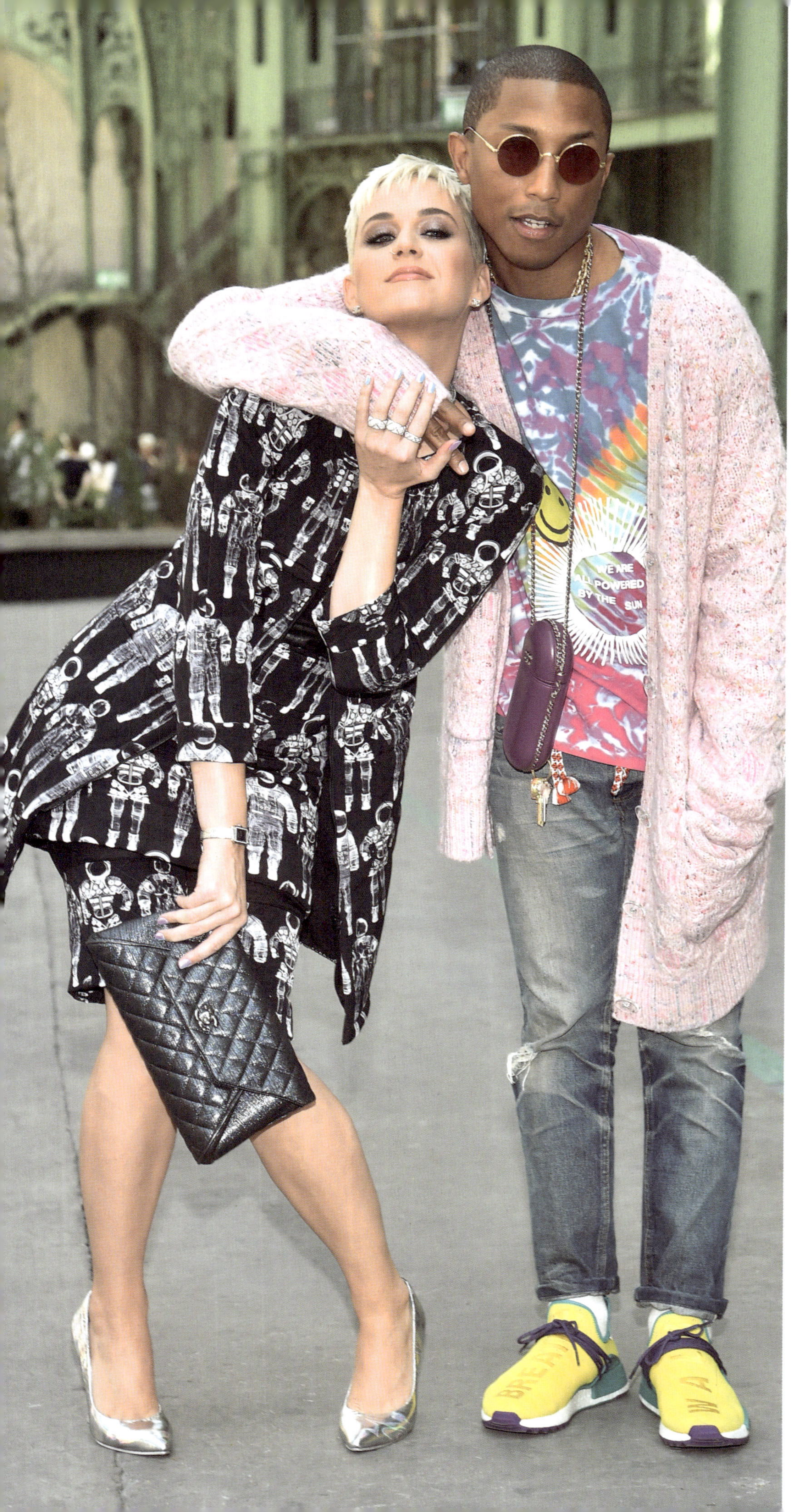

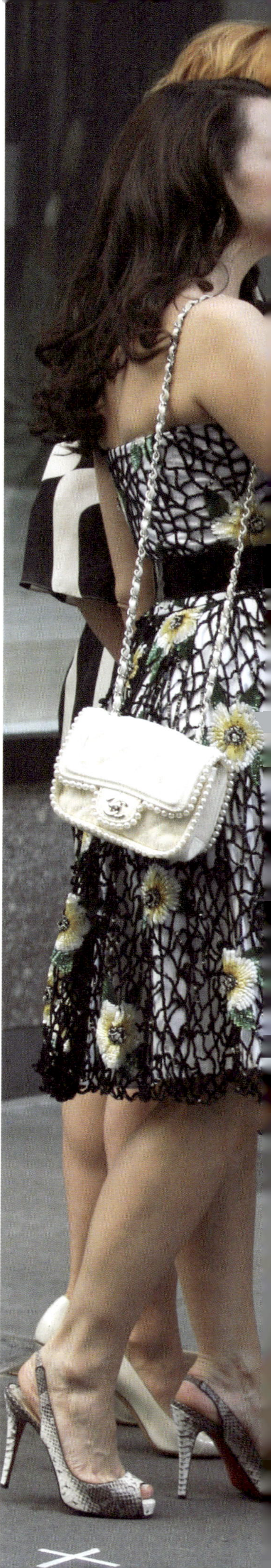

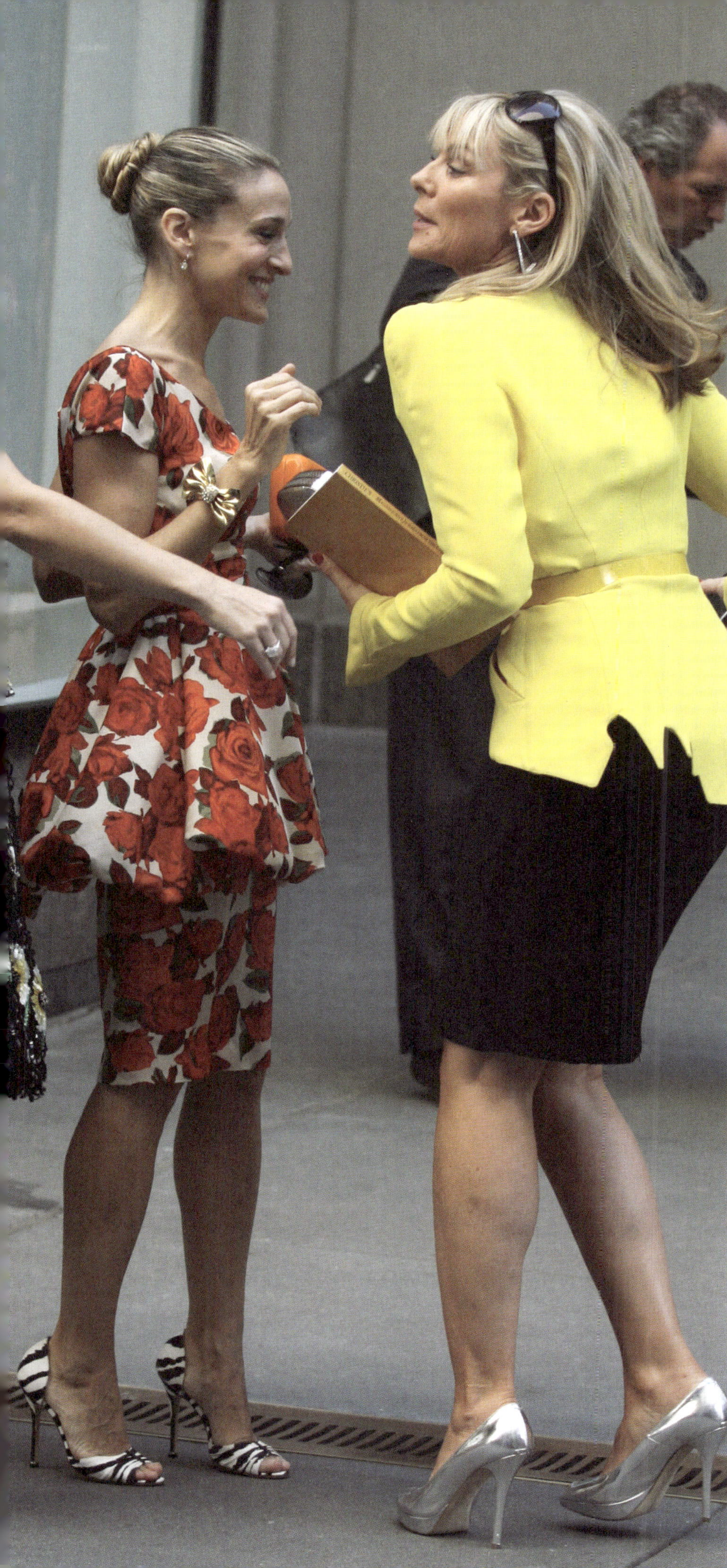

Previous page: Katy Perry and Pharrell Williams attend the Chanel Haute Couture Fall/Winter 2017 show in Paris, 2017. Perry is carrying a Chanel clutch

This page: On the set of *Sex and the City: The Movie*, Kristin Davis, as her character Charlotte York, carries a flap bag in New York City, 2007

Next page: Kristin Davis is seen on the set of *And Just Like That*, wearing a WOC in New York City, 2024

Pages 156/157: Kate Moss on the runway at Chanel's Fall/Winter ready-to-wear 1993 fashion show in Paris

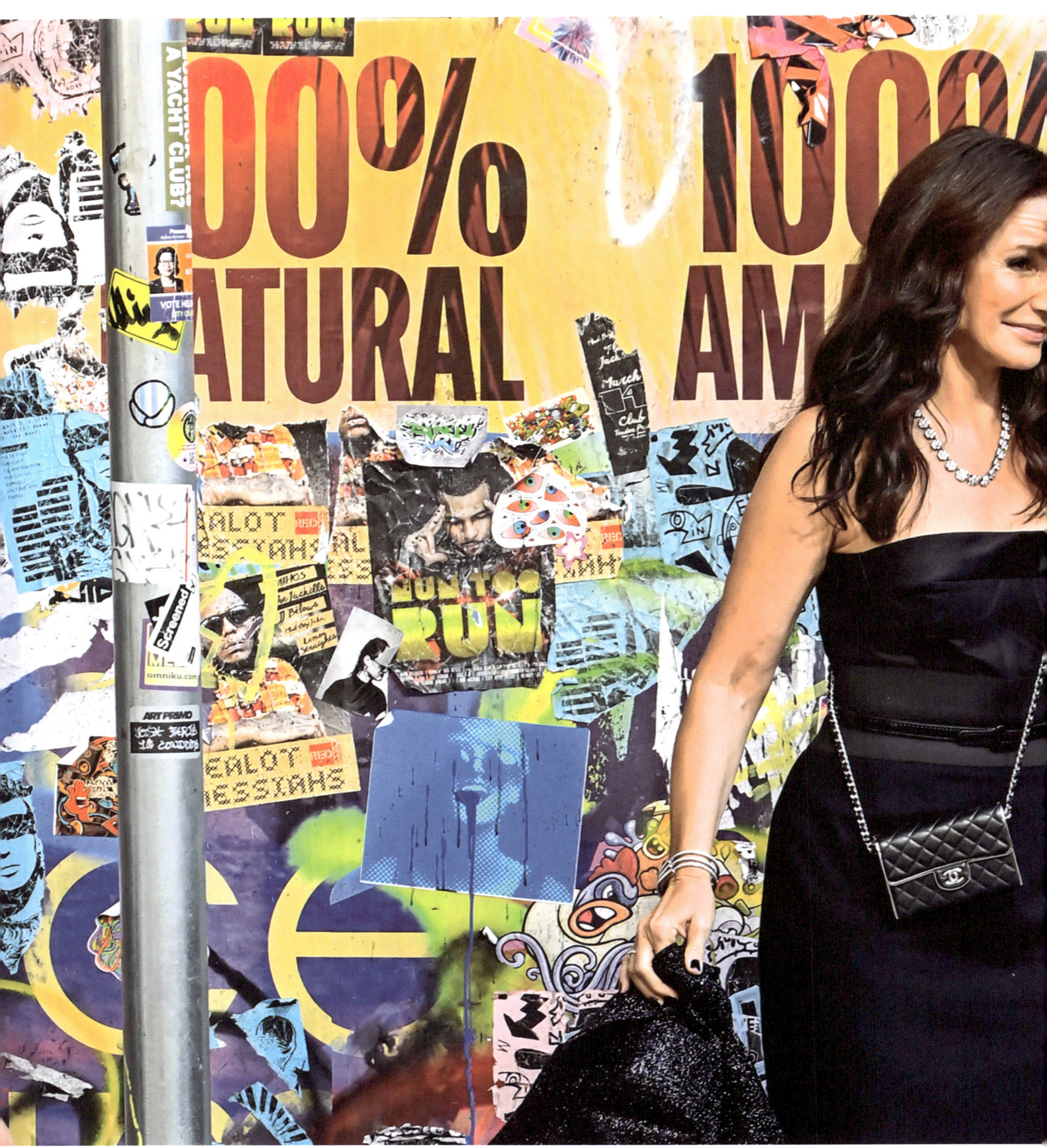
A YACHT CLUB?
00%
ATURAL
100
AM
EALOT
ESSIAHS
Screened
omniku.com
ART PRIMO

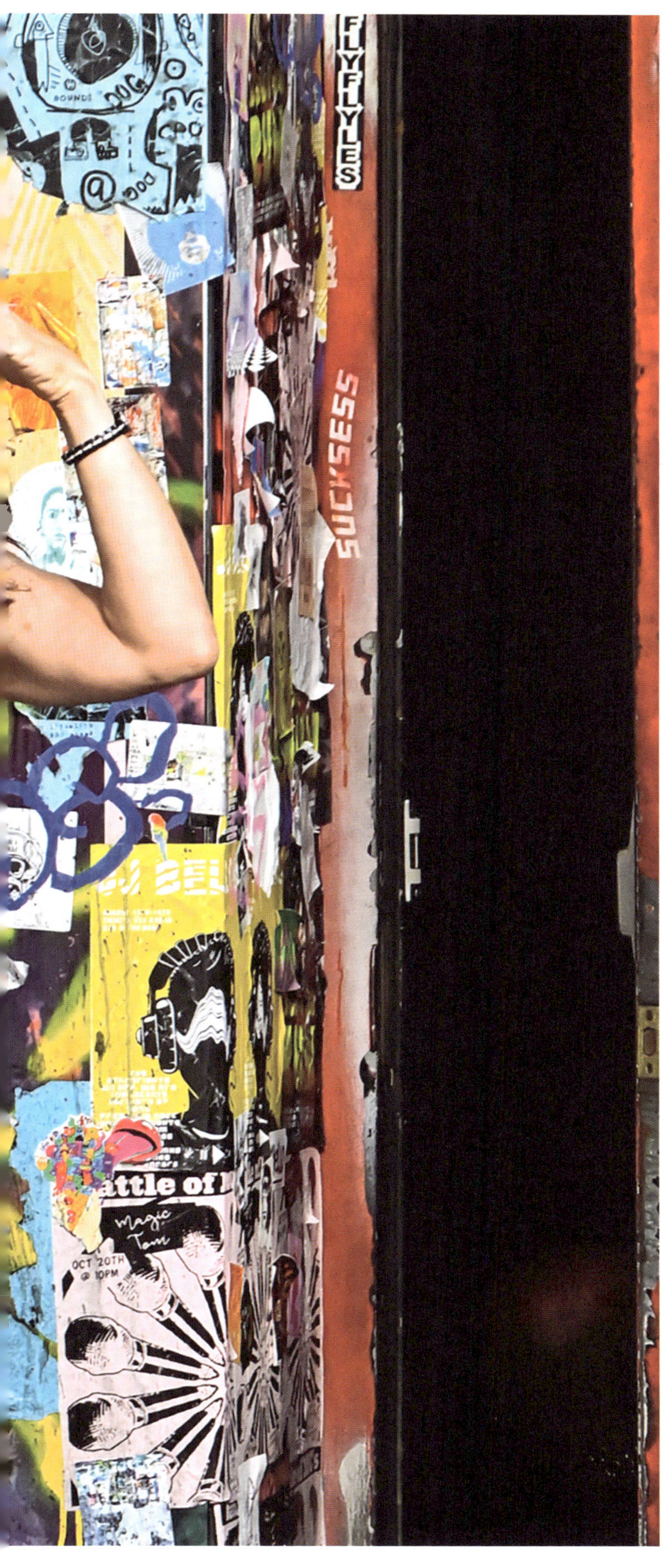

ner, "he falls in love with her and hardly acknowledges that I've been sitting there." Kardashian's response is to sob hysterically in the bathroom. Kim had hoped to pass a bag on to her daughter and ensured that Jenner bequeathed the bag to North in her will. Perhaps Jenner's entirely vintage Chanel look endeared her to Lagerfeld, proving vintage Chanel is always a wise investment.

Wiz Khalifa would agree, having titled his 2013 hit *Old Chanel,* while Katy Perry sang "All my girls vintage Chanel, baby" in *This Is How We Do* (2013). Camilla Cabello recorded an ode to *Chanel No.5* (2024), but Chanel namechecks are most popular in hip-hop. Nicki Minaj released *Coco Chanel* (2018), with Young Thug, A$AP Rocky and Young Jeezy all dropping double CC mentions.

Chanel is eager to build on creative relationships across all genres, handpicking nascent icons to become ambassadors. Jennie Kim, singer in Blackpink, was named a brand ambassador in 2017, having already fronted a Chanel Beauté campaign. Lupita Nyong'o and Riley Keogh (granddaughter of Elvis Presley) both joined the *maison* in 2024 alongside Willow Smith, who was named an ambassador in 2016. Smith posted on Instagram at the time, "Thank you Karl Lagerfeld and the entire team at Chanel for expanding the perceptions of 'beauty' by picking me to be the new Chanel ambassador. I am honored. #BLACKGIRLMAGIC."

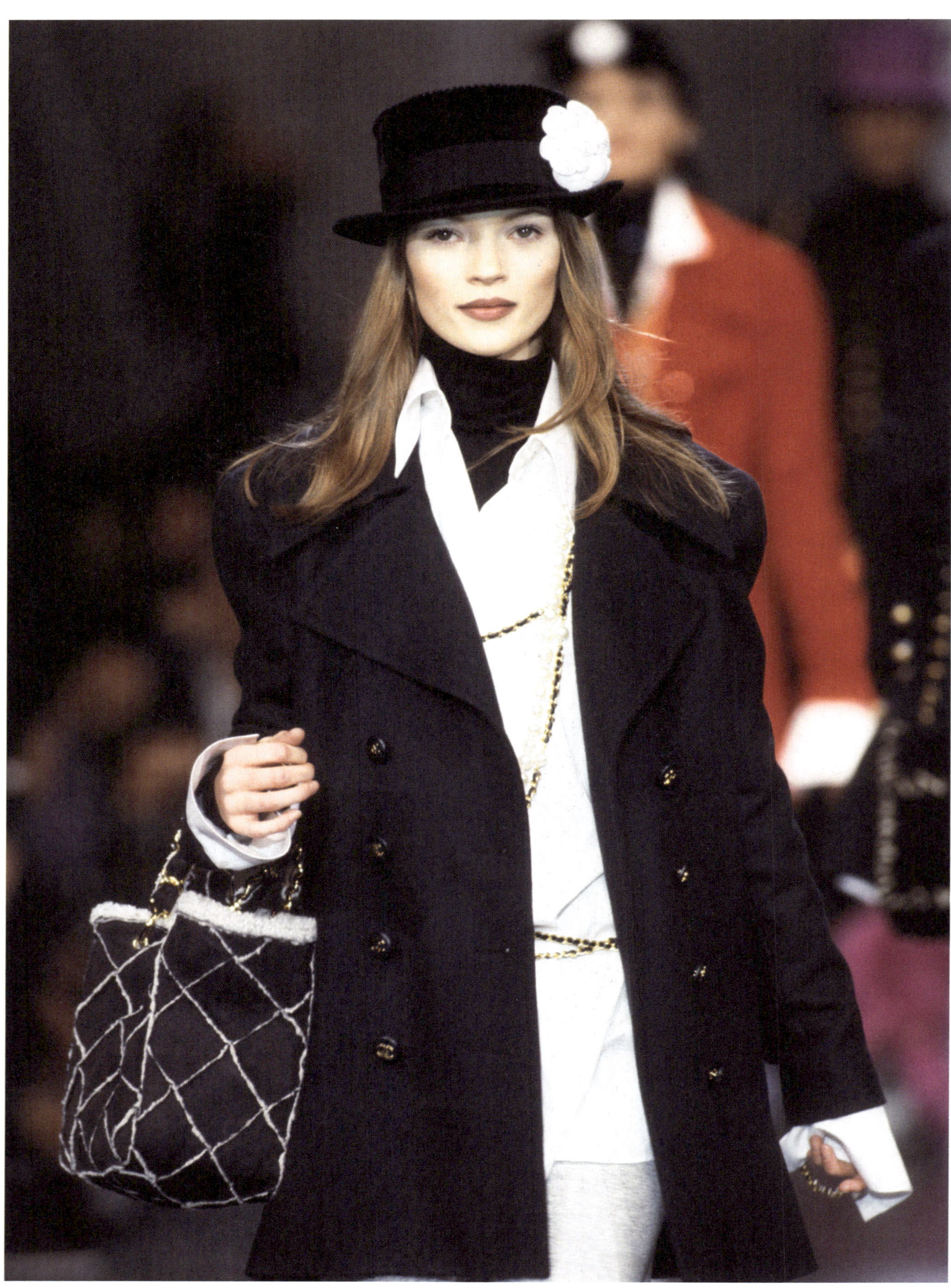

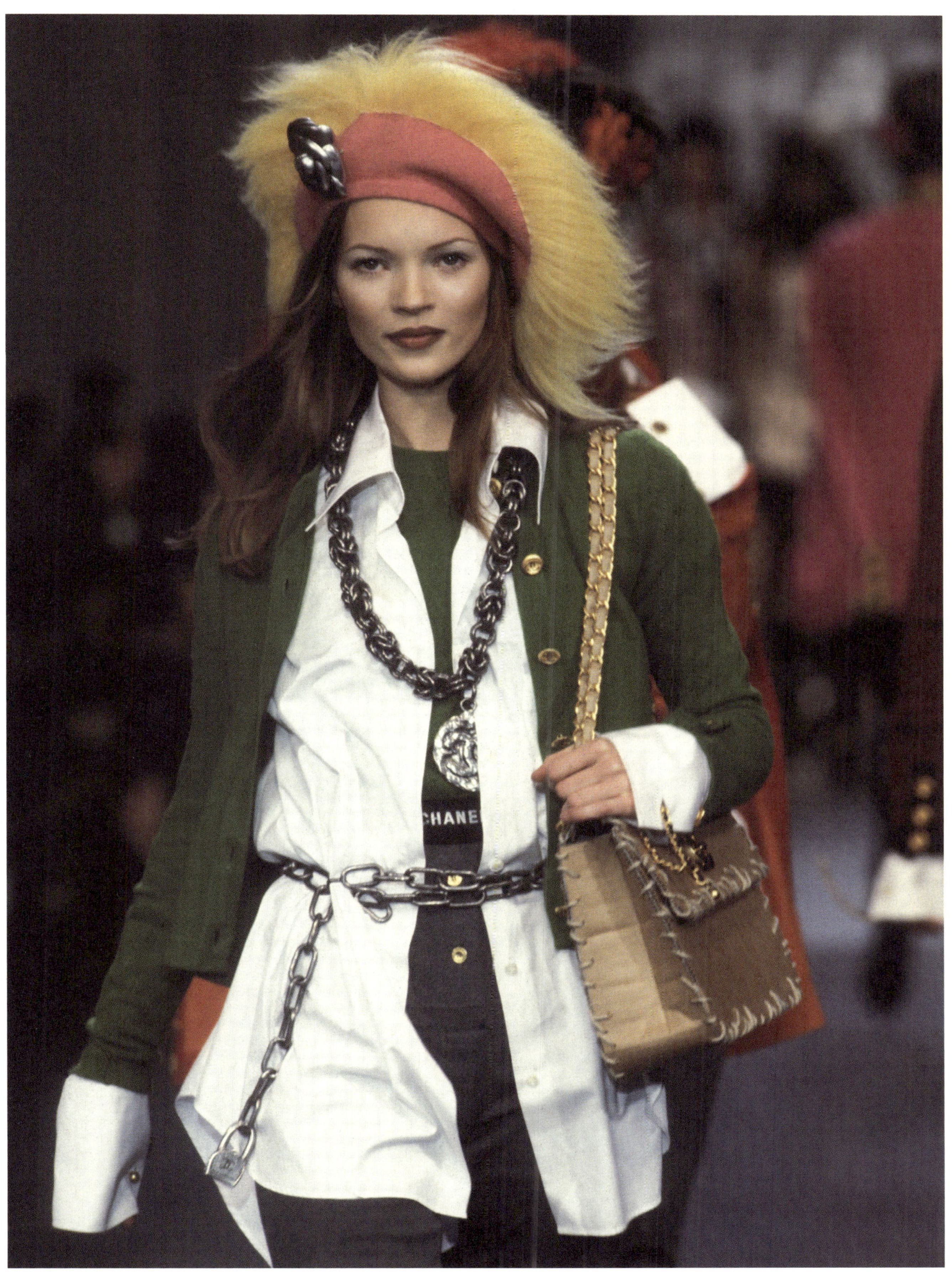

This page: Brand ambassador Riley Keough is captured on the Upper West Side with a 22 bag in New York City, 2024

Next page: Nicki Minaj carries her pale pink Top Handle Flap bag at DJ Khaled's "The Keys" Book Launch Dinner in Los Angeles, 2016

Page 160: Brand ambassador Jennie Kim of BLACKPINK, in Incheon, South Korea, 2024.

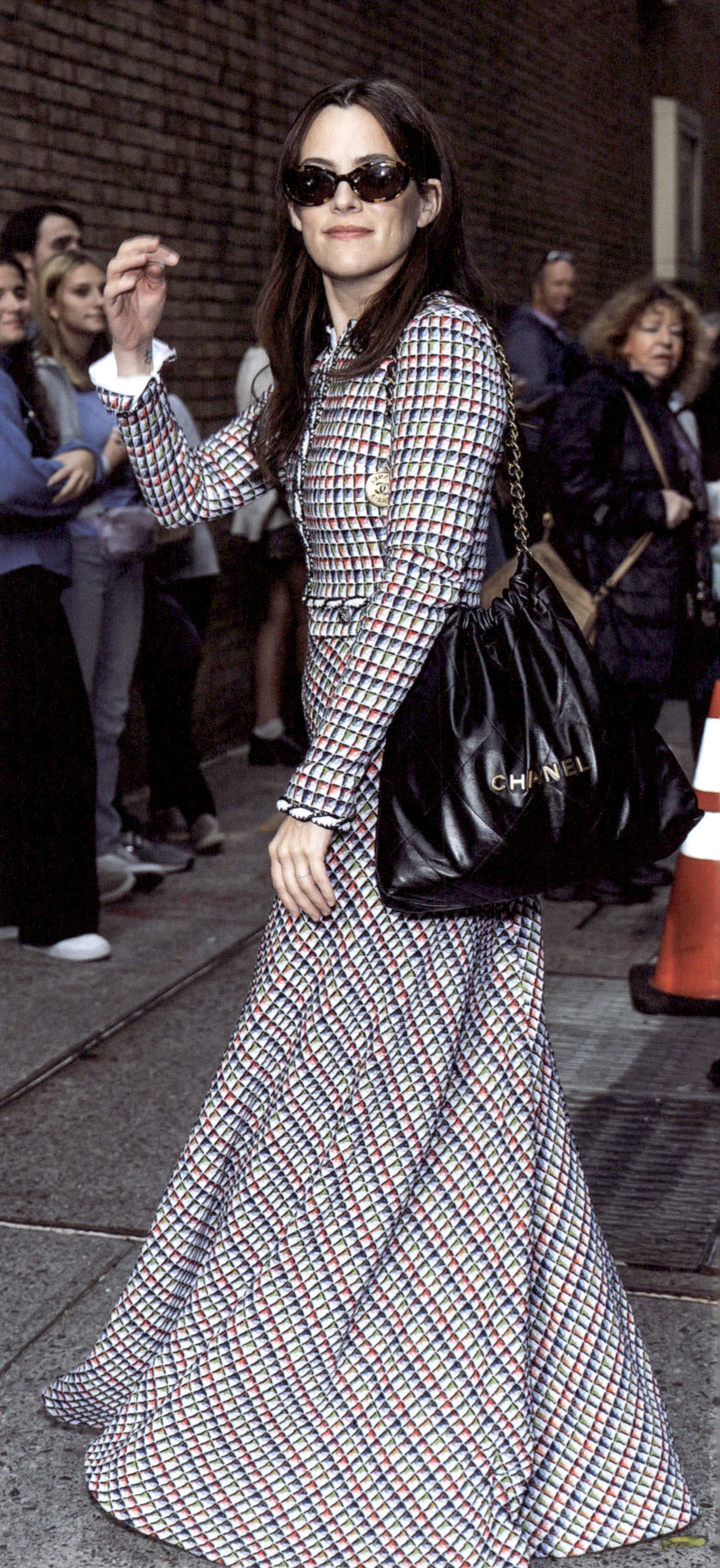

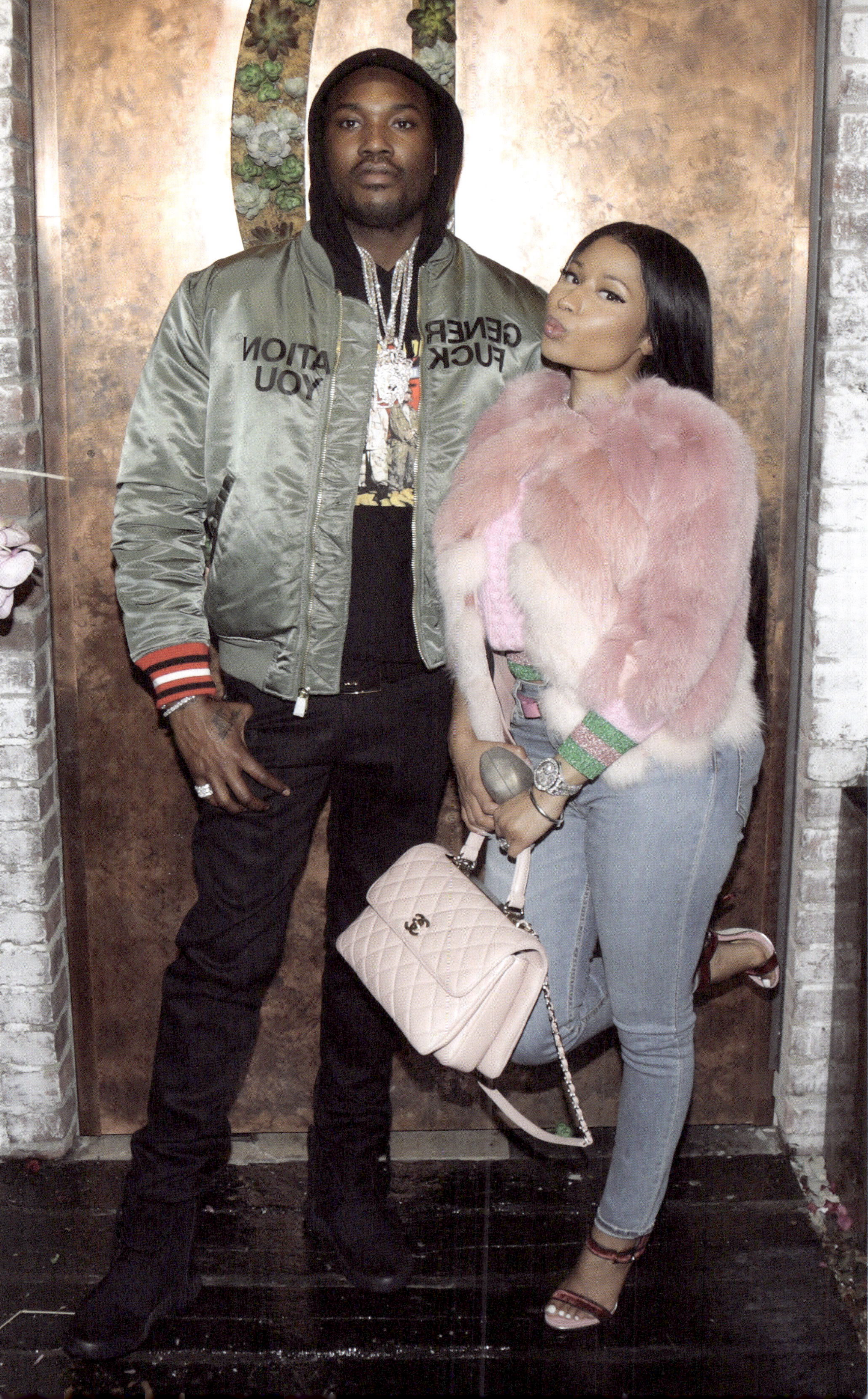
ATION
YOU
GENER
FUCK

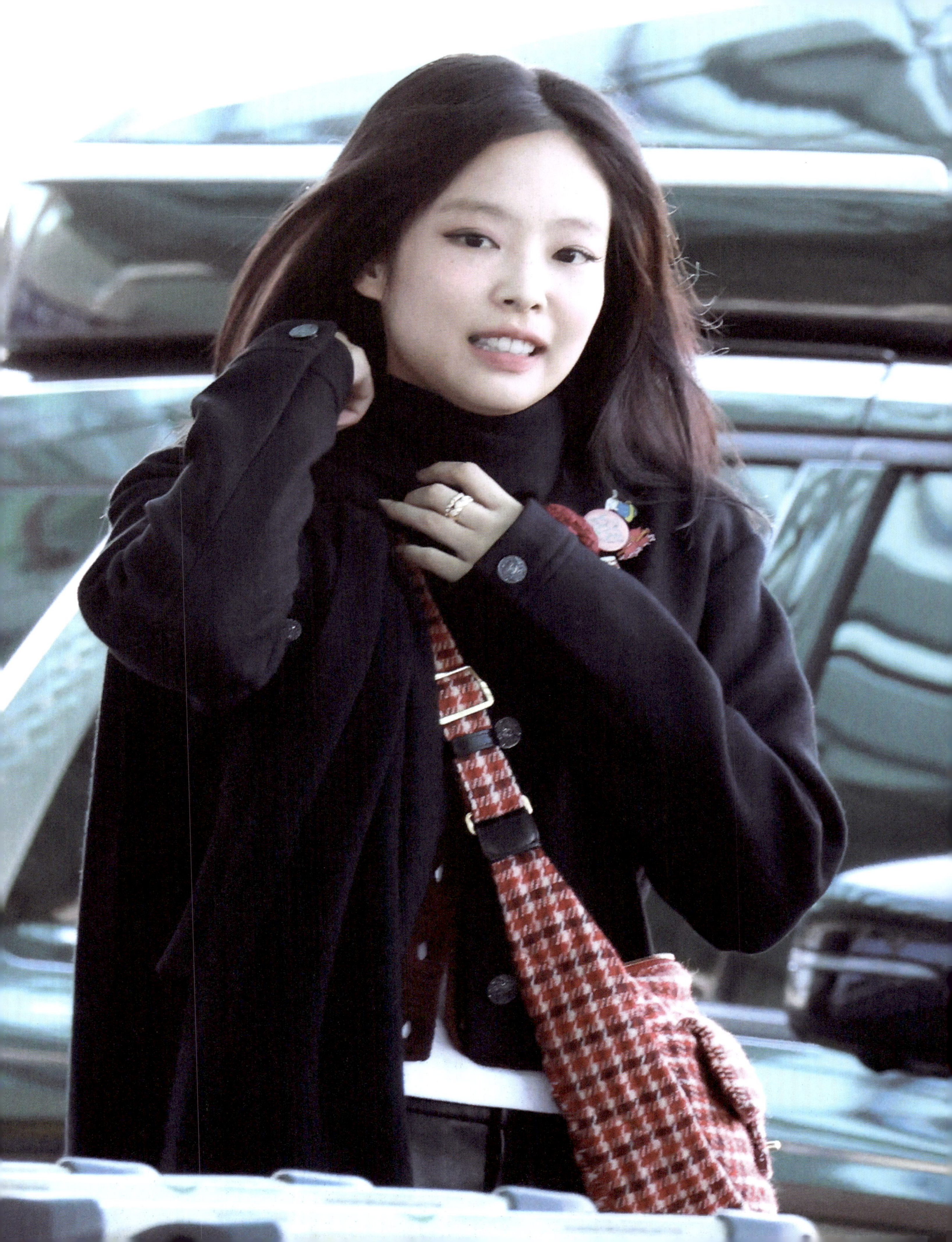

JENNIE KIM, SINGER IN BLACKPINK, WAS NAMED AS BRAND AMBASSADOR IN 2017

This page: Lily Collins is seen exiting the Chanel store on rue Cambon with a Girl bag in Paris, 2015

Next page: Whitney Peak departs the Chanel Fall/Winter 2023 fashion show with a pale pink vanity case in Paris, 2023

Page 164: Nicki Minaj is observed at Charles-de-Gaulle airport with a Chanel Gabrielle bag and a Chanel backpack in Paris, 2018

Page 165: Cameron Diaz is pictured with her Cerf Tote in New York City, 2011

Page 166: Paris Hilton arrives at the Chanel Cruise 2023 fashion show at Paramount Studios in Los Angeles carrying a pale pink tweed top handle bag, 2023

Page 167: Betty Bachz, holding a WOC, attends the private viewing of "Gabrielle Chanel. Fashion Manifesto" at The V&A on September 13, 2023 in London

Pages 168/169: Close-up of a rainbow-colored Classic Flap, Paris, 2023

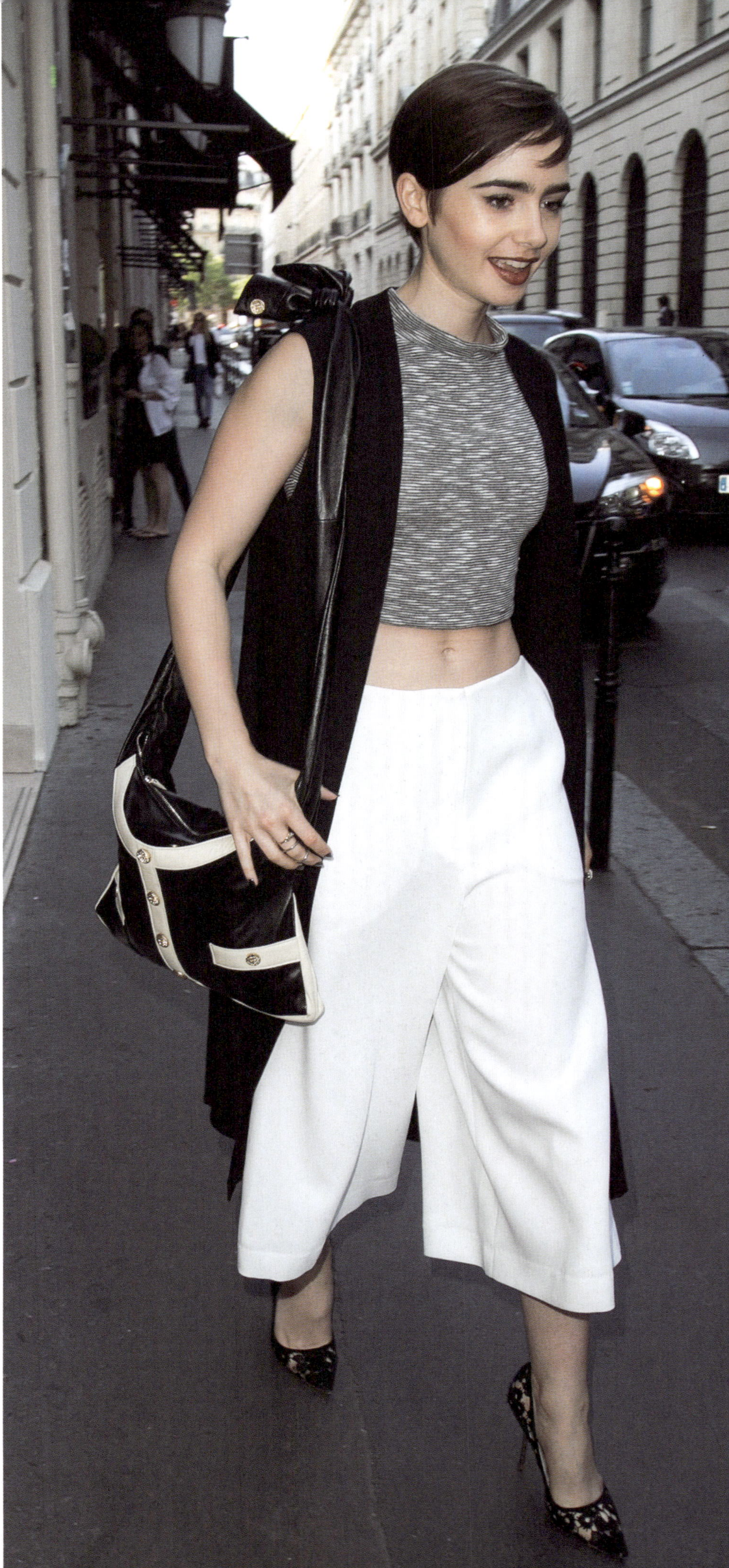

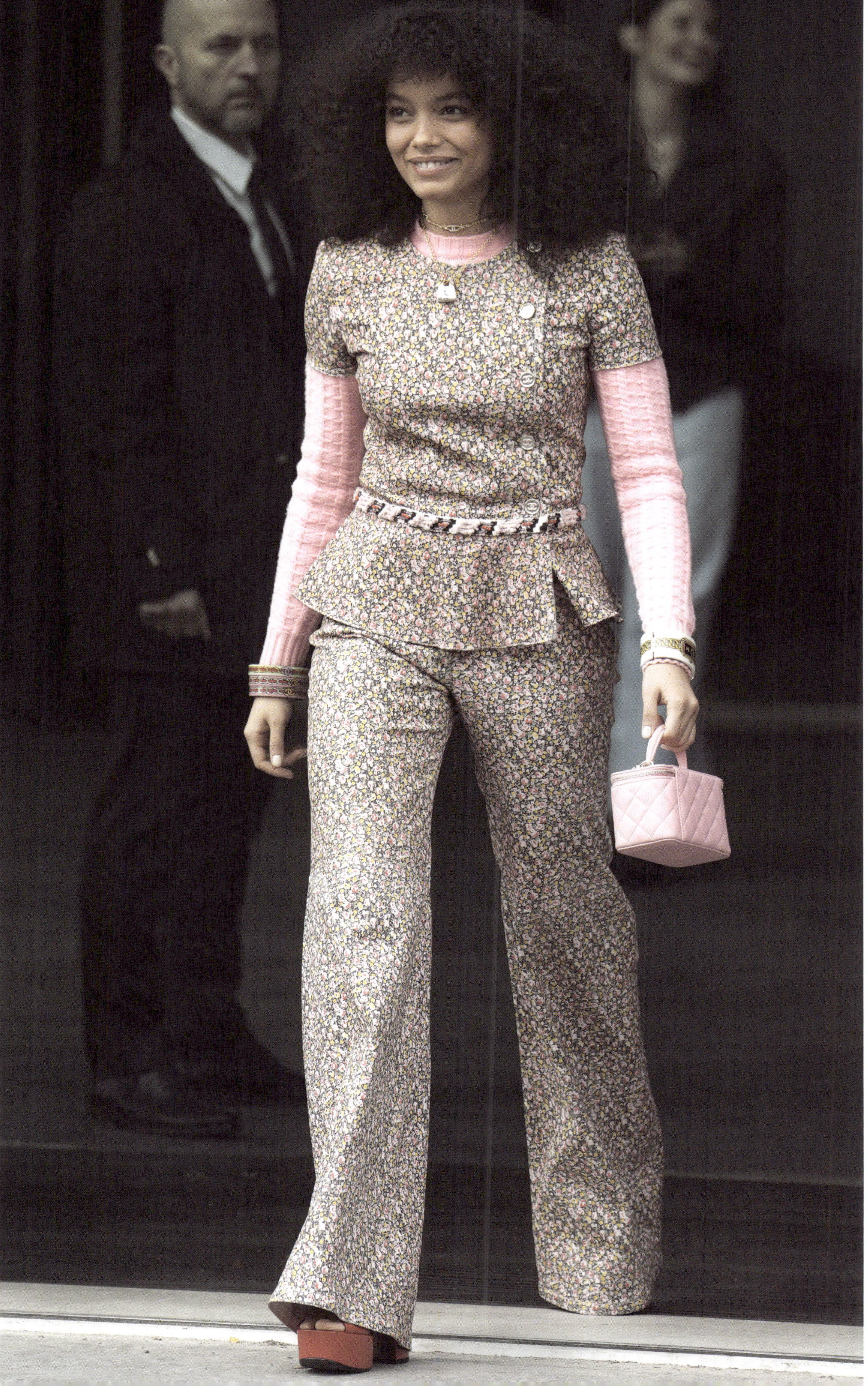

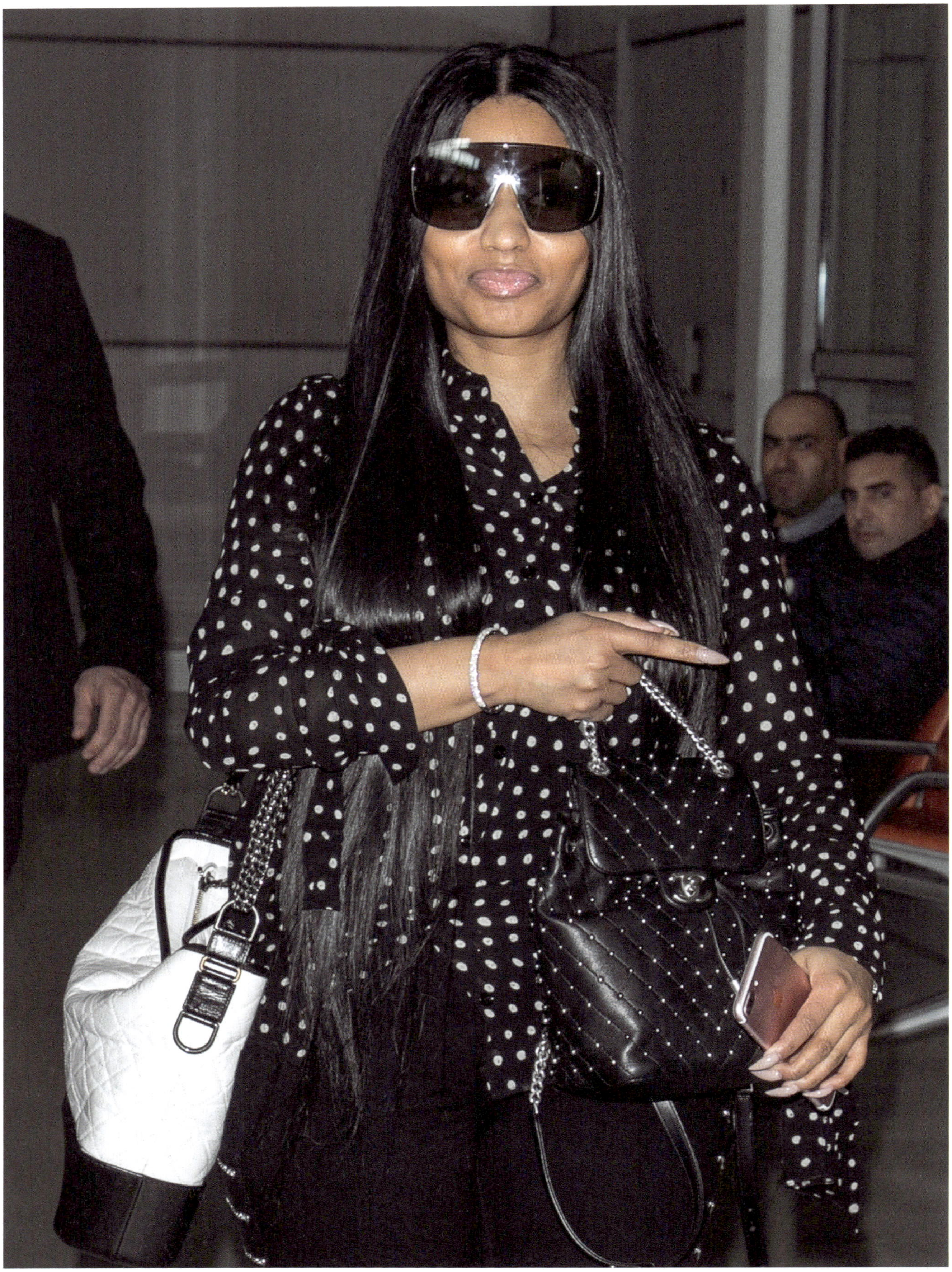

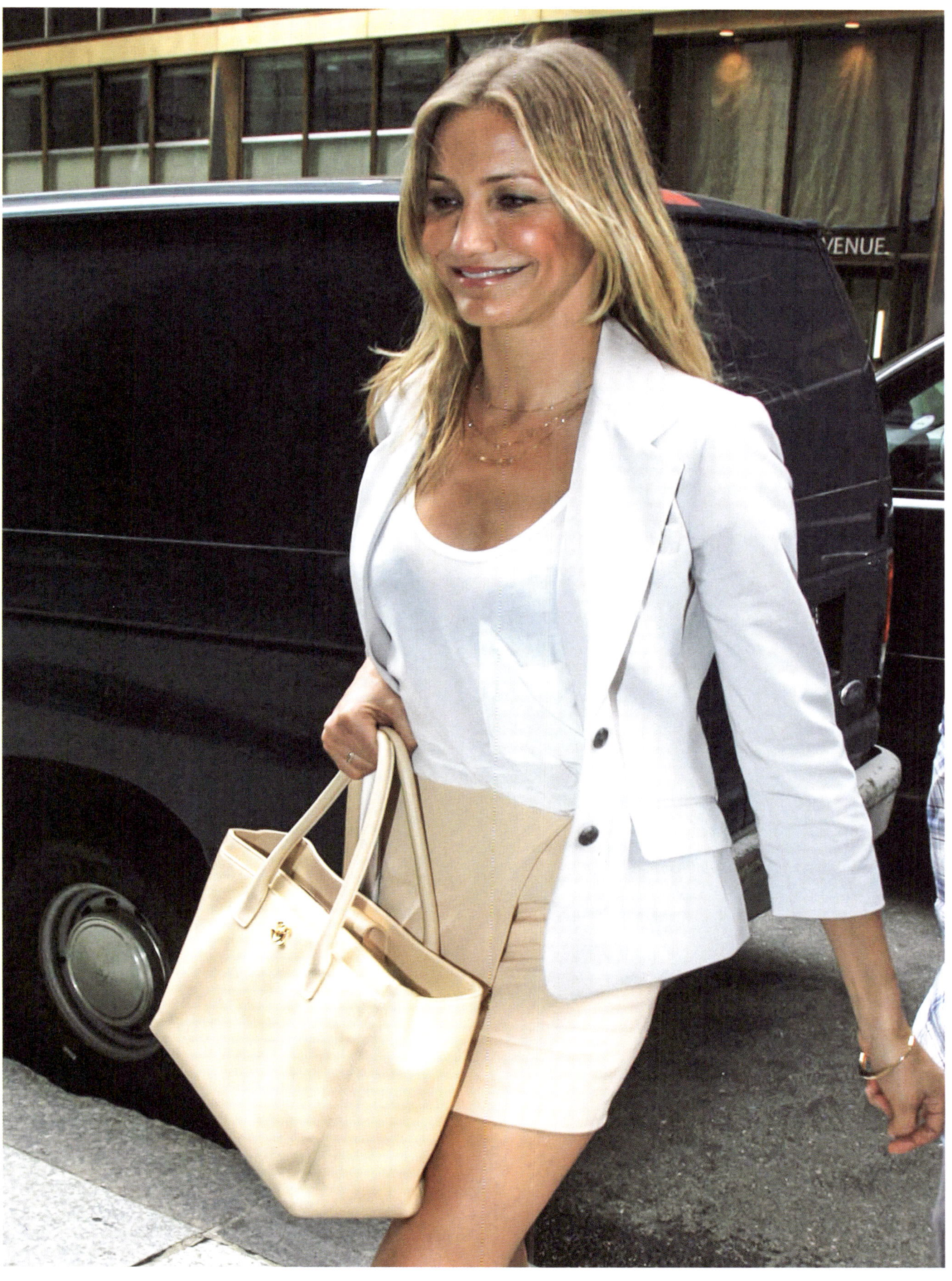
VENUE

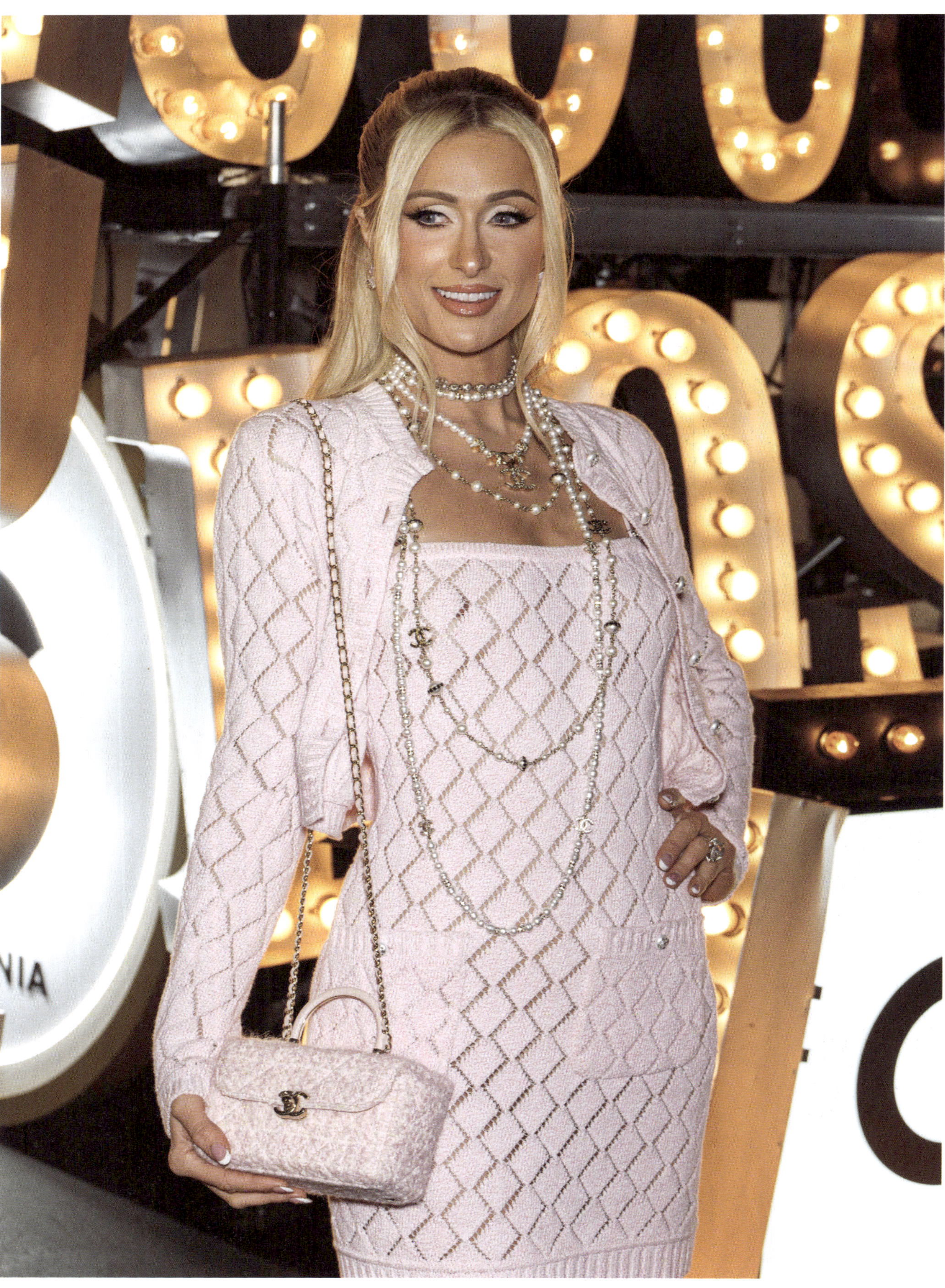
NIA

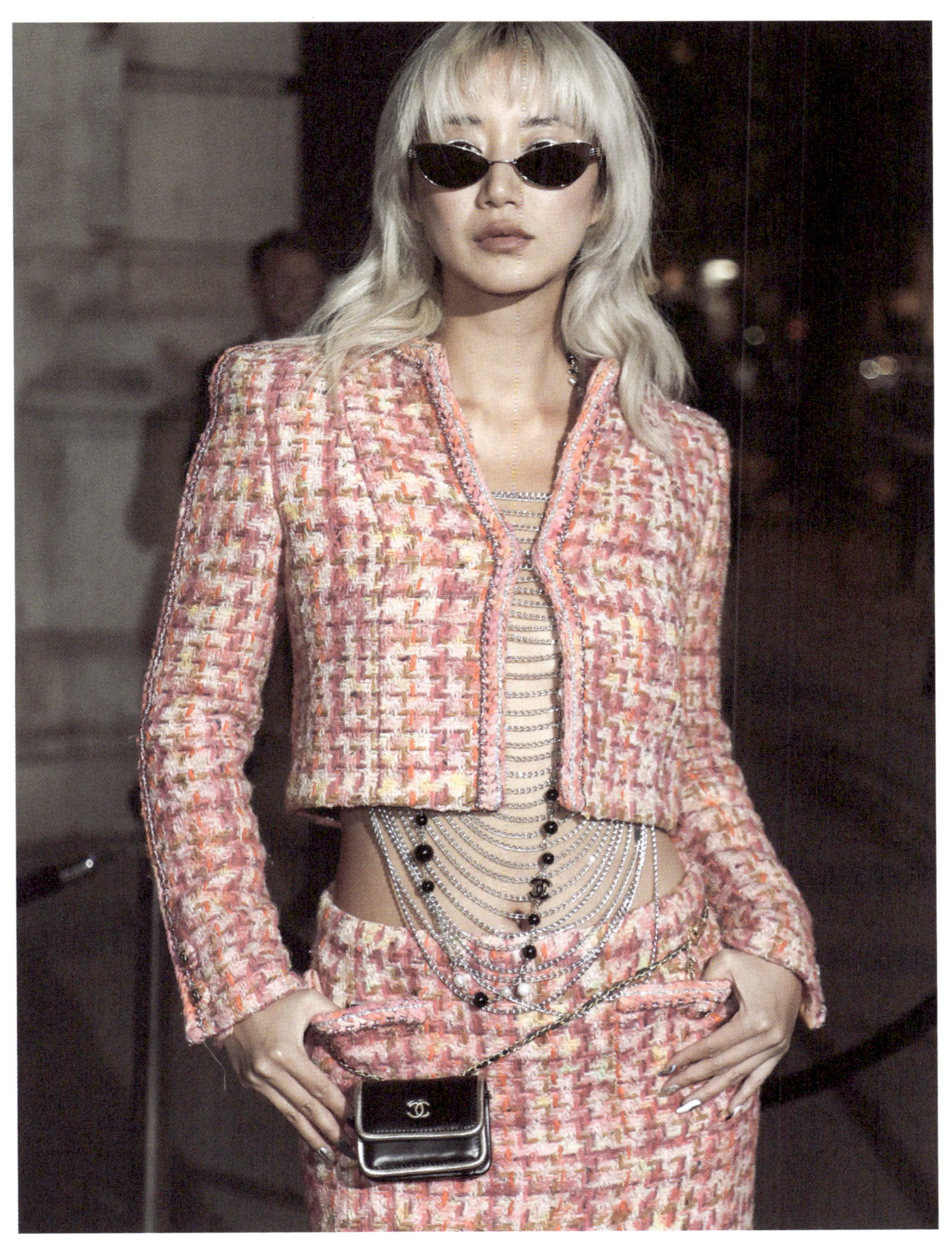

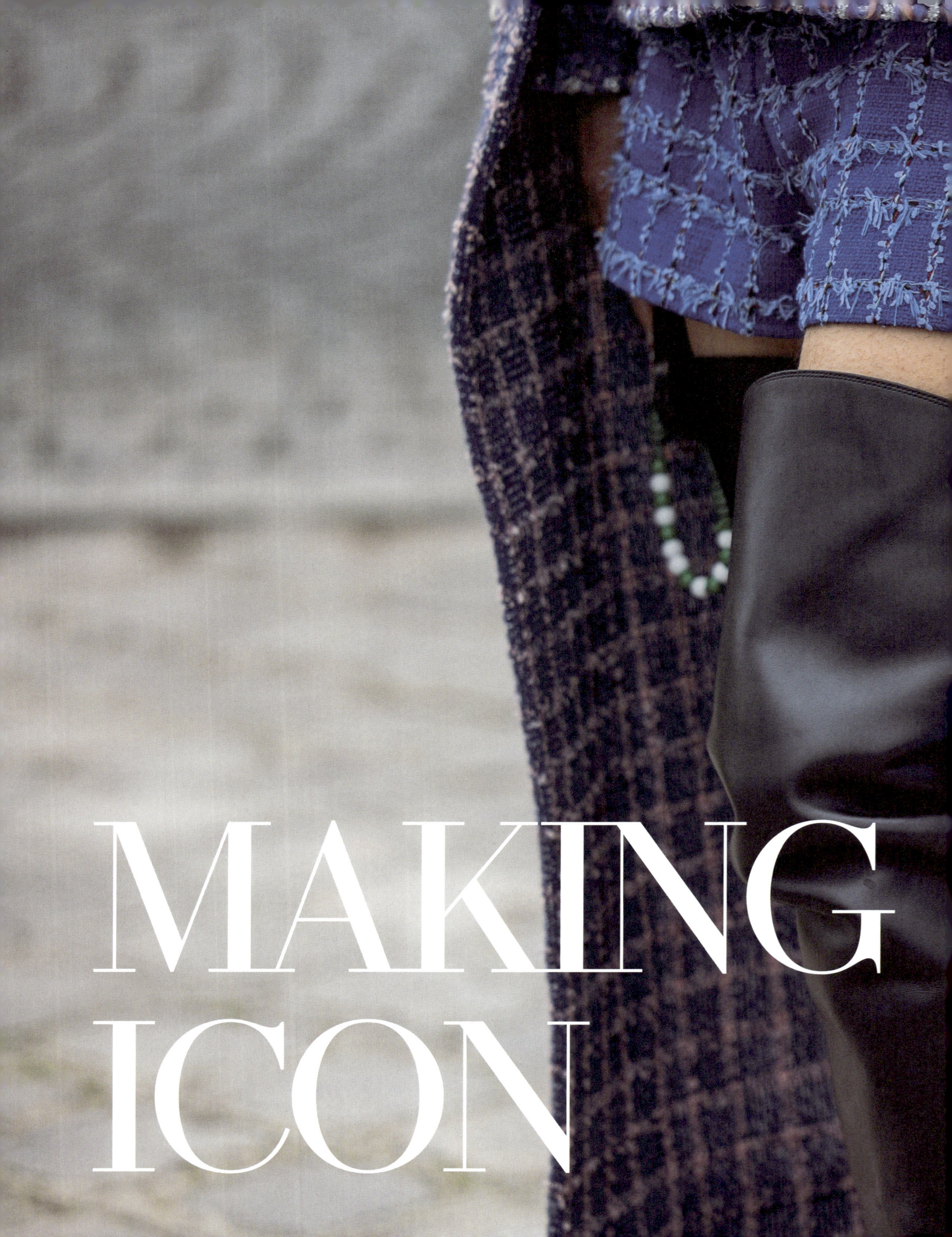

MAKING ICON

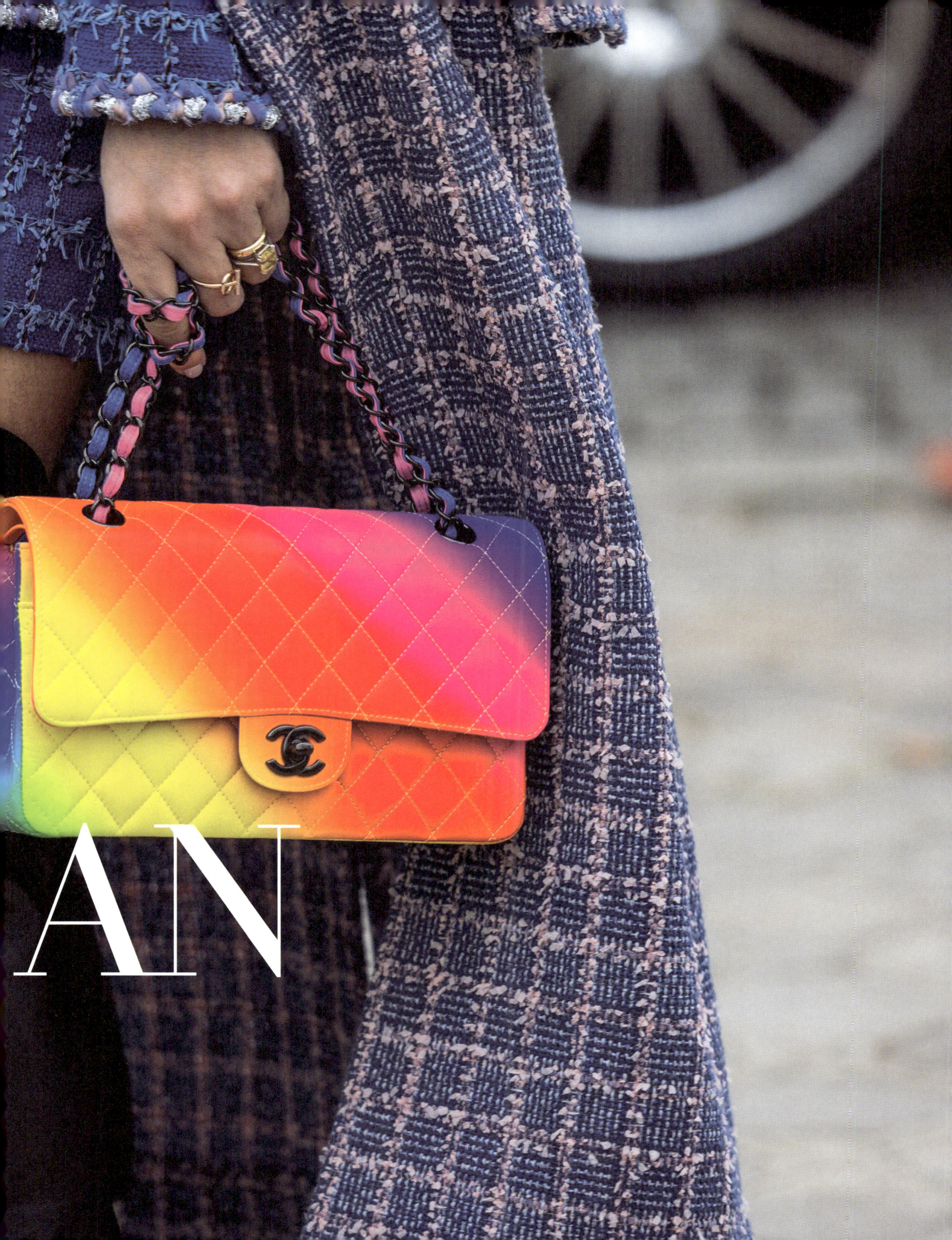
AN

THE CRAFT OF CHANEL

The allure of Chanel is multifaceted, but the combination of craftsmanship and high-quality materials required to create each piece surely plays a significant role. Most bags are made at Les Ateliers de Verneuil-en-Halatte, a slick warehouse north of Paris, where visitors are tightly monitored and the building has a secretive air akin to Willy Wonka's chocolate factory.

Creating a Chanel bag requires trained artisans who build the bags by hand and oversee certain machine-led processes. The *savoir faire* needed to make bags of such high quality takes time. Employees undergo four to five years of rigorous training to ensure they are able to make the immaculate accessories the house is famous for. Chanel does *not* tolerate—or sell—'seconds.' Depending on the specific style, up to 15 different artisans may work on each bag, spending 18 hours on production. Bags can also undergo 180 different procedures from ideation to creation.

As Chanel's fame has grown, so too has their vulnerability to counterfeiters. Therefore, the exact details that go into each bag's design are kept under wraps, and the *maison* has developed many ways to stay several steps ahead of the fake-makers, introducing new details and shapes each season.

Although illegal, there is a misguided belief that fake bags are a victimless crime. *Harper's BAZAAR* launched a campaign in 2007 to raise awareness that the counterfeit trade is also linked to child labor, human trafficking, forced sex work, drug production and terrorism. While some fakes may look good, the quality is always inferior to an authentic item, and some items have been found to include high levels of dangerous chemicals. Fakes are *never* in fashion.

Beyond making a purchase from a Chanel store, those looking to invest in a Chanel bag have a few ways to ensure authenticity. Shopping at a credible retailer is a start. Many purveyors of pre-loved pieces have sophisticated verification strategies that can validate a bag's provenance. The Entrupy method, which employs a combination of AI and microscopy, is 99.1% accurate and is widely used at pre-owned retailers.

If you are shopping online, beware of stores with multiples of the exact same item and too-good-to-be-true prices. In every shopping situation, check the bag's original accessories. Beyond a receipt, Chanel bags will come in a dust bag with an authentication card, although these can also be faked. While a card may be real, it may not match the bag being sold. Cards should be printed immaculately with even spacing. The language should be correct; fakes sometimes use incorrect grammar or syntax.

Serial numbers are one of the easiest ways to confirm a pre-owned bag is a genuine Chanel and also allow you to determine the bag's production date. Check that the date of manufacture matches the style, and double-check when that specific style was made. Ensure

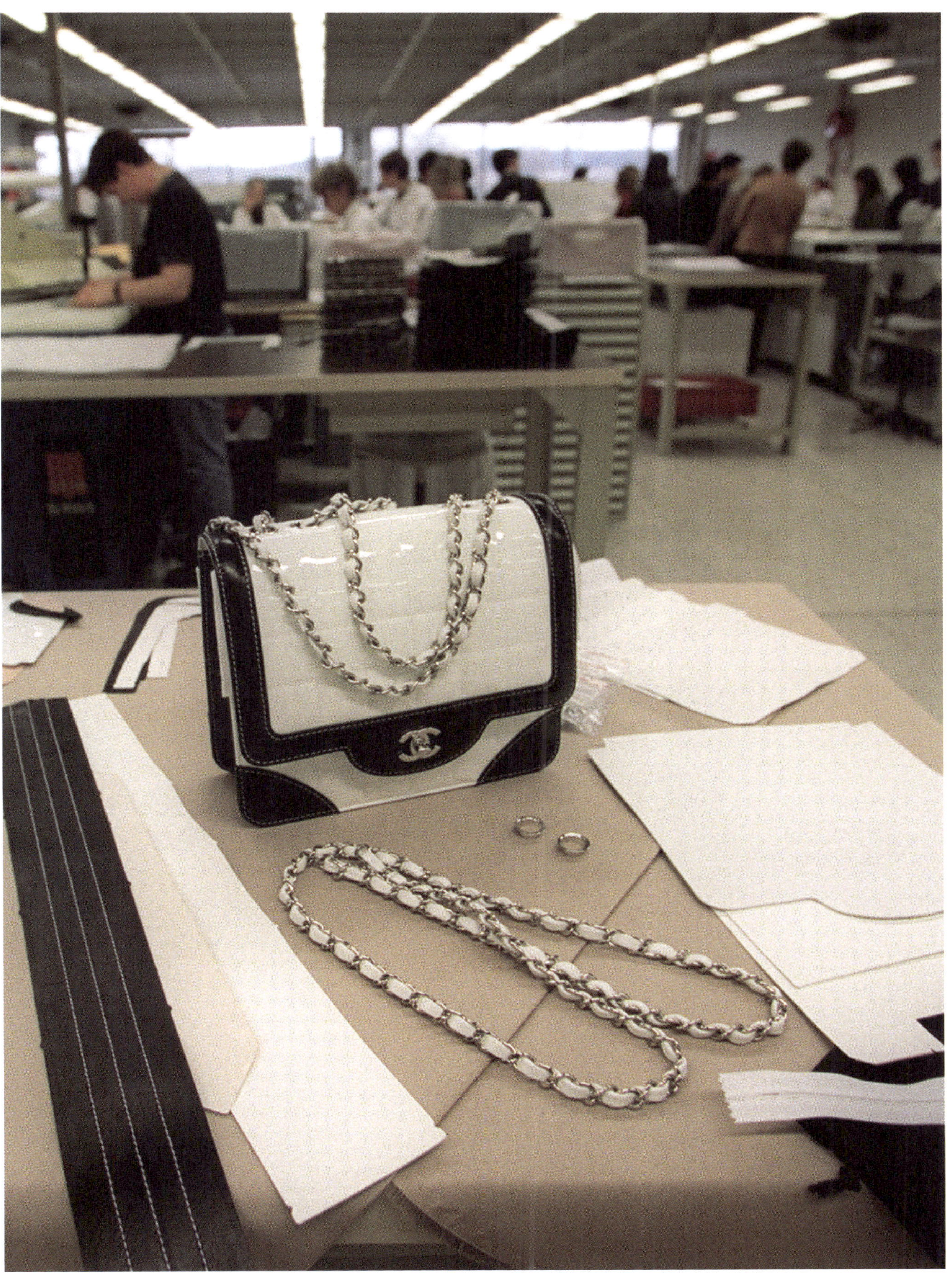

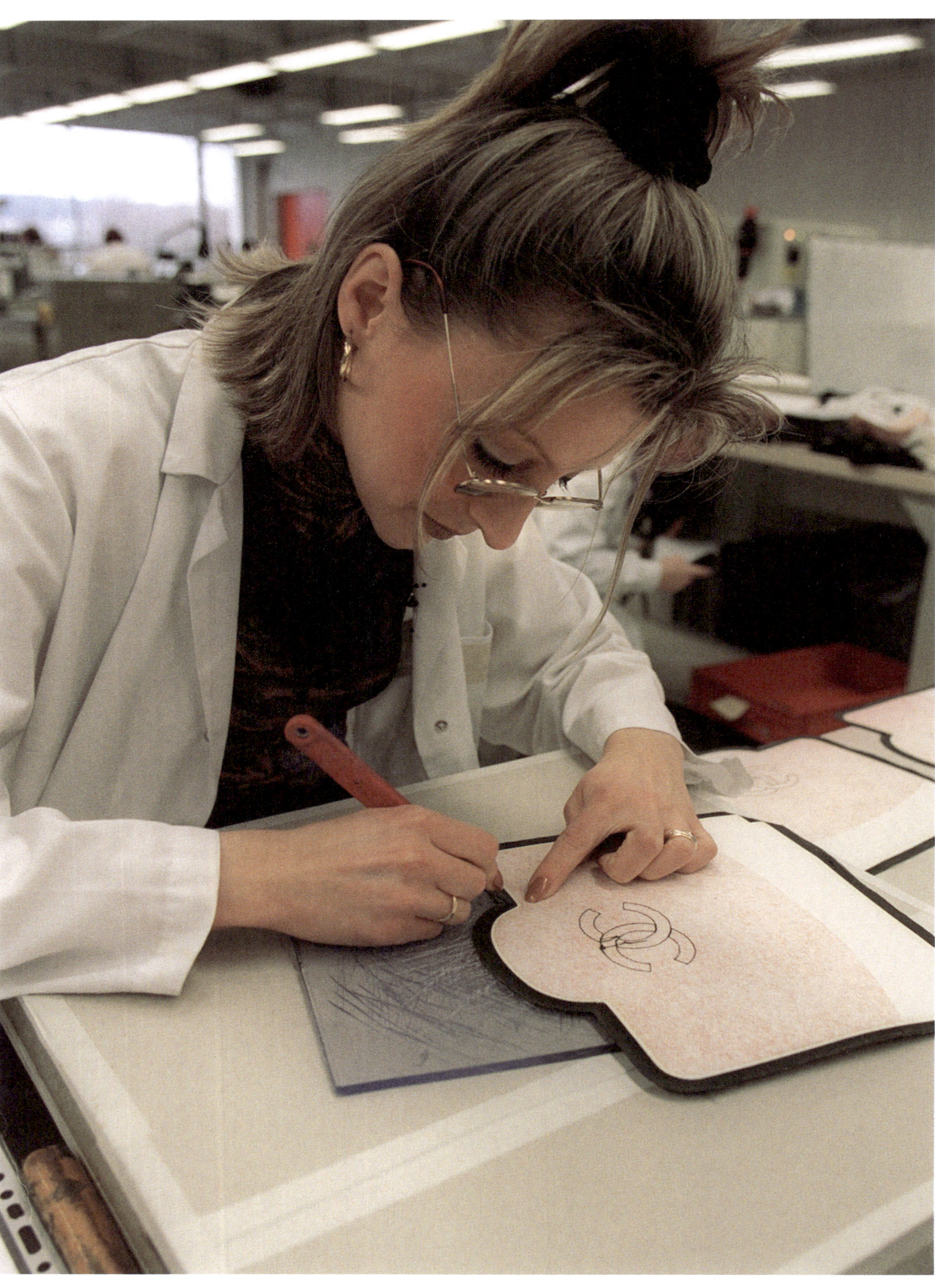

the serial numbers on the card and bag match, too. Serial numbers were introduced in 1986 when a numbered sticker was placed in each bag.

Over the years the numbers increased in sequence with the initial digits increasing from 0, 1, 2 and so on. By 2010, at the 13 series, Chanel was producing so many bags that a serial sticker no longer sufficed. From the early 2000s, serial stickers were protected by a hologram on a piece of clear tape. Sometimes the stickers had several interlocking double CC logos on them too, or came with fine golden speckles in the finish. You can further authenticate your bag by checking whether the 0s have strikethroughs, or whether the 1s are in a serif style, and cross-checking this against the supposed year of manufacture. Be aware that the protective film can sometimes detach, especially on older bags. Metal serial plates were introduced in 2021, and these are now linked to a microchip, which is read by Chanel's computer system and provides secure verification.

For each style of bag, Chanel may use a different method of quilting. The number of stitches can vary depending on the style and the age of the bag, but there will never be loose threads, wonky stitches or misaligned quilting. There should never be fewer than 10 stitches per row of quilting. If the bag of your dreams has a leather-threaded chain, Chanel uses four specific techniques to ensure a clean, neat finish; fake finishes look lumpy. For any zip fastenings, a real bag will always have a Lampo metal-toothed zipper. Counterfeiters often skip this detail to use a cheaper zipper instead.

Smelling the bag may be one of the quickest ways to determine authenticity. Fakes often have a synthetic aroma of glue and plastic, rather than rich, real leather. They also may be unrealistically rigid, indicating a cardboard-based structure, or overly floppy with no structure at all. Inside, check the quality of the lining—whether fabric or leather—and note the stitching and detail. On real Chanel bags, the finish will be tight and lie flat with immaculate stitching.

With an interlocking double CC clasp, the right C overlaps the left at the top, and this detail is reversed at the bottom. That's a reliable indicator of an authentic bag, but the hidden elements are just as important to Chanel. Tiny screws in the backplate of the clasp are either flathead or star-shaped; the supplier makes them exclusively for Chanel. All of the remaining hardware should be smooth and lie flat against the bag's fabric.

The interior leather stamp is included on either a leather patch or an embossed brand stamp. The logo should always be printed in capitals, accompanied by a ™ logo, and "Made In Italy" or "Made In France," depending on the specific bag style. Stamps that aren't embossed or mention a city rather than a country are fake. Likewise, make sure the hardware color is consistent throughout the bag and that the colorway matches the stamp.

As with any high-value purchase, it pays for the buyer to be aware of all of the details above before parting with their money. Buying a brand new bag from Chanel is obviously the safest option, but beyond new season items, searching for pre-owned items can give the shopper a wider choice of rare or limited edition pieces along with the possibility of securing a lower price than current items. Chanel doesn't sell their bags online, but if you can find a reputable retailer, the ease of 'add to cart' can work wonders.

So, where to start the search for a Chanel bag? Online auction sites and community marketplaces such as Vinted and eBay are working hard to ensure fakes are removed from their sites, and both have recently introduced an extra level of physical inspection and authentication for further peace of mind for buyers. However, there are also specific retailers that only deal with high-end designer fashion. Vestiaire Collective sells items from individuals as well as taking pieces on consignment from high-profile names in the fashion industry and offers individual item authentication. Sellier, Love Luxury and 1st Dibs are all specialist stores carrying a mix of classic pieces and rare items that collectors crave. Eager to be part of the boom in pre-loved fashion, which is predicted to be a $100 billion market by 2026, traditional department stores are also partnering with resale businesses to offer pre-owned bags. The Handbag Clinic is the UK's longest standing independent luxury bag restorer, but it also offers bags for sale at Fenwick, and you can even find some pre-owned designer brands on Amazon and TK Maxx.

It's sensible to consider renting a bag to get a feel for the authentic details before making such a significant purchase. By Rotation offers peer-to-peer rentals on their game-changing app. Bag Borrow or Steal is US based—and had a cameo appearance in the *Sex and the City* movie (2008). Cocoon Club is dedicated solely to designer handbag rentals (you can purchase pieces that have been rented, too).

Beyond something borrowed, auctions offer an adrenaline rush *and* a glorious chance to find an incredible bag that no one else will own. Depending on your budget, you may find the simplest, smallest Classic Flap at a sale near you with a reserve of a couple of thousand pounds. However, prices skyrocket for the most intricate and sought-after designs. The most expensive Chanel bag sold at auction—and the highest priced Chanel bag ever—was designed by Karl Lagerfeld in 2008. Following the silhouette of a Classic Flap bag, only 13 Diamond Forever bags were ever made. As one would expect from the name, each one is encrusted with 334 diamonds on the clasp weighing a total of 3.56 carats. To match its white gold hardware, the alligator leather bag also had a chain made of 18-karat gold. With the winning bid coming in at $261,000, it was auctioned for amfAR's Cinema Against Aids benefit dinner. Madonna carried the bag at auction, including a personal touch for the winning bidder—a handkerchief with a kiss, and her own red lipstick.

After Karl Lagerfeld's death, it was his own Chanel bag that commanded the highest price at auction. Lagerfeld famously said, "In Chanel, I look like my mother" and the designer rarely wore his own designs, although his embellished fingerless gloves and his brooches are exceptions to the rule. The black crocodile embossed lambskin tote had over 500 bidders vying for ownership of the rare prototype, which was never presented on the runway or sold in Chanel's boutiques. As such, the bag was utterly unique and a piece of fashion design history. It sold for $107,000.

Other than the charity auction, Chanel's priciest bag at auction was the black lucite Matryoshka evening bag with gold hardware from the Métiers D'Art Paris-Shanghai collection of pre-Fall 2010. The show was inspired by all things Chinese, and the resulting *minaudière* fetched a record-breaking $32,500 at Christie's New York in 2018. If you are looking for tips on where to invest next, Chanel Kelly bags are some of the consistently most expensive pieces and are currently experiencing a resurgence. Originally created in the 1990s,

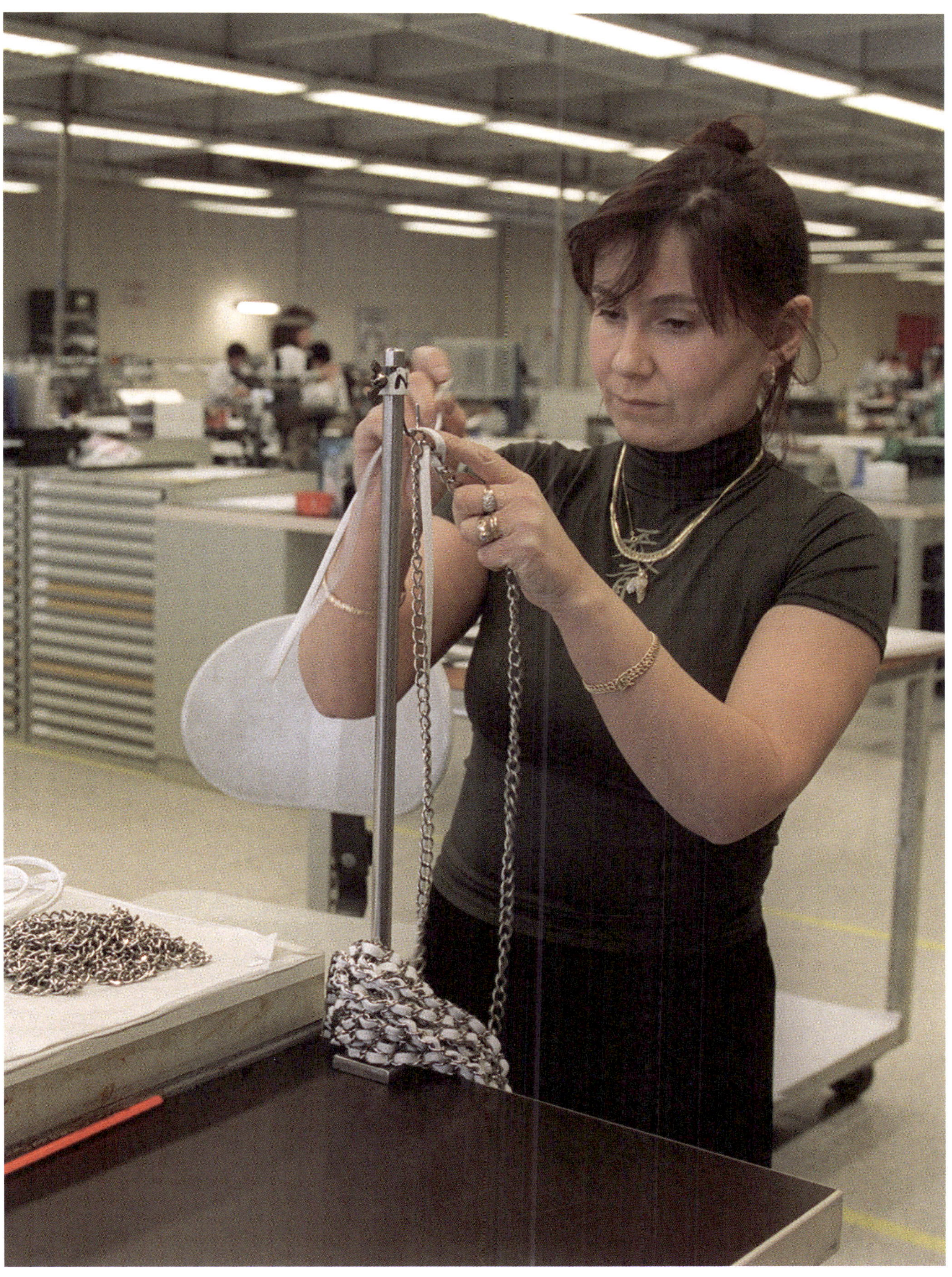

Chanel reinstated the Mini Nano Kelly in 2023, and both the reissues and the vintage originals have been hot commodities ever since. A Green Crocodile Mini Kelly from 1997 is currently for sale on 1stDibs.com for $220,900. Some predict that Kelly styles will become a classic on the collector's market, although it should be noted that Chanel stopped the use of all exotic skins—such as crocodile or alligator—in 2019.

Fantasy-worthy auction prices notwithstanding, a Chanel purchase is still a sound investment. While luxury brands are suffering from a global financial downturn, Credit Suisse has suggested that high-end handbags will outperform art and jewelry purchases in coming years. The designer bag market is projected to grow to $42 billion by 2029. With a clever purchase, and by keeping your bag box-fresh with all *accoutrements*, you could secure a healthy return on your investment. Chanel bags hold their value and appreciate over time. The downside is, of course, that you could never wear your bag, which would be no fun.

Perhaps one of the reasons Chanel remains so successful is their fabled annual price increases estimated at approximately $800-$1000 per bag in 2025. The price of a medium 11.12 bag increased by 140% between 2010 and 2021, and most bag prices were raised by 6% in 2024.

There are several reasons why Chanel increases their prices, one of which is their desire to remain exclusive. This may explain why they discontinued bags like the Grand Shopping Tote to concentrate on producing more expensive models. Material costs are increasing right along with labor costs and production costs, so Chanel needs to raise their prices to reflect this. Chanel bags are also some of the most in-demand bags in the world, and the repeated price increases have failed to quash demand. The brand's timeless allure, its storied history and its exciting future make Chanel a forever buy. If you want to secure the most favorable financing for your Chanel purchase, *now* is always the best time to invest in Chanel.

Pages 171–177: In February 2001, Chanel's workshop in Verneuil-en-Halatte (Oise) produces its iconic bags through a detailed process. A worker cuts leather slabs for one of the 70 pieces needed for a bag, which involves 253 operations taking four hours from cutting to packaging. The latest model, reference 16.524, continues the legacy of the Chanel bag introduced in 1955. The process begins with selecting lamb or calf skins and involves gluing, trimming, reinforcing, and quilting. Each bag ultimately receives its logo, eyelets, clasps, and a certificate of authenticity before being numbered and packaged. This factory employs 350 people, making it the primary site for Chanel bag production.

Pages 184/185: Jewelry Box *minaudière*, showcased during Paris Fashion Week, 2019

Pages 188/189: La Pausa Coco Lifesaver round bags from the Cruise 2019 collection, Paris Fashion Week, 2019

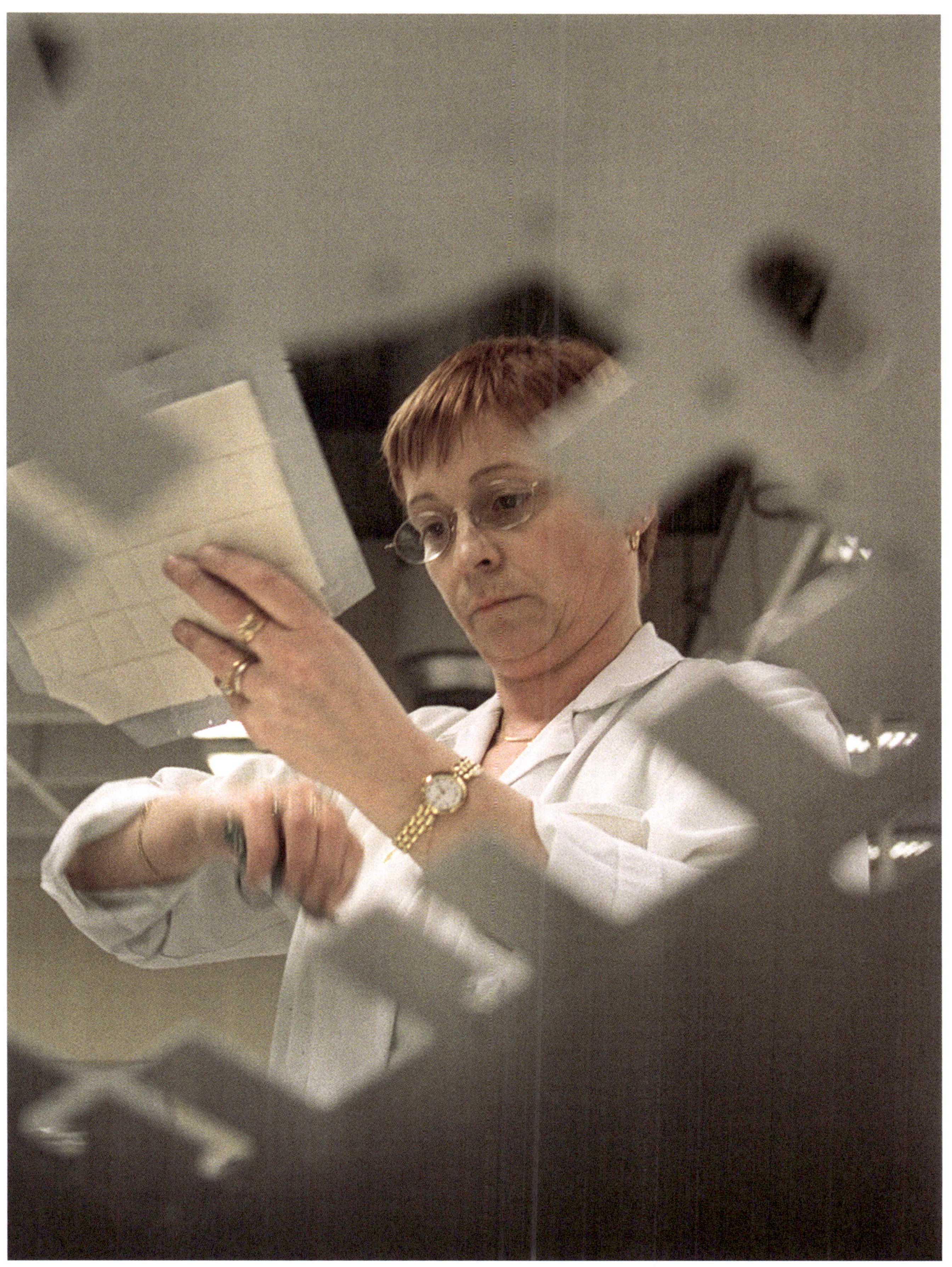

BUYING CHANEL AT AUCTION

Q&A with Meg Randell, Head of Bonhams Designer Handbags and Fashion Department

How do you assess the condition of a bag?

Condition is crucial when it comes to value, so we carry out a thorough assessment of each bag—both inside and out—before offering it at auction. There are the obvious things to look out for, such as stains, scratches, scuffs, or any structural damage like broken hardware or loose stitching. But more subtle signs also play a role: creasing, indentations to the leather from storage, loss of shape, fading or dryness in the materials, and general signs of age or use. These aren't always easy to define, but they contribute to an overall impression of how well the bag has been looked after. We also do our best to assess whether a piece has been restored by means such as recoloring because this can affect the bag's value.

Which grades are there and what do they mean?

We assign condition grades to all our bags so that buyers can bid with confidence. These grades provide a quick reference point, but we also offer full, detailed condition reports for every piece. Our grading scale ranges from A+ to D, with A+ representing a bag in perfect, unused condition, often with its original packaging, and D indicating a piece in need of restoration.

How does the selling and purchasing process work?

Typically, those looking to sell their handbag collections will begin by sending images of their pieces. From these photographs, we can usually provide initial auction estimates—subject to in-person inspection—and advise on suitable upcoming sale dates. We hold Luxury Goods auctions three times a year in London, and globally, the department conducts around 35 auctions each year with salerooms in Paris, Hong Kong, Los Angeles and New York. Occasionally, we also host special standalone sales such as the dedicated Chanel auction in 2023.

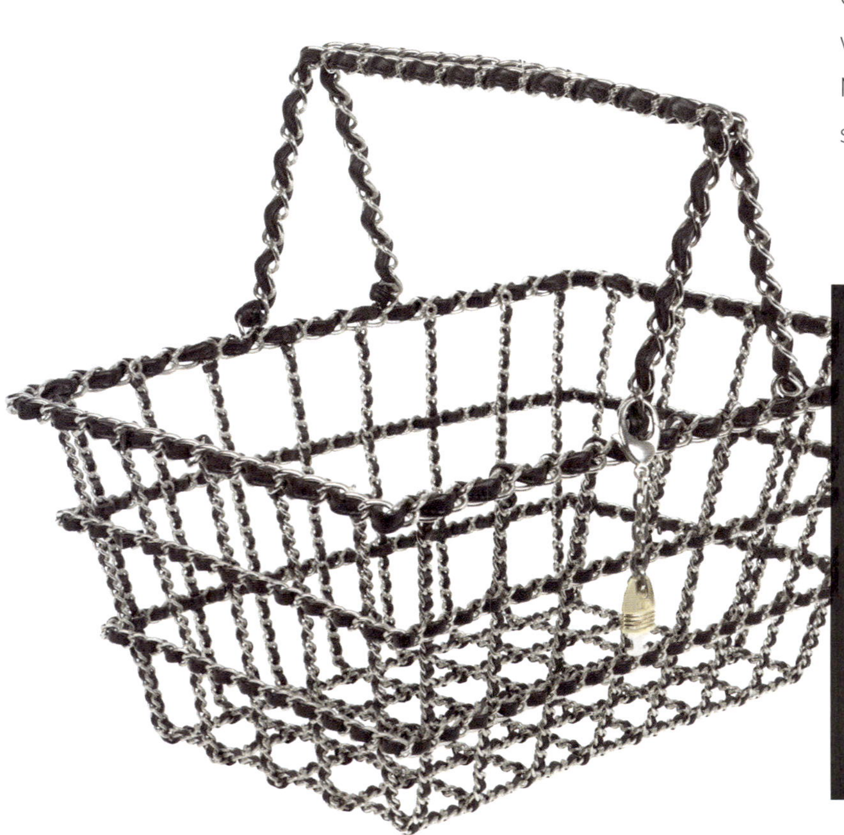

SUPERMARKET SHOPPING BASKET

Year: 2014

Material: Black interwoven leather on silver tone metal frame

This basket was carried down the runway of Chanel's Fall/Winter 2014 "Supermarket" collection

Sold at auction at Bonhams London for £11,520 in 2024

Most of our sales include a public viewing exhibition before the auction, and we always encourage clients to attend in person to view the collection. As a global auction house, we also sell internationally through our website and app, and many buyers choose to participate remotely without seeing the handbags in person. This is why detailed condition reports are essential—they help ensure that all buyers, wherever they are in the world, can bid with confidence.

How many Chanel bags go up for auction each year?
A typical London Luxury auction will have between 40 and 50 Chanel handbags (as well as Chanel accessories and ready-to-wear pieces), but we have also held Chanel-only auctions with 150 handbags, so it can vary quite a bit.

What was the most exceptional (expensive) Chanel bag you've auctioned?
We've offered some truly exceptional pieces over the years, but one of my personal favorites was the Chanel 2014 Supermarket Basket. This example was carried down the runway by a model and was gifted by Karl Lagerfeld himself to the vendor. The baskets are extremely rare, and the fact that it was used on the runway made it extra special. It sold at auction for £11,500, although examples have been listed online for over £100,000. Another standout piece was a black patent leather heart-shaped vanity bag from the Spring/Summer 1995 'Barbie' collection. The bag was part of the dedicated Chanel auction in 2023. It's an incredibly iconic piece by Karl Lagerfeld, and it achieved £17,920 at auction.

BLACK PATENT LEATHER HEART VANITY BAG

Year: 1995

Material: Quilted black patent leather, gold chain and leather threaded top handle

Sold at auction at Bonhams London for £17,920 in 2023

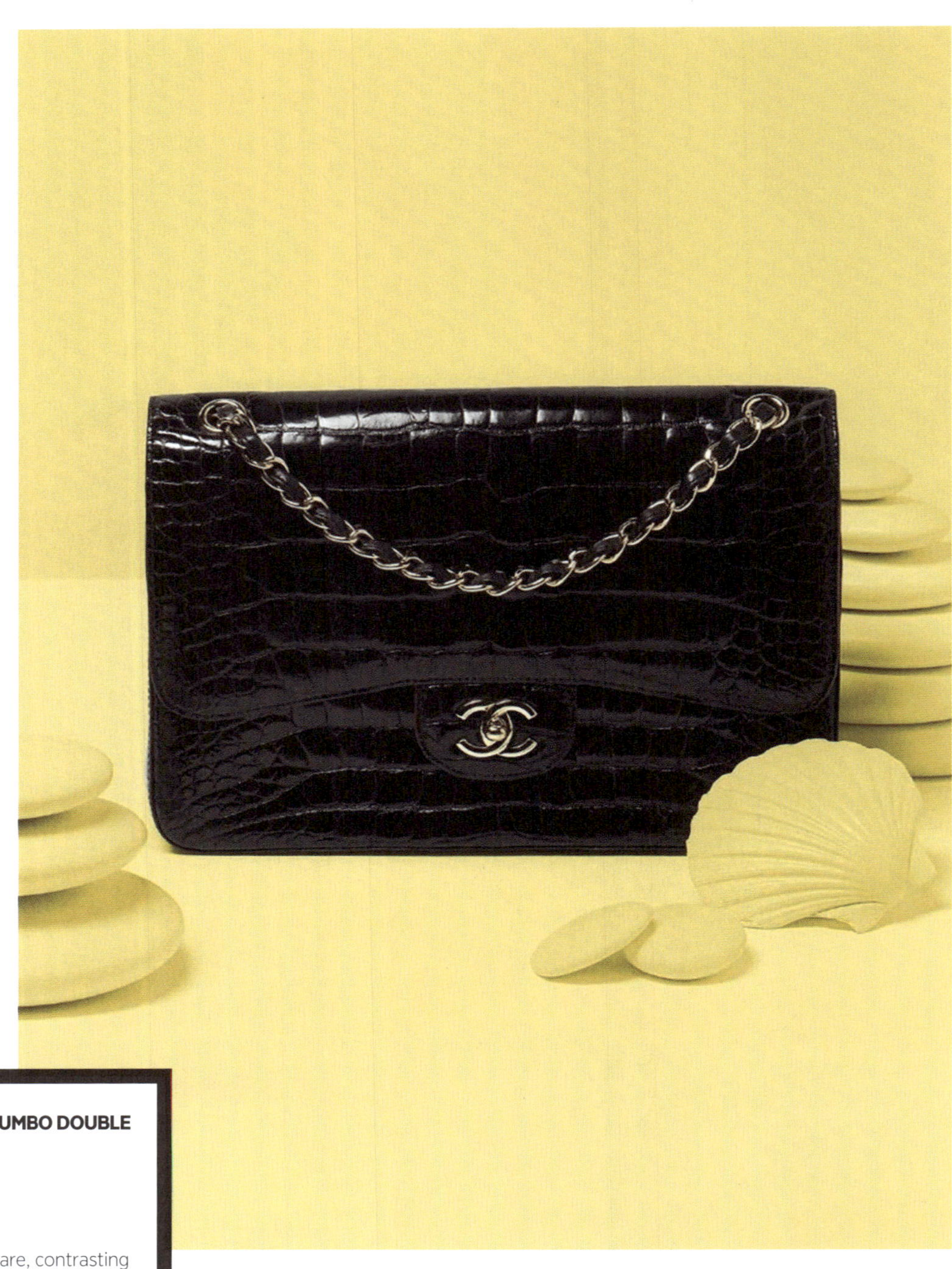

BLACK ALLIGATOR JUMBO DOUBLE FLAP BAG

Year: c. 2010–11

Material: Gold hardware, contrasting red lambskin lined interior

Sold at auction at Bonhams London for £10,200 in 2021

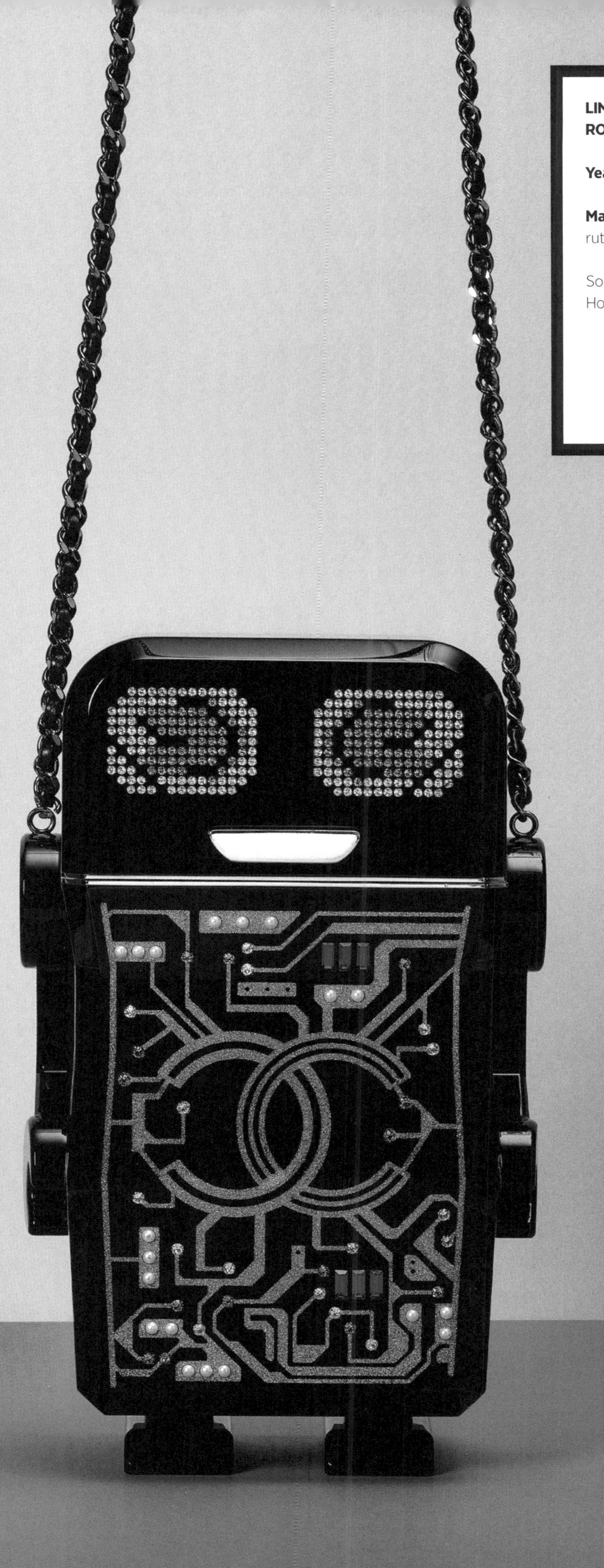

LIMITED EDITION BLACK ROBOT MINAUDIÈRES BAG

Year: 2017–2018

Material: Plexiglass, ruthenium hardware

Sold at online auction with Bonhams Hong Kong for HK$76,800 in 2025

Are there any interesting anecdotes about Chanel bags at auction?

One standout example was a black crocodile Mini Flap bag with the classic CC turn lock closure. What made this piece particularly special—beyond the rarity of the model—was that the vendor still had the original receipt tucked inside the box, showing it had been purchased in December 1987 from the Old Bond Street boutique for £1,490. The bag was offered with an estimate of £4,000–6,000 and achieved £6,650 at auction. A few years following the sale, we were able to facilitate a private sale on behalf of the buyer, as a dedicated collector had been searching for that exact piece. The bag ultimately sold privately for just under £10,000, demonstrating the strong demand for rare and well-documented vintage Chanel items.

What model is most sought after?

Unsurprisingly, the Classic Flap bag remains consistently popular, especially in Caviar leather, which tends to be more durable and resistant to wear than lambskin.

The Diana Flap Bag, named after the late Princess Diana, has seen a resurgence in recent years, becoming increasingly sought after. Prices have risen significantly from around £1,500 a few years ago to £3,000 or more at auction today. Another in-demand model is the Chanel GST (Grand Shopping Tote). Although now discontinued, it remains highly desirable. A recent example in one of our sales had an estimate of £1,500–2,000 and ended up selling for nearly £4,500, demonstrating just how competitive the market can be for classic Chanel styles.

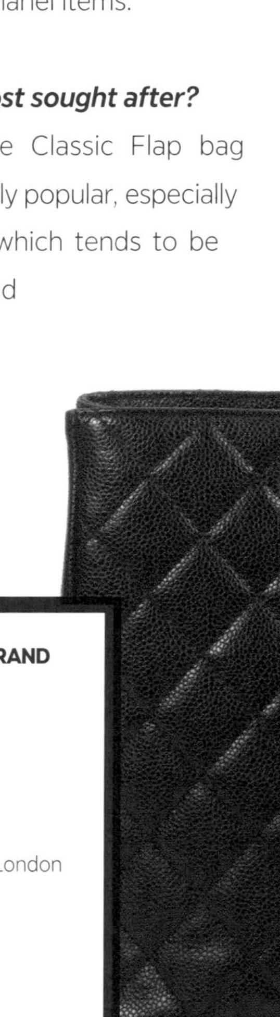

BLACK CAVIAR LEATHER GRAND SHOPPING TOTE (GST)

Year: 2013–2014

Material: Silver hardware

Sold at auction at Bonhams London for £4,480 in 2023

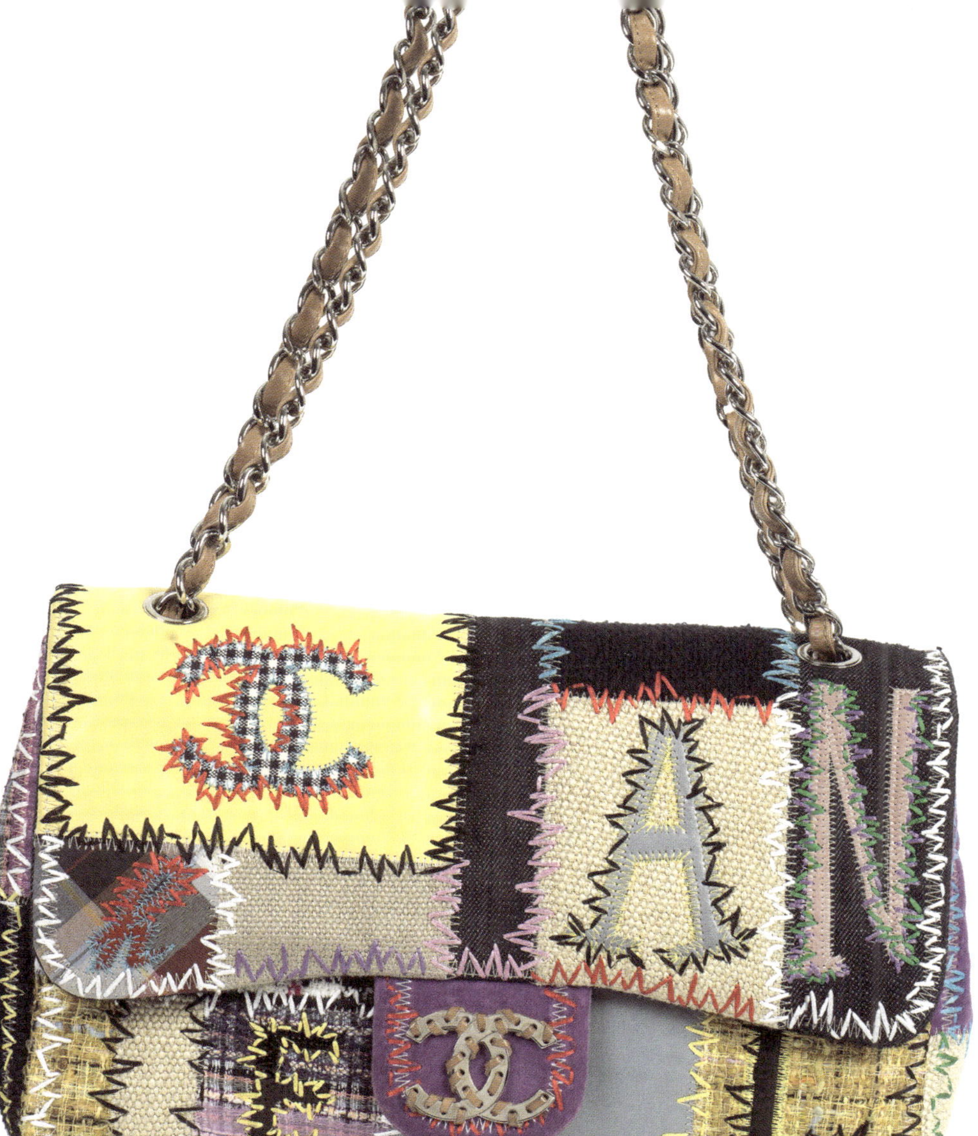

PATCHWORK JUMBO SINGLE FLAP BAG

Year: 2011

Material: Multicolor lambskin, tweed, velvet, and denim embroidered patches, leather woven silver chain shoulder strap and magnetic popper fastening

Sold at auction at Bonhams London for £5,760 in 2023

SMALL VANITY BAG WITH CHAIN

Year: 2021

Material: Quilted lambskin

Sold at auction at Bonhams Hong Kong for HK$20,400 in 2021

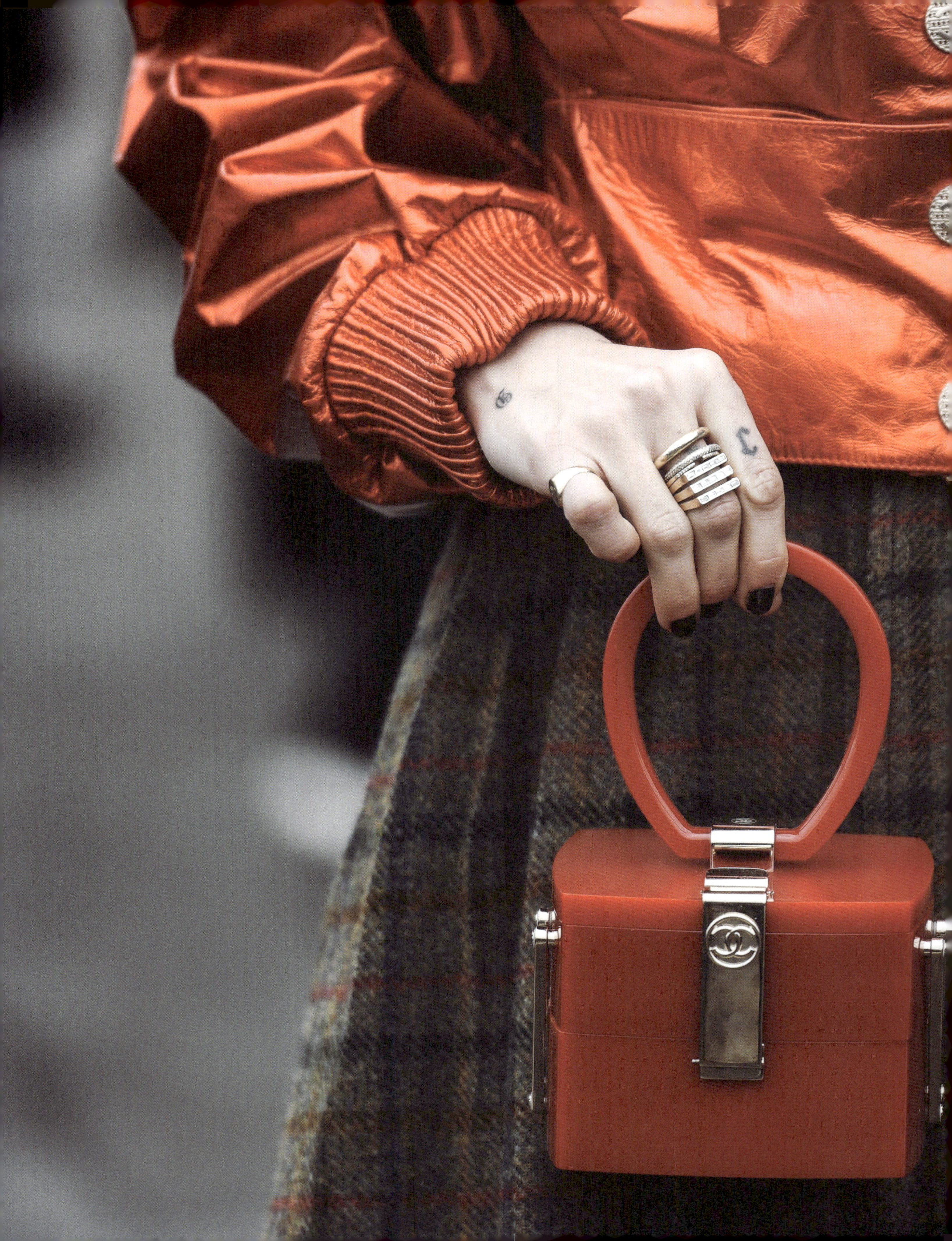

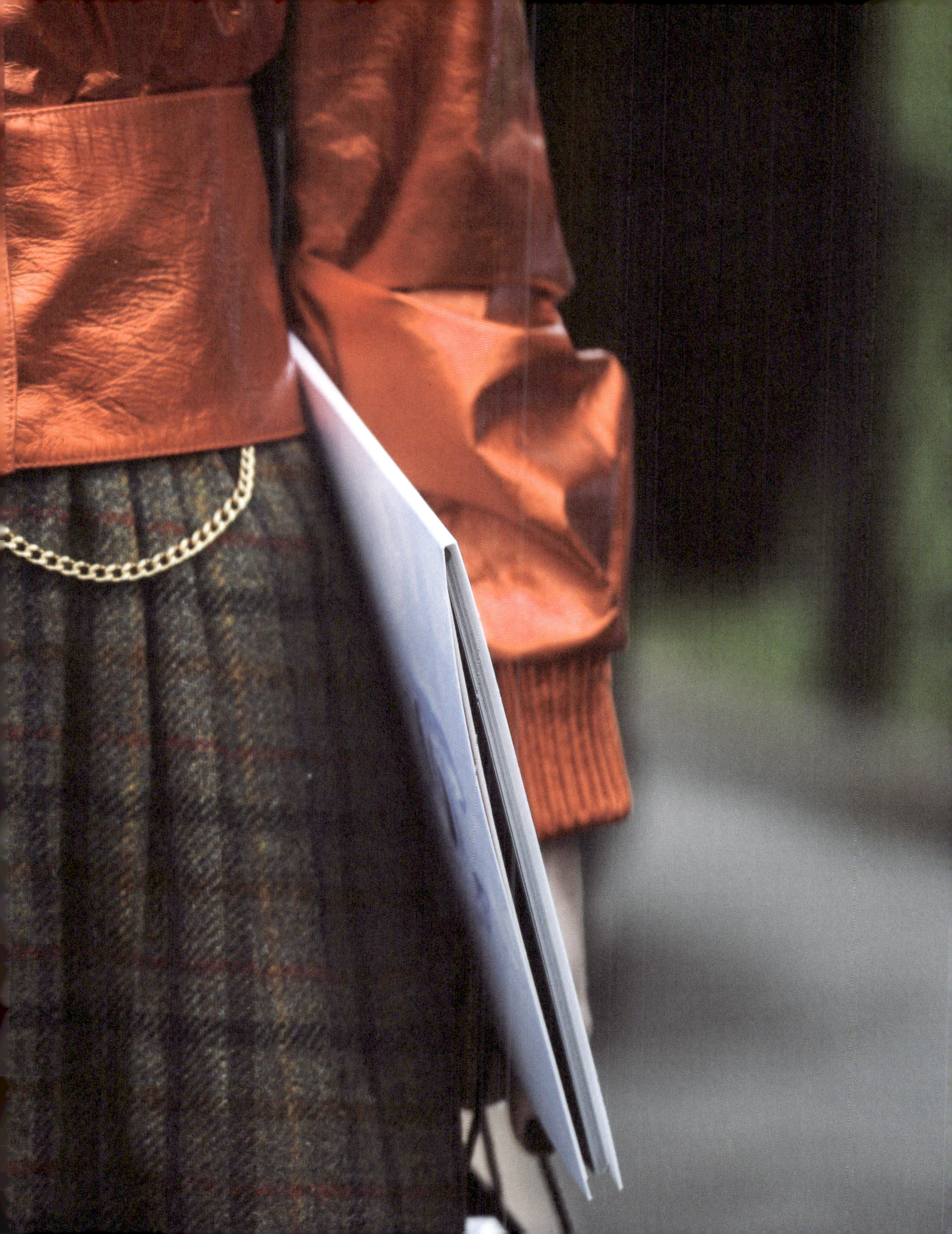

BIBLIOGRAPHY

- The Allure of Chanel, Paul Morans
- Coco Chanel: the Legend and the Life, by Justine Picardie
- Gabrielle Chanel, edited by Oriole Cullen and Connie Karol Burks
- The Story of The Chanel Bag, by Lara Farran Graves
- Vogue Handbags by Carolyn Asome
- Sleeping with the enemy, by Hal Vaughan

RETAILERS

- Chanel http://chanel.com/
- Vinted https://www.vinted.co.uk/
- Vestiaire Collective https://www.vestiairecollective.com/
- Sellier https://www.sellierknightsbridge.com/
- Love Luxury https://loveluxury.ae/
- 1st Dibs https://www.1stdibs.com/
- The Handbag Clinic https://www.handbagclinic.co.uk/
- Fenwick https://www.fenwick.co.uk/
- Amazon https://www.amazon.co.uk/
- TK Maxx https://www.tkmaxx.com/uk/en/
- By Rotation https://byrotation.com/
- Bag Borrow or Steal https://www.bagborroworsteal.com/
- Cocoon Club https://www.cocoon.club/
- Bonhams www.bonhams.com

RESOURCES

- https://www.chanel.com/
- https://www.sothebys.com/
- https://loveluxury.co.uk/topics/chanel-19-bag-history/
- https://www.voguescandinavia.com/articles/history-of-chanel-2-55-bag-through-imagery
- https://saclab.com/chanel-2-55-vs-classic-flap-bag/
- https://fairlycurated.com/blog/2021/4/27/chanel-reissue-255-bag-review
- https://www.forbes.com/sites/pamdanziger/2024/05/29/chanel-holds-as-luxurys-number-two-brand-but-herms-is-gaining-ground/
- https://www.harpersbazaar.com/uk/fashion/a44542758/chanel-2-55-bag/
- https://www.purseblog.com/guides/chanel-flap-bag-facts-history/
- https://stylefrizz.com/200712/short-history-of-the-famous-chanel-255-bag/

- https://www.yoogiscloset.com/chanel/guide
- https://bagpad.com/blogs/blog/chanel-most-iconic-handbags
- https://www.vogue.co.uk/fashion/article/virginie-viard-chanel
- https://www.vogue.co.uk/article/dua-lipa-chanel-25-bag
- https://blog.fashionphile.com/chanel-255-reissue-guide/
- https://www.sellierknightsbridge.com/collections/buy-an-authentic-chanel-2-55-reissue-bag
- https://www.zoemagazine.net/
- https://finance.yahoo.com/news/exclusive-chanel-launches-ad-campaign-050054919.html
- https://www.vogue.com.au/culture/features/karl-lagerfelds-best-quotes/image-gallery/a9639f89c5c56ebb8ecf45808b4a1288
- https://editorialist.com/fashion/chanel-boy-bag/
- https://www.chanel.com/br/moda/news/2012/06/boy-capel--br--by-justine-picardie.html
- https://saclab.com/all-about-the-boy/
- https://www.glamourmagazine.co.uk/article/chanel-19-handbag
- https://cocoapproved.com/
- https://etoile-luxuryvintage.com/
- https://www.refinery29.com/en-us/chanel-shell-bag
- https://lovethatbagetc.com/
- https://demibang.com/
- https://www.vam.ac.uk/collections?type=featured
- https://www.zoemagazine.net/184171-chanel-and-cinema/
- https://www.vogue.fr/culture/article/chanel-costumes-films-cinema
- https://www.heyuguys.com/coco-chanel-films/
- https://www.shopyourtv.com/
- https://pagesix.com/2022/05/26/inside-kim-kardashians-30000-piece-fashion-archive/
- https://www.classical-music.com/
- https://wwd.com/lists/chanel-ambassadors-1236763091/sofia-coppola/
- https://www.standard.co.uk/lifestyle/what-really-goes-into-making-a-chanel-handbag-behind-the-scenes-at-its-topsecret-paris-workshop-a3184881.html
- https://www.1stdibs.com/blogs/the-study/fake-chanel/
- https://wwd.com/feature/most-expensive-handbags-1235687288/

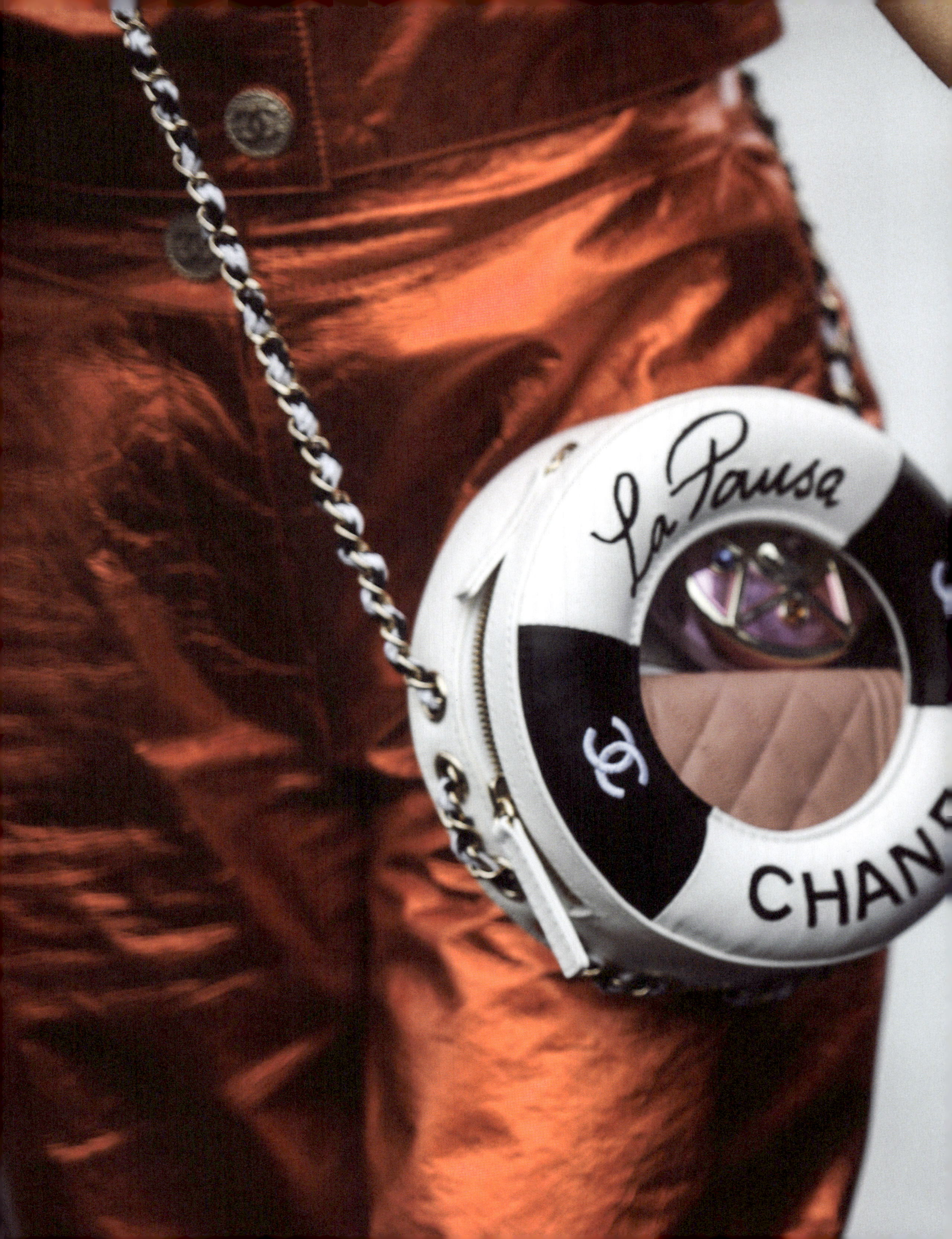

La Pausa
CHAN

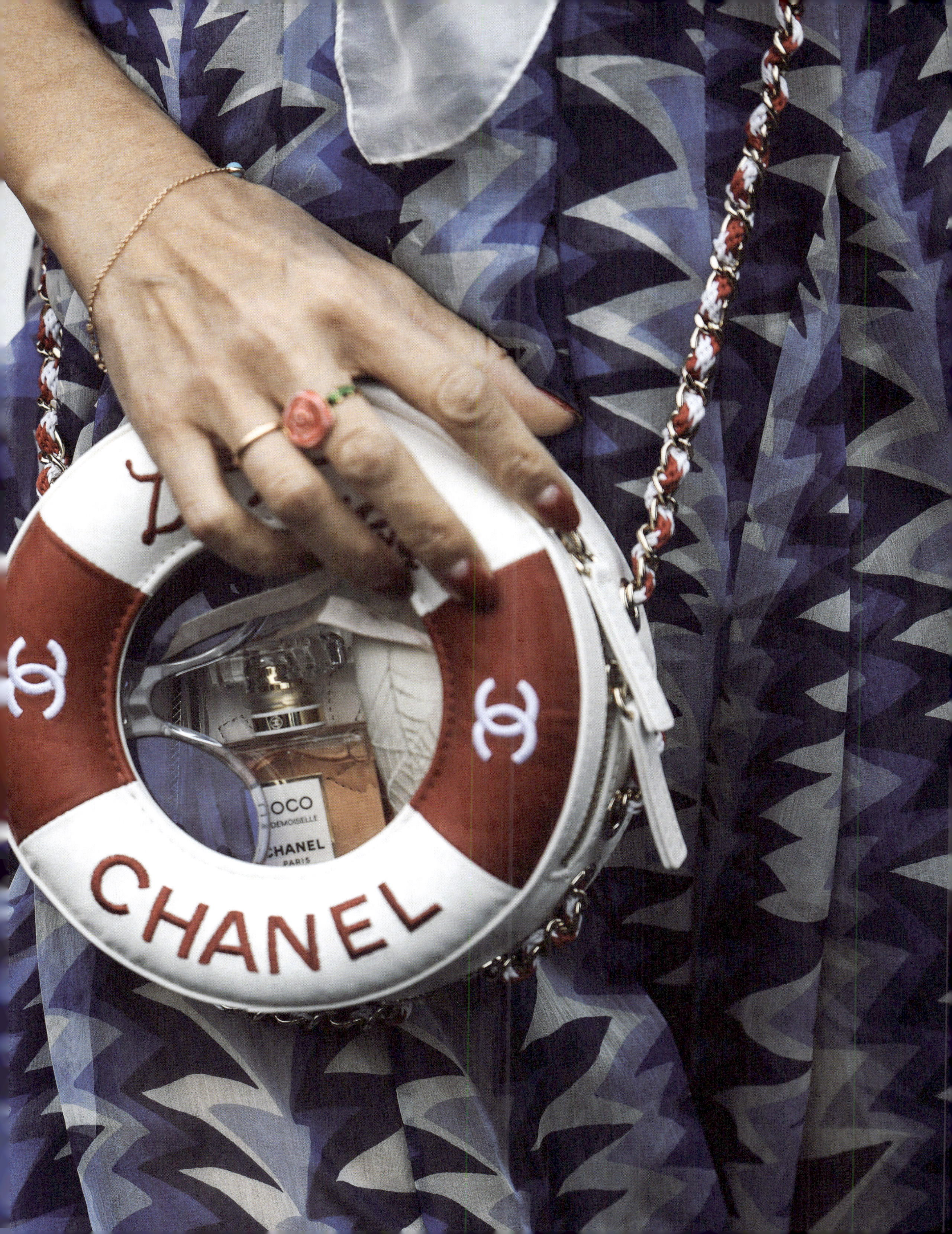
CHANEL
CHANEL
PARIS

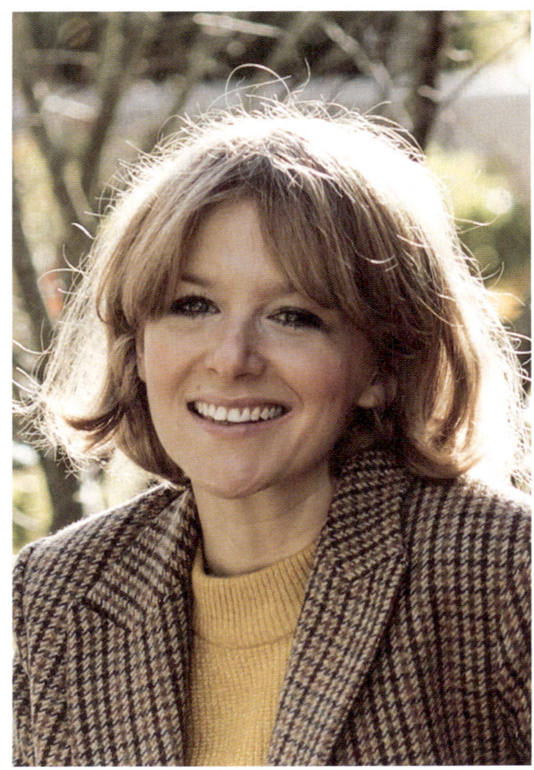

ALEXANDRA FULLERTON

Alexandra Fullerton is an Essex Girl by birth and former Londoner, however she now resides in Norfolk, having done a pandemic pivot towards a more rural life. She lives in a small village with her husband, daughter, long-haired chihuahua Ozzie and Nibbles the rabbit. The majority of Alex's career has been spent on magazines as a fashion director (7.5 years as Fashion director at Stylist magazine, 5 years as fashion director at large of Glamour UK) which meant styling A list actors, musical icons and celebrities (including Kylie Minogue, Rosie Huntington-Whiteley, Sophie Turner, Florence Welch and Kelly Rowland), travelling the world to shoot fashion stories and sitting front row at fashion shows. Now Alex is self-employed and has a portfolio career that combines fashion writing for The Telegraph and Bazaar Arabia, commercial styling (brands she has worked with include Stella McCartney and Marks & Spencer), personal styling, ghostwriting, writing her own books and running a shopping platform My3Words.co. When not working, Alex loves to explore provincial charity shops and dreams of unearthing a stash of Hermès Birkin bags. alexandrafullerton.com/@alexandrafullerton

IMAGE CREDITS

Cover Illustration: Jasmin Taeschner

p. 3: © mauritius images/Alamy Stock Photos; pp. 4/5: © Creative Lab/Shutterstock.com; p. 7: © Pascal Le Segretain/Getty Images; pp. 8/9: © Apic/Hulton Archive/Getty Images; p. 11 © Henry Clarke/Condé Nast via Getty Images; pp. 12/13: © Apic/Hulton Archive/Getty Images; p. 15: © Keystone-France/Gamma-Keystone via Getty Image; p. 16: © Evening Standard/Hulton Archive/Getty Images; p. 17: © John van Hasselt/Corbis via Getty Images; pp. 20/21: © FashionStock.com/Shutterstock.com; pp. 22/23: © Christian Vierig/GettyImages; p. 25: © Edward Berthelot/GettyImages; p. 26: © Frédéric Vielcanet/Alamy Photo Stock/mauritius images; p. 29: © Christian Vierig/Getty Images; p. 31: © Claudio Lavenia/GC Images; pp. 32 & 33 (top left): © agcreativelab – stock.adobe.com; p. 33 (bottom): © mauritius images/Helen/Alamy/Alamy Stock Photos; pp. 33 (top right) & 34: © Creative Lab/Shutterstock.com; p. 35: © photo-lime – stock.adobe.com; p. 36: © Jeremy Moeller/Getty Images; p. 37: © Christian Vierig/Getty Images; pp. 40/41: © agcreativelab – stock.adobe.com; pp. 42, 43 & 45 (bottom left): © Christian Vierig/Getty Images; p. 45 (top left): © agcreativelab – stock.adobe.com; p. 45 (top right): © Alya108k/Shutterstock.com; p. 45 (bottom right): © Creative Lab/Shutterstock.com; pp. 46/47: © Christian Vierig/Getty Images; pp. 48/49: © photo-lime – stock.adobe.com; p. 51: © Kristy Sparow/Getty Images; pp. 52 & 54: © Edward Berthelot/Getty Images; p. 58: © SAVIKO/Gamma-Rapho via Getty Images; pp. 59 & 60/61: © Edward Berthelot/Getty Images; p. 63: © Whitley – stock.adobe.com; p. 64: © photo-lime – stock.adobe.com; p. 65: © yu_photo - stock.adobe.com; p. 67: © Stephane Cardinale - Corbis/Corbis via Getty Images; p. 68: © Swan Gallet/WWD via Getty Images; p. 69: © Raimonda Kulikauskiene/Getty Images; pp. 70/71: © agcreativelab – stock.adobe.com; pp. 72/73: © Edward Berthelot/Getty Images; p. 74: © Stephane Cardinale - Corbis/Corbis via Getty Images; p. 75: © Whitley – stock.adobe.com; pp. 76/77: © agcreativelab – stock.adobe.com; p. 78: © WWD/Penske Media via Getty Images; p. 79: Creative Lab/Shutterstock.com; p. 80: © Merilyn Smith/WireImage via Getty Images; pp. 81 & 82: © Christian Vierig/Getty Images; p. 83: © Jeremy Moeller/Getty Images; p. 85: © Swan Gallet/WWD/Penske Media via Getty Images; pp. 86 & 87: WENN Rights Ltd/Alamy StockFoto/mauritius images; p. 88: © Pascal Le Segretain/Getty Images; pp. 90/91: © Edward Berthelot/Getty Images; p. 93: © Jeremy Moeller/Getty Images p. 94: © Kevin Winter/FilmMagic; p. 95: © photo-lime – stock.adobe.com; p. 96: © Raimonda Kulikauskiene/Getty Images; pp. 98/99: © WWD/Penske Media via Getty Images; p. 100: © James Devaney/GC Images via Getty Images; pp. 102/103: © agcreativelab – stock.adobe.com; p. 105: © Whitley – stock.adobe.com; p. 106: © photo-lime – stock.adobe.com; pp. 108/109: © Kirstin Sinclair/Getty Images; p. 110: yu_photo – stock.adobe.com; p. 111 (top left): © Whitley – stock.adobe.com; p. 111 (top right): © mauritius images/Dimitri MOONEESAWMY/Alamy/Alamy Stock Photos; p. 111 (bottom left): © Frédéric Vielcanet/Alamy Stock Foto/mauritius images; p. 111 (bottom right): © Christian Vierig/Getty Images; p. 112 (top left): © Peter White/Getty Images; p. 112 (top right): © Stephane Cardinale - Corbis/Corbis via Getty Images; p. 112 (bottom left): © Pascal Le Segretain/Getty Images; p. 112 (bottom right): © Edward Berthelot/Getty Images; p. 113: © Aitor Rosas Sune/WWD/Penske Media via Getty Images; pp. 114/115: © Edward Berthelot/Getty Images; pp. 116/117: © Whitley – stock.adobe.com; p. 118: © Stephane Cardinale/Corbis via Getty Images; p. 119: © Fairchild Archive/Penske Media via Getty Images; pp. 120 & 121: © WWD/Penske Media via Getty Images; pp. 122/123: © Pascal Le Segretain/Getty Images; pp. 124/125: © Creative Lab/Shutterstock.com; p. 126: © Whitley – stock.adobe.com; p. 127: agcreativelab – stock.adobe.com; pp. 128/129: © mauritius images/Pictorial Press Ltd/Alamy/Alamy Stock Photos; p. 131: © Jun Sato/WireImage via Getty Images; p. 132: © Jose Perez/Bauer-Griffin/GC Images via Getty Images; p. 133: © Bertrand Rindoff Petroff/Getty Images; p. 134: © Pascal Le Segretain/Getty Images; p. 135: © Alain BENAINOUS/Gamma-Rapho via Getty Images; p. 136: © Julian Parker/UK Press via Getty Images; p. 138: © Valerie MACON/AFP © VALERIE MACON/AFP via Getty Images; p. 139: © Pierre Suu/GC Images via Getty Images; p. 140: © picture alliance/United Archives | IFTN; pp. 142/143: Farabola/Bridgeman Images; pp. 144 & 145: Miller/INTERFOTO; p. 146: © picture alliance/ASSOCIATED PRESS | Leslie Priest; p. 147: © picture alliance/Everett Collection | Courtesy Everett Collection; pp. 148: © Kristy Sparow/Getty Images; p. 150: © thecelebrityfinder/Bauer-Griffin/GC Images via Getty Images; p. 151: © James Devaney/WireImage via Getty Images; p. 152: © Stephane Cardinale - Corbis/Corbis via Getty Images; p. 153: © ZUMA Press, Inc./Alamy/Alamy Stock Photos/mauritius images; p. 154: © Raymond Hall/GC Images via Getty Images; pp. 156 & 157: © Pool ARNAL/GARCIA/Gamma-Rapho via Getty Images; p. 158: © TheStewartofNY/GC Images via Getty Images; p. 159 © Jerritt Clark/WireImage via Getty Images; p. 160: © The Chosunilbo JNS/Imazins via Getty Images; p. 162: © Marc Piasecki/GC Images via Getty Images; p. 163: © picture alliance/Scott Garfitt/Invision/AP | Scott Garfitt; p. 164: © Marc Piasecki/GC Images via Getty Images; p. 165: © Gardiner Anderson/Bauer-Griffin/GC Images via Getty Images; p. 166: © picture alliance/Willy Sanjuan/Invision/AP | Willy Sanjuan; p. 167: © Mike Marsland/WireImage via Getty Images; pp. 168/169: © Christian Vierig/Getty Images; pp. 171, 172, 175 & 177: © MANOOCHER DEGHATI/AFP via Getty Images; pp. 178–183: Courtesy of Bonhams; pp. 184/185: © Alberto Grosescu /Alamy Stock Photos/mauritius images; pp. 188/189: © agcreativelab – stock.adobe.com; p. 190: Photo by Rekha Damhar

IMPRINT

The Ultimate Guide to Chanel Bags
This book was conceived, edited, and designed by teNeues.

Text by Alexandra Fullerton
Proofreading by Amanda Ennis, Nadine Weinhold, Benine Mayer

Editorial Management by Nadine Weinhold
Design by Marcus Taeschner
Layout by Marcus Taeschner
Picture Editing by Heide Christiansen
Production by Sandra Jansen-Dorn, Nele Jansen
Color Separation and Prepress by Jens Grundei

Printed in the Czech Republic by Finidr
Produced in Europe

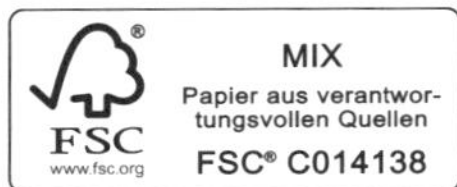

Published by gestalten, Berlin 2025
ISBN 978-3-96171-711-8

2nd printing, 2026

The German edition is available under
ISBN 978-3-96171-729-3.

For more information, and to order books, please visit
www.teneues.com and www.gestalten.com

Die Gestalten Verlag GmbH & Co. KG
Mariannenstrasse 9–10, 10999 Berlin, Germany
hello@gestalten.com

Krefeld Office
Uerdinger Str. 265 / Villa Pattberg
47800 Krefeld, Germany
verlag@teneues.com

teNeues Press Department
press@gestalten.com

Bibliographic information published by the Deutsche Nationalbibliothek. The Deutsche Nationalbibliothek lists this publication in the Deutsche Nationalbibliografie; detailed bibliographic data is available online at www.dnb.de

https://instagram.com/teneuespublishing

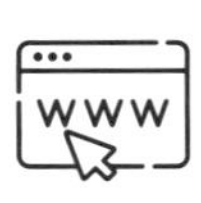

www.teneues.com